Affirmative Action and Justice

MICHEL ROSENFELD

Affirmative Action and Justice

A Philosophical and Constitutional Inquiry

Yale University Press
New Haven and London

Portions of chapters 7 and 10 have been adapted from Affirmative Action, Justice, and Equalities: A Philosophical and Constitutional Appraisal, *Ohio State Law Journal* 46:845 (1985), copyright 1985 by the Ohio State University; and Decoding *Richmond:* Affirmative Action and the Elusive Meaning of Constitutional Equality, *Michigan Law Review* 87:1729 (1989).

Library of Congress Cataloging-in-Publication Data

Rosenfeld, Michel, 1948–
Affirmative action and justice : a philosophical and constitutional inquiry / Michel Rosenfeld.
p. cm.
Includes bibliographical references and index.
ISBN 0-300-04781-9 (cloth)
0-300-05508-0 (pbk.)
1. Affirmative action programs—Law and legislation—United States. 2. Equality before the law—United States. 3. Affirmative action programs. 4. Equality. I. Title.
KF3464.R65 1991
342.73'0873—dc20
[347.302873] 90–37995
CIP

A catalogue record for this book is available from the British Library.

Designed by April Leidig-Higgins.
Set in Trump Mediaeval type by The Composing Room of Michigan, Inc., Grand Rapids, Michigan.
Printed in the United States of America by Vail-Ballou Press, Binghamton, New York.

The paper in this book meets the guidelines for permanence and durability of the Committee on Production Guidelines for Book Longevity of the Council on Library Resources.

10 9 8 7 6 5 4 3 2

To Evelyn, Maia, and Alexis

Contents

Acknowledgments ix

Introduction 1

PART ONE Liberal Political Philosophy and Affirmative Action

ONE Definition of Key Concepts and Delimitation of Scope of Analysis 11

TWO Libertarian Justice and Affirmative Action 52

THREE Contractarian Justice and Affirmative Action 65

FOUR Utilitarian Justice and Affirmative Action 94

FIVE Egalitarian Justice and Affirmative Action 116

PART TWO Constitutional Equality and Affirmative Action

SIX Constitutional Equality and Equal Protection 135

SEVEN The Constitutional Dimension of Affirmative Action 163

PART THREE Equality, Difference, and Consensus: Toward an Integrated Conception of the Justice of Affirmative Action

EIGHT The Limitations of the Major Liberal Philosophical Conceptions of the Justice of Affirmative Action 219

NINE Justice as Reversibility, Equality, and the Right to Be Different 239

TEN Toward an Integrated Philosophical and Constitutional Justification of Affirmative Action 283

List of Cases 337
Notes 339
Bibliography 353
Index 359

Acknowledgments

I have accumulated many debts in writing this book. I am most grateful to my colleague David Carlson, who selflessly and patiently read through the entire manuscript, contributing innumerable valuable suggestions. I am also very grateful to Kent Greenawalt, who read early drafts and whose always incisive and detailed comments saved me from many egregious errors. Among the many others who read or commented on some part of the book, or with whom I have had enlightening discussions on some of its themes, thanks are due to Andrew Arato, Jean Cohen, Drucilla Cornell, Arthur Jacobson, Charles Larmore, David Richards, Lawrence Sager, and Charles Yablon. Finally, special thanks are due to Harry Wellington for his kind encouragement and support, starting in the early stages of the project.

Last but not least, I owe debts of a different kind to my family. To my wife, Evelyn, I owe the deepest gratitude for her love, friendship, wise counsel, good humor, and steadfast encouragement, which prompted me to persevere notwithstanding numerous seemingly formidable obstacles. To my children, Maia and Alexis, I also owe a great deal, as their insatiable intellectual curiosity and countless imaginative insights have vividly exemplified the exhilarating possibilities open to the inquisitive mind dedicated to the pursuit of knowledge.

Introduction

For the past two decades, affirmative action has ranked among the most controversial publicly debated issues in the United States. Between 1978, when the celebrated *Bakke* case was decided, and January 1, 1990, the U.S. Supreme Court has decided ten closely divided major affirmative action cases. Furthermore, the relation between affirmative action, justice, and equality has been extensively examined by numerous legal scholars and philosophers.[1] No doubt some progress has been made on both the constitutional and philosophical fronts, as various issues have been significantly clarified and diverse positions given cogent articulation. Yet the debate over affirmative action has recently intensified, with advocates and foes as bitterly divided as ever.[2]

The stridence of the recent debate over affirmative action is, to a significant degree, a reflection of the increasing political polarization in the United States concerning civil rights issues. Fueled by efforts of the Reagan Administration to restrict the scope of civil rights and to dismantle existing affirmative action programs,[3] a strong backlash against preferential treatment for minorities and women has developed.[4] On the other hand, civil rights advocates have warned that the termination of existing affirmative action programs would nullify hard-won strides toward parity and turn back the clock to the days when women and minorities were systematically excluded from desirable positions.[5]

The clash between those who view affirmative action as a means to provide handouts to minorities and women and those others who believe that the abolition of affirmative action will lead to a return to "the good ol' boy network"[6] may appear to be a simple political dispute concerning the allocation of scarce social goods. However, something more profound is involved. The passionate opposition against affirmative action, for example, cannot be simply explained in terms of resentment against departures from the meritocratic system in the award of jobs or of scarce educational opportunities. People lose in the competition for places at universities or for jobs because of nepotism or preferences for veterans, but those clear departures from the ideal of the meritocracy hardly arouse the kind of passion that race- or gender-based preferential treatment does. Thus, in the context of the *Bakke* case, a state medical school's rejection of a more qualified white applicant to make room for a less qualified minority applicant ignited an intense national debate. But that the same medical school favored children of friends of high-ranking university officials over more qualified applicants for admission barely provoked any reaction.[7]

The intensity of the debate over affirmative action is due to the shared belief of all participants that they are engaged in an important moral debate concerning fundamental notions of justice and equality. Moreover, not only does this debate have important constitutional and philosophical implications, but it is in a sense a unique moral debate. Indeed, for all its vehemence, the contemporary debate over affirmative action is, at least in the United States, an intramural debate among partisans of equality. Other divisive contemporary moral debates with important constitutional and philosophical ramifications, such as that regarding abortion, for example, are debates among persons who appear to adhere to sharply different values. In the familiar language of the slogans, the abortion issue divides those who are "pro-choice" from those who are "pro-life." In sharp contrast, however, the affirmative action debate is not between persons who are "pro-equality" and others who are "anti-equality." Both the most ardent advocates of affirmative action and its most vehement foes loudly proclaim their allegiance to the ideal of equality.[8]

Equality also provides the nexus between affirmative action, the equal protection clause of the fourteenth amendment to the United States Constitution, and philosophical conceptions of justice. Moreover, there is a significant overlap between philosophical and constitutional questions regarding equality and affirmative action, but there have been far too few cross-references between the extensive bodies of legal and philosophical scholarship on these questions. Also little has been done to date to integrate the philosophers' and the legal theorists' insights into affirmative action, or to determine to what extent philosophical conceptions of equality and affirmative action might be relevant to the resolution of the constitutional issues posed by affirmative action. A principal aim of this book is to provide an interdisciplinary analysis of affirmative action with an eye toward integrating philosophical and constitutional assessments of affirmative action where appropriate and toward determining the proper place of philosophical insights in the constitutional assessment of the legitimacy of affirmative action under the equal protection clause.

That both proponents and opponents of affirmative action are partisans of equality has the effect of both constraining and intensifying the debate concerning the legitimacy of affirmative action. The debate is constrained insofar as there is a convergence in the understanding of the meaning of equality at higher levels of abstraction. On the other hand, the debate is intensified as a consequence of the fact that as more people subscribe to the ideal of equality, there seems to be less and less agreement concerning the concrete meaning of the term.

Both proponents and opponents of affirmative action generally agree that racial and sexual differences should not be used to the disadvantage of racial minorities or women. This consensus breaks down, however, when the issue is whether such differences may properly be taken into consideration in support of policies that favor racial minorities or women. Foes of affirmative action stress equal treatment regardless of race or gender, and contend that the preferential treatment of racial minorities or women is as reprehensible as the preferential treatment of white males. Partisans of affirmative action, in contrast, argue that equal treatment may be used to perpetuate existing inequalities and that whereas the preferential treatment of white males would exacerbate such inequalities, favoring racial minorities and women would contribute to the elimination of race- and gender-based inequalities.

Even among those who believe that equality is not incompatible with departures from equal treatment and who are willing to acknowledge the legitimacy of affirmative action, there are sharp disagreements concerning its permissible scope. For example, there appears to be much greater judicial acceptance of preferential treatment in job hiring than in job layoffs.[9] To lose a job that one already holds may be more painful than failing to win the competition for a job that one covets. On the other hand, if affirmative action in job hiring is justified on the grounds that equality requires integration of the workplace, then rejection of affirmative action in job layoffs may be inconsistent. Indeed, by preserving the customary order of reverse seniority in layoffs—whereby employees with less job seniority are laid off ahead of those who possess greater job seniority—one is likely to nullify the gains toward integrating the workplace achieved through preferential treatment in job hiring. Because the beneficiaries of affirmative action tend to be among the most recently hired employees, they are the first to be laid off under the reverse seniority system.

Several other key issues cannot be settled exclusively on the basis of consensus on the meaning of equality at the highest levels of abstraction. Thus, agreement that all members of society should be considered equal does not settle whether equality is compatible with departures from the practice of awarding scarce jobs to the most qualified applicants regardless of race or sex or whether all such departures should stand on the same footing. Is it possible, for instance, consistently to support preferential treatment of veterans but to oppose affirmative action in favor of racial minorities or women? Would it be defensible to argue that equality cannot require affirmative action in the hiring of heart surgeons or airline pilots, but that it is compatible with the preferential hiring of state troopers, fire fighters, and road dispatchers (which are some of the positions involved in affirmative action cases thus far decided by the Supreme Court)? Should the legitimacy of race- and gender-based affirmative action in hiring depend on its likely effects on economic efficiency?

A proper resolution of these issues and a principled and systematic evaluation of the legitimacy of affirmative action consistent with the existing agreement on the meaning of abstract equality requires an integration of diverse conceptions of equality operating at different levels of abstraction, ranging from the most concrete to the most abstract. This kind of integration is generally lacking in the existing philosophical and constitutional assessments of affirmative action. These assessments nevertheless achieve partial integrations and can thus serve as building blocks in a scheme of comprehensive integration. Accordingly, one of the principal tasks that I undertake in this book is the reappraisal of the principal existing philosophical and constitutional evaluations of affirmative action to determine how far integrated they are and how they might contribute to a project of comprehensive integration. Moreover, this task is rendered manageable by the recent development of a structural grammar of equality that provides essential tools for discovering the links between more abstract and more concrete conceptions of equality.

As I previously mentioned, agreement concerning the meaning of equality, even if only at the highest levels of abstraction, does constrain the debate over the legitimacy of affirmative action. In the United States, moreover, two broad propositions over which there is widespread agreement (at least in the context of public discourse) foreclose the acceptability of certain justifications of affirmative action. First, there is a broad-based public consensus on the proposition that first-order discrimination is morally wrong because it violates the inherent equality of all persons. First-order discrimination is discrimination against blacks or women on the grounds that they are inferior or different. First-order discrimination, furthermore, is to be distinguished from "reverse" discrimination or "benign" discrimination, which is discrimination in favor of those who have been targets of first-order discrimination. In short, because of the repudiation of first-order discrimination, no justification of affirmative action that would also legitimate first-order discrimination is acceptable.

Second, it is widely accepted in the United States that the individual rather than the group is the subject of equality. In other words, regardless of what equality may require in concrete situations, it is the individual rather than the group who is entitled to such equality. As a consequence, purely group-related justifications of affirmative action become unacceptable. Thus, for example, a group proportionment argument advocating affirmative action to eliminate glaring group-related imbalances in a particular workforce would have to be rejected as inconsistent with the conviction that the individual rather than the group is the proper subject of equality.

Operating within the constraints imposed by acceptance of these two broad propositions, I seek to answer the following question in this book: What consistent set of assumptions, conditions, and arguments operating at the various relevant levels of abstraction would lend support to the claim that affirmative action is legitimate in terms of both a suitable philosophical conception of justice and a suitable constitutional conception of equal protection?

In this book I discuss the ten affirmative action cases decided by the Supreme Court between 1978 and January 1, 1990. All these major affirmative action cases raise the issue of whether affirmative action is permissible under the appropriate constitutional or statutory standard. Because of this and of the complexities involved in attempting to delimit the nature and scope of permissible affirmative action under the relevant sets of constraints, I, by and large, confine my focus on the determination of when, and under what circumstances, affirmative action might properly be deemed permissible. A determination that affirmative action is permissible does not, of course, necessarily foreclose the possibility that it could also be justified as mandatory. Accordingly, any conclusion that I reach concerning the legitimacy of permissible affirmative action should be interpreted as leaving open the question of whether mandatory affirmative action could be justified under the same circumstances.

I have characterized the current debate in the United States concerning the justice of affirmative action as an intramural debate among partisans of equality. That proponents and opponents of affirmative action share at some level a common identity, however, should not obscure the deep rift that sets them one against the other. One need only be reminded that civil wars are often the most bloody. Furthermore, the struggle over affirmative action forms part, and is illustrative, of a larger struggle being currently waged in the United States in the name of equality. This larger struggle is in essence a struggle between two conflicting visions of equality: equality as identity and equality as difference. Indeed, as the voices against equality have receded from the public arena, the question has shifted from *whether* equality to *what* equality.

Identity and difference may bear different relationships to equality. Difference, for example, can be made into a badge of inferiority, and blacks and women subordinated and marginalized. In that case, equality is closely linked to identity. But equality as identity may be either exclusive or inclusive. If it is exclusive, then only white males may enjoy the status of equals. If is made inclusive, however, then blacks and women are no longer to be excluded on account of their race or their gender, respectively, provided they conform to the dominant perspective of the white male. On the other hand, one may attempt to achieve equality as difference—that is, to abolish the need to profess allegiance to the values of a dominant "other" as a precondition to treatment as a fully deserving equal.[10] In the context of equality as difference, everyone enjoys the status of an equal without having to compromise his or her perspective. Consistent with these observations, first-order discrimination appears linked to equality as exclusive identity; formal equality and equal treatment regardless of differences to equality as inclusive identity; and affirmative action, which may be broadly viewed as an equality that accounts for differences, to equality as difference.

Application of the structural grammar of equality and integration of various conceptions of equality operating at different levels of abstraction reveal that the struggle between equality as identity and equality as difference is much more complex than it initially appears. Ultimately, equality cannot be achieved either through pure identity or pure difference, but must rely on some kind of dynamic relationship between the two. Similarly, affirmative action cannot be systematically justified by relying on a vision of equality as difference. I will explore these issues more fully in the last part of the book. Moreover, while I will focus primarily on affirmative action, my analysis will bear upon the broader debate concerning the possibility of achieving equality without the suppression or subordination of legitimately held differences.

The book is divided into three parts. Part One is devoted to a critical assessment of the principal philosophical arguments made for and against affirmative action from the standpoint of liberal conceptions of justice. In chapter 1, I define key terms and concepts used in the subsequent analysis, delimit the scope of analysis, and describe certain of the most salient features of the structural grammar of equality. Chapters 2 through 5 each examine the treatment of affirmative action under one of the four principal liberal conceptions of justice. These are the libertarian, contractarian, utilitarian, and egalitarian conceptions.

In Part Two I explore the relationship between constitutional equality as it emerges from the jurisprudence of the equal protection clause and affirmative action. Chapter 6 focuses on the relevance of philosophical conceptions of equality to constitutional interpretations of the equal-protection clause and assesses existing judicial interpretations of equal protection. Chapter 7 is dedicated to a critical analysis of the ten major affirmative action cases decided before 1990 by the Supreme Court.

In Part Three I attempt to construct an integrated philosophical and constitutional conception of the justice of affirmative action, based on an understanding of the dynamic relationship between identity and difference, and on the implementation of a dialogical conception of justice. Chapter 8 examines the crucial relationships between autonomy and welfare and between identity and difference, and then, on the basis of that examination, explains why the four liberal conceptions of the justice of affirmative action examined in Part One are ultimately inadequate. In chapter 9, I construct a dialogical model to account for the complex dynamic relationship between equality as identity and equality as difference. Drawing upon Kohlberg's conception of justice as reversibility and upon Habermas' theory of communicative ethics, I propose adopting a principle of justice that I call "justice as reversible reciprocity" as the best means to achieve the integration of various relevant perspectives and to provide a comprehensive philosophical and constitutional justification of affirmative action. Finally, in chapter 10, I posit and seek to justify the various elements that must be combined to provide an integrated philosophical and constitutional justification of affirmative action. I conclude by articulating the nature and scope of the constitutional justification of affirmative action in the context of adherence to the principle of justice as reversible reciprocity.

PART ONE

Liberal Political Philosophy and Affirmative Action

CHAPTER ONE

Definition of Key Concepts and Delimitation of Scope of Analysis

Whether philosophical notions of justice and equality and the constitutional constraints imposed by the equal protection clause can justify affirmative action without thereby legitimating first-order discrimination depends on the meaning of such key terms as *justice, equality,* and *affirmative action.* The meaning of those terms, however, is far from settled. Moreover, many variables are likely to affect the validity of philosophical arguments for and against affirmative action. Because of this it is important to provide a definition of key terms and concepts and to delimit carefully the scope of analysis. Accordingly, in this chapter I offer a definition of key terms and explore the distinctions between *distributive justice, compensatory justice,* and *procedural justice,* that between *equality of result* and *equality of opportunity,* and that between *formal equality of opportunity* and *fair equality of opportunity.* Further, I delimit the scope of analysis, by means of a series of assumptions concerning certain variables, to permit full concentration of the principal and most contested philosophical issues raised by affirmative action.

The concept of equality, perhaps more than any other, has become increasingly elusive as its growing prescriptive role tends to obscure the nature and scope of its descriptive uses. Since the eighteenth century almost all social systems regard equality as a positive value (Feher & Heller 1980, 152). But with the widespread embrace of equality as a desirable positive value comes the apparent dilution of its meaning (Gutmann 1980, ix–x). Accordingly, it is not surprising that the very idea of equality has been attacked as being empty (Westen 1982) and that it has been invoked by both proponents and opponents of affirmative action.[1]

It would be, however, a serious mistake to discard the concept of equality as empty. Indeed, as Gutmann points out, "once one specifies a context, a purpose, and a conceptual framework, the relevant meanings of equality become more limited and the concept of equality takes on an importance for our normative concerns in political philosophy" (Gutmann 1980, x). With this in mind, I shall attempt to narrow the range of meanings of equality and other key concepts for purposes of evaluating affirmative action by specifying a relevant context, purpose, and conceptual framework. The context shall be contemporary society in the United States. The purpose shall be assessing the legitimacy of affirmative action in the face of rejection of first-order discrimination in accordance with the constitutional right to equal protection. Finally, the conceptual framework shall be that of liberal theory.

Narrowing the range of possible meanings to render a key concept manageable does not necessarily bridge the gap between theory and practice. To illustrate, let us suppose that based on sharing the same conceptual framework we agree with the following theoretical proposition advanced by Dworkin: "Government . . . has an abstract responsibility to treat each citizen's fate as equally important" (Dworkin 1986, 296). As Dworkin goes on to point out, "rival conceptions or theories of equality are rival answers to the question of what system of property would meet that standard." Thus, for instance, Dworkin states that "libertarian conceptions of equality suppose that people have 'natural' rights over whatever property they have acquired in certain economical ways and that government treats people as equals when it protects their possession and enjoyment of that property" (ibid., 297). On the other hand, welfare-based conceptions, according to Dworkin, "deny any natural right in property and insist instead that government must produce, distribute, and regulate property to achieve results defined by some specified function of the happiness or welfare of individuals."

To determine whether the libertarian or welfare conceptions of equality are better suited to lead to the fulfillment of the abstract government responsibility mentioned by Dworkin, we must carry out at least two different tasks. First, the relevant conceptual framework would have to be sufficiently elaborated to allow for a more precise understanding of the prescription that government treat each citizen's fate as being equally important. Second, after we had reached a more precise understanding, it would become necessary to compare the practical results likely to follow from an actual implementation of each of these conceptions of equality. Indeed, only on the basis of such a comparison would it become clear whether the libertarian or welfare conception of equality would be better suited to promote the government's treatment of each citizen as being of equal importance under a given set of historical circumstances.

The gap between equality in theory and equality in practice can be filled through application of a "structural grammar of equality." Indeed, by providing a "middle term" between theory and practice (Rae et al. 1981, 14–15), the structural grammar of equality elaborated by Rae can assist in determining the consequences of rival theoretical conceptions of equality. To understand how this may be, we must focus first on Rae's central insight that to the move from theory to practice there corresponds a move from equality to equalities (ibid., 19). In the most general terms, in any complex sociopolitical universe, the implementation of any theoretical conception of equality promotes not equality in general but certain particular equalities that are necessarily accompanied by correlative inequalities.

To illustrate this last point, let us suppose that a particular theory of equality requires that individuals within a given society be treated equally according to merit. In that society, an equal lot should be received by all those whose merit is alike. Moreover, as a corollary, unequal lots should be received by those whose merits are unlike, with a greater lot going to persons with greater merit and a smaller lot to those with lesser merit. Now, suppose that the individual needs of the members of this society do not necessarily correspond to their individual merit, so that two persons who have the same needs may well be unlike with respect to merit. In that case, equality according to merit would entail inequality according to need. More generally, in Rae's words, "because of the antagonisms between one equality and another, *there must always be some inequalities.* For any society with structural complexity, there must be choices among equalities, hence equalities left out" (ibid., 144).

It is important to specify relevant prescriptive propositions and to provide a description of the particular equalities and inequalities that would be promoted by rival theories. Indeed, this should make it possible to determine in a systematic way which (if any) of those rival theories is capable of leading to the realization of certain identified prescriptive aims. More particularly, in the case at hand, a proper account of prescriptive and descriptive equalities is essential in order to determine whether, consistent with the prescriptive presuppositions behind the equal protection clause, it is possible to settle on a philosophically coherent theory that would legitimate the public use of affirmative action.

1. Definition and Specification of Key Terms and Concepts

A. Justice, Equality, Equalities, and Inequalities

Since the Greeks, justice has been equated with equality (Ross 1958, 268).[2] On the other hand, in the words of Owen Fiss, the equal protection clause has "given constitutional status to the ideal of equality" (Fiss 1977, 85). Moreover, both judicial proponents and opponents of affirmative action have sought to justify their respective positions by reference to adherence to the ideal of equality.[3]

There is no agreement among philosophers concerning the meaning of substantive justice. Perelman, however, has articulated a principle of formal justice designed to be consistent with all the plausible conceptions of substantive justice. According to Perelman, formal justice is "a principle of justice in accordance with which beings of one and the same category must be treated in the same way" (Perelman 1963, 16). The principle of formal justice commands equal treatment of those who are alike and, as a corollary, the unequal treatment of those who are not alike—or in other words, that equals be treated equally, and unequals unequally. But since this principle does not provide a criterion for determining who is equal to whom, or in what respect one person might be equal to another, it is, as Perelman notes, reducible to a principle of consistency (ibid., 21–22). Accordingly, Perelman's principle of formal justice seems to be equally compatible with a substantive criterion that treats persons unequally according to their race or sex and with a diametrically opposed criterion which provides that mere differences of race or sex do not justify treating persons as unequals.

The equal protection clause, on the other hand, appears, at the very least, to elevate compliance with the principle of formal justice to a constitutional requirement. In the words of Chief Justice Rehnquist, "equal protection does not mean that all persons must be treated alike. Rather, its general principle is that persons similarly situated should be treated similarly."[4] Moreover, as Chief Justice Rehnquist also points out, one of the principal aims of the framers of the fourteenth amendment was to invalidate racial classifications as the basis for treating blacks as inferior to whites.[5] These specifications, however, do not provide a sufficient basis for determining the constitutionality of affirmative action. They do not, without further elaboration, permit a determination of whether the intended beneficiaries of affirmative action are for relevant purposes similarly situated to nonbeneficiaries. Furthermore, the prohibition against using racial classifications to treat blacks as inferiors does not prima facie militate for or against affirmative action involving a preference designed to *benefit* blacks.

Since the combination of adhesion to the principle of formal justice and repudiation of first-order discrimination cannot settle the justice of affirmative action, it is necessary to appeal to principles of substantive justice. Application of the vast majority of plausible principles of substantive justice would inevitably result in the establishment of complex sets of particular equalities standing in opposition to particular inequalities (Rae et al. 1981, 130). Also, as I shall explore more fully below, the concept of justice is not monolithic. It encompasses such diverse notions as justice in distribution, justice in compensation, and procedural justice. Further, as a consequence of the complex nature of the concepts of justice and equality, the equal protection clause, as stressed by Fiss, cannot fulfill its constitutional mission of implementing the ideal of equality without adopting a suitable mediating principle (Fiss 1977, 85).

A more comprehensive grasp of the likely relationships between equalities and inequalities is essential in order to permit a systematic assessment of the justice of affirmative action. Indeed, as already indicated, in any complex universe—such as one in which subjects are classified both in terms of merit and needs—equalities seem inextricably linked to inequalities in a process of mutual determination.[6] Moreover, as the relevant universe becomes more complex, it is possible to distinguish among a greater number of classes of subjects, and the implementation of any relevant set of principles of substantive justice is likely to produce a greater number of equalities and of corresponding inequalities. Also in such a universe choices must be made not only between equalities, but also concerning the proper subject of equality, the proper domain of equality, the proper domains of allocation and account, and the proper aims of equality-seeking policies in terms of promoting marginal or global equality. To obtain a better grasp of these terms introduced by Rae, I shall now provide a brief account of each of them, in the context of their roles in his structural grammar of equality.

The subject of equality is determined by the response to the question of "who is to be equal to whom" (Rae et al. 1981, 20). There are two different possible answers to this question. The first is that each individual member of a relevant class is the equal of every other individual member of that class. This means that the individual is the subject of equality and that, to use Rae's expression, "individual regarding equality" is involved. An example of an individual-regarding equality is provided by the "one-person-one-vote" principle, which defines a class comprised of all those who are citizens and which grants each individual member of that class the same right to vote as any other member of that class (ibid., 21).

The second possible subject of equality is the group (ibid., 20). Once the class of all those who are to be treated equally has been defined, then in contrast to cases of individual-regarding equality, equality is not between individuals but between *subclasses* (ibid., 32). To illustrate, let us assume there is a class of one hundred persons divided into two subclasses, S1 and S2, of fifty persons each. Let us assume further that there are two hundred equal lots of good G available for distribution to the class. Group-regarding equality would be satisfied if S1 and S2 each received one hundred G's. Moreover, group-regarding equality but not individual-regarding equality would remain satisfied no matter what the particular distribution of G's made by each subclass among its own members. Thus, group-regarding equality is as compatible with equal distribution *within* each subclass as with equal distribution in one subclass but not the other (e.g. two G's for each member of S1, and one G for half of the members of S2 and three G's for the other half of the members of S2) and with unequal distribution within both subclasses.

As demonstrated by the following example, group-regarding equality may well *produce* inequalities between individual members of different groups. This would be the case if group S3 has fifty members, group S4 one hundred members, each group receives one hundred lots of G, and each group adheres to a rule of equal distribution among its members. Under those circumstances each individual member of S3 would receive two G's whereas each individual member of S4 would receive only one G. Moreover, individual-regarding equality produces group-regarding inequality whenever the relevant groups are of different sizes. Thus, if every individual is to receive one G, and if group S5 is comprised of one hundred individuals but group S6 of only fifty, S5 will receive twice as many G's as does S6.

If we assume agreement on a particular subject of equality, the next logical task seems to require the determination of what Rae terms the "domain of equality." According to Rae's definition, domain of equality refers to the "classes of things that are to be allocated equally." Moreover, a domain of equality may be broad or narrow. Taking any two domains of equality, Domain I and Domain II, Rae stipulates that "Domain I is broad in relation to II if, first, everything in II is also in I, and, second, some of the things in I are not in II." Thus, for instance, if Domain I were to consist of 100 tons of gold and one peanut and Domain II of 100 tons of gold, Domain I would be broad in relation to Domain II (ibid., 45–46).

Rae argues that the distinction between broad and narrow domains of equality highlights a persistent difficulty confronted by all proponents of equality since Locke. As Rae indicates, Locke advocates equal individual rights before the state but finally rejects any right to equal allocation of all goods susceptible of being divided into equal lots for purposes of allocation to the relevant individual-regarding subject-class (ibid., 47). Once one advocates the equal allocation of *certain* classes of things, however, the question arises: Why only those classes of things and not other classes of things? Why not *all* classes of things? Moreover, since, according to Rae, almost no political thinkers have seriously endorsed "equal everything in the world for everyone in the world" (ibid., 48, 166), these difficult questions arise for a broad spectrum of political thinkers extending from Nozick to Marx.[7]

It is obvious that Rae's structural grammar of equality does not of itself provide the means to justify choosing broad or narrow domains of equality. Moreover, even if all proponents of equality shared an essentially similar conception at the highest levels of abstraction, such justification would still be contingent on the various intermediate theoretical conceptions that might serve as vehicles for the implementation of agreed-upon abstract principles. Nevertheless, Rae's concept of domains of equality and his articulation of criteria making it possible to classify such domains according to their breadth do provide an important analytical tool, in that they facilitate the comparison of otherwise seemingly irreconcilable political theories. Thus, for example, "market liberals (corresponding roughly to American 'conservatives')," argues Rae, "are not so much *anti*egalitarian as they are *narrowly* egalitarian. Milton Friedman, Murray Rothbard, and Robert Nozick do not oppose equality, for the very heart of their appeal is universal—that is, equal—distribution of formal property rights and certain civil and political rights. But they oppose the *broadening* of equality beyond the narrow limits of this domain" (emphasis in original; ibid., 47).

By contrast, as Rae further argues, "Leftward ideologies, no matter how various in other respects, all seek to broaden the domain to which equality is to be applied. All forms of Marxian thought resist narrow equality. Marx and his successors argue that narrow equality leaves the weak at the mercy of the strong, and thus lets the strong use a form of equality to cover and justify inequality of accumulation and exploitation" (footnotes deleted; ibid., 47–48). Based on this analysis, moreover, Rae concludes that it is more accurate to characterize the ideological conflict between market liberals and Marxists as one between "equality in the narrow" versus "equality in the broad," rather than one pitting "liberty" against "equality" (ibid., 48). Finally, although this may not be readily apparent at this point, the breadth of relevant domains of allocation seems bound to have an impact on whether, and to what extent, affirmative action may be justified. Thus, a very narrow domain of equality restricted to formal property rights appears much less compatible with affirmative action than do broader domains.

Brief mention of a couple of additional distinctions made by Rae in the course of his elaboration of structural grammar of equality is also in order. The first of these is that between "domain of allocation" and "domain of account." Rae defines a domain of allocation as "the class of things that a given agent (or agency) presently controls for the purpose of allocation." Moreover, he adds, "The domain of allocation *defines the range of resources with which a given agent can act upon a demand for equality.* No claim to equality can be meaningfully addressed to an agent who controls no means for its satisfaction" (emphasis in original). On the other hand, Rae defines a "domain of account" as "the class of things over which a given speaker seeks equality." Further, he emphasizes the following important distinction between a domain of allocation and a domain of account: "A domain of allocation is attached to the agent *to* whom a demand for equality is addressed, and a domain of account is cited by the agent *from* whom such a demand issues" (emphasis in original). Consistent with this distinction, a domain of allocation may or may not "cover" a given domain of account (ibid., 48–49). Thus, let us suppose, for example, that the domain of account involves a demand for equal education for all the children in a given country and that the agent of allocation to whom that demand is addressed is the government of that country. In that case, the domain of allocation would cover the domain of account, if the government possessed sufficient resources to provide equal education for all the children in the country. If, however, the relevant domain of allocation did not encompass all the requisite resources, it would then fail to cover the domain of account. For example, if the constitution of the country in question forbade government to enter the field of education, or if it imposed a ceiling on the amount of taxes that such a government could exact from its citizens, such that it would be impossible for such a government to amass the necessary resources, then the government's domain of allocation would fail to cover the domain of account.

The relationship between domain of allocation and domain of account is particularly important in the context of constitutional equality, in view of certain inherent limitations in the rights afforded by the equal protection clause. Indeed, one of the fundamental prerequisites of a valid equal protection claim is that the requirement of "state action" be met.[8] In general, to satisfy the state action requirement, it is necessary for a state or one of its subdivisions to control directly or indirectly the domain of allocation that encompasses the goods targeted by the relevant domain of account. Direct state control could be said to exist, moreover, whenever a state or one of its subdivisions is the agent of allocation for a given domain of allocation; indirect control, by contrast, when the state has a significant "nexus" with a private agent of allocation,[9] or when the latter performs a "public function."[10]

In view of the constraints imposed by the state action requirement of the equal protection clause, it is conceivable that the demands for equality emanating from a given domain of account may be deemed to be philosophically justified without thereby acquiring any constitutional validity. To illustrate, let us suppose that there are philosophically convincing reasons for requiring equal opportunities in education for all children. If the relevant state government is the agent of allocation for the domain of allocation capable of covering the relevant domain of account, then the philosophical and constitutional justifications of the right to equal opportunity in education may well be coextensive. If, however, the state's government is neither directly nor indirectly in control of the relevant domain of allocation, then there would seem to be no basis for a constitutionally guaranteed right to equal opportunity in education, even in the face of the strongest possible philosophical support for the provision of such right. Consistent with this analysis, and assuming that affirmative action would contribute to the satisfaction of a legitimate domain of account, there may be sound philosophical support for its implementation without thereby being any similar constitutional support.[11]

The second important distinction drawn by Rae, for our purposes, is that between "marginal equality" and "global equality." In Rae's words, "Marginal equality is defined with respect to (often small) *changes* from the status quo, with the changes being equal in magnitude for all. Global equality is defined with respect to holdings above zero, with their *amounts* or end states being equal" (emphasis in original; Rae et al. 1981, 51). To illustrate this difference, let us draw upon Rae's own example and imagine a business with two employees X and Y, who have different salaries; X earns $20,000 per year, while Y earns only $15,000. Now, if both X and Y are given a $5,000 raise, marginal equality will be accomplished, but not global equality. On the other hand, if X's and Y's employer wishes to achieve global equality, she would have to resort to marginal inequality. Indeed, in that case, the employer could either give Y a $5,000 raise, leaving X's salary unchanged; or reduce X's salary by $2,500 and increase Y's salary by the same amount; or else give both X and Y different size raises, such as a $5,000 raise for X and a $10,000 raise for Y, so as to provide both of them with the same salary. In short, whenever one is faced with a state of global inequality, any subsequent marginally equal distribution will preserve the initial global inequality, and any course of action designed to lead to the achievement of global equality among the relevant subject class will necessarily involve some marginally unequal pattern of distribution.

The preceding review of some of the principal elements in Rae's structural grammar of equality reveals that, for any complex society placed within the flow of history, any allocation of divisible goods according to a noncontradictory conception of equality seems bound to create certain particular equalities and correlative inequalities. What Rae's structural grammar of equality does not reveal, however, is which, if any, of the possible conceptions of equality can be given a comprehensive and satisfactory normative justification. Thus, for instance, Rae's analysis provides the means to classify various domains of equality in terms of their breadth but does not indicate whether narrow or broad domains are more likely to be just. The descriptive configurations of equalities and inequalities derived from the structural grammar of equality do not in and of themselves point to any set of norms capable of delimiting legitimate prescriptive bounds for the concept of equality. Accordingly, such norms must be sought elsewhere.

B. The Postulate of Equality

Rae's structural grammar of equality is compatible with a virtually unlimited number of sets of norms, including the most antiegalitarian ones. Within the particular conceptual framework circumscribed by modern liberal theory, however, the range of acceptable norms is much narrower. Moreover, although different values, such as liberty and state neutrality, have assumed a paramount role in certain versions of liberal theory, at the highest levels of abstraction, equality can be viewed as the principal operating norm of liberal theory. At the lower level of abstraction, where such versions of liberal theory as the libertarian, contractarian, utilitarian, and egalitarian conceptions operate, there may be disagreements as to whether liberty or equality should be ranked higher than the other. At the highest levels of abstraction, however, all versions of liberal theory are united in rejecting claims of a natural hierarchy in favor of the assertion that all human beings are in some fundamental sense equal to one another (Gutmann 1980, 18).

According to Gutmann, equality is an idea that, "is basic to the modern doctrine of individualism, equal respect for the human dignity of all people being essential to the realization of individual autonomy, the protection of privacy, and the opportunity for self-development" (ibid.). Gutmann further emphasizes that equality lends support to

> the peculiarly modern view that each human being is uniquely dignified: that every person must be presumed rational until his actions prove otherwise. This presumption of universal rationality is difficult for modern theorists to override. Liberal democratic theorists by no means prove their cases for equal treatment of persons. Rather, they choose not to carry the burden of disproof. The presumption in favor of human equality therefore remains strong for both rationalist and utilitarian schools of liberal thought. (Ibid., 43)

Based on these statements, it can be said that modern liberal theory has embraced the normative proposition that all individuals are morally equal qua individuals. This proposition, to which I shall refer as the "postulate of equality," is counterfactual in the sense that it does not depend for its validity on any empirical proof of the existence of particular (descriptive) equalities.[12] Further, to distinguish the kind of equality involved in the postulate of equality from that which emerges from the interplay of equalities and inequalities revealed through application of the structural grammar of equality, I shall refer to the former as "prescriptive equality" and to the latter as "descriptive equality." With that in mind, what is crucial in the context of liberal political theory are not descriptive equalities of race, physical strength, intelligence, and the like, but rather, as Gutmann indicates, a broadly conceived equal "ability to abide by the law and to choose a reasonable plan of life," as well as an equal capacity for "self-respect and human dignity" (ibid., 45).

Not only has the postulate of equality been a central tenet of liberal political theory from Locke and Kant to Nozick, Rawls, and Dworkin, but it has also been a cornerstone of the American form of constitutional government. This is clearly evidenced by adherence to the famous dictum that "all men are created equal" contained in the United States Declaration of Independence.[13] In explaining the meaning of this dictum, tenBroek has emphasized its prescriptive nature: "'All men are created equal' is not a declarative sentence; it is an imperative. It is not a statement but an exhortation. It is not an affirmation or description. It is a command. Whatever its form, its function is directive. It says in substance, within certain limits and for certain purposes, that we should treat men as if they were the same, although we know full well that they are not" (tenBroek 1969, 19).

While the postulate of equality does not itself specify which equalities and inequalities are justified, it does represent an advance in specificity over the principle of formal justice. Indeed, consistent with the postulate of equality and with its individualistic underpinnings, it is the individual who is the proper subject of equality.[14] Similarly, the U.S. Supreme Court has declared that the proper subject of constitutional equality is the individual.[15] In addition, the postulation of the moral equality of all individuals precludes the use of certain actual differences as the basis for justifying unequal treatment. By placing the postulate of equality within its proper historical perspective, one is reminded that it first emerged as a moral weapon against the privileges of status and birth characteristic of the feudal order (Benn & Peters 1965, 132). Accordingly, at the very least, the postulate of equality condemns using differences of status or birth as the basis for treating persons unequally.

Inasmuch as endorsement of the postulate of equality entails a commitment to the proposition that all individuals are equal in some important respects, theories that espouse the postulate of equality are more egalitarian than rival theories relying on status and hierarchy. It does not follow from this, however, that an adherent to the postulate of equality who might be considered as an egalitarian at the highest levels of abstraction must also commit himself or herself, for the sake of consistency, to an egalitarian middle-level political theory. Gutmann accounts for this distinction, in the context of classical liberal theories, in the following terms:

> To say that classical liberal theories were characterized by assumptions of human equality of course does not imply that classical liberalism was an egalitarian doctrine. Hobbes' theory clearly sanctioned enormous inequalities of power between sovereign and subjects, and Lockean liberalism justified great inequalities in the distribution of property, at least once consent to money was assumed. These political and economic inequalities may have been even

> greater than those sanctioned by previous hierarchical views of politics. (Gutmann 1980, 19)

In other words, commitment to the moral equality of all individuals does not necessarily entail commitment to political or economic equality for all. Although all the middle-level theories generating the arguments for and against affirmative action discussed in the following chapters are committed to the postulate of equality, the libertarian, contractarian, utilitarian, and egalitarian theories differ, as we shall see, in their conception of which social and economic goods ought to be distributed equally (or distributed unequally for purposes of achieving an equal result).

As a general proposition, a theory can be said to be more egalitarian than another if it either supports a larger subject class of equality or a larger domain of equality. For example, if two theories A and B differ only in that A postulates that the class of subjects of equality comprises all the male members of society, while B postulates that such a class comprises both all male and female members of society, then B is a more egalitarian theory than A. Furthermore, if two theories C and D differ only in that C postulates as its domain of equality the class of all political goods, while D postulates that class and in addition the class of all economic goods, then D is a more egalitarian theory than C.

It may be difficult or impossible to determine which of two competing theories is more egalitarian if those theories differ both with respect to the definition of the proper subject class of equality and the proper domain of equality. But it is not necessary to deal with this problem in the context of the present analysis. This is because the alternative middle-level theories giving shape to the various arguments for and against affirmative action to be considered in subsequent chapters do not differ in any significant respect in their respective conceptions of the relevant subject class. Indeed, none of these theories holds that blacks or whites or men or women ought to be excluded from the relevant class that should be made the subject of equality. Rather, these theories differ in their conceptions of what constitutes a legitimate domain of equality, and consequently, each of them can be classified as being more or less egalitarian than the others.

C. Equality of Result and Equality of Opportunity

As I have already mentioned, the postulate of equality posits that individuals are entitled to equal autonomy and equal respect as subjects of moral choice capable of devising and pursuing their own respective life plans.[16] Accordingly, it would seem that the aims of the postulate of equality could be completely satisfied if enough goods could be distributed for each individual to realize fully the goals of his or her own life plan. If this were possible, individuals would most probably receive unequal lots, since not all individual life plans are likely to require the same number or the same kinds of goods for their fulfillment. These unequal lots, however, would merely represent marginal inequalities necessary to realize global subject-regarding equality among all individuals—that is, global equality in the sense of equal satisfaction of each life plan, but not global equality in the sense of an end state in which each individual possesses an equal lot.

In the absence of the abundance required to fulfill everyone's life plan, however, a difficult question is raised concerning the just distribution of scarce resources. Assuming, for example, that several individuals need to obtain a scarce good in order to be able to fulfill his or her own chosen life plan, and that each such individual is equally morally entitled to such good, how could distribution of the scarce good in question be reconciled with adherence to the postulate of equality? If a group of one hundred persons is accidentally trapped in a life-threatening situation, and each such person is equally entitled to be rescued, but available resources are limited in a way such that only fifty persons can be rescued, then a difficult question arises concerning the course of action consistent with adherence to the postulate of equality. Indeed, each of those trapped has an equal need to be rescued regardless of his or her particular life plan, as remaining alive is prerequisite to the satisfaction of every conceivable life plan. Moreover, since it is assumed that none of those trapped is in any way responsible for his or her predicament, none can lay a stronger moral claim to being rescued than any other. Equal treatment for all taken in a literal sense would require not rescuing anyone.[17] Wasting fifty lives that might otherwise be saved for the sake of equal treatment, however, seems morally unjustifiable. On the other hand, assuming that fifty of those trapped are white and fifty are black, selecting those slated for rescue solely on the basis of race would likewise seem morally unjustifiable.

A possible solution relies on the distinction between equality of result and equality of opportunity. As Rae's analysis illustrates, equality of result may entail different outcomes in different circumstances. Thus, the result will probably vary depending on whether lot-regarding or subject-regarding equality of result is deemed the appropriate goal. If lot-regarding equality of result is involved, the distinction between equality of result and equality of opportunity can be stated in the following way: equality of result means that each member of the class designated as the subject of equality ends up with an equal lot (of the good being allocated). Equality of opportunity, on the other hand, means that each member of the subject class has the same opportunity as every other member to obtain some scarce good, but that all members will not end up with an equal lot, as some but not all will succeed in acquiring the scarce good. In Rae's words, equality of opportunity means that "opportunities of power, right and acquisition are to be equal: power, right, and acquisition themselves are not" (Rae et al. 1981, 64).

As Rescher has argued, justice requires the implementation of equality of opportunity whenever equality of result would be mandated if it were not impossible to achieve. In Rescher's view, "a distribution that does not give all equally deserving claimants an equal share must, in the interests of justice, at least preserve an 'equality of opportunity.'" Rescher emphasizes, moreover, that equality of opportunity ought only be implemented if equality of result is impossible to achieve. Thus, he states: "Resort to the concept of 'equality of opportunity' is a *faute de mieux* procedure, a counsel of despair, as it were. It represents a means for achieving an equalization of opportunities (and risks) in cases in which a direct allocation of shares to claims is infeasible" (Rescher 1966, 94).

There is a solution to the moral dilemma posed by the case of the one hundred persons trapped in a life-threatening situation. That solution relies on a scheme that establishes equality of opportunity. Indeed, if each of the one hundred persons involved is given an equal opportunity of being rescued—as would be the case if a fair lottery were carried out to select the fifty persons slated for rescue—it seems possible to avoid both unnecessary deaths and selection for rescue on a morally reprehensible basis such as race. All those trapped are assumed to be equally deserving of rescue and therefore ought to receive equally the good they seek—namely, the services of a rescuer. But since there are not enough rescuers to save everyone, providing each person in need of rescue with an equal opportunity of being rescued would satisfy the requirements of justice. Furthermore, a fair lottery giving everyone in need an equal opportunity of rescue does not violate the postulate of equality, as would selection of who shall live and who shall die solely on the basis of their race. In short, in terms of the distinction drawn by Dworkin, equality of opportunity may not result in *equal treatment,* but it does (in the context of the above case) respect every person's right to *treatment as an equal.*[18]

In the case under consideration, it is, strictly speaking, possible to achieve equal treatment and equality of result. This would happen if *none* of those trapped were rescued. Nevertheless, in the case of rescue it seems intuitively morally wrong to tolerate fifty needless deaths for the sake of achieving equality of result.

Taking into account Rescher's view, we can draw the following conclusion: where equality of result is morally justified—that is, where no morally relevant differences are found that would justify inequality of result—it can nevertheless be set aside if there is a compelling reason to do so, provided that all those originally entitled to equality of result have an equal opportunity to receive the scarce goods to which they would be morally entitled absent scarcity. Moreover, where equality of result would be warranted, equality of opportunity is justified only if there is a scarcity of the good that everyone wants and deserves. Indeed, if, in our example, there were no scarcity of available rescuers, so that all one hundred trapped persons could be saved, than it would clearly be morally wrong to save only half, even if a fair lottery were conducted to determine who would be slated for rescue.

The type of equality of opportunity achieved by means of a lottery, such as in the case of the trapped persons in need of rescue, is what Rae has defined as "prospect-regarding equality of opportunity." In such a case, the lottery grants each person in need of rescue an equal probability of being rescued. In Rae's definition prospect-regarding equal opportunity means that "two persons, j and k, have equal opportunities for X if each has the same probability of attaining X" (Rae et al. 1981, 65).

Rae contrasts "means-regarding equality of opportunity" with prospect-regarding equality of opportunity. In a case involving means-regarding equal opportunity, the competitors for a scarce good possess the same tools for obtaining the good they seek. Rae defines means-regarding equality of opportunity as follows: "Two persons j and k have equal opportunities for X if each has the same instruments for attaining X" (ibid., 66).

While it is possible for equal means and equal prospects to coincide, in many cases, equal means will lead to unequal prospects and equal prospects will require unequal means. To illustrate this, let us suppose that two persons, one being twice as strong as the other, compete for a single good G that can only be obtained through the exertion of physical strength. Without tools other than their brute strength, their prospects for obtaining G are unequal. Moreover, if they are both given the same instrument—say an instrument that is capable of increasing its user's physical strength by a factor of two—they will both possess means-regarding equal opportunity, but their prospects would remain unequal. Conversely, to grant them prospect-regarding equality of opportunity, it will be necessary to provide them with unequal tools for enhancing physical strength. In this latter case, the allocation of unequal means becomes a prerequisite to the achievement of prospect-regarding equality of opportunity.

As Rae points out, when two competitors receive the same instruments, what is achieved is *marginal* means-regarding equality of opportunity. Rae contends, moreover, that "most if not all forms of means-regarding equal opportunity are marginal." This means, in turn, that "some means of success are equalized while others, which affect the use of the first, are allowed to fall unevenly" (ibid., 74). In other words, in the context of inequality in initial circumstances—that is, the prevailing circumstances immediately preceding the allocation of equal means—the institution of marginal means-regarding equality of opportunity is unlikely to bring about equality of result or prospect-regarding equality of opportunity.

To the extent that justice requires the establishment (or preservation) of *marginal* means-regarding equality of opportunity, it is necessary to determine *which* among the total number of means likely to have an effect on the outcome of the competition for scarce goods should be singled out for equal allocation. To illustrate, let us suppose that the domain of relevant means in the context of the competition for scarce jobs can be reduced to the following: the education received by the job applicant and the values imparted to the applicant by her family, such as a strong work ethic. Under these circumstances, both inequalities in education and inequalities in family-imparted values would contribute to inequality of prospects. Moreover, the combination of disparities in education and disparities in family values, pitting applicants with sound educations and family values against others with inadequate educations and weak family values, would compound the difficulties of the latter and increase the inequalities of prospects. Assuming it were possible to provide either equal family values or an equal education, but not both, then it would be necessary to determine which of the two alternatives would better comport with the requirements of justice.

This determination cannot be made in a principled manner without reference to the positions advanced by an intermediate-level theory. The postulate of equality and the structural grammar of equality do not alone indicate *which* means ought to be equally allocated (or equally protected from interference) in order to achieve a legitimate form of means-regarding equality of opportunity. Regardless of the particular forms of means-regarding equality of opportunity ultimately claimed to be justified, however, the legitimacy of means-regarding equality of opportunity is inextricably linked to the *prospects* of success of the subjects of such means-regarding equality. Indeed, if the prospects fall below a certain threshold, then there is no "opportunity," let alone "equality of opportunity." On the other hand, if equal means lead to equal prospects then, as will be more fully explained below, affording means-regarding equality of opportunity would seem to be superfluous.

Westen has argued that, for there to be an opportunity, the subject of the opportunity must not confront an insurmountable obstacle that makes it impossible for her to obtain the good in relation to which she is supposed to have an opportunity (Westen 1985, 839–40). In Westen's words, an opportunity is something more than a "mere possibility" and less than a "guarantee" (ibid.).[19] Combining Westen's point that an opportunity requires more than a mere possibility of success with Rae's observation that marginal means-regarding equality of opportunity makes for equality with respect to some but not all the instruments that a competitor must possess to realize her goal, we find the following. Let us assume, for example, that a demand for means-regarding equality of opportunity arises in the context of the competition for a scarce good that can only be obtained through the employment of several distinct means (e.g., education, effort, perseverance, the display of social graces). In that case, allocating marginal equality with respect to some but not all of these means would fail to provide all competitors with a real opportunity—much less an "equal" opportunity—if some of them were to possess less than a mere possibility of obtaining the scarce good in question *after* the allocation of marginally equal means. In other words, if marginal equal allocation of certain means leaves some of its beneficiaries with such a low prospect of success that they enjoy less than a mere possibility of success, then it fails to satisfy the substantive requirements of equal opportunity. Accordingly, in determining which means ought to be equally allocated, and which can legitimately be allowed to remain unequal, it is necessary to rule out those choices that would leave certain members of the subject class with prospects amounting to no more than a mere possibility of success.

As I previously pointed out, equality of means—and particularly marginal equality of means—generally goes hand in hand with inequality in prospects. Moreover, this relationship between equal means and unequal prospects often seems to be particularly desirable. For example, if scarce jobs are allocated pursuant to a competition among a group of candidates who have all been provided with the same education, those who possess greater natural talents would clearly enjoy higher prospects of success. All other things being equal, those with greater talents will obtain the scarce jobs. Provided that equalizing educational experiences renders the competition for scarce jobs just and fair, this result may represent the best possible way, under the circumstances, of allocating scarce goods in conformity with the postulate of equality. If, however, all the competitors possessed exactly the same natural talents, then the competition for the scarce jobs would fail to lead to the desired outcome. Indeed, assuming that test results are an exclusive function of natural talents and previous education, then all the competitors would end up with the same score, and it would become impossible to award the jobs on the basis of test results alone. In other words, when means-regarding equality of opportunity leads to equal prospects for all, it loses its usefulness as a device for the allocation of scarce goods.

Not only would a truly *global* means-regarding equal opportunity requiring the full equalization of all means be superfluous, it would also most likely be unbearably intrusive. As Rae points out, to achieve a full convergence between means and prospects, "One would have to include a great deal under the domain of means—for example, genetic endowments (cloning equals?), the family (raising children under common conditions), schooling (a perfectly standardized curriculum for genetically standardized children). With these draconian measures, equal means would lead toward equal prospects" (Rae et al. 1981, 75).

Even assuming that equality of means requires prospects amounting to more than a "mere possibility" but less than a "guarantee," the question remains whether to choose marginal or global equality with respect to certain individual means. Supposing that means-regarding equal opportunity in the competition for scarce jobs is realized if all the competitors have obtained an equal education, and that the competition is open to all, there is a question as to whether the competitors are entitled to marginal or global equality in education. If the competition for scarce jobs is deemed just, provided that all competitors have received the same number of years of education in the same subjects regardless of their educational achievements, then marginal equality in education would be sufficient. If, however, the job competition were not just unless all competitors had achieved the same level of educational proficiency, then what would be called for would be global equality in education. In this latter case, the achievement of a genuine means-regarding equality of opportunity in the competition for jobs would depend on the realization of equality of results in education. It becomes apparent that equality of opportunity with respect to the allocation of one scarce good may sometimes depend on the achievement of equality of result with respect to the allocation of another good.

A distinction is often drawn between "formal equality of opportunity" and "fair equality of opportunity." Fullinwider gives the following definition of formal equality of opportunity: "X and Y have equal opportunity in regard to A so long as neither faces a legal or quasi-legal barrier to achieving A the other does not face" (Fullinwider 1980, 101). If we view this definition in terms of the preceding analysis, formal equality of opportunity can be considered as a form of means-regarding equality of opportunity. It requires that laws and quasi-legal devices not be used to deprive subjects of means already in their possession or within their present capacity to obtain in the future. Thus, for example, a law that forbids blacks from competing for certain scarce jobs would deprive them of formal equality of opportunity. Similarly, a law that makes it illegal for blacks to obtain the education that would make them eligible for certain scarce jobs would also deprive them of formal equality of opportunity with respect to the allocation of those jobs.

"Fair equality of opportunity," on the other hand, requires, according to Rawls, that "those with similar abilities and skills should have similar life chances . . . irrespective of the income class into which they are born" (Rawls 1971, 73). Moreover, in Goldman's words, fair equality of opportunity requires that

> individuals should be afforded the means of fulfilling their natural capacities. The social system assumes responsibility for overcoming initial disadvantages that have social causes—for example, disadvantages owing to low income or social class of one's parents. Individuals from all economic and social classes should be able to achieve those skills they are naturally suited for achieving. Thus, with respect to the award of jobs or socially desirable positions, . . . (fair equality of opportunity) . . . demands correction for socially relative disadvantages. (Goldman 1979, 171)

In other words, assuming that the totality of separate means capable of affecting the relative prospects of the various competitors for scarce goods could be divided into two distinct categories relating respectively to "natural" and "socially generated" abilities and skills, then fair equality of opportunity would require that the latter, but not the former, be equalized for all. Put yet another way, fair (means-regarding) equality of opportunity requires that differences in prospects among competitors be an exclusive function of differences in natural abilities and skills.

Eliminating socially caused differences in prospects may require the institution of global means-regarding equality of opportunity with respect to those instruments whose acquisition depends on socially relative factors. Indeed, to accomplish the goal which Rawls contemplates for fair equality of opportunity, marginal means-regarding equality of opportunity may often be insufficient. Let us assume that, for several generations, members of the elite class have received outstanding educations while members of socially disadvantaged classes have received virtually none. In that case, merely prescribing the same education for all might fail to end socially relative differences in prospects in the competition for scarce jobs. Indeed, the elimination of all socially relative differences in prospects might well require remedial programs for the disadvantaged, or some other *marginally* unequal treatment of the privileged and the underprivileged likely to lead eventually to global equality in education. In short, inasmuch as fair equality of opportunity requires the eradication of social disadvantages, it may justify unequal allocations of certain relevant goods.

D. Distributive, Compensatory, and Procedural Justice

Let us assume, for the sake of argument, that justice requires the institution of formal equality of opportunity. From the prospective standpoint of a sociopolitical order about to be set into operation, this means that the government shall not impose any legal or quasi-legal obstacles to the competition for scarce goods. From the retrospective standpoint of a government confronted with claims for the redress of injuries suffered as the result of past violations of the right to formal equality of opportunity, on the other hand, the matter may not be nearly as clear. It may be that the removal of wrongful legal or quasi-legal obstacles imposed in the past would suffice, and lead to the restoration of the kind of competition envisaged initially. It may also be, however—particularly, if the illicit obstacles have been in place for a long period of time—that the mere removal of such obstacles would not suffice to restore the kinds of conditions that existed (or would have existed) prior to the imposition of such legal or quasi-legal obstacles. Thus, for example, it is conceivable that long-term legal obstacles imposed on some but not other members of society have put the former at such a disadvantage that the removal of the obstacles would not improve their prospects of success in the relevant arenas of competition to more than a "mere possibility." In short, even if there were unanimous agreement on a single principle of justice, its proper application would most likely differ from one type situation to another. Accordingly, at the very least, a distinction must be made between justice in distribution and justice in compensation.

The distinction between distributive justice and corrective or compensatory justice dates at least as far back as Aristotle.[20] According to Aristotle, "distributive justice" relates to the distribution of public goods by political authorities, whereas "corrective justice" applies to private transactions. As understood by Rescher, "Aristotle's *distributive justice* requires the state to act equitably in its distribution of goods (and presumably also of evils) among its members. Aristotle's *corrective justice* requires the individual to act equitably in actions or transactions affecting the interests of his fellows" (Rescher 1966, 6). Philosophers do not agree on the definition of "distributive justice," as certain modern conceptions of it are much broader than Aristotle's. It is nevertheless important to settle on some definition of distributive justice, particularly since the nature and scope of the relationship between distributive and compensatory justice is likely to vary as a function of the adoption of narrower or broader domains of application for the principle of distributive justice.

Feinberg points out that, notwithstanding the traditional meaning given to the term distributive justice, "it has now come to apply also to the goods and evils of a nonpolitical kind that can be distributed by private citizens to other private citizens. In fact, in most recent literature, the term is reserved for *economic* distributions, particularly the justice of differences in economic income between classes, and of various schemes of taxation which discriminate in different ways between classes" (Feinberg 1973, 107). Feinberg also indicates that distributive justice can be used to refer to acts of distribution as well as to states of affairs that follow from some distribution. Moreover, the term *distribution* is itself ambiguous, and this may account, in part, for the kind of uncertainty that exists concerning its proper scope. In Feinberg's words, "there is, of course, an ambiguity in the meaning of 'distribution.' The word may refer to the *process* of distributing, or the *product* of some process of distributing, and either or both of these can be appraised as just or unjust" (emphasis in original; ibid, 107–8). Not only can considerations of justice be applied to both the *process* and the *product* of a distribution, but they can be applied to them even if no *deliberate* scheme or process of distribution is in place. As Feinberg states, "a 'distribution' can be understood to be a 'product' which is *not* the result of any deliberate distributing process, but simply a state of affairs whose production has been too complicated to summarize or to ascribe to any definite group of persons as their deliberate doing. The present 'distribution' of American wealth is just such a state of affairs" (ibid., 108). Consistent with Feinberg's analysis, distributive justice will be understood here in its broadest meaning, which encompasses both the *process* and the *product* of distribution, whether such distribution is deliberately planned or the unintended result of the combination of social, political, and economic forces.

One of the advantages of a narrow conception of distributive and compensatory justice, such as the traditional one espoused by Aristotle, is that it seems to minimize the potential for conflict between the aims of distributive justice and those of compensatory justice. Indeed, if the domain of distributive justice is limited to certain public goods in the exclusive possession of the state, and that of compensatory justice to the realm of private transactions, then conflict seems entirely avoidable as the two domains do not appear to overlap. With as broad a conception of distributive justice as the one adopted here, however, conflicts between distributive and compensatory aims cannot be as easily avoided. Not surprisingly, in the context of broader conceptions of distributive justice, several contemporary philosophers have noted that the aims of distributive justice are likely to conflict with those of compensatory justice.[21] Before attempting any further examination of the relation between compensatory and distributive justice, however, we must take a closer look at the meaning of the term *compensatory justice.*

As in the case of distributive justice, there are different conceptions of compensatory justice (Coleman 1983, 6). Aristotle's account of compensatory justice, at least according to Weinrib, "considers the position of the parties anterior to [a] transaction as equal, and it restores this antecedent equality by transferring resources from defendant to plaintiff so that the gain realized by the former is used to make up the loss suffered by the latter. In this focal and paradigmatic instance the gain is equivalent to the loss" (Weinrib 1983, 38). Weinrib goes on to contrast compensatory justice with distributive justice. Compensatory justice involves an "impingement" of one party over the other, whereas distributive justice does not. He states that, in the context of distributive justice, "the relationship between the claimants—who can in theory be any number—is always mediated by the scheme of distribution" (ibid.).

Coleman also contrasts compensatory justice with distributive justice. In Coleman's words, "Corrective justice is a matter of justice . . . *not* because it promotes justice in the distribution of holdings, but rather because it remedies unjust departures from the prevailing distribution of holdings" (emphasis in original; Coleman 1983, 6). Further, Coleman maintains that compensatory justice provides an independent principle of justice "precisely because it may be legitimately invoked to protect or reinstate distributions of holdings which would themselves fail the test of distributive justice" (ibid., 7). In analyzing the principle of compensatory justice in the context of affirmative action, Goldman identifies the following case as the paradigm: "The paradigm case to which the principle of compensation applies involves an intentional infliction of injury in violation of right, resulting in a measurable loss to the victim and benefit to the specifiable perpetrator. In this case it is clear that the guilty party ought to restore his ill-gotten benefit to the victim" (Goldman 1979, 67–68). In the strongest possible case fitting within this paradigm, moreover, the ill-gotten gain of the violator would be the exact equivalent of the loss suffered by the victim. This would be true in cases in which a violator has stolen a given good from the victim. In such cases, the measure of the loss suffered by the victim is equal to the measure of the gain obtained by the violator—at least from the standpoint of lot-regarding equality.[22] In those cases in which the unjust enrichment of the violator corresponds exactly to the wrongful loss incurred by the victim, application of the principle of compensatory justice can completely restore the equilibrium that existed immediately prior to the transaction giving rise to a claim for compensation.

Extrapolating from the cited views, and focusing exclusively for the moment on the paradigm case of the misappropriation of particular goods, one could say that compensatory justice requires the transfer of goods from one subject to another in order to restore the equilibrium that existed between these two subjects prior to their voluntary or involuntary involvement in a transaction that resulted in a gain for the violator and a loss for the victim. The subjects in question may be individuals or groups. War reparations by one country to another as compensation for wrongful expropriation of property, for example, would constitute an instance of the use of compensatory justice to restore a prewar equilibrium between groups. Compensatory justice may be invoked in the context of a "voluntary transaction" such as a contract if, after performance by one of the parties to the contract, the other party were to breach the contract by refusing to perform his own contractual obligations. Thus, if one party to a contract for the sale of a good delivers that good to the other party, but the latter then refuses to pay for the good received as agreed, then compensatory justice would require that the illicit gain resulting from possession of a good for which payment was unjustly refused be wiped out. An "involuntary transaction" could be involuntary from the standpoint of the victim only, or from the standpoint of both the victim and the wrongdoer. Theft provides an instance of the former, as the victim is involuntarily drawn into the theft "transaction," whereas the thief voluntarily engages in it. By contrast, the following situation provides an example of a transaction that is entered into involuntarily by both parties. Suppose A purchases a good G from a merchant M and pays M for it, with delivery due subsequently. Suppose further that M delivers G by mistake to B, who lives next door to A. In this case both A and B could be said to have entered into a transaction *involving the other* involuntarily. Yet if B simply refuses to return G to A, after knowing that he received G by mistake, then A would clearly seem to have a compensatory claim against B.

Given the broad conception of distributive justice adopted above, and assuming a continuing adherence to the same principle of distributive justice, the relationship between distributive and compensatory justice might either be one of harmony and complementarity or one of conflict and contradiction. The former is likely to be the case where an overriding principle of justice governs all social interaction and where justice in distribution and justice in compensation are treated as two distinct embodiments of the same overriding principle. It is also likely in those cases in which the concerns of distributive justice loom as paramount and those of compensatory justice as being subordinate to them. On the other hand, distributive and compensatory justice are likely to clash in those cases in which each of them is used to advance the goals of distinct and incompatible principles of justice.

Before I provide examples of the three kinds of relationship between distributive and compensatory justice identified above, it is important to be aware of the following point made by Weinrib regarding compensatory justice: "Restoration of equality with reference to an initial position does not specify either the relevant notion of equality or the relevant initial position. . . . Corrective justice in itself is devoid of a specific content, which, accordingly, must be sought elsewhere" (Weinrib 1983, 40). Thus, in a breach of contract after performance by one party, for example, although compensatory justice requires that the breaching party compensate the nonbreaching party, it does not itself provide the proper measure of compensation. Supposing the nonbreaching party has delivered a good to the breaching party, what should the proper measure of compensation be? The market value of the good delivered? The contract price the breaching party had agreed to pay for that good? As Weinrib's observations suggest, one cannot provide a principled answer to this question without referring to certain norms that are not inherent in the concept of compensatory justice. In short, regardless of which possible relationship between distributive and compensatory justice may be deemed applicable, the concept of compensatory justice does not of itself provide a legitimate measure of compensation.

An example of a situation in which compensatory and distributive justice emerge as two distinct embodiments of the same overriding principle of justice is provided by the view that justice requires the enforcement of contracts.[23] One may assume that this view, which may be referred to as justice as contract (Rosenfeld 1985a), is grounded on the belief that a society based on free exchange is uniquely suited to promote individual autonomy and respect. On the other hand, in a sociopolitical order governed exclusively by the principle of justice as contract, no deliberate pattern of distribution could be legitimately imposed. Nevertheless, it is conceivable that *any* or *all*, or even *any and all*, configurations of holdings that may result from the free exchange of goods pursuant to contracts might be deemed to be fair and just. In other words, so long as the *process* of distribution is an exclusive function of the execution of freely concluded contracts, any or all (or any and all) *products* of distribution emanating from such a process would necessarily satisfy the relevant criterion of distributive justice. A further consequence of the postulation that the terms of a freely concluded contract are necessarily fair and just, moreover, is that the measure of compensation for a breach of contract should be determined by reference to the terms of the contract. Thus, the proper measure of the value of the good received by the breaching party is supplied by the good which that party was contractually obligated to deliver to the nonbreaching party. If one party has performed under the contract and the other party refuses to do likewise, compensatory justice could fully restore the requisite equilibrium by commanding that the breaching party carry out his obligations under the contract. Under these circumstances, the performance of all the obligations arising under the contract would both satisfy the aims of compensatory justice and promote those of distributive justice. In the context of justice as contract, therefore, distributive and compensatory justice are in harmony and they both contribute to the achievement of the same goal.

An example of a situation in which the principle of compensatory justice appears subordinate to that of distributive justice is provided by the following set of circumstances. Let us suppose that distributive justice requires formal means-regarding equal opportunity with respect to job allocations. The reason for this requirement is the desire to have jobs allocated to the most qualified to hold them and the belief that this would occur if each applicant is given an opportunity to demonstrate possession of the relevant qualifications. The justification for the distribution of jobs to the most qualified is the belief that such a distribution will produce greater efficiency and thus eventfully benefit everyone.

Let us now imagine that a person who has demonstrated that he is the most qualified candidate for a given job is nevertheless not chosen to fill that job. If immediate compensation for the violation of his right were available, and if it took the form of awarding him the job in question, then both compensatory and distributive justice could be satisfied by the single act of awarding him the job he was unjustly denied. If, however, there is a significant lapse of time between injury and compensation—say six months—an apparent conflict could well develop between the aims of distributive justice and those of compensatory justice. Indeed, let us assume that six months after our victim has been unjustly denied the job, it becomes available again. From the standpoint of compensatory justice, awarding the job to the victim would be appropriate. But if when the job becomes available for the second time there are candidates who are better qualified to hold it than our victim, then awarding it to him would seem to violate the dictates of distributive justice.

Goldman argues that when the need for compensation arises out of the violation of a prevailing distributive norm, there is a solution to the dilemma posed by apparently mutually contradictory distributive and compensatory aims. The solution he proposes holds that compensation for past violations of the principle of distribution should take precedence over distributive considerations, even if that entails temporarily suspending application of the distributive principle (Goldman 1979, 65–67). Thus, a violation of equal opportunity rights in the domain of job allocation might have to be compensated by awarding the victim a subsequently available job, even at the price of suspending a nonvictim's right of equal opportunity to the latter job. According to Goldman, this solution is nevertheless justified, for, unless compensatory claims are given precedence over distributive claims, those who violated the victim's rights could completely and with impunity undermine a legitimate distributive principle (ibid.). To prevent this, and ultimately to preserve the integrity of a violated distributive principle, paradoxically, one may have to set the principle temporarily aside.

In terms of Goldman's analysis, the above example presents no genuine long-term conflict between compensatory and distributive justice. The chief concern is to protect the continuous long-term functioning of an established principle of distributive justice. Accordingly, the principal function of compensatory justice may be to contribute to the long-term realization of just distributive aims.

Let us turn finally to an example of a situation in which the aims of compensatory and distributive justice seem to be squarely in conflict with one another. Based on Weinrib's claim that compensatory justice tends to be at odds with the principal aims of utilitarianism (Weinrib 1983, 40–41), one can conceive of a situation in which a utilitarian principle of distributive justice is supplemented by an independent principle of compensatory justice. Let us hence assume that just distributions are to be determined from the perspective of an act-utilitarian and that the independent criterion of compensatory justice requires, inter alia, that the victim of a theft be compensated by the thief in an amount equal to the market value of the stolen property. With this in mind, consider the following example: An impecunious mother steals a loaf of bread from an overweight millionaire in order to feed herself and her starving children. The day after the theft, the mother receives a charitable donation in an amount equal to the market value of a loaf of bread, which she intends to use to feed herself and her children. According to the prevailing principle of compensatory justice the mother ought to give the money she received to the millionaire as compensation for her theft of his loaf of bread. From the standpoint of the prevailing act-utilitarian principle of justice, however, she ought to keep the money, as the utilities she and her children would derive from that money would by far outweigh any utility that the millionaire would derive from this (to him) insignificant sum of money. Moreover, even if it is conceded that a net disutility might result to society as a whole if theft is generally tolerated, it seems plausible that the disutility resulting from the theft of food for the sole purpose of feeding starving children would be clearly outweighed by the utilities to be gained from the avoidance of starvation. Under such circumstances, there appears to be a strong distributive claim against compensation, and the aims of distributive justice seem therefore to be in clear conflict with those of compensatory justice.

Thus far we have assumed the existence of a paradigm case for compensation. Not all cases in which the law imposes a duty of compensation, however, can be made to fit within that paradigm. Indeed, whereas in the context of a theft the wrongful gain of the thief may be equal to the loss of the victim, the same would not be true in the context of negligent motoring leading to an injury-causing accident. Unlike the thief, the negligent motorist is not enriched by the accident caused by his or her negligence—or at least not enriched in an amount that is equivalent to the loss attributable to the injuries of the accident victim. This lack of equivalence between the negligent motorist's "gain" and the victim's loss leads Coleman, for one, to conclude that the obligation to make the victim whole for her injuries cannot be grounded exclusively on considerations of compensatory justice. In Coleman's own words,

> Because harmful, negligent motoring does not result in any wrongful gain . . . the obligation to repair the victim's wrongful loss cannot be entirely grounded on a foundation of corrective justice. There is, in other words, no wrongful gain corrective of the wrongful loss the faulty injurer imposes upon his victim; and no reason therefore as a matter of corrective justice alone for imposing the victim's loss upon his injurer. (Coleman 1983, 10–11)

Coleman argues further that a negligent injurer who secures no gain cannot be made liable as a matter of compensatory justice (ibid., 11).

As Coleman points out, the concern of compensatory justice is "wrongful gains *and* losses" (emphasis added; ibid.). From the standpoint of the victim who has suffered a wrongful loss, however, it may be irrelevant whether or not the wrongdoer enjoys a wrongful gain. Accordingly, in terms of the *legitimacy* of a victim's claim for compensation for a wrongful loss, it may not be particularly relevant whether or not there is any actual symmetry between such wrongful loss and the wrongful gain of the wrongdoer.[24] If, for example, a thief destroys the good he has decided to misappropriate from the victim in the course of stealing it, there may be no gain for the thief. Nevertheless, it still seems reasonable to maintain that the victim has a valid claim of compensation against the thief, in an amount equal to the value of the good destroyed as it was being stolen.

It may also be argued that a victim's legitimate claim to compensation does not depend on the continuing existence of the wrongdoer. Thus, the claim for compensation of a theft victim should not be deemed to expire with the death of the thief. Again, from the standpoint of the victim, the wrongful loss is the same whether or not the thief is alive, and the *moral* right to compensation should depend entirely on the nature and amount of the wrongful loss, not on the size of the wrongdoer's wrongful gain or on the contingent fact that the wrongdoer died before the victim's claim has been formally presented.

So long as a claim "to be made whole" is considered from the perspective of the victim who has suffered a wrongful loss, that claim can be said to come within the domain of compensatory justice. Having a valid claim to compensation, however, should not be taken to mean, in this interpretation, that the claimholder ought to have a guarantee of recovering the equivalent of her wrongful loss. There may be conflicting claims entitled to priority under the prevailing criteria of justice. In addition, and more importantly from the standpoint of the present analysis, the obligation to satisfy a valid claim for compensation is generally limited to the particular person or entity who is (morally and/or legally) responsible for the claimholder's wrongful loss. Further, unless the wrongdoer's gain is commensurate with the victim's loss, it is thus far unclear whether the victim should be entitled to full recovery from the wrongdoer.

Assuming the existence of a valid claim for compensation on the part of the victim, we now examine the question from the standpoint of the wrongdoer. In Coleman's view, all that compensatory justice requires of the wrongdoer is that his illicit gain be undone (Coleman 1983, 11). Consistent with this view, in cases in which there is an asymmetry between wrongful gain and loss, the wrongdoer's obligation under compensatory justice is limited to the return of the wrongful gain. Thus, even the victim's death (from unrelated causes) would not exonerate the wrongdoer from the obligation to divest himself of his wrongful gain. But, by the same token, if the victim's loss is much greater than the wrongdoer's gain, the latter's obligation *under compensatory justice* would still be limited to the amount of the wrongful gain. In this view, therefore, while it may be ultimately just to impose liability on a wrongdoer for the full amount of his victim's loss, any amount of liability that exceeds the wrongdoer's gain must be justified by something other than the dictates of compensatory justice.

Coleman's view seems to adopt too narrow a conception of the proper scope of compensatory justice. Indeed, it would be more reasonable both in terms of widely accepted legal and moral standards to define compensatory justice broadly enough to encompass the entire obligation of the one who is responsible for the wrongful loss of the victim, regardless of the amount of the wrongdoer's illicit gain. Therefore, so long as a victim's wrongful loss can be said (in a moral or legal sense) to be the fault of a wrongdoer, both the victim's claim and the wrongdoer's obligation to satisfy that claim will be considered for purposes of the present analysis to fall within the domain of compensatory justice. Unlike in Coleman's conception, in the one adopted here, application of the principles of compensatory justice does not always lead to a zero-sum result.

It may be objected that, unless the domain of compensatory justice remains within the narrow confines conceived by Coleman, the boundary between the realms of compensatory and distributive justice will become significantly blurred. In this view, merely restoring the status quo ante between wrongdoer and victim where the latter's loss exceeds the former's gain cannot be called, strictly speaking, a matter of pure compensation. In some cases, making the victim whole involves a net loss, and the proper allocation of that loss as between the wrongdoer and the victim can and should properly be viewed as a distributive matter.

In response to this last argument, one can point out that, even in a paradigm case under compensatory justice, the restoration of the status quo ante between the wrongdoer and the victim is likely to have independent distributive consequences. Indeed, as pointed out in the example of the destitute mother who steals a loaf of bread from a millionaire, the distributive consequences of requiring compensation would be a net decrease in utility. In general, it seems fair to assume that the totality of transactions made pursuant to the principles of compensatory justice will lead to changes in the total configuration of holdings in society, which may be deemed desirable or undesirable, depending on the prevailing criteria of distributive justice.

In view of the conception of distributive and compensatory justice adopted here, there are two types of cases that require further examination. These cases are not cases of mere asymmetry between gains and losses, but cases in which either the victim or the wrongdoer have altogether disappeared. In those two cases, the satisfaction of a claim to compensation or an obligation of compensation cannot be viewed exclusively in terms of compensatory justice. Unlike in other cases, where the entire transaction is governed by the principles of compensatory justice—albeit that such transaction *also* generates distributive consequences—in the two cases under consideration, the relevant transaction is governed in part by relevant principles of compensation, but also, in part, by relevant principles of distribution.

To illustrate this last point, let us imagine a case in which a thief steals some valuable goods from a victim who happens to die—in a manner completely unrelated to the theft—without leaving any survivors before the thief can be compelled to make the requisite compensation. Under these circumstances, compensatory justice would still seem to require that the thief be deprived of his wrongful gain. Compensatory justice, however, would provide no guidance in the determination of who should receive the goods that the thief must return. Distributive justice, on the other hand, might provide the necessary guidance. If, for example, the thief's wrongful gain is paid into a surplus fund to be distributed in accordance with the prevailing principle of distributive justice, then the ultimate disposition of the thief's wrongful gain will contribute to the promotion of distributive justice. From the standpoint of the obligation imposed on the thief, the transaction falls within the domain of compensatory justice; from that of the ultimate recipients of the goods returned by the thief, however, the transaction belongs to the domain of distributive justice. In short, taken in its totality, the transaction in question is in part compensatory and in part distributive.

A similar argument can be made in the case in which the wrongdoer has vanished before having had an opportunity to compensate his victim. As an example of such a case, let us imagine that an arsonist has completely destroyed his victim's home before disappearing without leaving any property behind. Let us assume further that the members of the victim's community decide to set up a fund and to contribute to it with a view toward enabling the victim to rebuild his home. From the victim's standpoint, replacement of his burnt house is a matter of compensatory justice; from that of the other members of the community, by contrast, contributing to the fund set up to help the victim clearly does not represent the fulfillment of an obligation under compensatory justice. Furthermore, if we postulate that the principle of justice embraced by the community makes it imperative for its members to contribute in certain prescribed proportions to the fund set up to compensate the arson victim, from the standpoint of the members of the community, the obligation to contribute to the compensation fund may reasonably be viewed as pertaining to the domain of distributive justice. Thus, just as in the case in which the wrongdoer's illicit gain is taken away although the victim has vanished, in the case in which the victim is "made whole" although the wrongdoer has disappeared, the transaction designed to rectify the relevant past wrong can be in part compensatory and in part distributive.

It is important to distinguish between cases involving compensation to the victim of a wrongful loss made by persons other than the wrongdoer and cases merely concerned with the equitable distribution of losses with respect to which no one has committed a wrong and no one has had a right infringed. Although in practice these two kinds of cases may on occasion be difficult to distinguish, in theory they remain distinct. For example, in the case of a natural disaster, such as an earthquake or a flood, certain members of society may absorb all the ensuing losses, but society, consistent with prevailing principles of distributive justice, may redistribute these losses so that these are ultimately spread proportionately among all its members. In such a case, the victims of the disaster would receive what may appear, on the surface, as a compensation for their loss, but should rather be viewed as a redistribution meant to eliminate their disproportionate initial share of the total losses.

The difference between compensation and a redistribution designed to spread a loss proportionately among the members of a group emerges even more clearly in the example of arson followed by the disappearance of the wrongdoer. Let us suppose that in that case the victim's home is twice as expensive as the standard home that every member of the community is entitled to. Moreover, each person in that community is entitled to a standard home pursuant to a principle of distributive justice that prescribes: "To each a decent shelter in the form of a standard home." Under these circumstances, the arson victim would presumably have, after the total destruction of his home, a distributive claim for a standard home, and a *compensatory* claim for a home costing twice as much as the standard home. If the community provides a standard home to the victim, then it discharges its distributive obligation to the victim, and the latter receives a good to which he is distributively entitled. If, on the other hand, the community provides the victim with a home worth twice as much as the standard one, then the victim would be receiving what he is entitled to under the principles of compensatory justice. To determine which of these two possible alternatives is preferable, however, it is necessary to refer to the applicable principles of substantive justice, or in other words, to norms that transcend the mere notion of compensatory or distributive justice.

In addition to consideration of compensatory and distributive justice, the achievement of justice generally depends on the implementation of just procedures. Indeed, if we assume that all the relevant substantive precepts of justice are firmly in place, it is doubtful that just results could be achieved in the absence of adequate procedures. For example, if justice requires that all criminals be punished for their crimes, but if the procedures used to determine who are the criminals are so inadequate that many noncriminals are punished while the majority of criminals escape punishment, then the lack of fair procedures would lead to the frustration of the aims of justice. Questions of procedural justice may therefore be important, and to the extent that they should figure in the determination of the justice of affirmative action, they will be addressed in the course of the following analysis. Moreover, in examining matters pertaining to procedural justice, I shall rely on the distinctions made on this subject by Rawls. According to him, there are basically two types of procedures leading to the achievement of justice (Rawls 1971, 85–87). The first requires both an independent criterion of justice to determine what would be a just compensation or distribution and a procedure to lead to the desired outcome as determined by the independent criterion. If the procedure assures the desired outcome, then one has, according to Rawls, "perfect procedural justice"; if it does not, then one has "imperfect procedural justice" (ibid., 85). As an example of the latter, Rawls mentions the criminal trial under the adversary system of justice. The adversary system does not always lead to the desired outcome—that is, the conviction of the guilty and the acquittal of the innocent. But it presumably works well in a sufficient number of cases to be arguably considered the best possible means of achieving the desired outcome consistent with adherence to fundamental individual rights. Accordingly, the criminal trial is procedurally imperfect but can nonetheless be deemed to be just, so long as no less imperfect alternative can reasonably be said to be available.

The second type of procedure considered by Rawls leads to what he terms "pure procedural justice." In contrast to perfect and imperfect procedural justice, pure procedural justice does not require the existence of an independent criterion of justice for its validity. Indeed, in Rawls' conception, in the context of pure procedural justice, any outcome is just provided that a fair procedure was properly followed (ibid.,

86). As an example of pure procedural justice Rawls suggests gambling. In his own words, "If a number of persons engage in a series of fair bets, the distribution of cash after the last bet is fair, or at least not unfair, whatever this distribution is." *Any* distribution resulting from a series of fair bets is just, but only as long as the bets remain fair. Thus, for instance, if the betting is marred by cheating, the resulting distribution would be unjust. Indeed, what each gambler who risks his own cash in the hope of winning a much larger sum counts on is prospect-regarding equality of opportunity (or means-regarding equality of opportunity if the particular form of gambling in question depends on skill as well as on chance) to win the larger sum at the culmination of a process of random selection. By subverting the random procedure, cheating alters the prospects of the gamblers and deprives them of equal opportunity. In general, where pure procedural justice is deemed appropriate, the main threat to justice stems from interference with the procedures designed to lead to the realization of pure procedural justice. Moreover, to the extent that the use of particular procedures is linked to the promotion of equality of opportunity, and that the acquisition of one good is likely to enhance the prospects (or means) of acquiring another, violations of pure procedural justice may pose vexing remedial problems. In many such instances, the mere restoration of the operation of the violated procedures may be insufficient to erase the unfair advantages gained as a result of their violation. Therefore, in a certain number of cases, the effects of interference with a purely procedural scheme are unlikely to be remedied by a mere return to the procedures originally designed to yield pure procedural justice.

E. The Meaning of Affirmative Action

There is much confusion concerning the meaning of *affirmative action* (Fullinwider 1980, 159) resulting, in significant part, from the vast array of often inconsistent practices and policies that fall under that rubric (ibid., chaps. 11, 12). The broad scope and seeming elasticity of the term emerges clearly from the following definition provided by Greenawalt: "'Affirmative action' is a phrase that refers to attempts to bring members of underrepresented groups, usually groups that have suffered discrimination, into a higher degree of participation in some beneficial program. Some affirmative action efforts include preferential treatment; others do not." (Greenawalt 1983, 17). In addition, affirmative action has also been associated with the imposition of "quotas" and "goals" (ibid.). Another term often associated with affirmative action is *reverse discrimination,* which, in Greenawalt's words, "means a difference in treatment that reverses the pattern of earlier discrimination" (ibid., 16).

Like the terms *discrimination* and *first-order discrimination,* the term reverse discrimination can be given a negative connotation. Indeed, if first-order discrimination consists in placing blacks at a disadvantage because they are black, for instance, then reverse discrimination might well be taken to imply the need to place whites at a disadvantage because they are white. But whereas the racist presumably wants to disadvantage his victims because of the latter's race, it is not the principal objective of the vast majority of proponents of affirmative action to place whites at a disadvantage *because* of their race. Accordingly, it is understandable that, as Greenawalt notes, "Some people who support (affirmative action) programs object to the term 'reverse discrimination' because they fear that the label will tag such programs with the assumption of unjustifiability that accompanies other practices they call discrimination" (ibid.).

To the extent that reverse discrimination is much the same as first-order discrimination, with a change only in victims, it is equally morally objectionable. Indeed, the postulate of equality precludes disadvantaging whites because of the color of their skin, just as much as it forbids disadvantaging blacks on the same basis. Because of this, and of the difficulties involved in dissociating the term reverse discrimination from its negative connotations, I shall avoid its use in the course of the following analysis.

Preferential treatment connotes the granting of a preference to one or several persons among a group of competitors, but as Greenawalt observes, not all such preferences constitute instances of preferential treatment (ibid.). For example, selecting the most gifted athlete for one's team indicates a preference for that athlete over all the others who also wish to make the team but is not properly characterized as an instance of preferential treatment.[25] Because the following examination of affirmative action will be largely confined to the contexts of university admissions and job hiring, I shall focus on the meaning that preferential treatment may be given in those specific contexts. Referring to the context of job hiring, and to the issue of race, Fullinwider provides the following definition of preferential treatment: "A black is preferentially hired over a white when the black, because he is black, is chosen over at least one better qualified white, where being black is not a job related qualification" (Fullinwider 1980, 17). Fullinwider's definition could easily be modified to be made applicable to the context of education by replacing "preferentially hired" with "preferentially admitted," and "being black is not a job related qualification" with "being black does not affect the educational abilities of a candidate for admission." Further, Fullinwider's definition can be expanded to cover preferential treatment on the basis of gender, merely by substitution of women and men for black and white, where appropriate.

Particularly since one of the assumptions I will make in the next section is that it is possible to ascertain academic and job qualifications with sufficient precision to be able to make a fair and meaningful comparison among competing applicants, Fullinwider's definition seems highly suitable for adoption. There is, however, one major problem with it. Fullinwider maintains that a black is preferentially hired when he is chosen *"because he is black"* over a better qualified white. Reading of the phrase "because he is black" in its literal sense seems to render Fullinwider's definition of preferential hiring ultimately indistinguishable from reverse discrimination in its pejorative connotation. Moreover, perhaps an even more unfortunate consequence of Fullinwider's inclusion of the phrase "because he is black" is his definition of preferential hiring is that the limitations it imposes would exclude many practices that clearly seem to involve preferential treatment.

For example, it seems reasonable to maintain that preferential treatment is involved when a black is hired over a more qualified white because blacks as a group are underrepresented in the labor force or because blacks as a group have been discriminated against in the past. Strictly speaking, in those cases a black is not hired *because* he is black, but because he is a member of an underrepresented group or of a group that has experienced discrimination in the past. Therefore, a sufficiently broad definition of preferential treatment should encompass both cases in which blacks are preferred over whites solely because of the color of their skin and cases in which the preference in question is grounded on any other reason that is not strictly related to academic or job qualifications.

It may be objected that the definition of preferential treatment adopted here would be too broad. For example, one might argue that when a black is hired over a more qualified white, but the black in question has personally been discriminated against in the past by the same employer who has now hired him, then what is involved is not preferential treatment but instead compensation for a past wrong. In reply, we can point out that, although principles of compensatory justice may provide a moral justification for the result achieved in the last example, the case nevertheless qualifies as an instance of preferential treatment. Indeed, it seems consistent to take the view that, in a competition for a scarce job, any award of the job on any basis other than job-related qualifications involves some kind of preferential treatment. This view is buttressed, moreover, by the fact that the subsequent reward of a job to a wrongfully rejected candidate is by no means the *only* conveivable form of acceptable compensation. It is quite plausible, for example, that at least in some cases the award of monetary damages would satisfy the relevant principles of compensatory justice. Accordingly, it seems amply justifiable not to equate the preferential hiring of a victim of job (first-order) discrimination with the satisfaction of compensatory justice.

One may seek to justify preferential treatment on distributive as well as compensatory grounds. One may, for instance, seek to justify certain types of preferential treatment for veterans to encourage voluntary service in the armed forces. Moreover, depending on the particular type of preferential treatment involved, on the applicable principles of justice, and on the circumstances, preferential treatment may be just or unjust, desirable or undesirable. In the last analysis, so long as one is willing to accept that preferential treatment itself is neither intrinsically good nor intrinsically evil, it seems appropriate to rely on the broad conception of preferential treatment adopted here and to leave to each particular case the determination of whether its use can be justified under the circumstances.

In the context of affirmative action, many believe that "goals" are good, but "quotas" bad (Fullinwider 1980, 162). Fullinwider maintains, however, that it is misleading to point to goals as being significantly different from quotas. Government regulations may tend to present goals as "flexible," but there is nothing inherent in goals or quotas that requires that this be the case. Indeed, argues Fullinwider, there can be "inflexible" goals and "flexible" quotas (ibid., 164).

In view of the confusions and disagreements that surround these terms, it seems advisable to settle on a particular definition for each of them. In the context of affirmative action, both goals and quotas relate to the relative proportion of the members of different groups in particular jobs or educational programs. To set a goal is to aim for the future achievement of some ratio of blacks to whites, or women to men, in a given workforce or university program. As I have already pointed out, a goal may be flexible or inflexible. Moreover, the time for its realization may be short or long, limited or unlimited; the means used to attain it, on the other hand, may involve no more than dedication to formal equality of opportunity or may be so extensive as to allow the unrestricted use of preferential treatment.

Quotas relate to particular allocations of jobs or of places in universities. Quotas require that a set number or proportion of the goods to be allocated be distributed on some basis other than, or in addition to, relative job or educational qualifications. A quota may require the allocation of a fixed number or percentage of the goods to which it applies to the members of a given group. For example, a quota may require that ten places or ten percent of the places in the entering class at a medical school be set aside for blacks. A quota may also impose a floor or a ceiling or both a floor and a ceiling. For example, a quota may require that a minimum of ten percent of blacks be admitted. Where two groups are involved, such as black and whites, a quota that imposes a floor with respect to one group also automatically imposes a ceiling with resect to the other group.

As already mentioned, quotas may be flexible or inflexible. An example of a flexible quota would be one that requires setting aside ten percent of the places in the entering class at a medical school for minority applicants, provided that such a quota can be lowered in proportion to any lack of minority applicants who are minimally qualified to enter medical school. Consistent with this flexible quota therefore, a medical school may well satisfy its obligations by filling fewer than ten percent of its available places with minority applicants. Further, although quotas are usually associated with preferential treatment, this need not necessarily be the case. Let us suppose, for example, that women have been prohibited by law from holding certain jobs for which a large number of them are qualified. The law in question is then repealed, and a quota imposed requiring that at least ten percent of the newly available jobs of the type involved be allocated to women. In this situation, it may well be that mere adherence to formal equality of opportunity would suffice to guarantee satisfaction of the quota. Finally, it is important to remember that quotas may be used not only in the pursuit of the aims of affirmative action—that is, to increase the representation of a previously underrepresented group in the workforce or in universities—but also as a means to further first-order discrimination, by forcing a decrease, or an artificially imposed limitation, in the representation of a group targeted for discrimination. To the extent that imposition of a floor for one group implies the imposition of a ceiling for another group, the determination of whether the quota involved is primarily one designed to advance an affirmative action or a first-order discrimination goal would seem to depend on certain variables, such as the relative ratios imposed by the quota and the intentions lurking behind the decision to adopt the quota.

In the last analysis, quotas in themselves, like goals and preferential treatment, would seem to be neither good nor bad, neither desirable nor undesirable. Whether any given quota is to be deemed just or unjust, good or bad, would seem to depend on the nature of the quota and on the (conceptual and historical) context in which it is sought to be inserted. Thus, for example, a flexible quota involving no preferential treatment and implemented for purposes of establishing a loose balance in the proportion of men to women at a coeducational college might well seem unobjectionable to a vast majority of the people. At the other extreme, a rigid quota setting a very low ceiling in order to drastically limit the number of members of a persecuted minority holding desirable jobs would undoubtedly be repugnant to anyone firmly committed to the postulate of equality.

A wide variety of practices are encompassed within the range of appropriate forms of affirmative action, as conceived by governmental agencies. To mention but one example, the Equal Employment Opportunity Commission, in its promulgated guidelines describing the types of affirmative action that would be appropriate under Title VII of the Civil Rights Act of 1964, specifically refers to the following practices, among others: adoption by employers of training programs that "emphasize providing minorities and women with the opportunity, skill and experience to perform [in given jobs]";[26] extensive recruiting programs;[27] or modifications in promotion and layoff procedures.[28] Moreover, these guidelines provide that an affirmative action plan may include goals, timetables, and "other appropriate employment tools which recognize the race, sex or national origin of applicants or employees."[29] Among the latter, the following are specifically deemed appropriate by the Commission: "a systematic effort to organize work and re-design jobs in ways that provide opportunities for persons lacking . . . skills to enter and, with appropriate training to progress in a career field"; "revamping selection instruments or procedures . . . to reduce or eliminate exclusionary effects on particular groups in particular job classifications"; and "a systematic effort to provide career advancement training . . . to employees in dead-end jobs."[30]

Given the broad range of practices that may be encompassed by the concept of affirmative action, we must settle on some precise meaning for the term. Moreover, given the aims of the present undertaking, it seems appropriate to concentrate on the most controversial practices. Indeed, if even these most controversial practices may be philosophically and constitutionally justified under certain circumstances—as I will conclude at the close of my analysis—then we can reasonably assume that less controversial practices would also be justified, at least under the same circumstances. For example, if quotas requiring preferential hiring are justified for American blacks under a given theory of compensatory justice, then it seems intuitively true that active recruiting of American blacks or job training programs designed for their benefit would also be justified under the same theory. Consistent with the above discussion, *affirmative action* shall be assumed henceforward to include some kind of preferential treatment. Specifically, affirmative action shall refer to the preferential hiring, promotion, and laying off of minorities or women, to the preferential admission of minorities or women to universities, or to the preferential selection of businesses owned by minorities or women to perform government public contracting work for purposes of remedying a wrong or of increasing the proportion of minorities or women in the relevant labor force, entrepreneurial class, or university student population. Moreover, such preferential treatment may be required in order, among other things, to achieve a defined goal or to fill a set quota. In the context of job hiring and promotion, preferential treatment shall include the hiring or promotion of a minority or a woman over a more qualified nonminority or male. In the context of layoffs, preferential treatment shall mean that a nonminority or a male with more job seniority shall be laid off prior to an otherwise similarly situated minority or woman who happens to have less job seniority.

2. *Assumptions concerning Certain Relevant Issues*

Even if we assume a consensus concerning applicable normative principles, the determination of whether affirmative action would be proper under given circumstances is likely to depend on a large number of variables. For example, in the context of Goldman's contractarian theory, hiring the most competent person satisfies the relevant principles of distributive justice, and both first-order discrimination and preferential treatment must be assessed in terms of the distributive rights of the most competent to scarce positions (Goldman 1979, 23–24). This, in turn, raises, among other things, questions concerning the criteria used to measure and compare relative competence, the validity of basing predictions about future performance on the job on past performance as a university student, and the proper weight to be accorded to cultural biases in the evaluation of credentials and of the desirability of certain skills (ibid., 49–51, 58–60). Thus, the validity of Goldman's thesis depends, at least in part, on the answers one can give to these questions. If, for instance, it were impossible to predict future performance on the basis of past performance, Goldman's distributive principle of awarding jobs to the most competent would be of limited value as it would be impossible to implement.

In general, in a society characterized by advanced forms of social and economic organization, the process of production and distribution of benefits and burdens is likely to be highly complex, making it very difficult to ascertain precisely the relative contribution of individuals engaged in collective enterprises. Moreover, even if such contributions were easy to measure, "in sophisticated economies," as Goldman observes, "there are forces—political muscle, organization, etc. that operate to effect reward out of proportion to contribution" (ibid., 32). Finally, even if individual contributions could be precisely measured and rewards made proportional to such contributions, the *worth* of each contribution would not be determined in the abstract, but in the context of particular processes of production depending on certain established patterns of hierarchy and, in some significant respect, on biased job selection procedures.[31] Given these complex variables, it may well be difficult to determine *when* the manifest underrepresentation of a particular group in a given segment of the labor force legitimately calls for remedial action, let alone *what* remedy would be proper once it is decided that one is necessary.

To foreclose further exploration of these variables in order to concentrate on the principal theoretical issues raised by the relationship between affirmative action and justice, I shall make the following assumptions without further reference to their possible empirical validity. My purpose in making these assumptions is to provide an admittedly oversimplified model of the current educational and job distribution systems, with a view to buttressing the proposition that the most qualified applicants should be entitled to the places or positions for which they compete. Accordingly, I shall assume the existence of a proper basis for the measurement, evaluation, and comparison of the qualifications of candidates for scarce places and positions, and that predictions concerning the probability of success in future performances based on an examination and evaluation of past performance can be sufficiently accurate to justify relying on them.

An important reason for making these assumptions is that the claim that the most qualified are entitled to scarce places and positions seems to provide strong support against first-order discrimination and to raise squarely the question of whether affirmative action may be justified notwithstanding that the most qualified applicants have a distributive right to scarce places and positions. To be sure, first-order discrimination may be condemned even in the absence of any such distributive right, as would be the case in the context of a normative system that made any such discrimination inherently wrong. Nevertheless, since the assumptions in question bolster the former claim without in any way detracting from the force of the latter moral proposition, they seem to be, at best, helpful and, at worst, harmless. Similarly, the claim supported by these assumptions may be very important for some theories concerning the justice of affirmative action. On the other hand, rejection of the validity of that claim by rival theories does not appear to be hampered in any way by continuing support for these assumptions. Indeed, nothing precludes one who believes that relative qualifications can be precisely measured, and that past performance is an accurate indicator of future performance, from maintaining that there ought not be any distributive rights to scarce places and positions for those who demonstrate that they are the most qualified.

To further simplify the relevant model in ways that do not seem to lead to a significant distortion of any of the principal issues to be examined, I shall also make the following assumptions. First, I shall assume that selection procedures for admission to educational institutions and the filling of scarce employment positions are not inherently biased in favor of or against any particular group. This does not mean, however, that members of given groups may not be disadvantaged with respect to certain selection procedures. It means, instead, that such disadvantages shall be assumed to follow as a consequence of past or present first-order discrimination rather than as that of the inherent nature of any selection procedure.

Qualifications relevant to the holding of particular places or positions shall be assumed to be the product of several factors, such as training, effort, and innate talents or capacities. In some cases, relevant qualifications may be primarily or even almost exclusively a function of the possession of innate talents. In any event, I shall assume that superior innate talents or capacities never provide *in and of themselves* a moral justification to claim a scarce place or position. This assumption, moreover, is based on the belief that individuals are no more responsible for the innate talents they possess than for the color of their skin. This assumption does not foreclose, however, the moral justification of awarding scarce places or positions to those who possess the most innate talent, so long as such justification is predicated on something besides the mere *fact* of possession of superior talents. Thus, for example, this assumption is not meant to preclude the award of scarce places and positions to the most talented because of the belief that it would lead to a net increase in utility or that it would be agreed to in the course of making a social contract.

The last assumption I shall make in this section relates to the role of race or sex as a job qualification. Cases that might otherwise fit within the definition of preferential treatment, but which involve instances of race or sex being bona fide job related qualifications, are not properly speaking preferential treatment cases. Depending on whether one embraces a narrow or broad view of race or sex as a job-related qualification, one could either substantially increase or decrease the number and types of cases that may properly be characterized as instances of preferential treatment. If one adopts a narrow conception of race or sex as a job qualification, according to which race and sex can only properly be considered job qualifications where the nature and a quality of the performance of the tasks required by the job would necessarily vary according to the race or sex of the jobholder, the vast majority of cases involving a preference on account of race or sex would be properly considered as preferential treatment cases. An example of a case in which sex would be properly considered a bona fide job qualification under this narrow conception would be a case involving a search for a young actress to play the leading female romantic role in a motion picture.

By contrast, under the broad conception, race and sex could be considered bona fide job qualifications, only if there is some likelihood that they would contribute to the enhancement of the performance of certain tasks directly or indirectly associated with the job to be allocated. For example, under the narrow conception, sex would not appear to be a proper job qualification for a college math professor. Nevertheless, under the broad conception, sex may well be such a qualification in filling a vacancy in an all male math department at a coeducational university. Indeed, the increased diversity of the math department that would follow from hiring a woman may have a positive effect on all its members. Also, by providing a positive role model for female students, the hiring of a female math professor may lead to an increase in motivation to study math among the female students.

Whether the narrow or the broad conception of race or sex as a job qualification ought to be considered ultimately more desirable is a matter of debate. For present purposes, however, I shall assume that the narrow conception is the correct one. The main argument in favor of this assumption is that, even if it turns out to be unwarranted, at worst certain cases that would have been justified as legitimate instances of affirmative action would prove to be justified, but for other reasons; on the other hand, certain cases *not* justified as legitimate instances of affirmative action would eventually prove to be justified for reasons unrelated to affirmative action.

Having completed the task of defining key terms and of enumerating the assumptions that will underlie the remainder of this analysis, I now turn to an examination of the principal liberal conceptions of justice in search of further valuable insights into the relation between affirmative action and justice.

CHAPTER TWO

Libertarian Justice and Affirmative Action

In this chapter, I examine libertarian arguments bearing on the justice of affirmative action. The libertarian position has its classic foundation in Locke's work and its chief contemporary advocate in Nozick (Pettit 1980, 75–76). This position stresses above all individual autonomy, very broad property rights, and a "minimal state" limited essentially to the following two functions: affording police protection to the lives and property rights of its citizens and enforcing contracts.[1] Consistent with this, one reasonably expects the lack of libertarian support for any form of state-run affirmative action. It is therefore hardly surprising that a survey of the relevant literature has not revealed any work that sets forth libertarian arguments in favor of affirmative action. Nevertheless, relying primarily on the views of Nozick, I will attempt to determine whether any such arguments can ever be plausibly made, in the context of state-sponsored affirmative action.

I begin by reviewing the libertarian argument against affirmative action. I then provide an account of Nozick's principle of rectification. Finally, I examine whether application of Nozick's principle of rectification would ever justify the use of affirmative action.

1. The Libertarian Argument against Affirmative Action

The libertarian position strongly rejects the legitimacy of imposing any affirmative action obligations. Based on the strong libertarian sense of the sanctity of private property and of freedom of contract, a libertarian seems unlikely to tolerate any interference with the right of an agent of allocation to award an available job to whomever she pleases. Moreover, this right is a function of a person's right to control the disposition of her property and of her right to freedom of association (Goldman 1979, 35). Thus, for example, if a corporation owns a factory fitted with machinery designed to transform certain raw materials into finished goods, and if it needs someone to operate its factory's machinery, it can purchase the services of whomever is seeking to sell such services. Because of their right to freedom of association, the members of the corporation are entitled to enter into contracts of employment with only those persons with whom they wish to be associated. To require them to do otherwise would force them to work with people they do not want to associate with and to lose complete control over the operation of their assets.

The corporation's property and association rights, moreover, are themselves ultimately legitimated by what Goldman refers to as the libertarian's desire for "the overall maximization of freedom" (ibid., 39). So long as a corporation is entitled to hold its assets—that is, so long as it has legitimately obtained them through lawful acquisitions and transfers[2]—the principle of overall maximization of freedom justifies it in selecting whomever it wishes to fill the jobs over which it is the legitimate agent of allocation. More generally, consistent with the postulate of equality, the principle of overall maximization of freedom can be interpreted as providing each individual with an equal right of free association and with an equal right to freely acquire and transfer property, provided only that such acquisitions and transfers do not interfere with the legitimately held property of others. In short, from the libertarian perspective, the postulate of equality finds concrete embodiment in the equality of free association and equality to acquire and transfer property freely.

One of the important consequences of the libertarian's acceptance of the principle of overall maximization of freedom is, as Goldman notes, that the libertarian "does not demand rational self-interest in contracts made or rules accepted. He accepts only actual contracts among actual individuals, not hypothetical contracts establishing rules among hypothetically rational or equal agents. Real individuals must be left free to make their own contracts and exchanges" (Goldman 1979, 35–36). Moreover, as Goldman further indicates, the libertarian does not believe that the rights to property and free association should be overridden by the "social interest in maximizing goods and services," by considerations of greater need, or in order to be able to achieve greater efficiency, Thus, "for the libertarian, freedom of choice normally takes precedence over welfare considerations" (ibid., 36–37).

As a corollary to the corporation's property and free association rights, applicants competing for corporate positions have no rights to them. The libertarian cannot justify prohibiting either first-order discrimination or affirmative action in the allocation of corporate jobs. Under the libertarian conception of justice, therefore, a corporation is as entitled to refuse flatly to hire blacks and women as it is entitled to grant them systematic preferential treatment.

Goldman raises two objections to the libertarian's seemingly unqualified endorsement of a corporation's right to hire whomever it pleases. First, the libertarian's conception of corporate job hiring does not correspond with the realities of contemporary society, as the libertarian misconceives the proper boundaries of the right to property. Second, the corporation's absolute right to hire whom it pleases does not necessarily result in the overall maximization of freedom sought by the libertarian.

According to Goldman's first objection, even if one accepts the libertarian's belief that rights cannot be overridden by considerations of social welfare, there is no need to recognize a right *prospectively* when it is plain that such a recognition would have significantly worse consequences than non-recognition (ibid., 36). The libertarian, however, is not likely to concede this point. Acceptance that a prospective right will lead to a decrease in utility does not compel refusal to support it. For example, as Goldman acknowledges, a libertarian could argue that even if we possessed a scientific means to match spouses so as to maximize their prospects for happiness, we would nevertheless continue to uphold the right of individuals freely to choose whom they wish to marry (ibid., 37).

Goldman replies that the analogy between the right to marry whomever one chooses and the right of the corporation to hire whomever it pleases is misleading. Indeed, the right to choose one's spouse, argues Goldman, is a fundamental right that relates to the right each individual has over his or her body and person. Hiring, by contrast, only involves a part of the corporation's right over its assets, and that right is already limited by several "exceptive clauses" (ibid., 37). Since numerous restrictions are imposed on a contemporary corporation's freedom to use its assets as it pleases, a further restriction involving its hiring practices would in no way be akin to a restriction of an individual's freedom to choose a spouse. Similarly, with respect to the right of free association, corporations are already restricted by antidiscrimination legislation. Thus, a corporation that runs a hotel or a restaurant cannot exclude black would-be patrons, even if it strongly objects to associating with them.[3] Unlike the fundamental association rights surrounding marriage, those involved in corporate hiring are more peripheral. Because of all this, concludes Goldman, obligating corporations to grant equality of opportunity to all job applicants should not raise serious objections. Indeed, the likely increase in social welfare attributable to the allocation of corporate positions to the most qualified candidates would clearly outweigh any corresponding added burden on the already restricted corporate rights to property and free association.

Goldman acknowledges that the libertarian would reject these arguments. The libertarian would maintain that imposition of an equal opportunity duty would violate the right to control what has been legitimately acquired (ibid., 38). Goldman advocates such a duty on grounds of justice and fairness (ibid., 39), but for a libertarian, as Nozick points out, fairness cannot "obviate the need for other persons' *consenting* to cooperate and limit their own activities" (emphasis in original; Nozick 1974, 95).

Consistent with the endorsement of Nozick's conclusion that "the minimal state is the most extensive state that can be justified" (ibid., 149), the libertarian might advance another argument against recognizing an equal opportunity right. Indeed, Goldman's claim that such a right would but add one more exceptive clause to the large number that already limit the scope of the corporation's right to property and free association may make perfect sense in the context of the welfare state. The libertarian, however, is not likely to accept the legitimacy of the welfare state. Rather, based on Nozick's views, libertarian justice requires the removal of most exceptive clauses in order to restore the rights to property and free association to their fullest potential under the minimal state. Accordingly, Goldman's argument for equal opportunity in the allocation of jobs seems clearly unacceptable under libertarian justice. In the last analysis, Goldman's argument does much more to indicate that the libertarian position might be incompatible with the maintenance of the status quo in contemporary American society than to provide reasons likely to lead a libertarian to embrace equal opportunity.

Goldman next contends that the libertarian is prone to misconstrue the true nature of the limitations that he agrees should be imposed on the right to property in contemporary society. Even the libertarian agrees that an individual's property right is limited by other people's similar rights. Thus, as Goldman points out, the libertarian recognizes that my right to use my knife does not include the right to insert it in my enemy's chest (Goldman 1979, 37). The libertarian, writes Goldman, "would grant that we cannot use our property in ways that directly harm other people, but he would allow total freedom short of this, including the freedom to ignore rational self-interest." Thus, the libertarian would agree that, while rights cannot be limited in order to maximize welfare, they must be limited in order to avoid direct harm to others. Goldman argues, however, that the distinction between preventing harm and maximizing welfare cannot be systematically maintained in the context of job allocation. For instance, if openings for airline pilots or surgeons were filled with incompetents, this would not only result in losses in efficiency but could also lead to the infliction of serious harm. Accordingly, suggests Goldman, the harm principle accepted by the libertarian may justify the imposition of the requirement to hire the most qualified job applicants (ibid., 38–39).

The libertarian is likely to reject the last argument as yet another attempt to put welfare considerations ahead of the right to property (ibid., 39). Drawing upon Nozick's assertion that legitimate constraints on freedoms must be determined in relation to the Lockean property rights possessed by people (Nozick 1974, 171), the libertarian can insist that there is a substantial difference between causing harm to the property interests (as broadly conceived by Locke) of another and causing harm to someone by virtue of merely failing to contribute to the maximization of welfare. To illustrate this, it may be useful to imagine that each person's legitimate Lockean property rights carve out a zone of autonomy within which that person has a complete freedom to use her property as she pleases. Each such zone of autonomy is, however, bounded by the respective zones of autonomy of every other person. Moreover, one person cannot legitimately enter the zone of autonomy of another without the latter's actual consent. Within this scheme, an unauthorized venture into another's zone of autonomy would constitute the kind of wrongful harm that the libertarian wishes to prevent even at the cost of restricting the freedom to use one's property. On the other hand, the failure to assist those who are incapable of achieving self-sufficiency may well cause harm and adversely affect the social welfare, but it involves no trespass on any zone of autonomy and therefore presumably does not justify limiting any property rights.

Let us suppose that an airline hires an incompetent pilot who causes the crash of the aircraft he was flying, killing all the passengers aboard and causing damage to the properties of several farmers located within a square mile of the crash site. Assuming that the airline makes full disclosure concerning the qualifications of its pilots to its prospective passengers, any of the latter who agree to fly on the airline can reasonably be deemed to have consented to assume the risk inherent in flying with an incompetent pilot. Hence, from a libertarian standpoint, no violation of the broad Lockean right to property of any such passenger would result from the airline's failure to hire the most competent pilots available. But the farmers whose property has been damaged by the crash present a more difficult case. Unlike the passengers, the farmers have not actually consented to the aircraft entering their zones of autonomy. On the other hand, the airline has not intentionally entered the farmers' zones of autonomy. (I am assuming, for purposes of this discussion, that the farmers' property rights to their farms do not extend thirty thousand feet into the atmosphere, where commercial passenger aircraft usually fly). Whatever the optimal libertarian solution to this apparent dilemma, that solution is not likely to include a requirement to hire the most competent. Indeed, unless adoption of such a requirement would put an end to all air crashes, the libertarian would not agree to it. Since several crashes result from causes other than pilot error, adoption of a rule to hire the most competent might decrease the prospect of a crash but would not insure the inviolability of the farmers' zones of autonomy. Under these circumstances, if the libertarian is unwilling to subject the farmers to any risk, then aircraft should be altogether banned from flying over their properties. If, on the other hand, the libertarian is willing to allow the operation of the airline notwithstanding the risk that the farmers might suffer an injury to their property rights, then a plausible solution might be to grant the farmers a right to compensation in case of injury.[4] In any event, the libertarian would have no reason to endorse a rule requiring that the most competent pilots be hired, as such a rule would interfere with the rights of the airline without eliminating the risks to the farmers. Although such a rule could significantly advance the welfare aims of the nonlibertarian, it ultimately seems unsuited to protect the property rights that override welfare considerations for the libertarian.

The line between harm to welfare interests and infringement of property rights may become blurred in the context of acts of commission, but not in that of acts of omission. Thus, in the previous example, both the property rights and the welfare interests of the farmers were adversely affected by the crash. Suppose, however, that a pharmaceutical company could manufacture a drug that would save the lives of the victims of a rare and otherwise fatal disease if it hired a uniquely qualified job applicant. Nonetheless, instead of hiring that applicant, the company fills the job with the son of its chief executive officer; the drug in question is not manufactured, and the victims of the rare disease die. From the standpoint of victim's welfare, it makes no difference whether the pharmaceutical company fails to manufacture the drug or whether it steals it from another company and then withholds it from such victims; in either case, the victims will die. From the standpoint of the legitimate property rights recognized by the libertarian, however, the two situations are clearly different. The failure to manufacture involves no violation of any person's zone of autonomy and is thus not illegitimate. The stealing of the drug, by contrast, involves an abridgement of legitimate property rights and is therefore unjustified.

In the last analysis, the libertarian can consistently refute the argument that recognition that property cannot be used directly to harm others justifies requiring corporations to hire the most competent job candidates. For the libertarian, I cannot insert my knife in my neighbor's chest because that would constitute an act of commission resulting in an unjustified invasion of another person's zone of autonomy. Failing to provide my neighbor with a lifesaving drug that only I possess, however, involves an act of omission and no trespass on any zone of autonomy. Hence, I am entitled to ignore my neighbor's plight and to decide not to contribute to the pursuit of her well-being.[5] From the libertarian perspective, therefore, the critical question is not whether the corporation's hiring practices are likely to harm the welfare of others, but rather whether such harm arises out of the violation of someone else's property rights.

Goldman also launches an altogether different kind of attack against the libertarian position. According to this objection, the libertarian view of corporate hiring ultimately leads the libertarian to an internal inconsistency. Goldman's argument is, in a nutshell, that if the libertarian justifies his rejection of equal opportunity as a necessary means toward the overall maximization of freedom, then the libertarian is mistaken. Far from leading automatically to an increase in overall freedom, granting corporations absolute freedom in hiring is likely to bring about decreases in overall freedom.[6]

Underlying Goldman's position is his observation that poverty and the lack of satisfaction of basic needs are impediments to freedom, as they inhibit the freedom to pursue one's chosen life plan and the ability to control one's life as desired (Goldman 1979, 39). Adoption of a rule of hiring that is bound to lead to the more efficient production of a greater number of goods and services would therefore serve, according to Goldman, not only to maximize welfare but also to increase overall freedom. In Goldman's words, "No social system that abandons those at the bottom to an enforced circle of dire poverty can be justified in the name of freedom. A free market society with severe racial biases and no rule for hiring results in that situation. Thus, we again arrive at the conclusion that society has the right to impose a rule for hiring against private corporations, justified this time in the name of freedom" (ibid., 40).

The libertarian is very unlikely to accept Goldman's argument, particularly since any move from an uninhibited freedom to hire whomever one wishes to any rule designed to maximize the production seemingly requires a weakening of historically acquired entitlements for purposes of accommodating essentially distributive concerns. According to Nozick, a person's property rights can be overridden for purposes of promoting fundamental welfare needs only in order to avoid a "catastrophe" (Nozick 1974, 181). Moreover, while his entitlement theory of justice essentially disregards the distributive consequences of acquisitions and transfers of holdings, Nozick acknowledges that it would be "disturbing" if people's reasons for transferring their holdings were arbitrary. Nozick is nevertheless confident that in a capitalist society individual transfers and transactions are largely reasonable (ibid., 159). Therefore, he concludes that in a free market system catastrophic conditions justifying abridging property rights are highly unlikely (ibid., 182). In the last analysis, the libertarian can overcome the charge of internal inconsistency, but only by embracing the proposition that the free market's "invisible hand" guarantees to everyone the minimum of subsistence that is a necessary precondition to the overall maximization of freedom.

If every free market participant were guided by the "invisible hand" of competition, job hiring would be subject to a de facto formal means-regarding equality of opportunity. If corporations seek to maximize profits, and if hiring the most competent person palpably increases the prospects for doing so, then it stands to reason that corporations will hire the most competent person in the pursuit of self-interest. There is, however, no guarantee that a corporation will be at all times exclusively motivated by its economic self-interest. The historical instances of racial and sexual discrimination in hiring are certainly abundant, and the libertarian would be unable to do much about it, because of his moral commitment against the imposition of rules of hiring. Moreover, in a society in which, for example, racism is pervasive, the purely economic self-interest of a hiring corporation may dictate, along the lines argued by Posner, that the corporation engage in first-order discrimination.[7] Thus, in a climate of racial hostility against blacks, it would be in a corporation's *economic* best interests to refuse to hire a black to handle customer relations, even if she had clearly proven to be the most qualified person—in the narrow sense discussed in chapter 1—for the job. Indeed, the corporation would incur a smaller risk of losing a significant percentage of its racist customers by hiring a less qualified white job applicant than an indisputably better qualified black applicant.

In conclusion, absent a "catastrophe," the libertarian flatly rejects the legitimacy of imposing any rule of hiring on private employers. Accordingly, a corporation is as entitled to engage in first-order discrimination as it is free to implement affirmative action plans. In neither case is state intervention justified. Furthermore, in neither case are those who consider themselves the victims of the corporation's hiring practices entitled to receive any compensation for what they perceive as their injuries. No one is entitled to a job unless he becomes a party to an actual contract with the employer entitled to allocate such a job. In the absence of an actual contract, no one has legitimate compensatory or distributive claim to any employment position.

It follows from the libertarian's rejection of the validity of imposing any hiring rule on private agents of allocation that it is equally impermissible for the state to forbid the hiring of blacks or women. In either case the private agent's property and free association rights would be equally abridged. Further, if the state institutes de jure first-order discrimination, it can cause injury not only to the rights of private agents of allocation but also to those of the members of the discriminated against groups. Indeed, if a black or a woman wants to work for an employer willing to hire him or her, a law forbidding the hiring of blacks and women would violate the freedom of contract and freedom of association rights of the prospective employees as well as those of the prospective employers.[8]

Even in the face of rejection of a hiring rule for private employers and of commitment to the minimal state, the question remains whether the libertarian would accept any hiring rule applicable exclusively to the allocation of nonelective government positions. In its Lockean conception, the minimal state is responsible for providing adequate police protection to safeguard the citizens' legitimate interests in life and property, and for supplying judges to guarantee the enforcement of contracts (Locke 1960, 398–99). This requires the state to allocate the positions of police officer and judge, to the extent that they are not subject to elections, in order to fulfill its legitimate function. Moreover, if the number of available candidates exceeds that of the vacancies to be filled, it is fair to ask whether the libertarian state can be charged with any obligation that could not be legitimately imposed on a private agent of allocation.

2. *Obligations of the Libertarian State as Agent of Allocation*

There is no single clear-cut answer to the last question, but the options that satisfy a libertarian seem rather limited. According to basic Lockean propositions, the principal purpose of society is to protect broadly conceived individual property rights; the proper function of government is to act as a trustee for the members of civil society; and once civil society has been constituted, its government should operate on the principle of majority rule (ibid., 247, 373, 375, 424). From this, it follows that the nature and scope of the state's obligations as the agent of allocation of public positions would be determined by the will of the majority. Thus, the libertarian position would seem to be equally compatible, at least in principle, with a state that acted as though it were just one more private agent of allocation, with a state obligated to hire public employees in accordance with the demands of equal opportunity, and with a state that decided to conduct its public hiring pursuant to an affirmative action plan.

As a practical matter, however, it is unlikely that a government that is truly responsive to the will of the majority would institute affirmative action plans favoring members of minorities. It is much less clear whether libertarians would impose upon the state an obligation to adhere to formal equality of opportunity. Nozick generally rejects the legitimacy of imposing equality of opportunity (Nozick 1974, 235–38). Hayek, however, specifies that the government ought to avoid arbitrary discrimination in the course of implementing publicly financed programs and appears to endorse the imposition of an obligation by government to provide formal equality of opportunity (Hayek 1979, 47–48). Indeed, unlike Nozick, Hayek is not an advocate of the minimal state in the context of contemporary society. In Hayek's words, "Far from advocating . . . a minimal state, we find it unquestionable that in an advanced society government ought to use its power of raising funds by taxation to provide a number of services which for various reasons cannot be provided, or cannot be provided adequately, by the market" (ibid., 41). Moreover, Hayek stipulates that, in the course of providing services other than those mandated by the minimal state, the government ought to adhere as far as possible to the rules of competition and "ought to be bound by certain general requirements of justice such as the avoidance of arbitrary discrimination" (ibid., 47–48).[9] Accordingly, Hayek would reject first-order discrimination against blacks and women and, consistent with his commitment to efficiency, would seem bound to require that the government as agent of allocation be committed to formal equality of opportunity.

Libertarians are likely either to require the same freedom for the government as for private agents of allocation or to demand that the government implement formal equality of opportunity. In the former case, there is no compelling argument in favor of or against the use of affirmative action; in the latter case, by contrast, the use of affirmative action seems clearly foreclosed. These results are hardly surprising in light of the libertarians' aversion to government intervention in the economic marketplace for purposes of promoting distributive justice. The preceding analysis, however, does not indicate whether libertarians might ever find affirmative action justified in the context of compensatory justice. To determine whether consideration of compensatory justice could lead a libertarian to accept affirmative action, we must first briefly examine Nozick's "principle of rectification."

3. *Nozick's Principle of Rectification*

According to Nozick, in a free market society different persons happen to exercise control over different resources and new "holdings" emerge out of voluntary exchanges or other actions of persons (Nozick 1974, 150). Further, Nozick maintains that justice in holdings is historical, in the sense that it depends on the actual sequence of events culminating in the acquisition of control by a particular person over a particular good. To determine whether a holding is just, Nozick maintains that it is necessary to satisfy the following definition of justice: (1) A person who acquires a holding in accordance with the principle of justice in acquisition is entitled to that holding; (2) A person who acquires a holding in accordance with the principle of justice in transfer, from someone else entitled to the holding, is entitled to the holding; (3) No one is entitled to a holding except by (repeated) applications of 1 and 2 (ibid., 151).

Where a present holding does not satisfy these criteria, the present holder is not entitled to her holding, and this raises the issue of compensation for past injustices. Ideally, it would be possible to locate the injustices in the past, to measure their effect on the configuration of present holdings, to determine what that configuration would have been in the absence of any past injustices, and then to compare the actual configuration of holdings with what would have been but for the past injustices. If a difference between the former and latter were found, moreover, justice would require a rectification in the form of a reallocation of holdings to the extent necessary to eliminate such a difference. Thus, Nozick's entitlement theory of justice embraces a principle of rectification, which in his own words, "presumably will make use of its best estimate of subjunctive information about what would have occurred (or a probability distribution over what might have occurred, using the expected value) if the injustice had not taken place. If the actual description of holdings turns out not to be one of the descriptions yielded by the principle, then one of the descriptions yielded must be realized" (ibid., 152–53).

Applying Nozick's principle of rectification, the proper measure of compensation for a victim of a past injustice would put that victim in the position that he would have come to occupy but for the past injustice. It thus would not suffice merely to return what was wrongly taken away or to give what was unjustly withheld, but it would also be necessary to provide compensation for the goods that the victim would have acquired over time as a consequence of the possession of the good of which he was unjustly deprived.

The minimal state envisaged by Nozick may have a very limited number of positive duties toward its citizens. Because of the libertarian belief that individuals should be left alone to develop their capacities and talents and to peacefully acquire and exchange goods as they best see fit, however, such a minimal state has an extensive negative duty to refrain from interfering with the individual's freedom to develop her talents and to enter into contracts. Any such interference would constitute an injustice and trigger the application of the principle of rectification. Let us suppose, for example, that a state has imposed slavery on a racial minority and made it a crime to provide an education to its members, as was once the case in the United States.[10] In that case, the principle of rectification would not only require that the state abolish slavery and repeal the law criminalizing educating the racial minority, but also that the state compensate the latter so as to put them in the position in which they would have been absent the state-imposed injustices.

4. A Libertarian Argument for Affirmative Action

Given the principle of rectification, a libertarian would seem bound to accept the legitimacy of affirmative action under the following circumstances. Suppose the minimal state pursuant to the will of the majority adopts the principle of formal equality of opportunity with respect to its allocation of scarce public employment positions. Suppose further that the state nonetheless systematically discriminates against black applicants for public employment positions. Now, assume that at time T_1, a black candidate A was the most qualified to hold the position P, but that because of racial discrimination, the state awarded P to B, the most qualified white candidate. Assume further that after one year of holding P, at time T_2, B quits his job, creating a vacancy for P, for which several candidates compete. At time T_2, A, who is competing anew for P, is no longer the most qualified candidate. Instead, the most qualified candidate at T_2 is C, a white candidate. Under those circumstances, Nozick's principle of rectification would require that P be awarded to A at T_2, even though A is not then the most qualified candidate for P, provided only that the following proposition be held to be true as an empirical matter: namely, that public employment positions are generally kept by those who hold them so long as their performance is satisfactory even if a more qualified candidate should become available after the position has been awarded (Goldman 1979, 125–26). Indeed, had the injustice not occurred at T_1, A would have been awarded P at that time and would have continued to hold on to that position indefinitely provided only that her performance on the job remained satisfactory. Under these circumstances, P presumably would not have become vacant at T_2, and hence C would not have been in a position to claim any entitlement to P, by virtue of being better qualified for P than A at time T_2. Thus, but for the injustice perpetrated by the state, A and not B or C would be entitled to hold P at T_2, and hence affirmative action—in the sense of a preference of A over C at T_2, even though, at that time, C is better qualified than A to hold P—would clearly seem called for by Nozick's principle of rectification. In this scenario, A would thus be entitled to affirmative action, while C could not legitimately complain that such affirmative action deprives him of any holding to which he has become entitled.

The libertarian argument in favor of affirmative action as a means of compensation for the actual victim of a specific injustice is a strong one. The range of circumstances under which affirmative action would have to be thus acknowledged as being legitimate by a libertarian, however, is rather narrow. Thus, if consistent with libertarian views like Nozick's the state chose not to abide by formal equality of opportunity in the allocation of public employment positions, its actions would not justify affirmative action. Indeed, if the libertarian state has no inherent obligation to institute equality of opportunity with respect to the domains of allocation under its control, implementation of a racially discriminatory public hiring procedure pursuant to the will of the majority would not deprive any member of the racial minority of any good to which she is entitled. Accordingly, for a libertarian, the legitimacy of affirmative action as a means of compensation may be limited to those contexts in which state allocation of public employment positions is supposed to be conducted in a racially neutral manner and in compliance with the principle of formal equality of opportunity, but is actually administered in a racially discriminatory manner.[11]

There seems to be no legitimate libertarian argument in favor of affirmative action from distributive justice. Under certain limited circumstances, there appears to be a strong libertarian argument in favor of affirmative action from compensatory justice. The most remarkable conclusion that emerges from the preceding examination is that even the libertarian appears to be compelled to acknowledge the legitimacy of affirmative action under certain (albeit narrow) circumstances.

CHAPTER THREE

Contractarian Justice and Affirmative Action

In this chapter, I consider contractarian arguments for and against affirmative action. The diversity of contractarian approaches to affirmative action is traceable in part, at least, to the existence of substantially differing conceptions of the contractarian position.[1] To be in a better position to assess contractarian views on affirmative action, we must first specify what will be understood here as the contractarian conception of justice.

I first provide a brief account of Rawls' conception of contractarian justice, then turn to Goldman's comprehensive analysis of affirmative action from the perspective of contractarian justice and his arguments for and against affirmative action. Finally, I briefly review the alternative contractarian justification of affirmative action proposed by Thalberg.

1. The Contractarian Framework

Contractarian theories postulate that, to be legitimate, principles of justice must be grounded on the consent of those who are supposed to be morally bound by them. The metaphor associated with contractarian justice is that of the social contract, according to which free and equal individuals enter into a mutual agreement concerning the normative principles that are to govern all their future intersubjective dealings in organized society. Moreover, from a contractarian standpoint, the purpose of the social contract is to generate an institutional framework suited to provide an optimal equilibrium between the achievement of the degree of social cooperation necessary to secure the proper functioning of society and the protection of each individual's right to pursue his own conception of the good.

Classical social contract theory as elaborated in the works of Hobbes, Locke, Rousseau, and Kant raises vexing problems concerning both the relative equality (of bargaining power) among the social contractors and the nature and scope of the requisite consent. To avoid these problems, Rawls formulates a contractarian theory that seeks "to present a conception of justice which generalizes and carries to a higher level of abstraction the familiar theory of the social contract as found, say, in Locke, Rousseau and Kant" (Rawls 1971, 11). Specifically, Rawls addresses the problem concerning equality by placing his social contractors in an original position in which they find themselves behind a veil of ignorance. Rawls also seemingly circumvents the problem regarding consent by stipulating that the contractors operating behind the veil of ignorance in the original position reach a hypothetical agreement on a particular conception of justice (ibid., 12).

Because of the veil of ignorance none of the parties in the original position "knows his place in society, his class position or social status, nor does anyone know his fortune in the distribution of natural assets and abilities, his intelligence, strength, and the like. The parties do not know their conceptions of the good or their special psychological propensities" (ibid.). Moreover, by depriving the parties in the original position of this information, the veil of ignorance appears to level the bargaining field so that no one has an advantage in bargaining power. Accordingly, the veil of ignorance is designed to permit every party in the original position to consent rationally only to those principles of justice that would be fair regardless of that party's position in society or conception of the good.

Given what the veil of ignorance conceals from the parties in the initial position, Rawls argues that it is reasonable for these parties to be risk averse and to follow the maximin rule in selecting principles of justice. In Rawls' definition, "The maximin rule tells us to rank alternatives by their worst possible outcomes: we are to adopt the alternative the worst outcome of which is superior to the worst outcomes of others" (ibid., 152–53).

With all these constraints, Rawls maintains that the parties in the original position would agree to the following two principles of justice. The first principle provides: "Each person is to have an equal right to the most extensive basic liberty compatible with a similar liberty for others" (ibid., 60). Moreover, Rawls specifies that this principle is lexically prior to the second principle, which is known as the "difference principle" and which requires that "social and economic inequalities are to be arranged so that they are both: (a) to the greatest benefit of the least advantaged . . . and (b) attached to offices and positions open to all under conditions of fair equality of opportunity" (ibid., 302). Further, Rawls also specifies—and this is important from the standpoint of assessing the justice of affirmative action in terms of his contractarian theory—that an inequality of opportunity is only acceptable if it enhances "the opportunities of those with the lesser opportunity" (ibid., 303).

Finally, Rawls specifies that his principles of justice are meant to apply not to every social problem but only to the "basic structure of society" that relates to "the way in which the major social institutions distribute fundamental rights and duties and determine the division of advantages from social cooperation" (ibid., 7). This raises the question of whether questions about the justice of affirmative action concern the "basic structure." For if they do not, then Rawls' contractarian approach would probably approach affirmative action as a matter of policy rather than of justice.

A strong argument can be made that questions concerning the justice of affirmative action do relate to the "basic structure" of American society. Not only does state-sponsored affirmative action raise important constitutional issues, but it also affects the distribution of fundamental equality-based rights and significantly affects the "division of advantages from social cooperation." Actually, affirmative action is meant to affect institutions and social practices that favor certain members of society over others in the allocation of desirable social positions and superior life chances. And as Rawls indicates, it is precisely the inequalities promoted by these institutions and practices "to which the principles of social justice must in the first instance apply" (ibid., 7). Therefore, it is appropriate to call on Rawls' principles of justice to determine the legitimacy of affirmative action consistent with a contractarian approach.

2. *The Contractarian Assumptions behind Goldman's Conception of the Justice of Affirmative Action*

A. Hypothetical Social Contract with Partially Lifted Veil of Ignorance

Goldman's assessment of affirmative action clearly operates within a Rawlsian contractarian framework (Goldman 1979, 12). Unlike Rawls, however, Goldman does not set his social contractors behind a full veil of ignorance. Indeed, Goldman's contractors are aware, among other things, of the structure of their society and of "their natural endowments," such as "intelligence" and "physical ability." Thus, under Goldman's partial veil of ignorance contractors are merely ignorant of "their social positions, race and sex" (ibid.).

Goldman argues that his allowing the contractors to have information concerning the structure of society is justified because, unlike Rawls, he is "not concerned with just relations among different societies at different times but with resolving a social problem in our own society" (ibid.). Under these circumstances, the contractors' knowledge about the structure of society appears to be unobjectionable. Their task is not to make a choice among several possible sociopolitical orders but merely to agree on a just solution for a vexing problem arising in their own sociopolitical milieu.

Goldman's lifting of the veil of ignorance with respect to the contractors' knowledge of their own natural endowments, by contrast, raises more difficult issues. Goldman seeks to justify his position as follows:

> My unwillingness to deny knowledge of [natural endowments] results from my uncertainty as to whether society has the right to nullify all natural differences among individuals, even those that are relevant to the performance of certain tasks and hence naturally useful to the individuals who possess them. If untalented or unintelligent individuals have no inherent claims upon the talents of others, and I do not see why they should, then it is not demanded, nor perhaps even permissible, that society nullify the distributive effects of these differences. (Ibid.)

Even if we assume that no one has an inherent claim upon the talents of others, it does not necessarily follow that there is only one legitimate way for society to deal with the range of possible distributive effects following from such differences in talent. If the individuals exercising their own talents were by and large self-sufficient, Goldman's position might seem compelling. But in a complex society where production requires a collective process of cooperation combining capital and labor, it may be neither desirable nor possible to devise a distributive scheme that relies heavily on differences in individual talents. In a society in which individuals are essentially self-sufficient, any redistribution of goods produced by a single individual may be viewed as an infringement on that individual's right to enjoy the fruits of her own efforts. In a society in which individuals are not basically self-sufficient, on the other hand, it is not self-evident how the products resulting from a collective effort ought to be distributed or redistributed.

If we assume that individuals are interdependent, then whether or not the hypothetical contractors know what natural endowments they possess makes a significant difference. If the contractors are not aware of their natural endowments, then applying Rawls' maximin principle, they might well agree to equal distribution according to need rather than to a distribution commensurate with talent. Indeed, if the latter distribution were incapable of securing the basic needs of the least talented, the contractors would most likely prefer distribution according to need. The most talented would lose less if their needs were met than the least talented would if relying on their meager talents they would fail to secure enough goods to satisfy their basic needs. On the other hand, if the contractors were aware of their natural endowments, the most talented would seem to have no reason to accept a distribution according to need that would undoubtedly be more disadvantageous for them than a distribution according to talent. The least talented would prefer a distribution according to need, although they might reluctantly consent to a distribution according to talent if the most talented would otherwise refuse all social cooperation. It is, however, precisely this kind of arrangement resulting from a great disparity in bargaining power among the contractors that Rawls and Goldman seek to avoid through introduction of the veil-of-ignorance device.

Goldman's lifting of the veil with respect to natural endowments is bound to have a significant effect on the contractors' deliberations concerning affirmative action. Indeed, insofar as affirmative action establishes a preference for some who are less talented over some others who are more talented, someone who knows her relative strengths would adopt a very different position than someone who is not aware of her own natural endowments. To illustrate this, let us consider a society that is 85 percent white and 15 percent black, and in which there has been past first-order discrimination against blacks. A proposal is made that 15 percent of future available positions shall be set aside for the most qualified black candidates regardless of whether there are more qualified white candidates. The remaining 85 percent of positions, on the other hand, are to be awarded to the most qualified candidates regardless of race. Moreover, those who must vote on the proposal know their own relative qualifications but not their race. As Goldman stresses, affirmative action plans, such as the one under consideration, benefit the best qualified members of the discriminated-against group and are likely to hurt most the least qualified members of the nonvictim group (ibid., 90–91). Hence, it seems clearly in the interest of the most talented members of society to adopt the proposal. Indeed, if a highly talented person turns out to be white, he would have little to fear from an affirmative action program that would result in the exclusion of less talented whites from the position. On the other hand, if a highly talented member turns out to be black, the existence of an affirmative action plan would either leave unaffected or enhance his chances of obtaining a coveted position.

Those who rank in the middle of the talent scale, on the other hand, are likely to find it difficult to determine whether accepting the proposal would be in their best interests. If a person in that group turns out to be black, affirmative action would enhance her prospects of obtaining a position. If that person turns out to be white, then affirmative action would threaten to reduce or eliminate his chances to secure a position.

Given that differences in talents may give rise to sharply diverging interests, social contractors aware of their natural talents might not reach any unanimous agreement concerning affirmative action. And if they did, there is no reason to assume that such agreement would be similar to that which they would reach without information concerning their individual talents. Without such information the social contractors would have to determine if they would be better off as the most disadvantaged under an affirmative action plan or as the most disadvantaged in the absence of affirmative action. In short, a contractarian who would not lift the veil of ignorance with respect to natural endowments might well find a significantly different scope of justification for affirmative action than does Goldman.

B. The Reversal Test

An alternative method for determining whether affirmative action programs can justified within a contractarian framework is provided by what Goldman labels the "reversal test" (Goldman 1979, 16). According to this test, the legitimacy of a state of affairs resulting from unequal treatment can be determined by imagining role switches among the individuals involved. In the context of affirmative action, "these role switches involve race or sex" and serve to probe our intuitions about whether unequal treatment based on race or sex is legitimate. As applied to determine whether a particular practice constitutes first-order discrimination, the reversal test requires an examination of whether a similarly qualified white male would have been given the position refused to a woman or a black. In assessing the legitimacy of an affirmative action plan, the test requires an evaluation of whether a similarly situated white male would have been given the position awarded to a black or a woman (ibid., 16–17).

In applying his reversal test, Goldman embraces what I have labeled the "narrow conception" of the role of sex and race as a bona fide job qualification.[2] Accordingly, Goldman's reversal test would certainly sanction considering only female candidates for a female role in a movie. This is because it is presumably unobjectionable to consider only men for male movie roles. On the other hand, the reversal test would not justify hiring a less qualified woman math professor over a more qualified male candidate on the grounds that women are underrepresented in the college math department allocating the position. This is because it would be presumably unacceptable to hire a less qualified male over a more qualified female to eliminate an underrepresentation of men in a college math department.

One important matter that Goldman does not address in his description of his reversal test is the precise nature and scope of the role switches among the individuals involved. A distinction can be drawn between a "limited role switch" and a "complete role switch." A limited role switch involves an exchange of places or of roles but not an exchange of perspectives. A complete role switch, on the other hand, requires not only an exchange of roles but also an exchange of perspectives. Under a complete role switch, I not only assume the role of another but also her perspective. This distinction will be more fully explored in chapter 9. For now, suffice it to point out that practices that can be justified on the basis of a complete role switch are not necessarily justifiable from the standpoint of a limited role switch. In evaluating the results obtained by Goldman through application of his reversal test, therefore, it will be necessary to determine whether they are justified in the context of a limited role switch, a complete role switch, or both.

C. Fair Equality of Opportunity

If jobs were abundant, and if every individual could obtain the position that she coveted, affirmative action would be superfluous. Positions, however, particularly those that are fulfilling, are bound to be scarce. On the other hand, available places for students at institutions of higher education need not be scarce. Whenever demand exceeds supply, the number of such places could, in principle, be increased to meet the excess demand. As a practical matter, however, time constraints may often make it impossible for the supply of university places to catch up with increased demand. More important, even if possible, increases in supply may not be advisable to the extent that higher education provides specific skills that are only useful in connection with a particular set of scarce positions. Under those circumstances, if the available pool of qualified candidates to fill such positions already far exceeds the number of available positions, then further expansions of university capacity could be wasteful, diverting scarce resources from other productive uses. Accordingly, at least in some cases, scarcity in university places should be considered as immutable as scarcity in certain desirable positions.

In our society, a university education and employment positions play an essential role in the quest to realize the aims of one's life plan. As Goldman points out, one's career "affects the quality of one's life as much as any other single factor" (Goldman 1979, 25). Particular positions are for many "a crucial ingredient in a sense of self-accomplishment, satisfaction or self-respect," while the acquisition of most social goods is mainly a function of one's job. Therefore, to obtain the social goods necessary to the fulfillment of one's life plan one should be able to fill the positions that provide the means to acquire such social goods (ibid., 25–26).

Based on the contractarian belief that each person is equally entitled to pursue his own life plan, it may seem, at first, that each person should have an equal claim to the scarce position most likely to lead to the fulfillment of his life plan. Goldman himself recognizes a "presumption or priority of an equal distribution of goods." In his own words, "The logical priority of equality follows directly from first moral principles, in fact from the definition of what it means to be moral (combined with some very general facts about the human condition). *Deviations from equality must be justified, since it is the morally preferred distribution ceteris paribus* (emphasis added; ibid., 175).

Because of the unavoidable scarcity in desirable positions that precludes achieving subject-regarding equality of result, it might seem that justice would require adoption of the principle of prospect-regarding equality of opportunity. Furthermore, the way to achieve prospect-regarding equality of opportunity for all the candidates for a particular position would be to conduct a lottery and to allocate the position in question to the winner. Goldman, however, rejects the legitimacy of such a lottery (ibid., chap. 2, 179) based primarily on the following two reasons. First, he maintains that productivity is an independent source of desert and that it is, therefore, a proper criterion for the award of jobs. Goldman, moreover, is careful to specify that it is productivity and not effort that ought to be rewarded (ibid., 32–33). But in that case rewarding those who are most productive with desirable positions may be, as a practical matter, tantamount to favoring those who have superior natural endowments, provided only that the acquisition of qualifications for positions is heavily dependent on the exercise of natural endowments.

If productivity is primarily a function of natural endowments, awarding scarce positions on the basis of productivity seems open to the same kind of objection as Goldman's lifting of the veil of ignorance concerning the social contractors' natural endowments. Thus, rejection of a job lottery in favor of an allocation of positions to the most talented could be interpreted as the result of the refusal of the most talented contractors to agree to any other alternative coupled with the least talented contractors' fear that left alone they would be unable to provide for their own welfare. Since such a compromise does not arise in a setting marked by equality in bargaining power, Goldman's suggested award of positions as rewards for greater productivity arguably fails to satisfy the contractarian criterion of justice.

Goldman's second reason against the adoption of a job lottery is based on considerations of utility (ibid., 155). Assuming that allocating scarce positions to the most qualified maximizes economic efficiency, it seems reasonable for social contractors to give up the job lottery in exchange for a greater proportion of the goods needed to pursue their life plans. Even if the contractors were unaware of their natural endowments, applying the maximin principle, the least talented contractor would be better off in a society that distributes scarce positions to the most qualified than in one that uses a job lottery. In the former society the least talented would not get any of the more desirable scarce positions but would get more goods than he would if he lost at the job lottery in the latter society.

Considerations of utility may justify awarding scarce positions to the most qualified, but they do not thereby justify awarding a *right* to a position to the most qualified candidate for it. It is indeed conceivable that under certain circumstances considerations of utility might dictate that a particular scarce position be awarded to someone other than the most qualified candidate competing for it. For example, in the face of racial unrest, considerations of utility might require awarding a position to a member of a racial minority, even if she is not the most qualified candidate available. Under such circumstances, a right of the most competent to a position would seem in conflict with clearly pertinent considerations of utility.

Goldman acknowledges that considerations of utility cannot explain why the most qualified has a right to a particular position. He maintains, nevertheless, that the contractors would agree on conferring such a right to the most competent, because of the great value that they would attach to security and to stability in expectations. Contractors would value rights because, as Goldman points out, rights free persons from dependence on the benevolence of others. Moreover, Goldman also stresses that security and stability are highly valued because of their importance to the maintenance of the dignity and inviolability of the person (ibid., 155–56).

In sum, if we discount the first reason Goldman advances for rejecting the job lottery—namely, that productivity provides an independent source of desert—as unpersuasive from a contractarian standpoint, the contractarian justification for the right of the most competent to scarce positions amounts, in essence, to the following. Contractors would agree to overcome the presumption of equality and to reject the job lottery because of considerations of utility requiring that positions go to the most qualified candidates for them. Utility alone does not justify granting a right to the most qualified job applicants, but the contractors' concern for the dignity and inviolability of the individual does, and thus overrides conflicting considerations of utility. Considerations of utility justify the move from the prospect-regarding equality of opportunity of the job lottery to the means-regarding equality of opportunity implicit in open competition for scarce positions. Concern for the dignity of the individual requires that individuals be accorded a right to means-regarding equality of opportunity. Finally, because Goldman's social contractors, like Rawls', are ignorant of their social position, they would not settle for formal equality of opportunity. Instead, they would insist on an individual right to fair equality of opportunity in order to nullify the advantages obtained through superior social position.[3]

Differences between groups may not stem from social injustice. Accordingly, one might wonder if the social contractors would not prefer a group proportionment principle for allocating scarce positions. A group proportionment principle would equalize group-regarding prospects. An individual belonging to a group that would fare better than others in an open competition for positions would enjoy lower prospects of success under a group proportionment principle. Conversely, an individual belonging to a group that would fare worse under open competition would enjoy higher prospects of success under the latter principle. It would appear, therefore, that contractors operating under the maximin principle might well opt for the group proportionment principle.

Goldman, however, rejects the legitimacy of the group proportionment principle because of, among other things, the necessity to respect individual rights (ibid., 184). Group proportionment exalts the group at the expense of the individual and tends to strip the individual of her inherent dignity and autonomy by virtue of its subordination of individual interests to those of the group. Therefore, concludes Goldman, "exact proportionate representation not only lacks positive rationale, but would also involve serious injustices to individuals if it were enforced" (ibid., 183). And because of this, the contractors would most likely embrace the following principle for the allocation of scarce (places or) positions: an open competition under conditions of fair equality of opportunity, with a distributive right to a particular position going to the individual who wins the competition for it.

D. A Contractarian Conception of the Relationship between Distributive Justice and Compensatory Justice

Adoption of the principle of fair means-regarding equality of opportunity to govern the allocation of scarce positions precludes, at least in the first instance, the legitimate use of affirmative action. Indeed, in the initial stages of a newly formed society in which no member enjoyed any advantage traceable to any difference in social position, application of the principle of fair equality of opportunity would require strict adherence to the practice of awarding scarce positions to the most qualified, thus clearly precluding both first-order discrimination and affirmative action. Moreover, so long as such a society would continue abiding by the principle of fair means-regarding equal opportunity, there would be no justification for affirmative action.

This, however, does not preclude the contractarian justification of affirmative action as a tool of compensatory justice, or even as a tool of distributive justice in certain instances in which the principle of fair means-regarding equal opportunity is made applicable to a society that has a past as well as a future. As discussed in chapter 1, according to

Goldman, compensation for past violations of a prevailing distributive rule should take precedence over distributive considerations, even if that entails temporarily suspending application of such a distributive rule (ibid., 65–67). As Goldman explains,

> The adoption of *any* distributive rule implies that when violations occur, perpetrators are to be held liable and victims compensated in order to keep distributions as consistent with the demands of the rule as possible. It would be irrational, or perhaps even meaningless, for hypothetical contractors to adopt a distributive rule without building stipulations regarding liability . . . and compensation for violations. If the results of violations are as a rule allowed to stand, then there cannot have been a sincere desire to distribute benefits according to the original principle. (Ibid., 65–66)

Goldman's principle of compensation is very similar to Nozick's principle of rectification. Thus, application of Goldman's principle of compensation involves counterfactual reasoning in the sense that it is necessary to determine what would have been the case had the injury for which compensation is sought not occurred (ibid., 68). Also, as we shall see below, Goldman justifies certain uses of affirmative action under compensatory justice that are very similar to those that can be legitimated under Nozick's principle of rectification.

Under the contractarian conception of justice, the institution of fair means-regarding equality of opportunity in an already existing society—as opposed to one exclusively projected into the future—makes possible the justification of affirmative action under distributive justice. If, for example, fair means-regarding equality of opportunity is introduced in a society with a long history of extreme disparities in the allocation of socially relative assets, a mere distribution of assets may be insufficient to equalize means within a reasonable time. In that case, such an equalization of means may be achieved through affirmative action. As we shall see in the next section, Goldman believes that distributive affirmative action is justified under certain limited circumstances.

3. *Goldman's Contractarian Argument for Affirmative Action*

A. Affirmative Action Justified under Compensatory Justice

Preferential treatment in education and job hiring offers a unique opportunity to provide the victims of discrimination of the basis of race and sex with compensation in kind (ibid., 64). This notwithstanding, however, Goldman only envisages a relatively narrow role for preferential treatment in the context of compensatory justice. He maintains that compensation in kind can only be justified if there is a clear answer to the relevant counterfactual (ibid., 69).

As I have stated, Goldman's compensatory justification of affirmative action is substantially similar to that under the libertarian principle of rectification. The principal difference between the two positions on this point stems from the contractarian's contemplation of a much broader domain of allocation for the state than that viewed as legitimate by the libertarian. Under the libertarian criterion of justice, as we have seen, the state has a very restricted domain of allocation, with presumably no inherent obligation to adhere to the principle of equality of opportunity. Under the contractarian criterion of justice, by contrast, the positive obligation of promoting fair equality of opportunity makes it imperative that the state assume responsibility for a much broader domain of allocation.

For Goldman, affirmative action is justified as compensation in kind for the actual victim of first-order discrimination in relation to the allocation of scarce employment positions. The paradigmatic case, in this connection, is that of a black or a woman who won the competition for a particular position but who was nevertheless not awarded that position as a consequence of racism or sexism. At some future time when the same or a substantially similar position is open, the previously wronged person is no longer the most qualified competing candidate. Notwithstanding that fact, the wronged person ought to be awarded the available position as compensation for the past wrong. Moreover, that wronged person has a superior claim to the latter position than a better qualified white male candidate. This is consistent with Goldman's position that the principle of compensation temporarily overrides the principle of distribution to redress injuries to distributive rights.

As far as the establishment of the relevant counterfactual is concerned, the victim of past first-order discrimination can certainly plausibly argue that but for such discrimination she would be occupying the very position that has now become open (or one that is substantially similar to it). On the other hand, the white male who wins the competition for the subsequently open position can also plausibly argue that he should be entitled to fill it. Accordingly, the key to the success of the relevant counterfactual argument depends on the acceptance of Goldman's observation that once a person is awarded a job, she will keep it, provided performance on the job is satisfactory, even if a more qualified candidate for the job in question should become available (ibid., 125). Goldman also adds that

> The reason we do not accept a general practice of firing those already in positions where more attractive younger candidates come along . . . is that the utility or efficiency that might be gained by such a practice would be more than offset by losses in job security. The prospect of having to defend one's job constantly by proving superiority to any other possible candidate would be too unsettling for most of us. Thus rational agents concerned for their security would not agree to such a rule. (Ibid.)

Consistent with this, if the very position to which a black or a woman was entitled at T_1, but which was awarded to a white male because of first-order discrimination, becomes vacant again at T_2, then under Goldman's conception of compensatory justice, the black or woman who was the best qualified for the position at T_1 should obtain it a T_2, even if there is a better qualified white male candidate at T_2. Indeed, applying the counterfactual, and assuming that the black or woman entitled to the position at T_1 would have, but for first-order discrimination, continued to hold it at T_2, then the position would have never become open at T_2, and the white male who happens to be the most qualified to hold that position at T_2, would have no valid claim to it at that time. Thus, under the preceding analysis, preferential treatment for an actual victim of first-order discrimination is justified on compensatory grounds, so long as the same (or a similar) position that was wrongfully denied to such victim becomes vacant at some subsequent time.

Because Goldman insists that the relevant counterfactual be established with a high degree of probability (ibid., 69), even a proven victim could only become entitled to preferential treatment within the confines of the same domain of allocation involved in the previous deprivation of that victim's distributive right. Thus, for example, if a woman is wrongfully denied a place at a university because of her sex, and as a consequence subsequently lacks sufficient qualifications to obtain a certain type of job, it would be unwarranted to grant her preferential treatment in the competition for the job, even if it were justified to accord her a preference in admissions to the university. Indeed, unless all those who entered the university were to become eventually entitled to hold the type of job question, one could not successfully contend that but for the educational discrimination the victim would have succeeded in the job competition.

Finally, compensatory preferential treatment must be limited to the very agent of allocation who bears responsibility for the violation sought to be compensated. If one employer has wrongfully denied a position to a victim, that employer, but not another with similar positions to allocate, may have an obligation to accord preferential treatment to the victim. Even absent any discrimination the innocent employer would not have been employing the victim at the time she seeks compensation. Thus, making such innocent employer responsible for compensation would clearly fail to satisfy the relevant counterfactual.

B. Affirmative Action Justified under Distributive Justice

Goldman maintains that future-looking concerns justify the institution of affirmative action on behalf of the chronically poor, at least under conditions of moderate scarcity (ibid; 191ff, 199). This future-looking justification of affirmative action depends on considerations of distributive justice relating to the principle of fair equality of opportunity. Over time, awarding positions to the most qualified may lead to the gradual undermining of equality of opportunity rather than to its continued preservation. Indeed, the greater rewards reaped by those who hold desirable scarce positions tend to allow them to exercise control over a greater portion of society's scarce goods, and thus enable them to enhance their children's prospects of obtaining the scarce positions for which the latter will eventually have to compete. Thus, the award of positions to the most competent would seem to clash with the maintenance of *fair* equality of opportunity.

Having embraced fair means-regarding equality of opportunity, the contractarian cannot sanction the award of scarce positions on the basis of competence as being completely just so long as substantial differences in prospects attributable to differences in social position are not eradicated (ibid., 198). Accordingly, for the contractarian the legitimacy of distributing scarce positions to the most competent depends on the neutralization of socially relative disparities of means. To be sure, the need to overcome such disparities does not in and of itself justify affirmative action. It is conceivable, indeed, that socially relative disparities could be sufficiently reduced by other means, such as free schooling and free remedial education. Goldman believes, however, that there is one group in society—the chronically poor—for whom schooling alone cannot be expected to provide the means to overcome the cumulative socially induced disadvantages from which they suffer (ibid., 173).

In Goldman's view, chronic poverty tends to lock its victims into a cycle of social deprivation and social disadvantage that leads to chronic lack of motivation (ibid., 191). Under these circumstances, nothing short of preferential treatment might enable the chronically poor to overcome their severe socially induced handicaps. Thus, as Goldman points out, preferential treatment instituted to combat the lack of motivation of the chronically poor accords with, rather than violates, the principle of fair equality of opportunity (ibid., 192). Although it may seem paradoxical, the long-term achievement of a fair system of distribution based on the allocation of scarce positions to the most competent in a context of fair equality of opportunity may well depend on periodic suspensions of the application of the rule that scarce positions must be allocated to the most qualified candidate until such time as chronic poverty is eliminated (ibid., 199).

Goldman's distributive justification of affirmative action is narrowly circumscribed, much as is his compensatory justification. Indeed, Goldman does not extend the scope of legitimacy of distributive preferential treatment beyond the chronically poor. In particular, as will be discussed in section 4D, Goldman does not believe that distributive justice legitimates preferential treatment of blacks or women.

4. Goldman's Contractarian Argument against Affirmative Action

Goldman maintains that contractarian justice does not support preferential treatment of blacks or women on either compensatory or distributive grounds. Concerning compensatory justice, Goldman does not believe that compensation ought to extend to a member of an often discriminated-against group who has not actually experienced discrimination, and he also does not believe that all women or all blacks have experienced discrimination in education or in the job market. On the other hand, Goldman also rejects affirmative action for blacks or women from the standpoint of distributive justice. His principal argument from distributive justice is that affirmative action favors the most competent members of the victim group while conversely penalizing the least competent members of the nonvictim group.

A. Constraints Imported from Tort Liability Law

As I stressed in the previous section, Goldman maintains that compensation through preferential treatment can only be justified when a clear answer can be given to the relevant counterfactual concerning the place the victim of first-order discrimination would have occupied absent such discrimination. Further, to properly establish the counterfactual, Goldman postulates that the wrong sought to be compensated must result in "clear and measurable" harm to the victim rather than in "remote, indirect or speculative" harm (ibid., 69). The reason for this stringent standard is stated by Goldman in the following terms:

> When there is no clear answer to the relevant counterfactual, awards of compensation according to the rule will be inconsistent in practice and without firm basis. Unsubstantiated answers would result in unjust overriding of legitimate prima facie rights, reducing these to no rights at all. Hence the epistemological problem here limits just application of the compensatory principle to harms that are direct, clear and measurable. (Ibid.)

Goldman points out, moreover, that this stringent standard has been long used in the law of torts.

In general, tort compensation can be viewed from at least two perspectives: that of the tortfeasor and that of the victim. Goldman divides tortfeasors into two classes according to whether their tortious acts are intentional or not. Intentional tortfeasors, he maintains, can, consistent with his conception of compensatory justice, be required to provide full compensation for their wrongs even if they have derived no benefit from their tortious acts. Further, Goldman specifies that an agent of allocation who engages in first-order discrimination is to be considered an intentional tortfeasor, even if he is not aware of his biases (ibid., 73–74).

An agent of allocation who has engaged in first-order discrimination has violated certain rights and ought therefore to be held liable for the damages flowing from such violations. Goldman asserts, moreover, that there is a retributive element in compensation, and that an intentional tortfeasor should accordingly not be heard to complain even if he is forced to compensate someone other than the actual victim of his wrong (ibid., 73). Consistent with this line of reasoning, the apparent justification for requiring establishment of the counterfactual does not stem from the plight of the tortfeasor or from any distributive windfall going to a nonvictim. Instead, such apparent justification derives from the need to avoid unjustly to override the prima facie valid distributive rights of innocent third parties. Thus, Goldman believes that affirmative action is warranted only in those cases in which the stringent tort liability standards are met, because the adoption of any looser standard would impinge on the distributive rights of the innocent nonvictims who have proven to be the most competent candidates for the places or positions proposed to be allocated on a preferential basis. As long as the stringent standard is scrupulously adhered to, the winner of the competition for a position awarded in compensation to an actual victim of past discrimination has no compelling distributive claim to the position that presumably would not have become available but for the discrimination.

Goldman's restrictive approach is open to criticism from a contractarian perspective, particularly in cases where widespread and systematic first-order discrimination has led to substantial injuries which cannot be measured with the degree of precision that he requires. Goldman's demand for precision is designed to safeguard prima facie valid distributive rights. But the more uncertain one becomes about the validity of any distributive claim the less justified it seems to reject prima facie valid claims for compensation because of the increasingly unlikely event that their vindication might lead to some violation of legitimate distributive rights. To illustrate this, let us suppose that as a consequence of systematic first order gender-based discrimination, women are altogether banned from competing for certain desirable positions.[4] Let us suppose, moreover, that absent any discrimination women would obtain fifty percent of the desirable jobs in society. In that case, the distributive claim of any man to any of the positions in question would drop to a fifty percent probability of being valid. Indeed, but for the injustice perpetrated against women, approximately half of the men who actually won a competition for a scarce position would have lost that competition to a more qualified woman. Under such circumstances one might well ask why it would be more objectionable to give compensatory preferential treatment to women than to deny men enforcement of dubious distributive rights earned in a flawed competition.

A contractarian critic of Goldman's restrictive position might maintain that the social contractors would relax the degree of probability with which a victim of discrimination would have to establish the relevant counterfactual in cases in which massive and systematic interference with the integrity of an accepted distributive system had taken place. Just as, in Goldman's own view, the need for compensation justifies the temporary suspension of the operation of an accepted distributive principle, dubious distributive claims arising out of a profoundly flawed system of distribution may have to be set aside to allow for the satisfaction of less than certain compensatory claims. Indeed, that might prove to be the best possible way to reestablish the integrity of a scheme of distribution that has been subjected to massive violations.

B. The Problematic Relationship between the Individual and the Group

One of the principal reasons for Goldman's rejection of compensatory preferential treatment for blacks or women derives from his analysis of the relation between the individual and the group. According to Goldman, given the kind of wrong sought to be compensated through affirmative action—namely first-order discrimination in education and employment—neither group compensation nor group liability are justified. But if only individual compensation is appropriate, then since not every black or every woman has suffered the kind of wrong for which preferential treatment would provide legitimate compensation, preferences for blacks or women as a group would be unwarranted.

Compensation to a group is warranted, according to Goldman, when a group is a victim. He argues that harm to a group can either be distributive or nondistributive.[5] The paradigmatic case of distributive harm to a group is the group involved in a class action suit (Goldman 1979, 76). For example, the class of all consumers who have been fraudulently induced to overpay for some consumer good is clearly a group that has suffered a distributive harm. The damages incurred by the class are nothing but the aggregate of the individual damages suffered by each and every member of the class. Accordingly, if the class recovers in a lawsuit an amount equivalent to the sum of all the overpayments made by individual members of the class, justice would require that the total sum awarded be distributed among the members of the class in proportion to their respective overpayments.

In the context of affirmative action, if the harm involved is the wrongful denial of university places or jobs, then Goldman asserts that since not all blacks or women are victims there is no distributive injury to blacks or women as a group. Even if all blacks or all women had been personally victimized, affirmative action would still not constitute an appropriate form of compensation in Goldman's view. If, for example, every black person has suffered a harm, then compensation should extend to all blacks. Preferential treatment, however, typically only benefits some members of the preferred group and would therefore constitute an inadequate means of compensation.

Goldman acknowledges that other harms, such as the loss of ambition and self-respect that results from systematic discrimination and perpetuation of negative stereotypes, may appear to be candidates for redress through affirmative action. As Goldman suggests, it may be argued that preferential treatment is the optimal means of compensation for motivational damages. Under this analysis, members of the victim group would experience "vicarious harm" from the denial of opportunities to other members of the same group. Compensation for such harm would be through "vicarious association" (ibid., 77). In other words, by providing preferential treatment—and hence coveted positions—for some members of the victim group, it would become possible to restore the self-respect of all of its members.

Goldman rejects the validity of using preferential treatment as compensation for as weak a distributive harm as the "indirect" psychological "vicarious harm" associated with possible loss of motivation due to stereotyping (ibid., 82). Among the reasons he advances for his conclusion are that individuals who have been harmed are unlikely to be satisfied by compensation made to others and that recognition of indirect motivational harm is likely to open the door to all kinds of irrelevant claims by groups who happen to be underrepresented in a particular job category (ibid., 81, 88).

Although motivational harm may be difficult to establish with a high degree of precision, one may disagree with Goldman's premise that it constitutes an indirect harm. Indeed, it seems reasonable to consider motivational handicaps traceable to first-order discrimination as significant harms. Actually, particularly in view of Goldman's conclusion that affirmative action is justified on distributive grounds to remedy the motivational deficiencies of the chronically poor, it is surprising that he refuses to give more weight to the motivational injuries caused by first-order discrimination. In any event, if one acknowledges that the motivational harms attributable to first-order discrimination may be substantial, then affirmative action may arguably provide the best and fairest possible means of compensation for the victims of such discrimination.

To illustrate this last proposition, let us assume that a series of scarce jobs is awarded solely on the basis of merit as determined by the relative scores on a single test taken by all the candidates. Let us assume further that as a direct consequence of first-order discrimination the members of the victim group suffer from motivational harm which results in an examination score that is ten points lower than it would otherwise be. Under these circumstances, the prospects of success of the members of the victim group are distributively diminished while those of the nonvictim group are correspondingly distributively increased. To be sure, this does not necessarily mean that all members of the victim group will fail to secure a job or that notwithstanding the ten point handicap several members of that group might not obtain a better score than certain members of the nonvictim group. Conversely, even if ten points were added to the test scores of all members of the victim group, most likely several of its members would still fail to secure a job. The most important point, however, is that first-order discrimination results in diminished prospects of success for its victims and in increased prospects for the nonvictims.

Given that, preferential treatment—in this case by adding ten points to test scores of all members of the victim group—would seem to be the optimal means of compensation. It would at once wipe out the handicaps flowing from motivational harm and eliminate the unwarranted increased prospects of success encountered by members of the nonvictim group. Moreover, since the measurable injury caused by first-order discrimination is a diminution in the prospects of success in the competition for scarce jobs, affirmative action provides real and not merely vicarious compensation to all the victims. Indeed, what each victim is entitled to under the circumstances is better prospects of success, and not a guaranteed job. Consistent with this analysis, social contractors operating behind a limited veil of ignorance might well agree to the use of affirmative action under the circumstances of the present example. Assuming agreement on the principle of equality of opportunity, and applying the maximin principle, members of the victim group would stand to lose more in the absence of preferential treatment than would members of the nonvictim group in its presence.

Goldman would most likely disagree with the above argument based on the distinction he draws between a wrong and a harm.[6] Although all the members of the victim group may have been wronged by first-order discrimination, some among them, because of their greater resilience, may not have been harmed. Returning to the last example, it may be that some members of the victim group, because of their particularly strong makeup, will score as well on the test as they would have in the absence of any past discrimination. In that case, adding ten points to the test scores of the latter would provide them with an advantage (and their competitors with a disadvantage), which they would otherwise have never experienced.

In reply, it may be argued that, if it were possible to measure with sufficient precision the motivational harm caused by first-order discrimination, then preferential treatment should be tailored to do no more than eliminate the actual differential in prospects of success attributable to first-order discrimination. Accordingly, if a given victim has suffered no harm then he should not be awarded any additional points to increase his test score. But, if he had experienced a greater harm than the average, then he should be awarded a greater number of additional points on the test than that awarded the average victim.

To the extent that motivational harm cannot be measured with a sufficient degree of precision, any form of compensation for such harm would lead to imperfect procedural justice. If one accepts this, then preferential treatment might conceivably provide the best means of compensation for reductions in the prospects of success attributable to first-order discrimination. Indeed, if systematic first-order discrimination has caused palpable motivational harm and led to wide discrepancies between the prospects of success of members of the victim group and those of the nonvictim group, then the equalization of group-regarding prospects of success (leading to an increase in the prospects of success of individual members of the victim group and to a corresponding decrease in the prospects of their nonvictim counterparts) might amount to the best available remedy.

As mentioned above, another of Goldman's concerns is that providing compensation for motivational harm would open the door to a multitude of irrelevant claims by groups underrepresented in the workforce. This concern would appear to be easily met, however, if the right to compensation is limited to those instances of motivational harm that arise as a consequence of the commission of a clearly identifiable wrong. Thus, for instance, in the case of American blacks it would seem fairly obvious that there might be a strong link between motivational harm resulting in underrepresentation in the workplace and prolonged and nearly universal exposure to systematic first-order discrimination. In such a case, affirmative action would be justified as a means of compensation. In other cases, in which underrepresentation of a group is primarily a result of other causes, such as cultural idiosyncracies, however, such underrepresentation would not give rise to legitimate claims for compensation.

In addition to distributive harm to a group, Goldman argues that there may also be nondistributive harm to a group. As a paradigm of such nondistributive harm, Goldman refers to a sports team whose star player's arm is deliberately broken by an opponent. In that case, the team suffers a harm—that is, a substantial loss in competitive efficiency—which cannot be redressed by means of separate compensation for each of its players. In the case of nondistributive harm to a group, Goldman argues that preferential treatment is never justified. Thus while he believes that blacks who were second-class citizens by law suffered a nondistributive harm as a group, he does not believe that preferential treatment would be an appropriate form of compensation for such harm (ibid., 82–86). The reason for this position, moreover, is that preferential treatment benefits certain individual members of the group rather than the group as a whole.

Goldman acknowledges that if a group is characterized by "mutual concern," cultural and political identification, and "shared values and interests," and if each member prefers that a benefit go to a group member rather than to an outsider, then "benefits to any member may be said to benefit all." This notwithstanding, Goldman still argues that preferential treatment would not be appropriate, because he believes that third-party preferences ought not to outweigh the rights of "those for whom the benefits are directly at stake," and because he is convinced that victims of first-order discrimination would rather be personally compensated than have another member of their group enjoy the principal benefits of such compensation (ibid., 87).

It may be argued against Goldman that, particularly in the case of a cohesive victim group that possesses a high degree of solidarity, preferential treatment may well be a particularly appropriate means of compensation for nondistributive harm. If, for example, the principal harm deriving from first-order discrimination is a severe decrease in collective pride and self-esteem, then preferential treatment leading to the placement of several group members in positions of power and prestige might produce a substantial boost in the collective self-image of the group. Under these circumstances, although affirmative action would benefit certain individuals more than others, it would also produce a tangible benefit for the group as a whole.

Before determining whether a particular form of compensation is appropriate, we must establish not only to whom compensation is owed but also who properly owes such compensation. In considering *who* owes compensation to the victims of first-order discrimination, we are again confronted with the problematic relation of the individual and the group. At least two classes of subjects usually bear the burden of compensating the victims of discrimination through affirmative action: the agent of allocation who must award positions on a preferential basis and the class of those who compete for preferentially awarded positions and who would have been awarded such positions but for the implementation of an affirmative action plan. Imposing an individual duty of compensation on anyone guilty of first-order discrimination would be clearly justified under the contractarian criterion of justice. But not every individual who would secure a place or position in the absence of preferential treatment is likely to have personally engaged in first-order discrimination. Therefore, it would seem that a duty of compensation could only be legitimately imposed on such an innocent individual on some theory of group liability or collective guilt. According to Goldman, however, first-order race-based or gender-based discrimination does not justify imposing collective liability.

Paradigms of collective guilt, in Goldman's view, include a bank robbery carried out by a group of persons, a multiple rape (ibid., 104), and other acts or omissions involving close-knit groups, peer pressure to conform, and group loyalty (ibid., 107). But even assuming that white males are guilty of widespread racism and sexism, Goldman maintains that they lack the cohesiveness necessary to justify imposing collective liability for the actions of some but by no means all of them (ibid.).

The paradigmatic cases cited by Goldman involve either some kind of joint enterprise or a situation in which every member of the group bears individual responsibility for the wrong sought to be compensated. Thus, for example, a bank robbery involves a joint enterprise, for which every participant bears responsibility regardless of whether his individual acts standing alone would be illegal. In a multiple rape, on the other hand, every rapist bears individual guilt because of the nature of his own act. By contrast, widespread racism and sexism cannot properly be said to amount to a joint coordinated enterprise of the kind involved in the joint planning and execution of a bank robbery. Moreover, since, even in the face of widespread racism and sexism, some white males have championed civil rights for blacks and equal rights for women, the collective guilt of white males cannot be predicated on a mere aggregation of instances of individual guilt.

Goldman acknowledges that collective liability might also be appropriate if every white male benefited from the injustices toward blacks and women (ibid., 108). He does not find, however, that the average white male has personally benefited from such injustices. Indeed, he maintains that, even if some white males have obtained jobs that they would not have absent first-order discrimination, because he believes discrimination to be generally inefficient, it is highly likely that white males as a whole are worse off because of discrimination.

This last conclusion seems highly debatable. If we concede that discrimination entails a loss in efficiency, it is nevertheless quite plausible that white males as a group would be better off by controlling a larger share of a smaller economic pie than by holding a smaller share of the larger economic pie produced by a discrimination-free society. Moreover, white males seem bound to enjoy a greater share of the power and prestige attached to desirable positions in a racist and sexist society than they would in a discrimination-free society. Finally, if a racist and sexist society has systematically deprived blacks and women of educational opportunities, white males are likely to enjoy greater prospects of success in the job market than they would have had in the absence of first-order discrimination.

If white males are better off because of first-order discrimination, one must determine whether a white male who is the innocent recipient of an undeserved benefit could be held liable to compensate the victims of discrimination under the contractarian principle of compensatory justice. To the extent that compensation includes a retributive element, such a liability would seem unwarranted. Retribution is usually associated with guilt in the context of criminal transgressions and is not ordinarily thought to be justified in the absence of culpable conduct. To the extent, however, that compensation encompasses an element of restitution—in the sense of eliminating an unjust enrichment and of using its proceeds to make up for an unjust loss—compensatory liability for innocent white males may be justified under certain circumstances.

To appreciate when such compensatory liability may be justified, let us focus on the distinction underscored by the following two examples. First, suppose that A purchases an automobile from B, pays B, and instructs B to deliver the automobile by leaving it in A's driveway. But B mistakenly drives the automobile to C's house and leaves it in C's driveway. Although C has not done anything to harm A., it seems fair to require that C give up possession of the automobile so that it can be delivered to A. Indeed, if C is allowed to keep possession of the automobile, C would be unjustly enriched and A unjustly impoverished.

In the second example, A contracts with B to have A's driveway repaved while A is away on vacation.[7] Mistakenly, B repaves C's driveway, which was as much in need of repaving as A's driveway. And C, who also happened to be on vacation at the time that B repaved his driveway, is very surprised to find his driveway repaved upon his return home. In this case, although C has received a benefit, it does not seem right to require C to pay B for that benefit. Thus, it may not be unjust to allow C to enjoy the benefit of a repaved driveway and to leave B's labor uncompensated. Even if the benefit to C is quantifiable as measured, for instance, by a net increase in the market value of C's house, it is arguably inappropriate to make C pay for a benefit he has not sought but cannot simply return. Clearly, C must be allowed to use his improved driveway, because the improvement may not be removable without causing the driveway to be put in a worse condition than it was prior to the repavement. On the other hand, C may not be required to pay, for he did not choose to have his driveway repaved, may have been perfectly happy to continue living with an unrepaved driveway, and have honestly preferred to put the money necessary to pay for such repavement to some other use.

Let us assume that innocent white males have benefited from first-order discrimination, by having acquired greater knowledge, skills, and qualifications than blacks or women. In light of the two examples discussed above, it would seem unjust to prohibit an innocent white male from making use of these acquired assets. Indeed, he may have worked hard to obtain them, and bears no personal responsibility for the deprivations of blacks and women. If anything, the case of the innocent white male to use his superior assets without incurring any compensatory liability seems stronger than that of the person whose driveway was repaved by mistake. On the other hand, however, because of these assets, innocent white males may enjoy greater *prospects* of success in the competition for jobs than they would have absent first-order discrimination. These increased prospects attributable to first-order discrimination arguably constitute an undeserved benefit that is separable from other benefits thrust upon them as a consequence of such discrimination. Imposing on innocent white males compensatory liability that merely requires them to give up a separable undeserved benefit would therefore seem as justifiable as requesting that a person who was mistakenly delivered a car give up possession of it. In sum, it seems fair for innocent white males to give up an undeserved increase in their prospects of success in order to wipe out the corresponding undeserved decrease in the prospects of success of blacks and women.

The compensatory liability of innocent white men for undeserved increases in prospect does not amount to collective liability—or, at least, to nondistributive collective liability. In theory, each innocent white man is only supposed to give up his own undeserved increase in prospects. In practice this will not always be the case, but that is a function of the inevitability in this context of imperfect procedural justice.

C. Affirmative Action Favors the Most Competent Victims and Conversely Penalizes the Least Competent Nonvictims

In what he considers to be perhaps the most important point of his book, Goldman argues that preferential treatment in education and hiring for blacks and women ought to be rejected because it tends to benefit the best qualified members of the victim group, who presumably need help the least, at the expense of its least qualified members, who are apparently in the greatest need of assistance. Conversely, according to this argument, preferential treatment is unjust to the members of the nonvictim group, in that it is much more likely to hurt the least advantaged among them than those who are most advantaged. Goldman points out that affirmative action provides advantage to the most competent members of the benefited group, who are most likely to end up with preferentially allocated places and positions. This, according to Goldman, is justified on distributive grounds. "What is wrong", however, "is that the principle of compensation and the distributive principle of hiring the competent pull in opposite directions here." Indeed, in Goldman's view, the most qualified members of the victim group are likely to have suffered the least discrimination, and the least qualified, the most discrimination. Under these circumstances, argues Goldman, preferential treatment directed to groups as a whole "will invert the ratio of past harm to present benefit" (ibid., 90–91).

In order to evaluate Goldman's argument properly, it is important to keep in mind that, absent any preferential treatment, the most qualified members of both the nonvictim and victim groups would be better off than the least qualified within their respective groups. This follows from adoption of equality of opportunity as the operating principle of distributive justice. Hence, it is because of Goldman's embrace of equality of opportunity, and not because of the imposition of affirmative action, that the best qualified victims and nonvictims will end up better off than their respective least qualified counterparts. Further, in a society that is supposed to abide by the principle of equality of opportunity in the allocation of scarce positions, first-order discrimination is more likely to harm the most qualified members of the victim group than their least qualified counterparts. Conversely, such discrimination is more likely to benefit lesser qualified members of the nonvictim group, who would not succeed in securing a scarce position in the absence of such discrimination, rather than its most qualified members, who would presumably have succeeded in any event.

Under these circumstances preferential treatment for the victim group as a whole seems equally justified on compensatory and distributive grounds, and best suited to reconcile the often-conflicting demands of compensatory and distributive justice. Ideally, such preferential treatment would simultaneously wipe out the undeserved increase in the prospects of success of the members of the nonvictim group and the corresponding unjust decrease in the prospects of the members of the victim group. In addition, awarding positions to the best qualified within each group minimizes the disruption of distributive schemes based on the principle of equality of opportunity.

The above argument rests on the assumption that first-order discrimination results in a marginally equal decrease in the prospects of success of every member of the victim group. It might be objected that such an assumption is completely arbitrary. This objection seems to be valid. Indeed, the prospects of success of an individual depend on many factors, such as natural talents, motivation, social class, cultural values, and the nature and quality of education. Therefore, it seems unlikely that there would be a simple correlation between the amount of discrimination experienced and the level of qualification attained by a particular individual. That fact taken alone, however, does not lend any support to Goldman's position. Quite the contrary, it buttresses the conclusion that the most talented have the most to lose as a consequence of first-order discrimination in the allocation of education and jobs.

Thus, in the context of racially segregated schools, for example, if black schools are significantly inferior to white schools, it seems logical that a naturally talented black would suffer a greater harm in relation to the marketplace for scarce jobs than a black with more modest natural gifts. Indeed, but for her inferior education, the more talented black would most likely succeed in the competition for scarce jobs while her much less talented counterpart would still in all likelihood fail. Accordingly, whereas segregation may be equally wrong with respect to the most talented and the least talented blacks, *regarding the competition for scarce jobs* the former are likely to suffer a much greater harm than the latter. So long as one focuses exclusively on that particular harm, therefore, preferential treatment may provide the best possible means of compensation. This is not to say that overall the least talented blacks have not been harmed as much as the most talented ones, or that the overall compensation due to the victims of racial discrimination ought not ultimately be divided in proportion to the overall harm suffered by each individual victim. For the harms suffered in the marketplace for scarce jobs, however, preferential treatment may well be the best possible remedy.

D. Preferential Treatment for Blacks and Women Not Justified under Distributive Justice

For Goldman, affirmative action is justified on distributive grounds for the chronically poor but not for all blacks or women. The legitimate function of forward-looking affirmative action, according to Goldman, is the establishment and maintenance of fair equality of opportunity for all members of society. Victims of chronic poverty and of a chronic lack of motivation may not be able to reach fair equality of opportunity without preferential treatment. Not all blacks or all women are poor, however, nor do they all lack motivation. Under these circumstances, race- or gender-based preferential treatment would be both overinclusive and underinclusive. In addition to favoring blacks and women who have already attained fair equality of opportunity, such preferential treatment would deprive chronically poor white males of fair equality of opportunity. Thus, according to Goldman, any reason offered to justify race- or gender-based preferential treatment as a means toward future equality of opportunity "will also constitute a reason for specifying the group to be preferred differently and more narrowly than by race or sex" (ibid., 195).

Whether Goldman's argument against extending affirmative action to all blacks and all women on distributive grounds is valid under the contractarian criterion of justice depends on whether all blacks or all women suffer from a similar socially induced handicap, which prevents them from attaining fair equality of opportunity. Moreover, such a handicap must be one that could be reduced or eliminated through preferential treatment. If, for example, women as a whole were proven to suffer from a unique motivational handicap resulting from the rigid imposition of certain traditional highly differentiated sex roles, then arguably women as a whole should be entitled to affirmative action as a matter of distributive justice. Therefore, the validity of preferential treatment on distributive grounds under the contractarian criterion of justice depends on the particular circumstances affecting the members of the group to be benefited.

5. Thalberg's Proposed Broader Contractarian Justification for Affirmative Action

Thalberg's argument in favor of a broader contractarian justification for affirmative action begins with an attack on the soundness of Goldman's rejection of preferential treatment because it favors the most qualified members of the victim group rather than its least qualified members. Thalberg concedes that it is likely that "the more vile and flagrant an injustice was, the more its victim will be hindered from developing the cognitive skills or ambition needed in today's job market" (Thalberg 1980, 143). Unlike Goldman, however, Thalberg does not believe that a scheme of compensation based on preferential treatment would necessarily benefit the least victimized members of the preferred group while leaving its most victimized members without any compensation.

According to Thalberg, Goldman is wrong to infer that the most qualified members of a group subjected to discrimination must also be those who have encountered the least amount of discrimination, as is shown by the following counterexample. In Thalberg's own words,

> Suppose the nonwhites who prosper through RD [Reverse Discrimination] happen to be individuals who were endowed at birth with uncommon resiliency—or perhaps they were fortunate to grow up in an exceptionally supportive milieu. Afterward they encountered "severe injustices"—enough to crush an average person. Yet, because of their unusual personality traits, they bounced back, often becoming more determined to achieve. (Ibid., 143–44)

Another deficiency that Thalberg sees in Goldman's analysis is the latter's apparent failure to recognize the most pervasive and insidious aspects of first-order discrimination. American racism, according to Thalberg, has not only left its imprint on every black, regardless of wealth or position, but has also fomented the development of the kind of self-doubt, self-hatred, and negative self-image that leads to an incapacitating sense of lesser worth (ibid., 146).

If this sense of lesser worth is as great a handicap in the job market as the lack of motivation that Goldman believes afflicts the chronically poor, then a contractarian could justify preferential treatment for blacks from the standpoint of distributive justice. Indeed, so long as that sense of lesser worth is not eradicated, the distributive system used to allocate scarce positions will lack substantial fairness. Under these circumstances, affirmative action in favor of blacks would presumably allow them to achieve fair equality of opportunity much in the same way as affirmative action in favor of the chronically poor would allow the latter to do the same. Indeed, what fair equality of opportunity requires is that differences in prospects attributable to differences in social conditions be eliminated so as to allow the outcome of competition to become a function of the differences in natural abilities among the competitors. A socially induced sense of lesser worth is likely to distort competition much in the same way as the lack of motivation resulting from socially created chronic poverty would. Similarly, just as preferential treatment for the chronically poor is likely to boost their motivation by demonstrating that success is not beyond their reach, so preferential treatment for blacks is likely to reduce their sense of lesser worth as their prospects of success increase.

Thalberg argues that, given Goldman's contractarian framework and his conviction that social advantages should not be allowed to increase the prospects of success in the marketplace for jobs, it is hard to understand why Goldman refuses to endorse affirmative action in favor of blacks. Given the setting in which Goldman has placed the social contractors, why—asks Thalberg—would they not reason as follows? "If I have the misfortune to be nonwhite in a society emerging from centuries of racism, I would prefer to see some kind of modification made in the absolute competence rule; and PRD [Principle of Reverse Discrimination] would be better than the compensation principle. Nor would I suffer as much under PRD if I'm white, as I would under the competence and compensation principles alone if I'm nonwhite" (ibid., 149).

Whether the social contractors would reason as Thalberg suggests would seem to depend on several factors, including whether or not they were aware of their natural abilities. Thus, if one assumes with Goldman that the contractors are aware of their natural abilities, a case can be made that they would split into two groups depending on their natural abilities. Those who possess the greatest natural abilities would favor the use of affirmative action to combat the effects of racism. Indeed, if it turns out that they are white, they would be the least likely members of their race to suffer its adverse consequences. If on the contrary, it turns out that they are black, they would stand the best chance of becoming the principal beneficiaries of affirmative action. Conversely, those who possess significantly fewer natural abilities would seem most likely to oppose affirmative action, as they would stand to gain little from it if it turns out they are black, and much to lose from it, if it turns out that they are white.

Assuming, on the other hand, that the social contractors are unaware of their natural abilities, the validity of Thalberg's argument depends primarily on whether the benefits of affirmative action for blacks are likely to outweigh the harms that it seems bound to impose on whites—*benefits* and *harms* being understood here in a broad sense that encompasses effects on self-respect and the integrity of the individual, rather than in any narrow utilitarian sense.

In the last analysis, whether Goldman's or Thalberg's approach is ultimately more justifiable within a contractarian framework, and whether the benefits of affirmative action would be deemed by a social contractor to outweigh its harms are issues that cannot be resolved satisfactorily within the confines of the contractarian position. The contractarian criterion of justice does not seem to allow for a sufficiently determinate definition of the legitimate scope of affirmative action. In order to understand the reason for this, however, it is necessary to critically evaluate the contractarian position from a broader perspective—a task that I will undertake in Part Three below.

CHAPTER FOUR

Utilitarian Justice and Affirmative Action

In this chapter, I examine utilitarian arguments for and against affirmative action. These arguments are generally forward looking.[1] The utilitarian arguments for affirmative action shall be divided into three, namely, what I refer to as the "pure utilitarian argument," the "limited utilitarian argument," and Dworkin's utilitarian argument. After completing my review of these arguments, I will discuss utilitarian arguments made against affirmative action.

1. Utilitarian Arguments for Affirmative Action

The utilitarian, who is principally concerned with maximizing welfare, can apparently avoid the most vexing problems confronting those who seek to justify affirmative action within a libertarian or a contractarian framework. Thus, if one seeks to justify affirmative action in favor of a group as leading to the maximization of welfare, it becomes unnecessary to confront the arguments against such policy in the context of compensatory justice—namely, that because not all individual members of the group have experienced first-order discrimination, compensatory justice does not justify group-based preferential treatment. Similarly, in the context of distributive justice, by focusing exclusively on welfare maximization, the utilitarian need not be concerned by the fact that preferential treatment in favor of a particular group tends to favor its most qualified members at the expense of its least qualified ones.

There is, however, a major problem confronting a utilitarian who endorses affirmative action. Any endorsement of preferential treatment as a morally justified means to maximize welfare may legitimate the use of first-order discrimination, as well. If social utility can be served by preferring blacks over whites or women over men, then—at least in principle—nothing would preclude social utility from being promoted by preferring whites over blacks or men over women. As Fullinwider indicates, even if the utilitarian could convincingly argue that under present circumstances affirmative action but not first-order discrimination would maximize utility, nothing precludes the possibility that the reverse would be true under different circumstances sometime in the future.[2]

This difficulty raised by the utilitarian approach arises because the single-minded pursuit of social utility is likely to frustrate the vindication of certain individual rights. In view of this, the utilitarian may recast his case for affirmative action in a way that takes as given the basic constitutional rights conferred by the equal protection clause.[3] Accordingly, utilitarian approaches to affirmative action can be divided for the most part into two: those that treat considerations of social utility as being paramount; and those others that treat such considerations as being legitimate, provided individual rights are properly considered. The former I call the "pure utilitarian approach"; the latter, the "limited utilitarian approach."

A. The Pure Utilitarian Argument

One of the principal virtues of the pure utilitarian approach is that it allows the focus on social utility to remain exclusive. Under this approach, as Fullinwider points out, questions of individual rights or deserts can ultimately all be reduced to questions of utility (Fullinwider 1980, 90ff.). As a consequence of this, an affirmative action plan can be deemed just if the benefits to society produced by it outweigh the harms to which it gives rise. Some of the most frequently mentioned benefits of affirmative action include more rapid integration of the workforce (Goldman 1979, 141), easing of tensions between sexes and races (ibid.), development of desirable role models and destruction of negative stereotypes (Greenawalt 1983, 64), achievement of diversity among the student body at institutions of higher learning (ibid.), and promotion of better services for minority communities (Fullinwider 1980, 18).

A practical problem confronting any assessment of the benefits and harms likely to be produced by particular affirmative action programs stems from the difficulty of projecting with any degree of accuracy the foreseeable consequences of any complex and far-reaching social policy (ibid., 19). Because any utilitarian justification of an affirmative action plan depends on whether it will result in a net benefit to society, the inability to project the likely consequences of a plan with a sufficient degree of accuracy could, as a practical matter, completely frustrate the utilitarian. With this in mind, our examination of the pure utilitarian argument for affirmative action shall concentrate on two broad issues: first, the relation between the benefits likely to accrue to the members of the group favored by an affirmative action plan and the harms likely to be suffered by others; and second, the possible justification of preferential treatment in the allocation of scarce employment positions given the assumption that awarding positions to the most qualified candidate is generally justified as leading to the maximization of utilities.[4]

Any pure utilitarian argument in favor of an affirmative action plan based on the claim that the plan is likely to produce a net benefit for society taken as a whole seems open to a serious objection. Indeed, as Fullinwider observes, in the context of an affirmative action plan designed to favor blacks, "It might be objected that the economic consequences of preferential hiring of blacks, in fact, be zero, since every black gain must be matched by a corresponding white loss, the losses and gains, cancelling each other out. Nothing is added to social utility by preferential hiring. The distribution of the economic total is merely shifted around among subgroups in society" (Fullinwider 1980, 69).

Notwithstanding this objection, Fullinwider believes that a strong case can be made that preferential treatment of blacks at the expense of whites can lead to a net benefit for society (ibid., 68ff.). Upon closer examination, the shift in the allocation of certain desirable positions from whites to blacks does not necessarily lead to a zero-sum result. Indeed, according to Fullinwider, a shift in the economic benefits attached to certain positions from whites to blacks can lead to a net increase in the total economic wealth at the disposal of society. Fullinwider goes on to argue that "the positive economic effects of the extra blacks, employed in higher paying jobs could likely be greater than the negative effects of white losses. This is because black poverty is concentrated. Consequently, a significant rise in the incomes of a substantial number of blacks will have a concentrated positive effect. We might truly say that black job gain will represent community gain while white job loss will represent individual loss" (ibid., 69–70).

Underlying Fullinwider's argument that affirmative action does not have to lead to zero-sum results seem to be two factual assumptions that are hardly self-evident. The first assumption is that allocating certain scarce positions to blacks on a preferential basis would lead to a greater increase in wealth (or a lesser decrease in wealth) than if they were to be allocated to whites pursuant to a straightforward competition based on competence. The second assumption is that the preferential award of a scarce position to a black will have beneficial effects on persons other than the successful candidate (and his or her immediate dependents), but will not have harmful effects on persons other than the unsuccessful white candidate who would have otherwise secured the position (and his or her immediate dependents).

To the first assumption, one can object that, in a nonexpanding economy, it is hard to imagine how allocation of a scarce position on a preferential basis could lead to a net increase in societal wealth. Indeed, all other things remaining equal, it seems unlikely that a less qualified preferentially hired person would produce *more* than the better qualified person who would have been hired but for affirmative action. In an expanding economy, on the other hand, it is conceivable—though by no means certain—that preferential treatment would lead to a net increase in wealth. This could happen if the implementation of affirmative action policies were to motivate hitherto demoralized blacks to enter the job market and to take advantage of increasing job opportunities. Under such circumstances, the whites who would be most directly adversely affected by affirmative action would nonetheless still find productive employment, while blacks who would have otherwise remained unemployed would enter the workforce and thus contribute to the generation of increased wealth.

The second assumption made by Fullinwider—namely, that black gains due to affirmative action will have a beneficial effect on society as a whole, whereas the corresponding white losses will only have a detrimental effect on those individuals who are directly affected—also seems open to serious objection. Again, in a nonexpanding economy, any gain brought by affirmative action to a black would seem to have to be offset by an equal loss to a white. Under such circumstances, for the black's gain to become a benefit to the community at large, or to blacks as a separate group, would seem to require the existence of special conditions, such as the greater sharing of individually earned income with other members of one's group among blacks than among whites, or greater group solidarity among blacks than among whites. Moreover, the extension of the benefits of affirmative action to the black community as a whole and the limitation of its burdens to isolated whites would seem to pull in opposite directions. Indeed, it would appear that the greater the number of black individuals who benefit directly from affirmative action, the more likely it would become that the black community would share the benefit. Conversely, the greater the number of whites who are denied desirable positions because of affirmative action, the more likely it would seem that whites would experience a sense of collective loss.

On the other hand, Fullinwider's second assumption could be defended on the theory that, all other things being equal, the psychological benefits that affirmative action is likely to produce for blacks clearly outweigh the psychological harms it is likely to inflict on whites. The reason for this is that the black gain would have a much greater repercussion on a concentrated black community than the white loss would on the white community. In the midst of poverty and a general lack of opportunities, visible success could quite possibly enhance hope and pave the way toward the improvement of prevailing material conditions. In contrast, a relatively small number of additional individual failures to secure scarce positions by whites are unlikely to have a great negative impact on the white community. So long as whites continue to hold on to most of the positions that wield power and prestige, their collective sense of worth and their general level of relative affluence would not seem threatened by isolated individual failures. In short, while individual black success would tend to lead to an increase in collective black self-esteem, individual white failures would not tend to lead to a decrease in collective white self-esteem.

The second broad issue raised by the pure utilitarian argument for affirmative action centers around the proposition that awarding scarce positions to the most qualified candidates leads to the maximization of utilities. If this is true, how can a pure utilitarian defend affirmative action plans that lead to the hiring of candidates who are not the most qualified for the position for which they compete?

There may be several contributing reasons why hiring the most qualified maximizes utility. One of them, for instance, might be that it is likely to satisfy most people's sense of justice, thus producing a generalized sense of satisfaction with the institutional practices of society. By far the most important reason, however, seems to be that hiring the most qualified leads to the achievement of the greatest possible measure of efficiency. Efficiency leads to the production of the greatest number of desired goods, and that, in turn, presumably makes for the greatest satisfaction of the greatest number of people.

To the extent that hiring the most qualified maximizes utility because it is efficient, the pure utilitarian proponent of affirmative action would have to be able to demonstrate that the kind of preferential treatment that she advocates would not reduce efficiency or that, if it does, such reduction would not lead to a decline in overall utility. As we will see, one can advance plausible arguments for both these propositions.

Race- or gender-conscious hiring policies may enhance efficiency in one of two ways. First, even under the narrow conception adopted in chapter I, race or gender may in certain cases constitute relevant job qualifications. Second, even where this is not the case, it would still be possible that an increased proportion of blacks or women in the workforce would enhance cooperation and harmony and thus eventually lead to enhanced efficiency.

In cases in which race or gender are genuine job qualifications, efficiency may be enhanced by race- or gender-conscious hiring policies, but, as indicated in chapter I, preferential treatment is not, properly speaking, involved. In other cases, preferential hiring may nevertheless lead to greater efficiency whenever diversity and balance would lead to greater overall productivity than the efforts of a more homogeneous group of workers hired only on the basis of possession of the highest directly relevant job qualifications. This is possible because, although in some cases the total efficiency of a group of workers is equal to the sum of its parts, in others, it can be greater than the sum of its parts. As

Fullinwider observes, sometimes efficiency is "additive," other times, it is "compositive" (Fullinwider 1980, 87). The efficiency of a group of workers is additive if it is "a simple function of each worker taken separately." On the other hand, it is compositive if the measure of success of an enterprise "depends not only upon the individual skills of the workers but also upon how well they interact with one another and how well others interact with them" (ibid.). Accordingly, preferential treatment may lead to greater efficiency in cases involving compositive rather than additive efficiency.

Fullinwider maintains that the efficiency of a particular group of workers is more likely to be additive or compositive depending, in significant part, on the level of skills necessary to perform the tasks at hand. Thus, where high levels of skill are at a premium, as, for example, in the case of heart surgeons, efficiency is more apt to be additive.[5] Where the level of the requisite relevant skills is substantially lower, compatibility and harmony among coworkers, and between the latter and the members of the public for whom they perform services, may be paramount. In the latter situation, efficiency would tend to be compositive, and affirmative action easier to justify.

One of the principal drawbacks of the pure utilitarian argument in favor of race- and gender-based affirmative action is that it seems to justify the use of race or gender for purposes of excluding blacks or women. Indeed, if, for example, whites are so hostile to blacks that hiring the latter would generate such tension and discontent on the job as to lead to a net decrease in efficiency, it would seem perfectly justified under the pure utilitarian position to refuse to hire blacks on account of their race. As Fullinwider points out,

> Once race is permitted to count as a job qualification, there is no way of preventing the racial sword from cutting both ways. There is nothing about the concept of qualifications itself which excludes or rules out race as a relevant job qualification. One may decide that, on balance, letting race be counted as a qualification is best; but this means being prepared, at least on some occasions, to view blackness not as an added qualification but as an added disqualification. (Ibid., 83)

Affirmative action may lead to a relative decrease in efficiency and still be justified in the eyes of a pure utilitarian. This would occur if the disutilities resulting from the losses in efficiency attributable to preferential hiring were outweighed by the utilities produced as a result of it. For example, preferential hiring in the manufacturing sector may lead to a relatively small decrease in the number of manufactured goods produced. That decrease may be completely outweighed, however, by the benefits flowing from preferential treatment, such as the lowering of racial tensions or the erosion of negative stereotypes about women.[6]

The pure utilitarian approach permits a very broad justification of affirmative action. Its most glaring weakness, however, is that it seems to allow for as broad a justification of first-order discrimination. One way to attempt to overcome this weakness would be to embrace a more limited utilitarian approach that makes room for the vindication of rights independently (or to a large degree independently) of their consequences.

B. The Limited Utilitarian Argument

Upon initial consideration, the principal advantage of the limited utilitarian approach seems to be its ability to provide better protection to rights than does the pure utilitarian approach. Accordingly, the limited utilitarian approach may provide a particularly appealing alternative to utilitarians who are concerned about respecting individual rights sanctioned by the Constitution. Essentially, as envisioned by J. J. Thomson, affirmative action is justified from a limited utilitarian standpoint under two different sets of circumstances: first, whenever its implementation would maximize utilities without violating any rights; and, second, where, although it would lead to violations of rights, such violations would not be offset by a mere gain in utility, but rather by the achievement of a great benefit.[7]

Thomson points out that affirmative action could maximize utilities without violating any rights when a black or a woman is given a preference over an equally qualified white or male candidate. When two competitors for the same scarce position tie in the competition for the position, none of the two are entitled to the position. Thus, although both competitors would be wronged if the position were awarded to a less qualified third person, neither of them would suffer a violation of a right to the position if it were awarded to the other. Under such circumstances, moreover, using the maximization of utilities as the criterion for breaking the tie between equally qualified candidates might clearly seem preferable to the use of some other method, such as a lottery. Therefore, to the extent that preferential treatment on the basis of race or gender would lead to a net increase in utility, it would seem justified as applied to equally qualified candidates.[8]

Even if the above argument were unobjectionable, limiting affirmative action to the role of a tiebreaker would relegate it to a rather insignificant position. The number of instances where a black and a white or a woman and a man have precisely the same qualifications for a scarce position are likely to be very modest in relation to the total number of claims to preferential treatment. More important, it may be objected that even this limited form of affirmative action could not be implemented without the violation of important rights other than the right of the most qualified candidate to be awarded the position for which he has applied. For example, a systematic preference for blacks in all race-related tiebreaking instances would arguably be violative of the non-preferred whites' right to equal respect.

The second kind of limited utilitarian argument in favor of affirmative action depends on the validity of overriding rights in the pursuit of certain particularly important benefits. Thomson, a chief proponent of this kind of argument, claims that "it is . . . widely believed that we may without injustice refuse to grant a man what he has a right to only if *either* someone else has a conflicting and more stringent right, *or* there is some very great benefit to be obtained by doing so—perhaps that a disaster of some kind is thereby averted" (emphasis in original; Thomson 1977, 33). To determine whether this belief is warranted, we must assess under what conditions the preferential treatment of blacks or women may produce such great benefits as would justify overriding the right of a white male to a scarce position.

According to Thomson, compensation to blacks and women provides a legitimate justification for overriding the rights of white males to scarce positions (ibid.). Unlike Goldman, however, Thompson advances a broad conception of compensation which contemplates that the benefit of compensation can extend beyond the class of those who personally experienced first-order discrimination (ibid., 35–36). With this in mind, the main thrust of her claim seems to be that the great benefit—as measured by a considerable increase in utility—of broad-based compensation to blacks and women through preferential treatment overrides whatever rights white males may have to scarce positions.

Specifically, Thomson argues that a white male has only an equal opportunity right to the job for which he competes. The job itself, in her view, belongs to the community that is responsible for its allocation. Moreover, Thomson believes that the community may, if necessary, limit the white male's right to equal opportunity in pursuit of a great benefit. She believes that compensating those whom one has wronged is compelling and likely to provide great benefits; that the community has wronged blacks and women in the past, for which it owes them compensation; and that preferential treatment amounts to a just and suitable means to achieve such compensation (ibid.).

By proposing that a scarce job belongs to the community rather than to the white male who is the best qualified candidate for it, Thomson seeks to avoid the following familiar criticism: it is unjust to take something away from one who is innocent of any wrongdoing for purposes of compensating the victim of someone who can no longer be made to account for his wrong. Moreover, in response to another familiar objection to compensatory affirmative action, namely, that many of those who are entitled to benefit from preferential treatment are not the personal victims of first-order discrimination, Thomson argues that

> Even those [who] were not themselves downgraded for being black or female have suffered the consequences of the downgrading of other blacks and women: lack of self confidence, and lack of self-respect. For where a community accepts that a person's being black, or being a woman, are right and proper grounds for denying that person full membership in the community, it can hardly be supposed that any but the most extraordinary independent black or woman will escape self-doubt. (Ibid.)

Finally, Thomson also stresses that many white males have directly benefited from their community's wrongs against blacks and women (ibid., 39).

Since Thomson views affirmative action as a necessary means to restore the self-confidence and self-respect of blacks and women, one could interpret her justification of preferential treatment as resting on the resolution of a conflict between the fundamental right to equal respect and the somewhat less fundamental right to equal opportunity.[9] Given our present concentration on the limited utilitarian approach, however, the thrust of Thomson's argument will be recast as follows: the benefits to society that could be achieved through the preferential hiring of blacks and women would be so great that they justify limiting the equal opportunity rights of white males to the extent necessary to promote the integration of the workforce.

As a general matter, the proposition that rights may be limited, offset, or overridden to achieve a great benefit seems highly defensible. For example, it seems unreasonable to maintain that a landowner's right against trespass ought not to be temporarily suspended for purposes of saving several lives. Actually, the less fundamental the right to be offset or overridden, and the more important the benefit to be achieved, the more it appears that one would be justified in subordinating the right to the achievement of the benefit. Even if a right is particularly important, a relatively minor curtailment of it may be warranted if necessary to produce a sizable benefit. Accordingly, to properly assess Thomson's above argument as cast in limited utilitarian terms, it seems useful to take a closer look at the innocent white male's equal opportunity rights.

Equal opportunity rights to compete for scarce employment are admittedly important. Such rights afford each candidate some degree of probability of winning the competition for the job. In most cases, that probability will fall far short of a virtual certainty. Each candidate's prospects of winning the competition will depend in part on the means at the disposal of competitors. Hence, the prospects of a candidate will generally vary depending on the size and quality of the pool of candidates against whom she must compete (Walzer 1983, 144).

Viewed in this light, affirmative action is likely to affect the prospects of a white male job applicant much in the same way as would an increase in the size or quality of the applicant pool in which he finds himself. Moreover, upon reflection, it would be misleading in a great number of cases to perceive preferential treatment as in effect depriving a white male of a job he covets, by reducing his prospects for the job to zero as soon as it is awarded to a less qualified black or woman. Actually, in a great majority of cases in which preferential treatment policies have been implemented—such as admissions to places at a university, the award of government contracts, or the hiring of policemen or firefighters by a municipality—a pool of applicants competes for a number of places or positions. In such cases, even if a quota is involved, the prospects of success of white males are not likely to fall off drastically. Thus, for example, if a university has one hundred places to allocate in its entering class, and one thousand applicants competing for admission, reserving fifteen places for minority candidates would reduce a white candidate's prospects of admission from 10 percent to approximately 8 percent. The same reduction would take place without a quota, if the numbers of applicants were to increase from one thousand to twelve hundred and fifty. In sum, if the principal *worth* of the right to equal opportunity is measured in terms of the prospects of success that it produces, affirmative action, while limiting that right, is unlikely to cause any major shift in the prospects of success of white male candidates.

If innocent white males are the beneficiaries of first-order discrimination, affirmative action may not at all lower the prospects of success of white males from what they *would have been but for first-order discrimination.* Indeed, first-order discrimination in education and other areas has most likely handicapped its victims, either reducing their prospects of success in the competition for scarce places or positions or discouraging them altogether from participating in the competition. Because of this, an innocent white male's prospects of success are bound to increase. The right to equality of opportunity, however, is certainly not meant to shield such increases in prospects of success. Accordingly, if an affirmative action program lowered a white male's prospects of success by the exact amount that such prospects were raised as consequence of first-order discrimination, the program could not fairly be considered as producing any real violation of that white male's right to equal opportunity. And under these circumstances, if what may amount to no violation or to no more than a trivial violation of a white male's right to equal opportunity is measured against the great benefit that society is likely to reap through the full integration of blacks and women into its workforce, Thomson's argument in favor of affirmative action seems highly persuasive.

On the other hand, Thomson's limited utilitarian argument in favor of affirmative action does seem to possess a major weakness. Indeed, nothing in her theory prevents the limitation of the equal opportunity rights of blacks or women in order to achieve some great benefit or to prevent some great harm. Thus, for example, a limited utilitarian approach would seem to justify first-order discrimination in a community that is so polarized along racial lines, that any attempted forced integration of the workforce would in all likelihood lead to violence. Moreover, the same would seem to hold even in less dramatic cases. Thus, it might be justifiable, for instance, in a society riddled by racism to curtail the equal opportunity rights of a small number of blacks for purposes of preventing substantial social unrest falling somewhat short of violence. Concerning the possible justifications of first-order discrimination, the differences between the pure utilitarian approach and that of the limited utilitarian appear to be much more a matter of degree than one of kind.

C. Dworkin's Utilitarian Argument

Dworkin has proposed an alternative utilitarian approach, which he claims justifies affirmative action without legitimating first-order discrimination. An important virtue of Dworkin's approach is that it takes into account the individual right to equality established by the equal protection clause (Dworkin 1977, 226). Dworkin's approach, which can be characterized as a limited utilitarian one, relies on two fundamental distinctions: the distinction between the right to equal treatment and the right to be treated as an equal; and that between personal and external preferences.[10]

In Dworkin's definition, the right to equal treatment is "the right to an equal distribution" (ibid., 227) of some good. The right to treatment as an equal, on the other hand, is not a right to receive an equal lot, but "the right to be treated with the same respect and concern as anyone else." Dworkin asserts, further, that the right to equal treatment is derivative, whereas the right to be treated as an equal is fundamental.

Dworkin's distinction seems to be in full accord with the postulate of equality. Indeed, the right to treatment as an equal follows from acceptance of the normative proposition that all individuals are equal in their capacity as moral agents. As discussed in chapter 1, it does not follow from this, however, that all individuals are entitled to equal treatment in all circumstances. Thus, for example, if the proper criterion for the allocation of scarce medicines is the health needs of those who wish to obtain them, equal treatment of persons with different health needs would be unwarranted.[11] If one person needs a medicine to survive and another needs it to speed up an otherwise certain recovery, and if there is only a sufficient amount of the medicine to satisfy the needs of one of the two, dividing the medicine into equal lots, or allocating it pursuant to the toss of a coin, would be manifestly unjust.[12] In view of the first person's much greater need for the medicine, equal treatment of the two persons involved would result in a violation of the first person's right to be treated as an equal, as that person's life would be accorded no greater weight than the other person's temporary comfort. Hence, the right to equal treatment is not only derivative, but also consistent with Dworkin's view that in certain cases adherence to the fundamental right to be treated as an equal *requires* unequal treatment.

A claim to equal opportunity to compete for scarce places or positions amounts to a claim to equal treatment with respect to the allocation of opportunities to compete. The fundamental right to treatment as an equal does not require, however, that all claims to equal opportunity be honored. So long as an individual's right to treatment as an equal is respected, Dworkin maintains that a policy refusing equal treatment may be permissible "if it seems reasonable to expect that the overall gain to the community exceeds the overall loss, and if no other policy that does not provide a comparable disadvantage would produce even roughly the same gain" (ibid., 227). Dworkin also makes clear that "an individual's right to be treated as an equal means that his potential loss must be treated as a matter of concern, but that loss may nevertheless be outweighed by the gain to the community as a whole" (ibid.). Based on this analysis, Dworkin concludes that affirmative action may be justified whenever the losses it causes innocent white males are outweighed by the overall gains it produces for society (ibid., 228ff.).

Thus far, Dworkin's justification of affirmative action appears to be essentially the same as that under the limited utilitarian approach discussed above. To preempt the contention that he only succeeds in legitimating affirmative action at the cost of also making possible the legitimation of first-order discrimination, however, Dworkin, invokes the distinction between personal and external preferences. In essence, Dworkin's position is that affirmative action, but not first-order discrimination, can be given a utilitarian justification, provided that external preferences are not counted in determining what policy would most likely produce the greatest benefit for society as a whole.

In Dworkin's view, utilitarianism can satisfy each individual's right to be treated as an equal. In his own words, "the utilitarian argument not only respects, but embodies, the right of each citizen to be treated as the equal of any other. The chance that each individual's preferences have to succeed, in the competition for social policy, will depend upon how important his preference is to him, and how many others share it, compared to the intensity and number of competing preferences" (ibid., 234).

Utilitarianism, however, can be "corrupted" in Dworkin's view, if the counting of preferences is done indiscriminately (ibid., 235). Such corruption can be avoided, according to Dworkin, by relying on the distinction between personal and external preferences and by excluding the latter from the calculus of utilities.

A "personal preference" is the preference of an individual "for his own enjoyment of some goods or opportunities" (ibid., 234). An "external preference," by contrast, is the preference of an individual "for the assignment of goods and opportunities to others." An external preference may be either altruistic or motivated by hostility to others.[13] External preferences may be in some cases inextricably intertwined with personal ones; in other cases, a single preference may be characterized as either personal or external. For example, a white male applying to law school might have a personal preference for first-order discrimination against black applicants because that would increase his own prospects of success, or an external preference for such discrimination as a consequence of his hatred against blacks (ibid., 234–36).

Although, on occasion, external preferences may be difficult to disentangle from personal ones, the former must be excluded from the calculus of utilities, according to Dworkin, in order to avoid transgressions against any person's right to be treated as an equal (ibid., 238). Moreover, once external preferences are excluded, Dworkin contends that affirmative action, but not first-order discrimination, may be justified on utilitarian grounds. For example, preferential treatment of blacks would be justified if it were to reduce racial tensions and thus enhance the welfare of most members of society (ibid., 232). On the other hand, first-order discrimination presumably would not be susceptible to utilitarian justification so long as external preferences are not taken into account. For example, even though a white male competing for a scarce position might benefit from first-order discrimination against blacks, such discrimination arguably could only be given a genuine utilitarian justification if external preferences were counted.

In fact, it seems consistent to argue that while a white male's desire to improve his prospects of success in the competition for a scarce position amounts to a personal preference, such desire, standing alone, would be insufficient to explain support for first-order racial discrimination. Since there are likely to be many different means to improve the prospects of success of any given candidate competing for a scarce position, the mere availability of racial discrimination as one among several alternative means to that end would fail to provide a sufficient reason for its selection. Supposing that changing the rules of the competition, age discrimination, height discrimination, sex discrimination, and racial discrimination would each equally improve the prospects of success of a given white male candidate, then all other things being equal, that candidate should be completely indifferent as to which one of these alternatives ought to be selected. If he prefers first-order racial discrimination over the other mentioned possibilities, therefore, it must be because in addition to his personal preference for increased prospects of success he also possesses an external preference for the disadvantaging of blacks based on hatred against them.

Two important objections have been raised by Simon against Dworkin's analysis. The first is that it may be indefensible to disregard external preferences; the second, that first-order discrimination may be justified, under certain circumstances, even if only personal preferences are taken into account (Simon 1979, 93–94).

Even if one agrees that the distinction between personal and external preferences makes sense in principle, the relationship between personal and external preferences is much more complex than would appear from a consideration of Dworkin's argument. Separation of personal and external preferences may make sense in the context an overly simplistic conception of the individual as essentially egocentric and atomistic, and as primarily devoted to the single-minded pursuit of a series of unconnected goods. From the standpoint of a more complex conception of the individual, however, personal and external preferences may be much more closely tied together and even, in some cases, mutually dependent. Thus, not only is it likely that a parent should have an external preference for the well-being of his child, but it would also seem quite normal for a parent to claim that the personal preference which he has for his own well-being depends in substantial measure on the well-being of his child. To the extent that personal and external preferences are mutually interdependent, therefore, disregard of the latter would seem to preclude adequate consideration of the former. Dworkin's proposal to disregard external preferences appears to stand ultimately on rather shaky ground.

The need to disregard external preferences could also be made dependent on nonutilitarian concerns, such as each person's right to be treated as an equal. Counting certain external preferences, such as those borne out of altruistic concerns, however, would not seem to contravene anyone's right to be treated as an equal. Taking into account the preference of a parent for the well-being of her child, for example, could be said to promote rather than threaten the latter's right to be treated as an equal. Moreover, giving full course to a parent's preference for the well-being of her own child would not seem to lead to the abridgement of any third party's right to being treated as an equal. If each person's pursuit of her own good is not deemed to interfere with another's right to treatment as an equal, merely assisting another in the legitimate pursuit of her own good, or incorporating another person's good as part of one's own, would not seem by itself to lead to any violation of a stranger's right to be treated as an equal.

If the disregard of external preferences is mandated neither on utilitarian nor on nonutilitarian grounds, Dworkin's limited utilitarian argument in favor of affirmative action is essentially circular. Dworkin's concurrent justification of affirmative action and rejection of first-order discrimination does not ultimately reflect any inherent schism between personal and external preferences. Instead, it seems entirely predicated on his belief that first-order discrimination violates the right to be treated as an equal, but that affirmative action does not.

Finally, even if disregarding external preferences were fully justified, Simon has demonstrated that there is a utilitarian justification of first-order discrimination that relies exclusively on personal preferences. As Simon points out, in a society that currently allocates scarce positions exclusively to white males because of systematic first-order discrimination of blacks and women, white males may have a perfectly natural personal preference for the preservation of the status quo (ibid., 93). Assuming that white males are in the majority, and that every white male has a personal preference for maintaining his present prospects of success in the competition for scarce positions, it would be justified for a utilitarian to continue endorsing first-order discrimination instead of attempting to open up the competition to blacks and women. Indeed, taking into account all the relevant personal preferences and no external preference, the aggregate personal preferences of the white male majority would certainly outweigh the personal preferences of blacks and women for open competition (ibid.).

In conclusion, although utilitarian arguments in favor of affirmative action are not without several important virtues, they all seem to share the same essential vice: they are incapable of justifying affirmative action without thereby also opening the door to plausible justifications of first-order discrimination.

2. *Utilitarian Arguments against Affirmative Action*

Utilitarian arguments against affirmative action display many of the same virtues and vices found in utilitarian arguments for affirmative action. In both cases, the justifications are forward looking, and the validity of particular arguments turns on a weighing of consequences. In significant part, utilitarian arguments for and against affirmative action reach opposite conclusions by placing different weights on the same factors.

The most often cited negative consequences of preferential treatment include reduction of efficiency associated with awarding jobs to the most competent candidates (Goldman 1979, 144); perpetuation of distinctions based on race and sex, and reinforcement rather than dissipation of negative stereotypes (Greenawalt 1983, 65; Goldman 1979, 144; Fullinwider 1980, 70); devaluation of achievements of beneficiaries of preferential treatment (Goldman 1979, 144); increases in racial tension (Fullinwider 1980, 70, 250; Goldman 1979, 144); damaging of the self-esteem of beneficiaries of preferential treatment by conveying to them the message that "they don't have it" and that "they will only get it if it is given to them" (ibid., 146); and significant increase in the chances that vehicles of preferential treatment, such as temporary quotas, will become permanent, thus vastly outliving any useful function (Fullinwider 1980, 248).

As pointed out in our discussion of the asserted benefits of affirmative action, it is difficult to project with any degree of accuracy the foreseeable consequences of any complex social policy, such as the implementation of preferential treatment. Because of this, the following examination of utilitarian arguments against affirmative action shall concentrate on the following claims: the distinction between maximizing welfare and preventing harm cannot be maintained in connection with the allocation of certain positions; the short-term utilities of preferential treatment are outweighed by the long-term utilities of hiring exclusively on the basis of competence; aiming directly at the general welfare is not always the best way to promote it; and, even if preferential treatment can produce the benefits that some utilitarians claim it can, it is sufficient to favor some blacks and women rather than either or both groups as a whole (Fullinwider 1977, 210).

A. Preferential Hiring Leads to Unacceptable Harms

As we have seen, the limited utilitarian argument for affirmative action is based on the proposition that certain rights can be overridden for purposes of achieving great benefits. A limited utilitarian argument against affirmative action, on the other hand, can be based on the proposition that the maximization of welfare must be set aside to the extent that it cannot be realized without causing substantial harm to individual members of society. To illustrate, let us assume that preferential treatment in the hiring of physicians and airline pilots would result in a net gain in utility, by promoting racial harmony, reducing stereotypes, and enhancing the self-image of members of the preferentially treated group. Let us also assume, however, that such preferential hiring will lead to the death and injury of a small number of patients and airline passengers who would not die if all positions were awarded to the most competent candidates for them. Finally, let us stipulate that, notwithstanding these harms, the benefits of preferential treatment in the hiring of physicians and pilots would still clearly outweigh its costs. Because of the substantial individual harms attributable to such preferential treatment, however, a proponent of the limited utilitarian approach would reject the legitimacy of affirmative action under the circumstances. More generally, consistent with this approach, whenever the loss in efficiency associated with an affirmative action plan would lead not only to a mere reduction in the number of goods or services produced but also to the infliction of a serious harm, the use of preferential treatment ought to be prohibited.

Acceptance of the above argument does not require rejection of all affirmative action plans. Arguably, the limited utilitarian argument against affirmative action only justifies banning preferential hiring with respect to jobs requiring high skill—such as airline pilots and heart surgeons.[14] Indeed, with respect to a job requiring medium skill, such as plumber, or a job requiring low skill, such as janitor, it seems highly unlikely that the differences in competence among several minimally qualified persons would in and of themselves lead to an increase in serious harms.

One may object that the limited utilitarian argument against affirmative action rests on premises that, if held to be universally applicable, would require the virtual abandonment of justifications based on the maximization of utilities. Indeed, if the strong likelihood of serious harm to a handful of individuals is deemed sufficient to warrant the elimination of practices and policies expected to maximize utilities, then very few of the undertakings in the modern welfare state would appear to be ultimately justifiable. For example, the construction of a much demanded new highway would have to rejected no matter how useful it would be, so long as traffic on such highway would inevitably result in certain fatalities that would not otherwise take place. Similarly, a whole range of modern products and services providing numerous benefits to a vast majority of the population would also have to be prohibited because in rare occasions they are bound to cause some serious injury or death. Because of this, opponents of the limited argument against affirmative action can contend that it is unpersuasive to the extent that its proponents refuse to extend it to apply to subjects other than job hiring. In other words, anyone who defends the conveniences of the modern industrial state, notwithstanding the inevitable harms that they cause, would not seem to be justified in rejecting preferential treatment in hiring on the sole grounds that it may lead to some instance of serious harm.

It seems that one would have to agree with Fullinwider that preferential hiring with respect to positions requiring high skill is less likely to be justified than with respect to positions requiring medium or low skill. To justify this conclusion on utilitarian grounds, however, one need not resort to the limited utilitarian argument. It would seem sufficient to argue that significantly greater disutilities attach to preferential hiring for high skill positions than for medium and low skill positions. Accordingly, whereas the costs may outweigh the benefits of preferential hiring for positions requiring high skill, the converse may be the case for those requiring medium and low skill.

B. Long-Term Utilities of Hiring the Most Competent Outweigh Short-Term Utilities of Preferential Hiring

The short-term utilities of preferential hiring may clash with the long-term utilities of hiring exclusively on the basis of competence. Indeed, even if hiring the most competent generally leads to the maximization of social utilities, the preferential hiring of blacks or women could still lead to a net short-term increase in utilities.[15] For instance, under certain sociopolitical circumstances, as Goldman points out, black students may profit from learning from a black teacher (Goldman 1979, 168). Furthermore, Goldman warns that the utilities which may tend to justify preferential hiring "are generally temporary and founded upon biases and misperceptions, rather than being those universal and long-range utilities connected with rewarding genuine dimensions of competence for providing goods and services" (ibid.). Thus, Goldman seems to claim not simply that long-term utilities outweigh short-term ones, but more specifically, that long-term "universal" utilities should be preferred over short-term utilities depending on "biases and misperceptions."

Two objections may be raised against Goldman's argument. The first denies that one can consistently justify the preference of long-term utilities over short-term utilities within a utilitarian framework. The second asserts that a utilitarian cannot without contradiction maintain a principled distinction between "universal" utilities and utilities based on "biases" and "misperceptions."

Turning to the first objection, one may begin by asking by what criterion a utilitarian could establish that the maximization of utilities requires the subordination of short-term utilities to long-term ones. To be sure, in some cases it seems quite obvious that short-term utilities ought to give way to longer-term ones. If an act were to produce an intense pleasure for one minute, but pain for several hours thereafter, it seems fair to assume that any reasonable utilitarian would forgo the moment of pleasure to avoid the prolonged pain. But in a large number of cases it is by no means evident that a utilitarian would opt for the long-term benefit rather than the short-term one. For example, it is not clear whether a corporation that has made a hefty profit ought to distribute the profit to shareholders through dividends or to reinvest it in the company, to obtain new equipment that will allow the corporation and its shareholders to reap even much larger profits in a relatively distant future.

If one remains within the confines of a utilitarian framework, there seems to be only one answer to that question—namely, that it depends on whether the shareholder considers the possibility of large future dividends a greater good than the present receipt of a smaller dividend. Since some people are gamblers by nature while others are risk averse, it seems fair to conclude that some shareholders would prefer to give up short-term benefits in favor of long-term ones, while others would prefer to do exactly the opposite. Similarly, if the members of society are faced with a choice between preferential hiring and hiring exclusively on the basis on competence, and if the former would reduce racial strife, produce greater harmony, and cause a rapid improvement in the prevailing social and political atmosphere—while the latter would maximize the long-term output of goods and services—then it seems reasonable to expect that some citizens would prefer to give up a future increase in wealth for a present reduction in racial tension, while others would rather settle for the opposite. Accordingly, within a purely utilitarian framework, it seems unwarranted to make a general claim that long-term utilities ought to outweigh short-term ones.[16]

The second objection rests on the denial that a utilitarian can, without contradiction, draw a principled distinction between "universal utilities" and utilities based on "biases." This denial is based, in turn, on the utilitarian's postulation that the individual is the best judge of her own interest.[17] If that is the case, then whatever she declares to be her interest ought to be taken at face value in the calculus of utilities regardless of whether what she views as being in her interest is a reflection of some bias. Thus, what the racist views as being in his best interest ought to be weighted in the same manner as what the civil libertarian claims is in his best interest. If the racist derives happiness from living in a racially segregated society then that happiness ought to count as much as the happiness which the civil libertarian would experience by living in a racially integrated society. To do otherwise, would be inconsistent with the premise that the individual is the best judge of her interest.[18]

C. A Rule-Utilitarian Argument against Affirmative Action

A utilitarian may reject the legitimacy of affirmative action based on the proposition that aiming directly at the general welfare is not always the best way to promote it (Fullinwider 1980, 240). As Fullinwider states, there "may be circumstances where there are special dangers of error in calculating the welfare benefits of various policies or where there is special liability of corruption of presumably welfare maximizing policies. Adopting and acting upon inflexible rules may prove the wiser course." Further, concentrating on race-conscious policies, Fullinwider argues that while such policies may produce net foreseeable benefits, they ought nonetheless be avoided. The reason for this, as Fullinwider puts it, is that "the use of race is a dangerous business; it lends itself to great abuses. If we allow policy matters to use race, we open the way to policies which do good but we necessarily also open the door to inevitable abuses which in the long run will outweigh all the good. Over the long run, general welfare is best served by our adopting an absolute prohibition against the use of race" (ibid.).

This argument may be interpreted either as a restatement of the proposition that long-term utilities outweigh short-term ones, or as an expression of the claim that rule-utilitarianism is preferable to act-utilitarianism. In the case of the former alternative the same objections already made would apply. Accordingly, I will now focus on the latter alternative.

Act-utilitarianism has been defined as "the view that the rightness or wrongness of an action is to be judged by the consequences, good or bad, of the action itself" (Smart and Williams 1985, 9). Rule-utilitarianism, on the other hand, is "the view that the rightness or wrongness of an action is to be judged by the goodness and badness of the consequences of a rule that everyone should perform the action in like circumstances" (ibid.). Keeping these definitions in mind, it seems plausible to argue that, although in particular instances preferential treatment may lead to more good than evil, the overall welfare of society would be better served by adherence to a single rule prohibiting race-conscious hiring practices and policies. Thus, consistent with the requirements of rule-utilitarianism, color-blind hiring policies ought to be implemented as a rule, even if concededly, following such a rule may in certain particular instances lead to a net decrease in utilities.

If the conclusion that the best route to the general welfare may not be the direct route is based on a rule-utilitarian argument, it seems open to the general objection that many have made against rule-utilitarianism. This objection—made, among others, by Lyons—is that rule-utilitarianism taken to its logical conclusion collapses into act-utilitarianism (Lyons 1965). According to this objection, even if a single rule leads to a greater good than no rule at all, if two rules will lead to a greater good than a single rule then the rule-utilitarian should be willing to adopt the two rules (or to accept an exceptive clause modifying the original single rule). Thus, for instance, let us assume that a rule barring race-conscious policies were to lead to a greater good than no rule at all. Let us assume further, however, that in certain types of particular instances, such as those that arise under conditions of intense and widespread first-order discrimination, preferential treatment of blacks would lead to greater net utilities than would color-blind policies. Under these circumstances, the rule-utilitarian should agree to a modification of her operative general rule and should incorporate an exceptive clause permitting the use of race-conscious policies where appropriate.

Moreover, so long as there remain other individual cases in which preferential treatment would lead to a net increase in utilities, the rule-utilitarian ought, by the same token, to refine her rules to effect an increase in the societal net quantum of utility. Taking this process to its logical culmination, the rule-utilitarian should be willing to modify her rule to account for every case in which an act-utilitarian could justify breaking such rule. Accordingly, "an adequate rule-utilitarianism would be extensionally equivalent to act-utilitarianism" (Smart and Williams 1975, 11).

A rule-utilitarian may reply that the modification and multiplication of rules themselves create additional disutilities, which should be taken into account when considering whether or not to impose a single rule. If the rule-utilitarian could demonstrate that the disutilities associated with rule proliferation would outweigh the utilities to be gained by means of that process, then adherence to a single rule would clearly seem appropriate. Intuitively, however, it would seem that implementation of a general color- and gender-blind rule with limited exceptive clauses permitting affirmative action would not be as unmanageable as to tip the balance of utilities. In view of this, the rule-utilitarian argument against affirmative action is at best speculative and uncertain.

D. Utilitarian Argument against Extending Affirmative Action to All Blacks and All Women

Fullinwider proposes another utilitarian argument against affirmative action which concedes that preferential treatment may lead to a net increase in utilities but maintains that it does not follow from this that preference in hiring should be extended to *all* blacks or *all* women (Fullinwider 1977, 210). Suppose, argues Fullinwider, that we accept that preferential hiring leads to a net gain in utility, by increasing the "well being of many persons," providing positive role models for blacks and women, undermining racial and sexual stereotypes, and making available better services to women and blacks (ibid.). This does not of itself explain why preferential treatment should extend to all blacks or all women. Indeed, in the case of positive role models and of the eradication of negative stereotypes, for example, what seems essential is that some women and some blacks occupy certain visible prestigious positions in which they have been traditionally underrepresented. To accomplish this, it does not appear to be necessary to extend preferential hiring to all women or all blacks. Instead, in Fullinwider's words, "It is probable that the enumerated goals, and other, could be accomplished by a policy of preferring in employment some blacks, some women, and some non-black males; and the net gains from such a policy would be greater than the net gains from preferring *all and only women and blacks*" (emphasis in original; ibid.).

While the validity of Fullinwider's claim ultimately depends on empirical factors, his claim seems most likely to be vindicated in a society that is sharply polarized along racial and sexual lines because of pervasive biases. In such a society, mistrust between blacks and whites, and between women and men, may be so deep seated, and negative stereotypes so accentuated, that blacks, for instance, are unlikely to learn from white teachers or to obey white policemen, and vice versa. Under such circumstances, where integration and assimilation do not loom as realistic goals, preferences for some blacks, some women, and some white males may maximize utilities by providing each of the antagonistic groups with greater freedom from the others. In other words, in a badly divided society, preferences for some members of each group may be better than preferences for all the members of some groups, as autonomy in segregation rather than integration and mutual respect seems to be the best realistic objective.

The utilitarian case against affirmative action seems tentative and inconclusive. None of the arguments reviewed above provide a firm basis for categorically opposing preferential treatment in the name of the general welfare. Moreover, it seems reasonable to expect that empirical comparisons of the costs and benefits of preferential treatment would lead to different conclusions depending on the circumstances under which each such comparison were undertaken. Finally, utilitarian arguments against affirmative action do not foreclose utilitarian justifications of first-order discrimination any more than do utilitarian arguments in favor of affirmative action. Indeed, so long as one believes that rule-utilitarianism is ultimately bound to collapse into act-utilitarianism, there seems to be no logical impediment for the preferences that underlie a rejection of affirmative action also to lend support to first-order discrimination.

CHAPTER FIVE

Egalitarian Justice and Affirmative Action

In this chapter, I turn to egalitarian arguments for and against affirmative action. Much like utilitarian arguments, these egalitarian arguments are primarily forward looking. Moreover, although this may seem surprising at first, to the extent that egalitarian justice requires a commitment to equality of result rather than to equality of opportunity, it seems much easier to formulate an egalitarian argument against the legitimacy of preferential treatment than in favor of it. Accordingly, the egalitarian argument in favor of affirmative action is but a limited one: it does not assert that preferential treatment is just, but merely that under certain circumstances it might not be unjust.

1. Egalitarian Arguments against Affirmative Action

A. Egalitarian Preference for Equality of Result over Equality of Opportunity

As conceived by Nagel, egalitarianism assumes that there is "moral equality between persons" (Nagel 1979, 111), and that each person has "an equal claim to actual or possible advantages" (ibid., 112). Moreover, besides being on the main forward-looking, egalitarianism "establishes an order of priority among needs, and gives preference to the most urgent." Consistent with this, Nagel puts forth a hierarchical principle of priority of needs: "Each individual's claim has a complex form: it includes more or less all his needs and interests, but in an order of relative urgency of importance. This determines both which of them are to be satisfied first and whether they are to be satisfied before or after the interests of others." Further, Nagel emphasizes that "the essential feature of an egalitarian priority system is that it counts improvements to the welfare of the worst off as more urgent than improvements to the welfare of the better off" (ibid., 117–18).

An egalitarian criterion of distributive justice conforming to Nagel's views would seem to require the pursuit of equality of result rather than of equality of opportunity. Indeed, equality of opportunity most often leads to inequality of outcomes, and thus seems less suited than equality of result to bring about the equal satisfaction of everyone's most urgent needs. For example, in a society characterized by inequalities in wealth, education, and natural abilities, equality of opportunity—and particularly means-regarding equality of opportunity—would lead to inequalities of result.[1] To assure the equal satisfaction of everyone's most important needs, the egalitarian would have to choose equality of result over equality of opportunity.

The preference for equality of result demanded by the egalitarian criterion of justice leads to further questions. Chief among them are the following: first, *which* equality of result does egalitarian justice seek? And, second, assuming equality of result is impossible to achieve or would lead to great harm, which, if any, kind of equality would be most compatible with egalitarian principles?

There are at least two kinds of equality of result: lot-regarding and subject-regarding.[2] A more crude form of egalitarianism may require exclusively lot-regarding equality of result, either by stipulating that equal lots be distributed to everyone, or that unequal lots be allocated with a view toward producing global lot-regarding equality of result. Under a different conception, however, egalitarianism may also require the pursuit of subject-regarding equality of result. For example, Nagel asserts that people with different talents may "deserve different opportunities to exercise and develop those talents," because "people are equally deserving of opportunities proportional to their talents" (ibid., 98, 98*n*.7). In other words, each person is equally entitled to receive the goods necessary to develop and exercise her talents, and to the extent that different talents require different goods for their development and exercise, their respective individual possessors may be entitled to unequal bundles of goods. In such a case, the allocation of unequal lots of goods would lead to subject-regarding equality of result for each recipient.

One may conceive of three different conceptions of egalitarianism, according to whether it is deemed to justify lot-regarding equality of result, subject-regarding equality of result, or a combination of both. An egalitarianism that relies exclusively on lot-regarding equality of result is rather unattractive in that it seems to ignore that different persons are likely to have different needs, interests, and talents. On the other hand, an egalitarianism that prescribes the full realization of subject-regarding equality of result appears to be impractical or merely utopian, so long as there is any scarcity of any coveted goods. Because of scarcity, a hierarchy of needs would have to be established so as to be able to satisfy everyone's most urgent needs before turning to anyone's next most urgent needs. But because this kind of egalitarianism relies on a subjective rather than an objective determination of the relative urgency of various individual needs, different needs are likely to assume different orders of importance to different persons. Accordingly, the duty to fulfill the most urgent needs of each person would likely require the satisfaction of different needs for different persons. This would be unmanageable, unless subjective needs were communicable, verifiable, and transformable. Indeed, if there is no way to verify claims concerning subjective needs, anyone could exaggerate the importance of his needs, and scarce resources could soon become insufficient to satisfy the most important needs of all members of society. Further, unless needs were transformable, strict adherence to subject-regarding equality of result would lead to repugnant outcomes. For example, a sadist's most important needs may require inflicting pain on others and may have priority over the needs of a masochist or of one indifferent to pain not to be used to satisfy the sadist's need.

An egalitarian position that relies on both subject- and lot-regarding equality of result seems well suited to avoid the most serious shortcomings of both of the conceptions of egalitarianism discussed above. For example, the third conception of egalitarianism could prescribe lot-regarding equality of result regarding certain fundamental needs, such as for food and decent shelter, while prescribing subject-regarding equality of result concerning other needs, such as for medicines or developing one's natural capacities. By stipulating that some of the most basic universally felt needs ought to be the subject of lot-regarding equality, the third conception of egalitarianism renders the task of satisfying everyone's most urgent needs much more manageable than its exclusively subject-regarding counterpart. On the other hand, by reserving certain important needs and interests for subject-regarding equality, the third conception of egalitarianism accounts for genuine differences among persons that cannot properly be taken into consideration by an egalitarianism entirely devoted to lot-regarding equality.[3]

As discussed in chapter 1, there are situations in which equality of result cannot be achieved—or, at least, cannot be achieved without causing great harm. For example, if there are one hundred starving persons who are equally morally deserving and only enough food for fifty to survive, rigid adherence to equality of result would require that none be given enough food to survive. In chapter 1, I argued that, consistent with the postulate of equality, fifty lives could be saved through implementation of equality of opportunity. The question here, however, is whether an egalitarian would under the circumstances justify a departure from equality of result.

Even the strictest adherence to the duty of satisfying needs in the order of their priority would not preclude the legitimacy of fulfilling some but not all of the needs that posses an equal rank in the relevant order of priorities. Accordingly, it would seem acceptable for an egalitarian under these circumstances to set aside equality of result for equality of opportunity (for example, in the form of a lottery that would determine which fifty persons would receive available food). In short, there appear to be circumstances under which commitment to equality of opportunity would be compatible with the egalitarian's beliefs that each person has an equal claim to advantages and that the most urgent needs of everyone should be satisfied before the less urgent needs of anyone.

Conceding that there can be circumstances under which the egalitarian should be willing to pursue equality of opportunity, the question becomes what circumstances justify the shift? Moreover, what kind of equality of opportunity—prospect regarding or means regarding—is the egalitarian most likely to accept? Resolving these matters is important, for as we shall see below, they have a bearing on whether the egalitarian might accept affirmative action in education or employment.

First, let us return to the example of the one hundred starving persons with only enough food to save fifty. That case seems to be an easy one, in that a great benefit—namely, the preservation of fifty lives—can only be obtained by setting aside adherence to equality of result. In less dramatic cases, however, the fact that a substantial benefit may only be obtained by deviating from equality of result might constitute a necessary but by no means sufficient condition for an egalitarian to embrace equality of opportunity. To illustrate, let us consider the following utilitarian argument against equality of result. According to Goldman, considerations of distributive justice may under certain circumstances justify inequality of result based on considerations of aggregate utility (Goldman 1979, 42). Goldman offers the following example: suppose that a group of four individuals faces the choice of receiving distribution of either eight units in equal shares of two or of fifteen units in three shares of four and one share of three. Goldman maintains that the distribution resulting in the larger aggregate is prima facie preferable and that to deny this is to attribute inordinate moral force to feelings of envy and pride (ibid.).

One need not mechanistically adhere to lot-regarding equality of result in order to reject Goldman's conclusion on egalitarian grounds. Indeed, as Nagel suggests, an egalitarian may reject an unequal distribution that results in a net gain in overall wealth and that increases the material well-being of the worst off on the belief that "some inequalities are bad even if they benefit the worse off, so that a situation in which *everyone* is worst off may be preferable if the inequalities are reduced enough" (emphasis in original; Nagel 1979, 110). In justification of that belief, Nagel adds that "the argument would be that improvements in the well-being of the lowest class as a result of material productivity spurred by wage differentials are only apparent: damage to their self-respect outweighs the material gains. And even inequalities that genuinely benefit the worst off may destroy nondistributive values like community or fraternity" (ibid., 110*n.3*). Thus, an egalitarian might reply to Goldman that a greater aggregate can only be preferable if it does not damage self-respect or undermine the possibility of community and fraternity. From this it follows that, even if adherence to equality of opportunity leads to the availability of more goods for everyone, that alone would not be sufficient for an egalitarian to agree to a shift from equality of result to equality of opportunity.

Nevertheless, particularly with regard to the allocation of employments, equality of result may be utopian; if not altogether beyond reach, it may require sacrifices that the egalitarian would be unwilling to impose. An eradication of the scarcity of desirable positions might severely deplete the stock of goods necessary to satisfy needs that the egalitarian would consider more urgent than possession of a desirable job. Thus, whereas a mere decrease in efficiency might not justify an egalitarian to abandon equality of result with respect to the allocation of jobs, a *severe* reduction in efficiency might do so. In such a case, equality of opportunity might well provide the most suitable means of safeguarding the egalitarian's design to fulfill individual needs in the order of their priority.

If she is willing to acknowledge the legitimacy of equality of opportunity under certain circumstances, an egalitarian must decide which kind of equality of opportunity might be consistent with her conception of justice. As discussed in chapter 3, contractarians opt for fair means-regarding equality of opportunity that makes prospects of success virtually exclusively a function of differences in natural abilities. Egalitarians, however, disagree. As Nagel states, "differential abilities are not usually among the characteristics that determine whether people *deserve* economic and social benefits" (emphasis in original; ibid., 97). Moreover, while Nagel acknowledges that voluntary differences in effort may have a bearing on economic and social desert, he nonetheless maintains that a person deserves neither her intelligence nor "the rewards that superior intelligence can provide" (ibid., 97*n.7*). Thus, whereas allowing success in the competition for scarce places or positions to turn on differences in natural abilities may satisfy Rawls' difference principle and maximize efficiency and utility,[4] it is unlikely to meet the requirements of the egalitarian criterion of justice. In view of this—and assuming that the realization of *global* means-regarding equality of opportunity requiring, among other things, genetic engineering is beyond the reach of present-day society—the egalitarian may have to opt for *prospect*-regarding equality of opportunity whenever she deems that a move from equality of result is required.[5] More specifically, with respect to the allocation of scarce places at the university or of scarce employment positions, the egalitarian might settle for selection based on a lottery among all minimally qualified candidates.[6]

The egalitarian claim that a person deserves neither his natural assets nor the rewards flowing from the use of such assets has been attacked by, among others, Goldman and Nozick. Essentially, what these critics contend is that it does not follow from the fact that one does not deserve one's natural assets that one likewise does not deserve the products generated through the use of such natural assets. In Goldman's view, the egalitarian claim "can be seen to rest upon a false principle. This principle states that all causal antecedents of features that enter into criteria for desert must themselves be deserved" (Goldman 1979, 45). Similarly, Nozick suggests, for example, that a painter is entitled to keep a painting that he made and that Rawls is entitled to praise for writing *A Theory of Justice,* even if neither the painter nor Rawls can be said to deserve their outstanding talents. So long as it is not illegitimate for them to have the talents with which they are blessed, Nozick maintains that they may deserve the benefits produced through the use of their talents, even if they do not deserve those talents (Nozick 1974, 225).

Goldman, moreover, draws a distinction between the role of natural assets and that of effort in the production of social and economic goods. Relying on that distinction, he argues that the fact that an individual may not deserve his natural assets does not mean that he does not deserve the product of his efforts (Goldman 1979, 44). Accordingly, Goldman insists that the random selection procedure advocated by the egalitarian leads to distributive injustice to the extent that it decreases utility and forecloses rewarding socially productive effort (ibid., 28, 44–45).

An egalitarian might reply that equality is good in itself and that the prospects of greater utility in themselves are insufficient to set aside the demands of equality. As Nagel states, if "equality is in itself good, then producing it may be worth a certain amount of inefficiency and loss of liberty" (Nagel 1979, 108). Accordingly, egalitarians can reject on principle Goldman's claim that the most competent ought to be entitled to scarce places and positions for reason of utility. Further, egalitarians can point out that Goldman's meritocracy rewards productivity rather than effort.[7] Greater productivity, however, does not necessarily go hand in hand with greater effort. For example, assuming that a person's productivity is a function of both that person's intelligence and of her efforts, then it seems reasonable to expect that a highly intelligent person could achieve greater productivity with much less effort than a significantly less intelligent person. Accordingly, an egalitarian could argue that the most competent are not necessarily those who have furnished the greatest efforts and that it is unjust therefore to reward them solely because they happen to be more productive.

Finally, an egalitarian may contest the validity of Nozick's assertion that it does not follow from the fact that natural assets are undeserved that the products dependent on them are likewise undeserved, along the following lines. It is significant that Nozick uses, as examples to buttress his point, cases of individuals working alone, largely severed from the productive efforts of others. Indeed, the work of a painter, or of an author such as Rawls, is individual work par excellence, rather than a collective enterprise requiring social coordination or teamwork. This kind of individual work fits well within the Lockean metaphor of the individual who through the expenditure of his own physical labor cultivates a previously unclaimed plot of land. Although such individual may not deserve his physical capabilities, it seems reasonable to argue that he rather than any other deserves the fruits of his own labor. Production in the corporate setting typical of contemporary industrial society, however, tends to be a collective process requiring social coordination and cooperation, as well as teamwork. Accordingly, the egalitarian can claim that it is by no means self-evident that the rewards flowing from a corporate endeavor ought to be divided in ways that reflect the relative intelligence (or productivity to the extent that it is a function of intelligence) of the various individual participants in the joint corporate enterprise. More generally, egalitarians may plausibly contend that the goods generated through the collective enterprise of production—including such goods as places in universities and positions of employment—ought to be distributed in accordance with the priority of needs rather than in proportion to contributions attributable to relative differences in morally undeserved intelligence.

B. Affirmative Action Perpetuates Inequality of Result

The main thrust of the egalitarian case against affirmative action is that preferential treatment may redress injuries arising from discrimination on the basis of race or sex, but that it does nothing to eradicate the inherent injustices of the prevailing system of allocation of educational and employment opportunities.[8] Claims for preferential treatment because of race or gender are most likely to be made in either of the following contexts: meritocracies marked by past or present first-order discrimination against blacks or women; or systems of allocation that do not even adhere to equality of opportunity, but that single out blacks or women for treatment as inferiors. The meritocracies in question may provide to white males either formal or fair means-regarding equality of opportunity in the allocation of educational and employment opportunities. The systems that do not rely on any form of equality of opportunity, on the other hand, may leave the allocation of the overwhelming majority of educational and employment opportunities in the hands of private agents of allocation. These agents are free to distribute the positions they control as they please, and operate in a social atmosphere marked by pervasive racism or sexism. Regardless of whether a meritocracy is involved, however, in none of these systems of allocation is equality of result or prospect-regarding equality of opportunity put into play. Accordingly, the egalitarian would find these systems of allocation themselves to be unjust, regardless of whether they were operated in a racist or sexist manner.

Both Nagel and Sher recognize that racism and sexism may cause injuries above and beyond those imposed by the prevailing system of allocation of educational and employment opportunities.[9] This raises the question of whether affirmative action should be viewed as a legitimate tool within an egalitarian framework, albeit a limited one capable of remedying only a fraction of the many prevailing injustices.

There seem to be at least two different possible egalitarian answers to this question. First, there may be comprehensive means that, if implemented, would concurrently eliminate the injustices attributable to racism and sexism and those directly linked to the prevailing system of allocation. Thus, if it were possible to effectuate the transition from meritocracy to an institutional arrangement leading to equality of result, affirmative action would be completely superfluous. If through suitable transformations of existing processes of production and distribution all members of society—including blacks and women—could be guaranteed equality of result, there would obviously be no need to secure higher positions in the meritocratic hierarchy for the victims of racism and sexism. It is with such a systemic solution apparently in mind that Sher states that "any egalitarian who argues for reverse discrimination will have to explain why we should stop at just the amount of equality which that practice would produce" (Sher 1979, 85).

Second, the egalitarian may answer that affirmative action serves to perpetuate the illegitimate hierarchies sustained by the meritocracy and thus stands in the way of realizing comprehensive egalitarian justice. Moreover, in Sher's view, affirmative action not only maintains existing inequalities but also contributes to the development of further inequalities. In his own words,

> To practice reverse discrimination is just to award certain contested goods to women and minority group members; and to award goods in this way is not to abolish, but merely to rearrange, the inequalities of distribution that now prevail. Moreover, since the goods to be awarded preferentially are themselves instrumental to the procuring of further goods, it is clear that any inequalities which are

> perpetuated by reverse discrimination must result in yet further inequalities in the future. (Ibid.)

Put somewhat differently, since a system of allocation based on means-regarding equality of opportunity tends to magnify initial differences in natural abilities and social and educational advantages, the preservation of any such system seems bound to exacerbate the inequalities of rewards among the members of society.[10] Accordingly, while affirmative action may close the gap between blacks and whites or women and men—that is, while it may equalize group-regarding prospects of success in the competition for scarce places and positions—it fails to produce any significant change in the pattern of seemingly ever-increasing inequalities among individuals.

To the extent that the egalitarian is committed to lot-regarding equality of result, the above arguments against the legitimacy of affirmative action seem to be persuasive. But what about the egalitarian who, like Nagel, believes that there are cases in which subject-regarding equality of result is called for? As we have seen, Nagel maintains that people deserve opportunities proportional to their talents. Suppose, however, that white males receive such opportunities but that women and blacks are denied them. Would such a situation justify the use of affirmative action to achieve subject-regarding equality of result with respect to the development and exercise of individual talent?

Consistent with egalitarian principles of justice, it may seem that, in a meritocracy where scarce places and positions are allocated so as to enable each applicant best to develop his natural talents, and where only blacks and women had been systematically denied such positions, affirmative action could be a useful remedial tool. Indeed, if as a consequence of prolonged first-order discrimination the natural talents of blacks and women remain somewhat underdeveloped or concealed, preferential treatment may well be the best means for them to secure positions enabling them to meet their potential.

There is, however, a profound egalitarian objection to the use of affirmative action under the circumstances described above. This objection is based on the distinction drawn by Nagel between different opportunities needed to develop and exercise different talents, and the differences in the order of magnitude of the social and economic rewards associated with different opportunities. In Nagel's view, "at present we have no way of divorcing professional status from social esteem and economic reward" (Nagel 1979, 104). And, while under subject-regarding equality of result one may deserve one's professional status if it is commensurate with one's talents, it does not follow that one also deserves the social and economic benefits which a meritocracy inevitably bestows upon those who enjoy a certain professional status. Thus, the egalitarian encounters a conflict between the following two maxims: "to each a professional position commensurate with his or her talents" and "to each the same economic and social benefits" (or "to each the economic and social benefits which he or she most urgently needs," if subject- rather than lot-regarding equality of result is deemed appropriate regarding a person's most urgent needs). Nagel both notes the existence of this conflict and proposes a solution to it. In his own words,

> There appears to be a conflict between justice in the distribution of educational and professional opportunities and the justice in the distribution of economic and social rewards. There is a presumption, based on something more than efficiency, in favor of giving equal opportunities to those equally likely to succeed. But if the presumption in favor of economic equality is considerably stronger, the justification for departing from it must be stronger too. So when "educational" justice and economic justice come into conflict, it will sometimes be necessary to sacrifice the former to the latter. (Ibid., 98–99)

Consistent with this analysis, to the extent that equal distribution of economic and social goods is inextricably linked to the satisfaction of needs more urgent than those met through allocation of educational and employment opportunities proportional to talent, the egalitarian would have to settle for equal distribution instead of the distribution that a meritocracy would produce. And, as previously discussed, where the meritocracy itself is deemed to be unjust, there seems to be no legitimate role for affirmative action.

As already pointed out, there may be circumstances under which an egalitarian might justify a shift from equality of result to prospect-regarding equality of opportunity. This raises the question of whether affirmative action might be appropriate in cases in which prospect-regarding equality of opportunity deemed justified by an egalitarian has been improperly withheld from blacks and women. To take an easy case, let us suppose that scarce places at universities are allocated on the basis of a lottery conducted among all minimally qualified applicants, except those who are black. In this case, each minimally qualified white candidate enjoys the same prospects of success as every other such white candidate, while all minimally qualified black candidates have no prospects of success. Furthermore, each white candidate has greater prospects of success than if blacks were not excluded from the lottery. Now, if first-order discrimination against blacks is outlawed, and if every minimally qualified candidate is allowed to participate in the lottery, then all such candidates will enjoy equal prospects of success, regardless of race. This notwithstanding, however, many of the places at the universities (for example, those occupied by students who are in their second or subsequent years) will have been filled prior to the abolition of first-order discrimination. Accordingly, the number of places occupied by whites would exceed the number they would have held absent past exclusion of blacks, and correspondingly the number of places filled by blacks would remain below what they would have been if no discrimination had previously occurred.

One way to accelerate the establishment of that proportion of blacks and whites which the lottery system would itself have produced had there been no racial discrimination would be to give preferential treatment to blacks to enable them to secure a greater proportion of available places. This could be done through the imposition of a quota. Assuming that one hundred places were available for allocation, one could impose a ten percent quota, according to which ten places would be reserved for blacks, while the remaining ninety would remain open to both blacks and whites. If the prospects of success of blacks are temporarily boosted at the expense of those of whites, it seems possible to arrive (as closely as possible) at the racial configuration that a series of racially neutral lotteries would have produced over time. Provided the egalitarian agrees with the objective of altering the racial configuration of university students to approximate what it would have been absent discrimination, affirmative action may be the best available means in the pursuit of that objective.

Upon closer examination, the preceding argument in favor of affirmative action seems unpersuasive. This is because the use of preferential treatment under the circumstances described above would neither further the egalitarian aim of providing prospect-regarding equality of opportunity nor furnish an appropriate remedy for the systematic violation of that equality. The purpose of instituting a lottery is to assure equality in the prospects of success of every minimally qualified candidate. A quota, however, does not advance that purpose. All it does is to increase the prospects of some candidates while correspondingly reducing the prospects of others. Therefore, from a purely forward-looking standpoint, affirmative action seems incompatible with an egalitarian implementation of prospect-regarding equality of opportunity.

From a backward-looking remedial perspective, affirmative action does not fare any better. The injustice created through the use of a racially biased lottery is the allocation of scarce places to more whites and to fewer blacks (or no blacks if they are altogether excluded from participation in the lottery) than would have been the case absent all discrimination. The remedy for this injustice is not the establishment of future quotas altering the prospects of success of persons who have suffered no harm. Instead, the most appropriate remedy under the circumstances would seem to consist of the following. As a first step, one could conduct a lottery among whites already holding places at the university, as a means to select a certain number among them who would then be forced to relinquish their place. Next, one would conduct a second lottery among the blacks who would have participated in the initial lottery for the places in question, but who were excluded because of racism. The winners of this last lottery would, in turn, be awarded the places vacated by the whites selected through the first lottery. Moreover, the number of places slated to change hands through these lotteries would be set so as to assure that the final racial configuration of place holders would approximate as much as possible the configuration that would have been established in the first place absent any discrimination. Unlike affirmative action, the remedy just described does not reward or penalize anyone not directly affected by the initial injustice. Although this remedy may be inefficient or even altogether impractical, it nonetheless appears to be just under egalitarian principles.

It is possible to make yet another argument for affirmative action within the context of an egalitarian pursuit of prospect-regarding equality of opportunity. This argument arises with respect to cases in which first-order discrimination leads to the reduction of the pool of available minimally qualified candidates belonging to the discriminated group. Suppose, for example, that as a consequence of racist policies the pool of minimally qualified blacks were reduced to one-half the size of what it would have been absent discrimination. Suppose further that the size of the pool of white candidates remains constant throughout the relevant period. If absent any discrimination there would be 80,000 minimally qualified white candidates, 20,000 such black candidates, and 20,000 places to be allocated, then approximately 16,000 whites and 4,000 blacks would be likely in the long run to secure places through the lottery process. If systematic discrimination were to lead to a reduction of the number of minimally qualified blacks to 10,000, then over time approximately 17,777 whites and 2,223 blacks would come to occupy the available places.

To prevent this latter result, one could have recourse to affirmative action. Indeed, by increasing the prospects of blacks and correspondingly reducing those of whites in an appropriate proportion one could cause the allocation made pursuant to the lottery to approximate the 16,000 to 4,000 ratio that would have prevailed absent discrimination. Further, although the use of affirmative action would reduce the prospects of minimally qualified white candidates and make them lower than those of their black counterparts, it would arguably be just inasmuch as it would give every white candidate the same prospects that he or she would have enjoyed absent discrimination. Because of this, affirmative action to deal with the effects of a reduced pool of minimally qualified blacks does not lead to the same problems that it raises in the context of attempts to use future lotteries to redress the imbalances produced through past discriminatory lotteries. Indeed, in the latter case, in which it is assumed that the relative pools of minimally qualified candidates remain constant, the reduction in the prospects of success of whites does not put them in the same position that they would have occupied absent any first-order discrimination: it puts them in a worse position.

On the other hand, affirmative action to counteract the effects of a reduced pool of minimally qualified blacks does provide the individual blacks who profit from it with a windfall benefit. Indeed, it increases the latter's prospects of success above what they would have been absent discrimination and the consequent reduction in the size of the pool. Arguably, this windfall benefit is not unjust as it does not put any white person in a worse position than he or she would have been in absent any discrimination. Upon further examination, however, an egalitarian could conclude that affirmative action as a response to a reduced pool of eligible blacks is, in the last analysis, unjust. Thus, the windfall benefit to some blacks may not be unjust when viewed in relation to whites, in contrast to when it is viewed in relation to those blacks who would have been in the eligible pool but for discrimination. Indeed, it is the injustice to the latter that ought to be redressed, and redress certainly should not consist of favoring those of their fellow blacks who have remained in the eligible pool. Accordingly, a more just remedy would be to bring those blacks who do not presently belong to the eligible pool into it. In light of this latter alternative, affirmative action ultimately appears to stand in the way of the full realization of egalitarian justice.

In sum, the egalitarian case against affirmative action appears to be a strong one. The egalitarian has a strong preference for equality of result, and affirmative action would stand in the way of its achievement. Moreover, even when the egalitarian might be persuaded to opt for prospect-regarding equality of opportunity, she would still be on the whole unlikely to find arguments for affirmative action persuasive. Hence, ultimately there appears to be little, if any, room for affirmative action from the perspective of egalitarian justice.

2. *Nagel's Egalitarian Argument in Limited Support of Affirmative Action*

Egalitarian justice may not justify affirmative action, but, according to Nagel, there may be circumstances under which an egalitarian would not consider it to be *unjust*. In those circumstances, moreover, Nagel maintains that affirmative action may be justified on grounds of social utility (Nagel 1979, 101). Thus, Nagel advances an argument for affirmative action that relies in part on egalitarian considerations and in part on utilitarian ones. Moreover, an important advantage that the mixed egalitarian and utilitarian justification for affirmative action can claim over its exclusively utilitarian counterparts is that the former is less prone to open the door to the legitimation of first-order discrimination than is the latter.

Although egalitarians generally consider meritocracies to be unjust, there may be situations in which it might be inadvisable or impossible to move away from the meritocratic system. In those cases, the question arises whether the use of affirmative action to counteract racism and sexism could be accepted by the egalitarian.

When the systemic inequities produced by the meritocratic process of allocation are beyond the reach of the would-be egalitarian reformer, the use of affirmative action cannot be accused of standing in the way of achieving greater justice. There are, therefore, as Nagel argues, circumstances under which affirmative action is not unjust from an egalitarian perspective, in the sense that it neither materially increases existing injustices nor does it render more difficult the pursuit of greater justice. This does not mean, however, that affirmative action is under the same circumstances just. Rather, Nagel's point seems to be that there are circumstances under which an egalitarian would maintain that affirmative action is neither just nor unjust.

Egalitarians recognize that there may be other injustices than those that are inherent to the meritocratic system. As Nagel indicates, first-order discrimination on the basis of race or sex produces serious injustices in the eyes of the egalitarian.[11] On the other hand, the egalitarian is likely to acknowledge that the use of affirmative action to alleviate added burdens imposed by racism and sexism on blacks and women, respectively, may lead to an increase in social utility.[12] When an egalitarian believes that affirmative action is not unjust, and that it may lead to increased social utility, it seems legitimate for her to accept affirmative action as a useful means to attack certain of the evil consequences of racism and sexism. At the same time, inasmuch as the justification for affirmative action is a utilitarian one, the egalitarian is reminded that preferential treatment cannot affect the deeper systemic injustices of the meritocratic system.

The mixed egalitarian and utilitarian justification of affirmative action has at least one important advantage over its exclusively utilitarian counterparts. Because the egalitarian's concern with social utility is clearly subordinated to her concern with equality, it is easier for the egalitarian than for the utilitarian to accept the legitimacy of affirmative action without thereby opening the door to the legitimation of first-order discrimination. According to Nagel, first-order racial and sexual discrimination is exceptionally unjust because "it attaches a sense of reduced worth to a feature with which people are born" (ibid., 102). Furthermore, Nagel specifies that

> A psychological consequence of the systematic attachment of social disadvantages to an inborn feature is that both the possessors of the feature and others begin to regard it as an essential and important characteristic, one that reduces the esteem in which its possessor can be held. Concomitantly, those without the characteristic gain free esteem by comparison, and the arrangement thus sacrifices the most basic personal interests of some for the interests of others, with those sacrificed being on the bottom. (Ibid., 102–03)

Affirmative action's principal virtue lies in its ability to contribute to the elimination of the "sense of reduced worth" of blacks and women who have been the victims of first-order discrimination. Moreover, although affirmative action could be said to discriminate against qualified white males who are turned away in favor of less qualified blacks and women, it does not seem to produce any significant change for the worse in the self-image of white males as a class. As Nagel explains,

> The self-esteem of whites as a group is not endangered by [affirmative action], since the situation arises only because of their general social dominance, and the aim of the practice is only to benefit blacks not to exclude whites. Moreover, although the interests of some are being sacrificed to the interests of others, it is the better placed who are being sacrificed and the worst placed who are being helped. The policy is designed to favor a group whose social position is exceptionally depressed, with destructive consequences both for the self-esteem of members of the group and for the health and cohesion of the society. (Ibid., 103)

Consistent with this analysis, the harms caused by the implementation of an affirmative action plan are altogether of a different kind than those perpetrated by first-order discrimination. Affirmative action seeks to enhance the self-worth of those who have been the object of systematic oppression and domination on account of certain group characteristics. It may harm the interests of certain members of the dominant group, but it is neither intended to, nor does it customarily, cause any sufficient diminution in the self-esteem of the members of that group. First-order discrimination, on the other hand, does tend to perpetuate inequality, by continuously and systematically eroding the sense of self-worth of its victims, while concomitantly inflating the self-image of its beneficiaries in proportion. In sum, the harm produced by affirmative action is only that necessary to eliminate the status of being more than an equal, while that imposed by first-order discrimination is that of forcing its victims to assume the status of less than equals. Given this clear difference, the egalitarian can endorse affirmative action without opening the door to the legitimation of first-order discrimination, even if it were proven to her satisfaction that the latter is best suited to enhance social utility.

Even if we accept it at face value, the mixed egalitarian and utilitarian argument for affirmative action advanced by Nagel seems weak. Since the desirability of affirmative action depends on its social utility rather than on its propensity to promote justice, an egalitarian should be prepared to reject it whenever it can be shown to be unlikely to enhance social utility. More important, because affirmative action generally leaves the injustices implanted by the meritocratic system of allocation intact, the egalitarian should opt for any viable alternative capable of combatting systemic injustices.

If one agrees with Nagel that opportunities ought to be proportional to capacities, but that differences in natural abilities do not justify corresponding differences in social and economic rewards, it would seem that the optimal course for an egalitarian is not one that includes affirmative action. Indeed, from this perspective, the ideal would entail an allocation of opportunities commensurate with capacities, and a redistribution of wealth so as to equalize the individual shares in the material rewards flowing from social and economic cooperation. Moreover, inasmuch as the capacities of blacks and women may have been diminished as a consequence of first-order discrimination, the proper remedy would seem to consist in the institution of special training and rehabilitation programs designed to develop their capacities to the level that they would have most likely achieved absent first-order discrimination. Particularly since opportunities would not be associated with social and economic rewards, this latter remedy would seem better suited to the aim of the egalitarian than a policy of preferential treatment that would allocate to blacks and women opportunities which would exceed their capacities for taking full advantage of them. On the other hand, blacks and women may have been deprived of just material rewards as a consequence of both first-order discrimination and the operation of a meritocratic system of allocation. In that case, the optimal egalitarian remedy would seem to consist in the allocation to blacks and women of fair shares in the course of redistribution of wealth designed to dismantle the meritocracy, rather than in the reservation for them of certain scarce places and positions as the beneficiaries of preferential treatment.

In view of the foregoing analysis, the mixed egalitarian and utilitarian case for affirmative action is both weak and narrowly circumscribed. It depends, on the one hand, on a finding that social utility will be enhanced rather than diminished by the institution of affirmative action.

It also depends, on the other hand, on the existence of a set of conditions such that it is impracticable for the egalitarian to pursue any legitimate course of action reasonably calculated to upset the meritocratic system of allocating social and economic rewards commensurate with natural abilities.[13]

PART TWO

Constitutional Equality and Affirmative Action

CHAPTER SIX

Constitutional Equality and Equal Protection

As indicated in chapter 1, equality provides the nexus between affirmative action, the concept of justice, and the constitutional requirements imposed by the equal protection clause. In Part One, I have focused on how philosophy deals with the concept of equality in both its descriptive and prescriptive dimensions. Operating within the confines of liberal moral and political theory, I have attempted to assess the legitimacy of affirmative action in the context of several different liberal theories of prescriptive equality—libertarianism, contractarianism, utilitarianism, and egalitarianism. In Part Two, I seek to elucidate the meaning of constitutional equality as it emerges from the equal protection clause. Specifically, I intend to use the structural grammar of equality and the distinctions between compensatory and distributive justice developed in chapter 1 in order to explore the meaning of the equal protection clause as it relates to the constitutionality of affirmative action.

As we shall see below, the equal protection clause constitutionalizes the norm of equality. Consistent with this, the principal objectives of Part Two are to determine which equalities and inequalities are, and which ought to be, promoted by constitutional equality and, based on the results of that inquiry, to assess the coherence of constitutional arguments for and against affirmative action.

Judges, lawyers, and legal scholars who engage in constitutional interpretation seek, like philosophers, to give determinate content to descriptive and prescriptive equality. Philosophical interpretation and constitutional interpretation constitute, however, different practices.[1] Thus, although there may be analogies, contiguities, and overlaps between the two practices, they are not mutually reducible, and insights produced through philosophical interpretation cannot be applied automatically *to* or *within* the practice of constitutional interpretation. With this in mind, I explore the place and relevance that philosophical insights into the concept of equality might have in relation to the constitutional interpretation of equality under the equal protection clause.

Later in this chapter, I examine constitutional equality as it emerges from the jurisprudence of the equal protection clause. As we will see, while the equal protection clause constitutionalizes the postulate of equality, this postulate cannot be directly applied as a constitutional standard. Instead, it requires the use of some suitable mediating principle. The mediating principle adopted by the Supreme Court for its analysis of equal protection claims is the antidiscrimination principle. That principle, however, is inadequate in that it lacks sufficient procedural neutrality to obviate the need to resort to a fairly elaborate conception of substantive equality.

Viewing the equal protection clause as imposing *some* conception of substantive equality, I undertake in the remainder of this chapter a review of Supreme Court equal protection decisions in order to determine the nature and scope of the conception of substantive equality that emerges from the Court's equal protection jurisprudence. Specifically, I will be searching for useful clues concerning the delimitation of a constitutionally legitimate domain of allocation for the state,[2] and the constitutional relevance of equality of result and of equality of opportunity.

1. The Nexus between Philosophy's Interpretation of Equality and the Constitutional Interpretation of Equal Protection

Like philosophy, constitutional interpretation seeks to elucidate the meaning of equality. Indeed, implicit in every constitutional claim alleging a violation of equal protection rights is a factual as well as a normative assertion concerning (constitutional) equality. Put differently, every allegation of a violation of equal protection rights asserts that a particular equality (equalities) that can be given descriptive content (for example, lot-regarding marginal equality in the allocation of particular divisible goods) has been frustrated (or promoted) through state action (or through the failure of the state or its agencies to act). Moreover, every such allegation also asserts explicitly or implicitly what constitutional equality prescribes as a norm. Thus, proving that a particular complainant has received from the state a particular thing that is smaller than that received by every other person within that state establishes that the state's allocation of the good in question has not resulted in marginal lot-regarding equality. But that factual finding does not in itself indicate whether the state in question has violated the claimant's constitutional right to equality. To elucidate that question, we must determine whether or not constitutional equality prescribes lot-regarding marginal equality where the state allocates divisible goods.

Although both philosophy and constitutional adjudication of equal protection claims can be viewed as interpretive practices seeking, among others things, to elucidate the descriptive and prescriptive meanings of equality, these two practices are by no means coextensive. The rules, norms, standards, and conventions that shape constitutional interpretation are not the same as those that define the practice of philosophical interpretation. As Greenawalt points out,

> Although law and ethics deal with many of the same problems and share forms of reasoning, a proper ethical resolution of an issue is not necessarily a proper legal resolution.
>
> When courts make decisions, they are largely guided by authoritative texts. These constitutional provisions, statutes, administrative regulations, and earlier judicial decisions do not always conform with a judge's personal views of what is ethically right; yet in the role of judge, he or she may be bound to follow them. . . .
>
> Ethical reasoning, as ordinarily developed in philosophical writing is different from legal reasoning in not starting with some authoritative text. (Greenawalt 1983, 7)

More specifically, to the extent that the constitutional interpretation of equality is constrained by the relevant constitutional text and by the specific intent of the framers of the Fourteenth Amendment, it is not in principle reducible to any philosophical interpretation of equality that is not subject to the same constraints.

The actual divergence between philosophical and constitutional interpretation of equality depends on what are considered the legitimate parameters of constitutional interpretation, a subject that has generated a considerable amount of debate.[3] It is important to emphasize, however, that no matter what degree of divergence separates these two practices, constitutional interpretations of equality can be assessed in terms of the philosophical understanding of equality. In other words, even if constitutional evaluations under the equal protection clause in no way depend on any philosophical interpretation of the concept of equality, a philosopher can determine whether such constitutional evaluations comport with philosophical notions of justice and equality.

To illustrate this point, let us assume that it is universally agreed that the only legitimate function of judges in an equal protection case is to follow the specific intent of the framers of the Fourteenth Amendment. Let us assume, further, that such intent consisted simply in having states act without any exceptions in a completely color-blind manner. Under these conditions, a quota in favor of blacks in public employment would have to be struck down under the equal protection clause. Moreover, this result would be mandated even if judges were convinced that it would be ethically desirable to impose racial quotas in public employment.[4] A philosopher, however, would be perfectly justified in assessing the judicial interpretation given to the equal protection clause, and in concluding, for example, that such interpretation leads to unethical outcomes. Thus, a utilitarian philosopher might plausibly conclude that racial quotas in public employment would maximize utilities and that consequently the constitutional restrictions imposed on these quotas were unjust.

The model of constitutional interpretation presented in the preceding example was pointedly extreme. Other models of constitutional interpretation make for practices that do not diverge as sharply from philosophical practice. It is certainly not possible here to do full justice to the lengthy debate on the proper nature and scope of constitutional interpretation. Nevertheless, among plausible competing models of constitutional interpretation, one can find some that give very significant play to philosophical arguments—that is, models that reserve a prominent place for philosophical arguments *within* the practice of constitutional interpretation. Moreover, in the context of such models, philosophy provides both a critical tool to evaluate existing constitutional conceptions and a building block of constitutional interpretation of the equal protection clause.

Before settling on a model of constitutional interpretation for the equal protection clause, it seems useful to outline briefly some of the salient features of the practice of constitutional interpretation. For this outline, I rely primarily on recent work by the legal scholar Richard Fallon. According to Fallon, most of those who engage in the practice of constitutional interpretation recognize the relevance of at least five kinds of constitutional arguments: arguments from the text of the constitution; arguments from the intent of the framers; arguments of constitutional theory "that reason from the hypothesized purposes that best explain either particular constitutional provisions or the constitutional text as a whole"; arguments based on judicial precedent; and "value arguments" making claims about justice, morality or social policy (Fallon 1987, 1189–90).

In Fallon's definition "value arguments" refer to

> claims about the moral or political significance of facts or about the normative desirability of outcomes. Defined in this way, value arguments assert claims about what is good or bad, desirable or undesirable, as measured against some standard that is independent of what the constitutional text requires. Value arguments do not claim that the particular value judgments they assert are necessarily ones that the framers intended to constitutionalize, or that they express the best constitutional theory. Rather, value arguments advance conclusions about what is morally or politically

correct, desirable, or expedient as measured against some standard. (Ibid., 1205)

Furthermore, Fallon indicates that value arguments have an accepted role in cases involving constitutional language, such as the equal protection clause, "whose meaning has a normative or valuative component." Following Dworkin,[5] Fallon maintains that the equal protection clause constitutionalizes the concept of equality. But this concept, as Fallon notes, is "essentially contestable." That means that, although the use of the concept is intelligible even to those who disagree with it, "consensus breaks down over the proper criteria" for deciding when the label "equal" is appropriate. In other words, "different people apply the term[] differently . . . because the full meaning of [the] term [equality] depends upon a background network of philosophical values and assumptions that is itself disputable." Consistent with this, decisions concerning the proper use of an "essentially contestable" term such as "equality" require normative evaluation and commitment of the kind that is customary within the practice of normative moral and political philosophy (ibid.).[6]

To the extent that value arguments are recognized as valid constitutional arguments, philosophical arguments can be said to play a legitimate role *within* the practice of constitutional interpretation. In discussing the sources of values to which a judge might legitimately appeal in the course of constitutional decision making, Fallon states: "One kind of value argument refers to some repository of values, outside of herself, that a judge or lawyer believes to be a legitimate source of authority in constitutional interpretation. That source might be traditional morality, consensus values, natural law, economic efficiency, or the original position liberal methodology of John Rawls" (ibid., 1208). Presumably, therefore, it would sometimes be appropriate for a judge faced with the task of deciding whether a particular affirmative action plan is constitutional to appeal, for example, to the arguments, values, and norms that inform the appraisal of the legitimacy of affirmative action under the contractarian theory of justice.

Accepting that value arguments have their place in the practice of constitutional interpretation, the next question is, when are they appropriate? Or, more generally, how are the five kinds of constitutional arguments identified by Fallon to be reconciled in particular cases? According to Fallon's theory, the various kinds of constitutional argument can lead to a single result in either of two ways: through a process of interpretive harmonization designed to "find the best arguments in all the categories to support, or at least not to be inconsistent with, a single result," or, when such process of harmonization fails to achieve coherence, through the assignment of a hierarchical order that ranks categories of argument in a descending order of authoritativeness with arguments in a higher category prevailing over inconsistent arguments belonging to a lower category (ibid., 1193). The most authoritative arguments, according to Fallon, are those from the constitutional text, followed, in descending order, by arguments based on the framers' intent, constitutional theory, precedent, and moral values (ibid., 1194). Although value arguments rank at the bottom of the hierarchy, Fallon asserts that they are likely to assume a much more important role than their ranking would suggest. Specifically, Fallon maintains that value arguments are likely to play a leading role in the process of harmonization designed to lead to the achievement of coherence (ibid., 1193–94).

Consistent with Fallon's theory, the most extensive possible role for philosophical argument in constitutional interpretation is realized in cases in which arguments from other categories are too indeterminate or contradictory to lead to a single coherent result. For example, in a case in which the constitutional text is particularly general, abstract, and vague; the intent of the framers difficult to ascertain; constitutional theory indeterminate; and relevant precedents lacking; the judges' decision may rely heavily on philosophical argument. In such a case, the weight of philosophical argument could determine the outcome of the process of constitutional interpretation.

Even if there are cases in which philosophical arguments play a decisive role, however, the practice of constitutional interpretation is never merely reducible to that of philosophical interpretation. Indeed, even in a case in which the right result is dictated by the force of philosophical argument, the judge must still operate within constraints that do not affect the work of the philosopher.[7] For example, the judge who engages in constitutional interpretation must endeavor to adhere to judicially manageable standards, and this may cause her to reject an otherwise commendable ethical norm. Likewise, as Greenawalt emphasizes, whereas the philosopher may legitimately stipulate certain facts, the judge cannot do so (Greenawalt 1983, 9). Thus, in chapter 1, I stipulated for purposes of philosophical analysis that it was always possible precisely to assess the relative qualifications of two candidates for the same position. In actuality, however, such comparisons may often lack sufficient reliability. This a judge should not ignore, and therefore she should not automatically adopt as a judicial norm an ethical norm which is justified, in part, based upon reliance on a factual stipulation that would be inappropriate in the judicial context.

Let us now turn specifically to the constitutional interpretation of the equal protection clause. A review of the arguments advanced in each of the relevant categories described by Fallon lends strong support to the conclusion that philosophical considerations of justice and equality ought to play a paramount role in the determination of the result in particular cases.

Starting with the constitutional text itself, it seems fairly obvious that arguments from the text are unlikely to provide any significant guidance in a great majority of cases. The relevant constitutional language prescribes that "no state shall . . . deny to a person within its jurisdiction the equal protection of the laws."[8] This language imposes minimal constraints on judicial action, as the phrase "equal protection of the laws" seems inherently vague and ambiguous (Bennett 1984, 495). Accordingly, one might at first glance be inclined to agree with Chief Justice Rehnquist that "the Equal Protection Clause is itself a classic paradox. . . . It creates a requirement of equal treatment to be applied to the process of legislation—legislation whose very purpose is to draw lines in such a way that different people are treated differently."[9]

Several legal scholars have asserted that no specific meaning can be extracted from the text of the equal protection clause.[10] Dworkin, for instance, maintains that the equal protection clause constitutionalizes the concept of equality without putting forth any particular conception of it (Dworkin 1977, 134–35). Because of this, he concludes that if "courts try to be faithful to the text of the Constitution, they will for that very reason be forced to decide between competing conceptions of political morality" (ibid., 136). Thus, as Dworkin emphasizes, the text of the equal protection clause does not reveal what kind of equality is constitutionally mandated, and much less does it provide any clue as to the constitutionality of affirmative action.[11]

There are also several legal scholars who do not believe that arguments based on the framers' intent are likely to be dispositive of a majority of constitutional claims made under the equal protection clause. The reasons that these scholars advance for their conclusions are manifold. One of these reasons is that the historical record is not clear concerning what the specific intent of the framers may have been.[12] Another is that even if the historical record were clear, the framers of the Fourteenth Amendment did not share the same political convictions, and hence it is highly implausible that they all had the same specific intent in framing a constitutional provision as vague and open-ended as the equal protection clause.[13]

A further reason that the framers' intent is unlikely to be a dispositive reflects the contrast between abstract and specific intent. It has been argued, for example, that it was not the specific intent of the framers of the Fourteenth Amendment to abolish segregation in education (Berger 1977, 117–33). But it has also been contended that, at a higher level of abstraction, the framers evinced the general intention that a person's fundamental rights should not be abridged because of race (Fallon 1987,

1216). Consistent with this distinction, *Brown* v. *Board of Education*, the landmark Supreme Court decision that held that laws designed to maintain segregated public schools violate the equal protection clause, cannot be reconciled with the specific intent of the framers of the Fourteenth Amendment, but it can with their abstract intent. Moving from the framers' specific intent to their increasingly more abstract intent appears to increase the likelihood of being able to reconcile important judicial decisions with the perceived ultimate aims of the framers. Such moves, however, also pose a vexing problem. In Fallon's words, "Once a consistent adherence to the framers' specific intent is renounced, there simply is no value-neutral way to choose among possible specifications of the framers' abstract intent" (ibid., 1217).

Finally, even if it were agreed that constitutional interpretation must stick to the specific intent of the framers, and that such intent is ascertainable in the case of the equal protection clause, one could still argue that the framers had no specific intent concerning affirmative action. Indeed, the possibility of preferential treatment of blacks in education and employment almost certainly did not occur to anyone at the time of the amendment's enactment (ibid., 1271). For this, as well as for the previously mentioned reasons, it seems fair to conclude that the framers' intent is hardly dispositive in the context of contemporary constitutional assessments of equal protection and affirmative action.

Although arguments from constitutional theory are "text focused," they do not rely on the precise meaning of the constitutional text or on the historically established specific intent of the framers (ibid., 1201). Instead, according to Fallon, these arguments "claim to understand" the equal protection clause, "by providing an account of the values, purposes or political theory" in light of which it becomes most intelligible (ibid., 1200). In other words, arguments of constitutional theory are those that assert that particular values or principles enjoy constitutional status because they provide coherence and intelligibility to constitutional provisions. Moreover, as Fallon emphasizes,

> A constitutional theory must seek not only to explain constitutional guarantees and prohibitions but also to do so in a normatively attractive way. And where more than one theory plausibly accounts for the text having been written as it was, an assessment along a normative dimension, whether undertaken consciously or unconsciously, becomes inevitable and desirable. The upshot is that the "derivation" of constitutional values can seldom if ever be a value-neutral enterprise. (Ibid., 1202)

More than one constitutional theory plausibly accounts for the purpose of the equal protection clause.[14] Dworkin, for instance, interprets the equal protection clause as imposing constraints on majority rule because of the moral rights that individuals have against the majority (Dworkin 1977, 233). Moreover, Dworkin claims that individual rights under the equal protection clause are matters of principle, and that such rights must be interpreted "as expressing a coherent vision of justice" (Dworkin 1986, 368). According to Karst, on the other hand, the core of the equal protection clause is "a principle of equal citizenship, which presumptively guarantees to each individual the right to be treated by organized society as a respected, responsible and participating member" (Karst 1977, 4). Similarly, O'Fallon maintains that the political theory embodied in the Constitution and in the equal protection clause requires adherence to a fundamental individual right to equal concern and respect (O'Fallon 1979, 57). Both the principle of equal citizenship and that of equal respect and concern very closely resemble the postulate of equality. In short, arguments from constitutional theory do not yield a single understanding of the equal protection clause. Moreover, as used to elucidate the purposes of the equal protection clause, these arguments often rely on philosophical conceptions of moral and political equality.

In the context of the equal protection clause, arguments based on precedent do not fare better than those in the three preceding categories. Indeed, precedents have often been indeterminate in the equal protection area and can hardly be expected to lead to single results in affirmative action cases. For example, in 1896, in *Plessy* v. *Ferguson*, the Supreme Court upheld the validity of state-mandated racial segregation on passenger railroad trains and endorsed the doctrine of "separate but equal." In its 1954 *Brown* decision, however, the Supreme Court did not follow *Plessy*, and held that state segregated schools were unconstitutional.[15]

By the time that the Supreme Court rendered its first decision on the constitutionality of affirmative action in the *Bakke* case in 1978, there were numerous equal protection precedents. As Fallon notes, however, these precedents could be combined in different ways, and could thus be made to support at least three different positions. The first of these is that the Constitution requires color-blindness; the second, that race-conscious classifications are justified only when necessary to advance compelling government interests; and the third, that there is no prohibition against racial preferences designed to eliminate the remaining effects of past discrimination (Fallon 1977, 1273). Depending on which of these three competing positions is chosen, arguments based on precedent would require different and even contradictory results in *Bakke* and in all subsequent Supreme Court affirmative action cases. Indeed, the first position would seem to bar all racial preferences; the second, to confine them largely to purely compensatory situations; while the third one would seem to sanction a much broader use of preferential treatment at least in part justified by distributive concerns.

In conclusion, in the case of the jurisprudence of the equal protection clause, neither arguments from the text, the framers' intent, constitutional theory, nor from judicial precedent are likely to lead often to determinate results. This leaves much room for value arguments in general and philosophical arguments in particular. Accordingly, as one commentator put it "insofar as the constitution contains fundamental ethical terms like . . . equality without expressly indicating how to interpret them, the constitution embodies some particular moral theories, namely, the most plausible ones, and the job of the judge is to identify and use them as bases for decision" (Morris 1984, 509). With this in mind, I now turn to a closer examination of constitutional equality.

2. *Equal Protection and the Postulate of Equality*

The equal protection clause has been interpreted as giving constitutional status to the ideal of equality (Fiss 1987, 85). Moreover, the Supreme Court has specified that the equal protection clause is designed to protect individual rights.[16] Combining these two propositions with the constitutional theory propounded by several legal scholars lends support to the conclusion that the equal protection clause constitutionalizes the postulate of equality.

According to several legal scholars, the equal protection clause should be interpreted as constitutionalizing the principle of equal citizenship or that of equal respect and concern. A closer look at these principles reveals that they amount to different expressions of the essential norms encapsulated in the postulate of equality.[17] According to Dworkin, for example, the equal protection clause constitutionalizes the concept of equality (Dworkin 1977, 134–35), but does not thereby mandate adoption of any particular conception of equality, such as the libertarian or the utilitarian (Dworkin 1986, 382). Dworkin, however, does specify some of the attributes of constitutional equality. Thus, he states that the "law must treat people as equals," and that government "must treat all its citizens as equals in the following sense: political decisions and arrangements must display equal concern for the fate of all" (ibid., 381–82). Implicit in this demand for treatment as equals and for the requirement to view the fate of each individual as being worthy of equal concern is the assumption that each person is the moral equal of every other person. Moreover, in light of Dworkin's distinction between equal treatment and treatment as an equal, discussed in chapter 4, it seems clear that he envisages constitutional equality as requiring equality of respect for each person within the state's jurisdiction, but not as necessarily requiring equal treatment or equality of result for all. Consistent with these observations, it seems that the constitutional equality that Dworkin has in mind is not the mere concept of equality taken at the highest level of abstraction, but rather the somewhat more determinate idea of normative equality embodied in the postulate of equality.[18]

Baker argues that the equal protection clause constitutionalizes the "equality of respect principle" that he views as requiring the community to "treat all its members with full and equal respect and concern as autonomous persons" (Baker 1983, 938*n.15*). Baker also adds that

> The assumption that the equal protection clause embodies such an equality of respect *principle* is not historically incongruous. The institution of slavery is our history's most glaring violation of this principle. Slavery denies that some people are fully and equally important, autonomous agents; . . . One can read the Civil War era amendments as a group, and particularly the Fourteenth Amendment which speaks most generally, as rejecting *any* violation of the principle. (Emphasis in original; ibid., 938–39*n.16*)

Based on these passages, Baker's equality of respect principle appears virtually indistinguishable from the postulate of equality.

Finally, as previously mentioned, Karst's principle of equal citizenship closely resembles the postulate of equality. According to Karst, the core of equal citizenship is "the dignity of full membership in the society" (Karst 1977, 5). Moreover, quoting Rawls, Karst asserts that the principle embodies "an ethic of mutual respect and self-esteem" (ibid., 6). Karst goes on to specify that equal citizenship requires "organized society to treat each individual as a person, one who is worthy of respect, one who "belongs." Also, Karst asserts that the equal citizenship principle is basically individualistic (ibid., 8), and that it is not incompatible with those inequalities that do not "belie the principle that people are of equal ultimate worth" (ibid., 10–11).

All of the views discussed in this section provide strong support to the claim that the equal protection clause constitutionalizes the postulate of equality. To be sure, these views are not unanimously held by all constitutional scholars. Nonetheless, these views demonstrate that it is quite plausible as a matter of constitutional theory to assert that, taken at a relatively high level of abstraction, the purpose of the equal protection clause is to constitutionalize the postulate of equality.

3. Antidiscrimination as the Mediating Principle in Equal Protection Jurisprudence

Exclusive reliance on the postulate of equality would not furnish judges with sufficient guidance to enable them to dispose of most equal protection claims in a principled manner. This is because the postulate of equality is too indeterminate to indicate which equalities and inequalities might be just in most individual circumstances. In a small number of cases, appeal to the postulate of equality would seem to be sufficient. These include cases involving laws permitting or mandating slavery or first-order discrimination against a group, if such discrimination is explicitly sought to be justified on the grounds that the members of the group in question are morally inferior. Beyond these very extreme cases, however, the postulate of equality does not seem to require any definite outcome. For example, suppose a state law imposes racial segregation in public education on the grounds that a segregated education will better enable both blacks and whites to realize the objectives of their respective individual life plans. The constitutionality of such law ought to turn on whether it treats all affected individuals as moral equals. The postulate of equality, however, cannot alone supply an answer to this question. Because of this, as Owen Fiss points out, judges need a mediating principle capable of furnishing them with greater guidance in their interpretations of the equal protection clause (Fiss 1977, 85).

The need for a mediating principle to supplement the postulate of equality within the practice of constitutional interpretation is analogous to the need to supplement the same postulate with particular conceptions of equality in the context of the philosophical interpretation of equality. Indeed, in both cases a mediating principle is needed to make possible a sufficiently determinate account of which equalities and inequalities can be justified under the postulate of equality. There are, however, important differences between particular philosophical conceptions of equality and mediating principles associated with constitutional equality. Chief among these is the fact that a constitutional mediating principle must be judicially manageable, so that it is within the competence of judges to apply it in such a way as to reach determinate decisions that are susceptible to implementation.

There is also another important difference between constitutional mediating principles and philosophical conceptions. Based on a particular philosophical conception of equality, it may be justified to prescribe a social, economical, political, and legal order requiring reforms, new laws, a radical transformation of the status quo, or even a revolution. Constitutional practice, however, requires that the judiciary refrain from interfering with the majoritarian policies codified by legislatures, except in those cases in which an enacted law contravenes a specific constitutional proscription.[19] Thus, unlike a philosopher, a judge deciding a constitutional claim cannot simply prescribe a conception of equality, no matter how persuasive. In the context of an equal protection claim, the judge cannot invalidate a state law, unless it violates someone's constitutional equality rights, and ought to be especially careful not to impose on the states particular conceptions of equality that are not constitutionally mandated.[20] Accordingly, a mediating principle designed to aid judges in constitutional adjudication must be crafted in such a way as to minimize interference with the integrity of the legislative process.

The Supreme Court has adopted the antidiscrimination principle as the mediating principle for interpreting the equal protection clause (Fiss 1977, 85). According to Fiss, the antidiscrimination principle essentially reduces the equal protection clause to a blanket prohibition against discrimination.[21] Further, Fiss asserts that the antidiscrimination principle "embodies a very limited conception of equality" which is "confined to assessing the rationality of means." Specifically, Fiss indicates that the antidiscrimination principle operates in three steps. First, it reduces the equality established by the equal protection clause to a purely formal requirement, insisting only that like cases be treated alike.[22] Thus far, therefore, the antidiscrimination principle seems virtually indistinguishable from the principle of formal justice discussed by Perelman, and mentioned in chapter 1.[23]

The second step in the operation of the antidiscrimination principle is necessitated by the fact that the very essence of the legislative process is to discriminate, in the sense of distinguishing and drawing lines. Laws classify, and at least some classifications that lead to unequal treatment are just, such as those that single out criminals for punishment. Accordingly, stresses Fiss, pursuant to the second step, the antidiscrimination principle cannot merely ban discrimination or classification, it only prohibits "arbitrary" or "invidious" classifications (ibid., 86). Moreover, for the antidiscrimination principle to be useful in distinguishing permissible from constitutionally prohibited legislative classifications, it must involve a third step. That third step, as Fiss indicates, includes identifying the criterion of discrimination employed in a particular legislative classification and determining whether the discrimination in question is sufficiently related to the state purpose to be served by the legislation to be constitutionally permissible (ibid.). In other words, the third step requires judicial review of the "fit" between legislative "means" and legislative "ends" (ibid., 97).

The fit between means and ends refers to the relation between the particular classification established by a given law and the ends sought to be achieved through the promulgation and implementation of that law. For example, a state law that provides that "no one under the age of eighteen shall be allowed to drive an automobile" classifies by dividing all persons within its jurisdiction into two groups: the group of all those who are eighteen and over, and the group of those who are under eighteen. Further, let us assume that the declared purpose of the law in question is to enhance traffic safety and to reduce traffic related deaths.

In the context of this example, the question of fit relates to the manner in which the classification contained in the law may contribute to the realization of the purposes for which this law has been enacted. In this case, the question of fit therefore boils down to the question of whether prohibiting those who are under eighteen from driving automobiles is likely to contribute to traffic safety and the reduction of traffic deaths.

In assessing the fit between legislative means and ends, a classification may either achieve a "perfect fit," or it may be "underinclusive," "overinclusive," or both underinclusive and overinclusive.[24] Returning to our example, for there to be a perfect fit all the traffic hazards and all traffic deaths would have to be attributable to those under eighteen *and* each member of that class would have to bear some responsibility for such increased hazards and deaths. If all the under-eighteen year olds bear some responsibility, but also some older persons do, then the classification is underinclusive. If some but not all under-eighteen year olds are responsible, but no one eighteen or older is, then the classification is overinclusive. Finally, if—as would be the case in the real world—some under eighteen years old and some older persons are responsible, then the classification would be both underinclusive and overinclusive.

According to Fiss, limiting a judge's role to a determination of the fit between legislative means and ends is attractive because it gives the impression that the judge's function is purely mechanical and the criteria for her decision purely quantitative and "value neutral" (Fiss 1977, 97). In Fiss's own words,

> The task of judicial judgment appear[s] to involve as little discretion as when a salesman advises a customer whether a pair of shoes fit. Moreover, under the antidiscrimination principle, whatever judgment there is would seem to be one about means, not ends, thereby insulating judges from the charge of substituting their judgment for that of the legislature. The court could invalidate state action without passing on the merit or importance of this end—a task, it might be argued, that is especially committed to the more representative branches of government. (Ibid., 97–98)

Because of its dependence on the implementation of the second and third steps described above, the antidiscrimination principle cannot be simply reduced to a purely formal device. Indeed, use of the means-end fit test makes the determination of the constitutionality of a challenged law dependent on a substantive criterion. That substantive criterion is apparently supplied, moreover, by the very legislature whose enactment is being constitutionally challenged. Indeed, the purpose of a particular piece of legislation provides a substantive normative objective that is posited as desirable. Thus, in the case of the last example, the normative objective is the achievement of greater traffic safety, which is presented by the legislature as a desirable social good. On the other hand, the classification introduced by the law is supposed to be legitimated by the substantive objective of the legislation, in the sense that the selection of those who are to be treated alike (or unalike) and the respects in which they are to be treated alike (or unalike) pursuant to the classification are supposed to be justified as contributing to the achievement of the normative objectives of the legislation.

Thus, to return to our example, treating those under eighteen years old differently than those who are older when it comes to the driving of automobiles is supposed to be justified in order to achieve greater traffic safety, which is clearly a desirable social end. And under these conditions, determining the justification of the classification, or the fit between means and ends, does indeed appear to be "value neutral," in the sense that it is the legislature and not the judiciary who provides the substantive norm that makes the carrying out of the requisite judicial task possible. In short, although it is inaccurate to characterize the antidiscrimination principle as being purely formal, it seems thus far warranted to claim that it does not rely on the judiciary for the selection of the substantive norms without which it cannot be intelligibly put into effect.

The antidiscrimination principle, however, is an inadequate vehicle for the constitutionalization of the postulate of equality. Indeed, to the extent that the substantive norms on which the antidiscrimination principle depends for its operation are provided by state legislatures, and to the extent that the latter are not inherently constrained by the postulate of equality, nothing would seem to prevent the choice of substantive norms that would violate the postulate of equality. For example, if a state legislature believes that the white race is superior, and that it is therefore of paramount importance to preserve racial purity, it may well pursue this avowed objective through the enactment of legislation mandating that racial segregation be maintained in all public places. Although such legislation designed to treat blacks as being morally inferior amounts to a glaring violation of the postulate of equality, there can be no serious question about the adequacy of the fit between the classification along racial lines and the legislative objective to keep the races separate.

At most, the antidiscrimination principle, as presented thus far, establishes a presumption of equality for each individual within the jurisdiction of the state. In essence, this presumption provides that each individual is entitled to equal treatment so long as the state does not pursue any objective in relation to which it could be justified to deny equal treatment to certain classes of individuals. This presumption, however, affords a purely formal and hence ultimately empty kind of protection. Accordingly, although the antidiscrimination principle proves not to be purely formal from the standpoint of its application, the protection it provides each individual seems to amount to no more than an empty formality.

Further inquiry into the supposed value neutrality of the judicial task of measuring the fit between legislative means and ends reveals, as Fiss demonstrates, another major flaw in the antidiscrimination principle. According to Fiss, "the promise of value neutrality is only an illusion" (ibid., 98). If Fiss is correct, then the second major virtue claimed for the antidiscrimination principle by its proponents is no more real than the first. And if the antidiscrimination principle is neither purely formal (from the standpoint of its application) nor value neutral, its application seems bound to require the judiciary to engage in precisely the kind of substantive normative evaluation that the proponents of the principle have steadfastly sought to avoid.

If the function of judges under the antidiscrimination principle were limited to a determination of whether a given legislative classification provides a perfect fit (that is, one that is neither over- nor under-inclusive) or no fit at all between means and ends, then it might be justified to characterize their role as being value neutral. Their function, however, has not been, and realistically cannot be, thus limited. Indeed, if the operative standard were the existence of a perfect fit, then the law prohibiting those younger than eighteen from driving automobiles would be unconstitutional even if it could be proven that a very high percentage—say ninety percent—of fatal automobile accidents are caused by drivers under eighteen. At the other extreme, assuming laws could only be declared unconstitutional in case no fit whatsoever exists between means and ends, a law commanding that all blacks be prohibited from driving automobiles in order to enhance traffic safety would have to be upheld as being valid under the equal protection clause, so long as at least one black person can be shown to have caused, or to be highly likely to cause, a fatal accident. Once one moves beyond these two extremes, however, then the question of how much of a fit is necessary or sufficient to pass constitutional muster becomes crucial to answer. To be able to answer that question, moreover, appeal must be made to some criterion justifying adopting an appropriate standard of fit. And whatever that criterion may be, it cannot be furnished either by the formal principle of justice of by the substantive norms inherent in the state legislation that has come under constitutional attack.

Judicial elaboration of the antidiscrimination principle has led to the adoption of standards of fit to be used in the assessment of the relation between legislative means and ends. To date, three different standards of fit have been adopted by the Supreme Court. The first of these, which is applicable in cases involving social and economic legislation, is the "minimum scrutiny" standard, and it requires that the classification be "rationally related" to a "legitimate" legislative end.[25] The next, more stringent standard, which is applicable in cases involving gender-based classifications, is the "intermediate level scrutiny." This standard requires that gender-based classifications be "substantially related" to the achievement of an "important" state purpose.[26] Finally, the most stringent standard, the "strict scrutiny" test, is applicable to classifications based, among other things, on racial and ethnic origin. To satisfy the strict scrutiny test, it must be shown that the challenged classification is "necessary" to achieve a "compelling" state purpose.[27]

As a practical matter, application of the "mere rationality" test almost invariably leads to a judicial upholding of the challenged legislation's constitutionality, whereas application of the strict scrutiny test almost always results in the constitutional invalidation of the disputed classification (Gunther 1985, 588–89). These facts, however, should not mislead one to believe that application of these various standards of fit can be rendered purely mechanical. As Fiss argues, the concept of fit does not have any "quantitative content" (Fiss 1977, 98). It is therefore impossible for a judge to specify a quantitative formula that would make it possible to know how underinclusive or overinclusive a given legislative classification could be and still be rationally related to the legislative end sought to be achieved. Fiss also adds that there is no value neutral way of determining what constitutes a compelling state purpose, or of defining with any precision the class of differences that ought to render a classification suspect (ibid.). Similarly, there is no objective standard to guide a judge in making decisions concerning the distinction between important state purposes and compelling ones, or between substantially related means and necessary ones. When added together, the lack of objective standards and the inherent imprecision of some of the key categories employed by the antidiscrimination principle leave ample room for judges to invalidate laws when they disagree with the ends sought by the legislature, based on their own conception of the public good. Thus, for instance, under the guise of finding an insufficient fit between a classification and the legitimate legislative purpose the classification is asserted to promote, a judge might invalidate a law because of her disagreement with its purpose. Moreover, by exploiting the inherent imprecision of the terms "compelling," "important," and "legitimate," a judge can lower or raise the burden necessary to overcome the presumption against using a particular difference as the basis of a constitutionally valid classification to suit her own vision of which equalities and inequalities are compatible with the constitutional standard of equality.[28]

Not only does the antidiscrimination principle fail to provide a purely formal or value neutral way of determining the requisite fit between legislative means and ends, but it is also incapable of limiting the constitutional inquiry in equal protection cases to an analysis of the relation between means and ends. This may not be readily apparent because so much constitutional analysis of equal protection is centered on the fit between means and ends that there may be a tendency to neglect the constitutional limitations on the ends pursued by the state. Nevertheless, even where the antidiscrimination principle tolerates the loosest fit between means and ends—that is in relation to general economic legislation—the range of permissible ends that the state may pursue constitutionally is significantly limited. As already mentioned, in the context of the mere rationality test, which requires the minimum level of scrutiny, the state's purpose for enacting the challenged legislation must be legitimate. That means that the state must have a purpose not otherwise prohibited by the Constitution (Novak, Rotunda, and Young 1983, 591). From a global constitutional perspective, therefore, the individual right to equal protection is linked, inter alia, to the individual civil and political rights guaranteed by the Bill of Rights, which imposes limitations on permissible legislative purposes. Accordingly, even in its weakest form, the antidiscrimination principle cannot avoid promoting certain substantive objectives—including those embodied in the Bill of Rights, such as freedom of speech, freedom from unreasonable searches and seizures, and the right to hold property—regardless of whether they conflict with the asserted objectives of the state.

Notwithstanding any appearance to the contrary, the antidiscrimination principle is not color-blind in theory or in practice. That it is not color-blind in theory follows from the fact, demonstrated above, that it does not even guarantee adherence to the postulate of equality. That the antidiscrimination principle is not color-blind in practice, on the other hand, is a consequence of the nature of the strict scrutiny test. Indeed, as will be remembered, application of the strict scrutiny test to racial classifications does not impose a blanket prohibition against such classifications, but merely requires that they be "necessary" to achieve a "compelling" state purpose. Accordingly, it would be quite consistent to uphold particular race-conscious laws under certain circumstances. And this precisely is what the Supreme Court did in the *Korematsu* case, where it upheld a classification based on ethnic ancestry as being "necessary" for the achievement of a "compelling" government interest in the context of World War II. This makes it plain that the antidiscrimination principle does not require by its own terms the adoption of a color-blind standard against which all legislation must be measured.[29]

A final shortcoming of the antidiscrimination principle that deserves some mention is its disproportionate concern with legislative classifications at the expense of the classes of persons who are advantaged or disadvantaged by particular classifications. This shortcoming becomes apparent in the context of affirmative action cases. As Fiss perceives the problem, while preferential treatment for blacks raises vexing constitutional problems,

> The antidiscrimination principle makes it more difficult than it is: the permissibility of preferential treatment is tied to the permissibility of hostile treatment against blacks. The antidiscrimination principle does not formally acknowledge social groups, such as blacks; nor does it offer any special dispensation for conduct that benefits a disadvantaged group. It only knows criteria or classifications; and the color black is as much a racial criterion as the color white. The regime it introduces is a symmetrical one of "color blindness", making the criterion of color, any color, presumptively impermissible. (Fiss 1977, 106)

A constitutional standard that places exclusive emphasis on classification may well be adequate in those contexts in which unequal treatment stems from first-order discrimination. Indeed, where first-order discrimination is the aim of the state, the classification will separate the (intended) victim class from the (intended) nonvictim class and saddle the former with some burden or disadvantage not shared by the latter. Under those circumstances, one is likely to reach the same result regardless of whether one considers the classification itself or the burden imposed on the victim class to be presumptively invalid. In the context of affirmative action, however, shifting the focus from classification to class may lead to a different outcome. To illustrate this, suppose that a state law mandates preferential hiring of blacks for certain public sector positions from which blacks have traditionally been excluded because of racism. Suppose further that the purpose of the law in question is purely remedial. From the standpoint of classification this law is indistinguishable from a racial segregation law: they both define the classes for which they intend different treatment along racial color lines. From the standpoint of the classes that they affect, however, these laws appear quite different. Thus, whereas the segregation law aims to stigmatize blacks and to treat them as inferiors, the preferential hiring law is designed to open for them certain doors that were previously shut because of invidious racism. On the other hand, while whites may be disadvantaged by the preferential hiring law, this disadvantage may not be comparable to that experienced by blacks under segregation laws and appears unlikely to stigmatize whites or to brand them as inferiors.[30]

The remedial use of race-based preferential treatment to eradicate the lingering effects of past first-order discrimination can certainly be justified by reference to the postulate of equality, as can be seen from several arguments made from the perspective of some of the philosophical conceptions of equality discussed in chapters 2 through 5 above. Where the law seeks to enshrine first-order discrimination, however, the postulate of equality requires, and the equal protection clause should demand, color-blindness. Accordingly, to use Fiss' terminology, applying strict scrutiny equally to stigmatizing preferences favoring whites and remedial preferences favoring blacks is to impose symmetry on situations that are essentially "asymmetrical."[31]

The inadequacy of the antidiscrimination principle in the context of affirmative action is perhaps most glaringly exposed, through a comparison of the discrepancies in result that it is likely to produce, depending on whether it is applied to preferential treatment of blacks or of women. As already indicated, under the antidiscrimination principle, racial classifications require strict scrutiny, while gender classifications require only intermediate scrutiny. This means that preferential treatment of blacks should survive constitutional attack only if "necessary" to achieve a "compelling" state purpose, whereas preferential treatment of women would be constitutionally permissible even if only "substantially related" to an "important" state purpose. With this in mind, let us assume that first-order discrimination in education against blacks has been more intense and has left deeper scars than similar discrimination against women. Let us also assume that a state enacts a single law prescribing preferential treatment of blacks and women in admissions to public universities, as a remedial measure to combat the lingering effects of past first-order discrimination. Because of the different levels of scrutiny that it imposes on racial and gender-based classifications, the antidiscrimination principle could quite conceivably require constitutional rejection of the racial preference while according constitutional legitimacy to the gender-based preference. Accordingly, the very same preference could be constitutionally accorded to a victimized group with a lesser need for remedial action, but not to a more victimized group with a substantially greater need for such remedial action. To the extent that this plausible result defies accepted notions of substantive justice and equality, it underscores the inadequacy of the antidiscrimination principle as a mediating constitutional principle.

The antidiscrimination principle is neither purely formal nor value neutral. Accordingly, it cannot obviate the application of substantive values by the judiciary in the process of assessing the constitutionality of equal protection claims. Moreover, the antidiscrimination principle has not been color-blind in its application. Finally, because of its overemphasis on classifications at the expense of classes, the antidiscrimination principle proves to be an unsuitable mediating principle in the context of affirmative action.

A corollary of the impossibility of purely formal or value neutral judicial review of constitutional challenges under the equal protection clause is that judges must impose *some* conception of substantive equality in the course of deciding equal protection cases. To be sure, whatever that conception, it is unlikely to be a full blown philosophical conception, such as those discussed in Part One. Nevertheless, in adjudicating equal protection claims, judges legitimate certain equalities and inequalities while rejecting others, and they vindicate certain claims of compensatory and distributive justice, while casting away others. In the rest of this chapter, I shall set aside the problem of finding an adequate constitutional mediating principle and concentrate on drawing a general picture of the conception of substantive equality that emerges out of the Supreme Court decisions in the equal protection area.

4. *Equal Protection and Delimitation of the State's Domain of Allocation*

There is no agreement among adherents to the postulate of equality concerning the proper delimitation of the domain of allocation—the class of things that a given agent controls for purposes of allocation[32]—under the (real or imputed through the state action doctrine)[33] control of the state. As discussed in chapter 2, under Nozick's conception of libertarian justice, the most extensive domain of allocation that a state ought to control is the very limited one associated with the minimal state. On the other hand, as indicated in the course of the discussion in chapters 3, 4, and 5, the contractarian, utilitarian, and egalitarian conceptions of justice are compatible with a much broader role for the state as agent of allocation, extending certainly as far as that assumed by the welfare state.[34]

In the constitutional context, the equal protection clause has not been interpreted as requiring that states be responsible for any particular domain of allocation.[35] Consistent with this, the Supreme Court has held that the state has no obligation to provide welfare rights,[36] enforceable voting rights,[37] appellate review of criminal convictions,[38] or a free public education.[39]

A state can thus, consistent with its constitutional obligations, choose to adopt a minimal government approach, relying primarily on the distribution of negative rights and calling for state control over a minimal domain of allocation. On the contrary, and also consistent with its constitutional obligations, a state could opt for an activist government with heavy reliance on the distribution of positive rights and the need to maintain state control over a vast domain of allocation. Be that as it may, once a state exercises control over a domain of allocation, it brings that domain within the ambit of the constitutional principle of equality.[40]

There are two principal ways in which a state can directly affect the allocation process of a particular domain. The first of these occurs when the state assumes control of a domain and becomes its agent of allocation. In that case, it is clear that the equal protection clause applies to the distribution. The second way a state can become significantly involved with a domain of allocation is by interfering with the distribution of a hitherto independent domain of allocation. While there is little question but that the interference triggers the application of the equal protection clause,[41] it is uncertain what the proper scope or duration of constitutional scrutiny ought to be in these circumstances.

To illustrate this problem, let us assume a society has a minimal government and relies on a free market economy as the domain of allocation of all material goods. Let us assume further that this arrangement is the most consistent with the postulate of equality, given the particular resources and potential of the society in question, which in this case include moderate scarcity and formal equality of opportunity for each individual—guaranteed by the self-regulating mechanism of the market—to compete for the scarce goods allocated by the market. Under these circumstances, all that the state has to do to preserve formal equality of opportunity is refrain from intervening in the economic marketplace. If the state enacts a law prohibiting blacks from competing for the goods allocated by the market, that law, which interferes with the integrity of the market, can be struck down under the equal protection clause. If the law in question is repealed or struck down as unconstitutional within a short period after its adoption, that may be sufficient to restore the integrity of the marketplace. This would justify refusal to apply the equal protection clause to remedy the inequalities arising as a consequence of the normal operations of the marketplace.[42]

But if the law prohibiting blacks from competing in the marketplace is enforced for several generations, its subsequent repeal is unlikely to be sufficient to lead to restoration of the equality of opportunity that existed prior to its enactment. In that case, because of the wrongful deprivations suffered during the course of several generations, blacks may no longer be on an equal footing with others who compete in the marketplace.[43] Thus, restoring formal equality of opportunity would not compensate blacks for their injuries. To remedy the situation and to restore the integrity of the marketplace, it might be necessary to give blacks a right to fair equality of opportunity or to distribute to them some other goods designed to enable them to become fully competitive again. But the grant of either of these would require positive state action. Hence, a dilemma would arise between the need for positive state intervention which would entail scrutiny under the equal protection clause, and the otherwise legitimate nonintervention by the state in the self-regulating market, which would mean that the equal protection clause is not applicable to the domain of allocation generated by the market.

The constitutional dilemma posed by the apparent need to sustain and deny simultaneously an equal protection right to equality of opportunity can, at least in theory, be resolved. This can be done along lines similar to Goldman's proposed solution to the conflict between the aims of compensatory justice and those of distributive justice, in the context of violations of an accepted principle of just distribution.[44] For the same reason that Goldman has argued that a compensatory scheme ought to be given precedence over a distributive scheme—lest the distributive scheme in question be in danger of being ultimately destroyed—one could claim that equal protection should be extended to a domain of allocation toward which the state has a policy of nonintervention if the integrity of that domain has been jeopardized by unwarranted state interference. Otherwise, the illegitimate state of affairs brought about by positive state-enacted legislation would likely continue indefinitely.

Two important points must be kept in mind as one seeks to discover the equalities promoted by the equal protection clause. First, consistent with currently accepted constitutional interpretation, it is initially up to the state to determine the domains of allocation over which it wishes to exercise control, and only once the state exercises such control does equal protection come into play. Second, the logic that links equal protection with the postulate of equality supports the argument that domains not intended to be controlled by the state, and equalities not contemplated by it, can be brought under the sweep of equal protection to restore an equilibrium upset by morally unwarranted state intervention. Once the equilibrium is restored, however, the affected domain of allocation would again be placed beyond the reach of the equal protection clause.

5. *Equal Protection and Equality of Result*

Only in very limited circumstances has the equal protection clause been interpreted to mandate the achievement of equality of result. These include basic political rights, such as voting, and fundamental personal rights, such as access to the courts in criminal proceedings. A state has no enforceable constitutional obligation to grant the franchise, but once it does,[45] each citizen is entitled to have an equal voice in the election process.[46] From the standpoint of the good distributed, namely voting, each individual is given exactly the same thing, one and no more than one vote, thus leading to equality of result. From the standpoint of the purpose for which the vote is distributed, to allow citizens to participate in the political process, however, each individual is given an equal opportunity—and in this case means-regarding and prospect-regarding equality of opportunity converge—to influence the course of political events.

Similarly, the state has no constitutional obligation to provide for appellate review of criminal convictions, but once it does, it must promote equality of result by providing equal access to each litigant, regardless of ability to pay.[47] In contrast to the situation of the political franchise, equality of result here is not achieved through equal treatment of all members of the relevant class. Instead, access by the indigent must be guaranteed by fee waiver[48] or by the state providing benefits free of cost, for which wealthier litigants would have to pay.[49] Thus, equality of access to rich and poor may require the state to provide marginally unequal treatment to achieve global equality. Equality of result is the goal from the standpoint of access to the courts. From the standpoint of preserving the integrity of the criminal trial process, however, equal opportunity to argue one's cause before the tribunal is paramount. In this instance, a means-regarding equality of opportunity is made necessary to insure that the litigants' prospects are determined by the merits of their case rather than by their relative wealth.

It is significant that in both cases—the political franchise and equal access to the courts—equality of result is a precondition to realizing equality of opportunity, rather than an end in itself. It is also significant that efforts to invoke the equal protection clause to achieve a limited measure of equality of result in the economic sphere have not met with success. Thus, in *Dandridge* v. *Williams* the Supreme Court rejected the proposition that the equal protection clause requires states to provide sufficient welfare benefits to satisfy "the most basic economic needs of [the most] impoverished [people]."[50] The Court's general aversion to imposing on a state a positive obligation to make marginally unequal economic distributions in order to promote some measure of global economic equality is forcefully conveyed in the following passage from Justice Harlan's dissent in *Douglas* v. *California:* "The Equal Protection Clause does not impose on the States 'an affirmative duty to lift the handicaps flowing from differences in economic circumstances.' To so construe it would be to read into the Constitution a philosophy of leveling that would be foreign to many of our basic concepts of the proper relations between government and society."[51]

6. *Equal Protection and Equality of Opportunity*

Standing in sharp contrast to America's dislike for equality of result is its widespread endorsement of the ideal of equality of opportunity.[52]

This ideal underlies Jefferson's notions of a natural aristocracy of virtue and talents emerging to replace the artificial aristocracy of wealth and birth.[53] Means-regarding equality of opportunity sufficient to allow the talents of each individual to determine the prospects of his or her own success is required for a natural aristocracy of talent to arise.

Support for the ideal of equality of opportunity can be found in Supreme Court equal protection opinions, congressional civil rights legislation, executive policy, and among some constitutional scholars.[54] For example, in his opinion in the *Bakke* case, Justice Brennan wrote: "the court today affirms the constitutional power of Federal and State Governments to act affirmatively to achieve equal opportunity for all."[55] Similarly, Title VII of the Civil Rights Act of 1964 imposes an obligation to provide equal opportunity in employment.[56] Furthermore, the third branch of the federal government, the executive, has also declared its commitment to equality of opportunity: "It is the policy of the government of the United States to provide equal opportunity in Federal employment for all qualified persons."[57]

Notwithstanding its declared support for equality of opportunity, the Supreme Court's overall record on this issue is not fully consistent. In cases in which the state has instituted or perpetuated inequality of opportunity on the basis of race, the Court has unequivocally endorsed the ideal of equal opportunity. In cases in which race is not involved, however, several of the Court's opinions seem difficult to reconcile with the equal opportunity principle. As shall be more fully discussed below, this discrepancy may be explained in part by the fact that commitment to equal opportunity does not entail compelling the state to assume responsibility for particular domains to be governed by the principle of equality of opportunity; in part, by the multi-tiered levels of scrutiny analysis adopted by the Supreme Court under the antidiscrimination principle, which seems ill-adapted to deal with the problems posed by inequalities in opportunities;[58] and, in part, because several of the critical factors that bear on the determination of whether equality of opportunity is achieved—such as a comparative scale of merits, qualifications, or talents, or the means precisely to rank diverse education offerings—are not sufficiently amenable to judicial evaluation.

To the extent that the Constitution does not compel the states to assume responsibility for any particular domain of allocation, a judge could consistently accept the constitutionalization of equal opportunity, and yet refuse to redress inequalities of opportunity relating to domains of allocation for which the state has not assumed responsibility. For example, formal equality of opportunity in employment can be achieved conceivably without government intervention through the self-regulating economic marketplace. Thus, if a private employer deprives a job applicant of an opportunity to compete for the position that she seeks, there would be a deprivation of equal opportunity but not a violation of the applicant's equal protection rights.

Once a state has decided to allocate scarce employment positions or to provide state-financed public education, however, judicial refusal to redress inequalities of opportunity with respect to those domains of allocation would seem difficult to square with the notion that equal protection constitutionalizes equal opportunity. As already mentioned, there are apparent inconsistencies in the Supreme Court's handling of equal opportunity claims arising in connection with state allocation of employment and education. Nevertheless, these apparent inconsistencies can be explained to a significant extent in terms of the second and third factors enumerated above—deficiencies in the antidiscrimination principle and the presence of factual issues not readily amenable to judicial evaluation.

When the basis for unequal opportunity has been race, the Supreme Court has unequivocally endorsed the ideal of equality of opportunity. In its landmark decision in *Brown* v. *Board of Education,* the Court struck down, as violative of equal protection, state laws mandating or permitting the racial segregation of public schools. The Court found racially segregated educational facilities to be "inherently unequal,"[59] a particularly significant finding in light of the Court's general perception of the central role of education in shaping future opportunities. In the Court's own words:

> Today, education is perhaps the most important function of state and local governments. . . . It is a principal instrument in awakening the child to cultural values, in preparing him for later professional training. . . . In these days, it is doubtful that any child may reasonably be expected to succeed in life if he is denied the opportunity of an education. Such an opportunity, where the state has undertaken to provide it, is a right which must be made available to all on equal terms.[60]

Strictly speaking, the individual right created by the Court in *Brown* is not an equal opportunity right, but instead a right to equality of result with respect to the allocation of a racially integrated public school education. In other words, pursuant to *Brown* every child living in a state that has decided to provide public school education is entitled to a place in a racially integrated public school. However, the equality of result mandated by *Brown* is best interpreted as being a necessary prerequisite to the acquisition of an equal opportunity "to succeed in life," which in the context of contemporary society can be understood to entail an equal opportunity to compete for scarce places in institutions of higher education and scarce employment positions.

Keeping in mind that the equality of result prescribed by *Brown* is necessary to promote the broader equality of opportunity "to succeed in life," the Court's broad language cited above could be interpreted reasonably as establishing a constitutional right to equal education, predicated on the Court's belief in the paramount importance of equality of opportunity. Moreover, as *Brown* and its progeny demonstrate, it is also constitutionally required that the state take the affirmative steps necessary to provide meaningful equality of opportunity to those persons who have been wrongfully cast as inferiors.[61] Hence, where equality of opportunity was purposefully undermined by state-imposed segregation, the equal protection clause mandates not only repeal of segregation laws but also achieving integration, a process that often necessitates undertaking such race-conscious and affirmative remedial steps as busing.[62]

By contrast, when race is not involved, certain Supreme Court decisions appear difficult to reconcile with the notion of the constitutionalization of equality of opportunity. In *Kotch* v. *River Port Pilot Commissioners*, river pilot jobs were awarded to relatives and friends of incumbents, but the Court rejected the equal protection challenge of disappointed applicants, principally because no suspect classification was involved. The dissent, however, stated that a standard of "consanguinity" was impermissible,[63] a position that is fully intelligible only in the context of adherence to the principle of equality of opportunity. Moreover, the majority opinion may have been heavily influenced by mechanical application of the antidiscrimination principle. Indeed, instead of focusing on whether a classification that separates relatives and friends from the rest of society is "suspect," the majority could have framed the issue before it in terms of whether the state's allocation of public employment to relatives and friends of incumbents is compatible with the state's obligation to comply with equal protection requirements. If the latter approach had been taken, it seems more probable that the majority would have sided with equal opportunity rather than with nepotism.[64]

In another case, *Personnel Administrator of Massachusetts* v. *Feeney*, an equal protection challenge to an absolute preference for qualified veterans to fill state civil service positions was rejected by the Supreme Court. The justification for this preference was to reward veterans, to ease their transition back to civilian life, and to encourage patriotic service.[65] Although the Court found veteran hiring preferences "an awkward—and, . . . unfair—exception to the widely shared view that merit and merit alone should prevail in the employment policies of government,"[66] it nonetheless held the state purpose to be legitimate and thus the state's requirements under the Fourteenth Amendment satisfied. Because the veteran preference in *Feeney* had a significant compensatory and distributive aim, as well as design to encourage conduct that would contribute to the public good, the Court's holding, unlike that in *Kotch,* is not necessarily inconsistent with a general adherence to the equal opportunity principle.

In the context of public school education, pursuit of the ideal of equality of opportunity suffered a setback when the Supreme Court refused to recognize a fundamental right to an equal education in *San Antonio Independent School District* v. *Rodriguez.* The plaintiffs in *Rodriguez* had charged that Texas' system of financing public school education, relying heavily on local property taxes, resulted in substantial inter-district disparities in per pupil expenditures.[67] In fact, state expenditures for the education of children living in wealthy neighborhoods were substantially higher than its expenditures for those living in poor neighborhoods.[68]

The decision in *Rodriguez* may be viewed as insensitive to the ideal of equality of opportunity. That view, however, may not be altogether warranted. Indeed, the Court emphasized that there was no absolute deprivation of a meaningful opportunity to enjoy the benefits of a public school education. At the same time, the Court pointed out that it was a matter of dispute whether a more expensive education was a better education.[69] Ideally, a state's decision to create and sustain a free public school system should create a fundamental individual right to an equal public school education. In practice, however, an individual's right to an equal education may not be susceptible to sufficient concrete definition to be protected consistently. As stated by the Court in *Rodriguez,* because "of the infinite variables affecting the educational process, [no] system [can really] assure equal quality of education."[70] Therefore, it may be that the Supreme Court refused to proclaim a fundamental right to an equal education more because of doubts about its feasibility than because of doubts about its desirability.

The equal protection clause, as interpreted by the Supreme Court, only rarely requires equality of result, and then only as a prerequisite to achieving some broader-based equality of opportunity. The principle of equality of opportunity, on the other hand, is deeply rooted in the American ideology and enjoys a definite constitutional dimension. The constitutional contours of this principle are by no means clear, as it has been applied somewhat inconsistently. Nevertheless the equal opportunity principle is clearly applicable in cases where morally reprehensible state action has interfered with the opportunities of those persons whom it has treated as inferiors.

CHAPTER SEVEN

The Constitutional Dimension of Affirmative Action

In this chapter, I examine the logical progression from racial segregation to affirmative action, by briefly retracing the Supreme Court's path from *Brown* v. *Board of Education* through various school desegregation cases, leading finally to the Court's encounter with affirmative action. After that, I analyze the ten principal affirmative action decisions that have been rendered by the Supreme Court before 1990. These cases either consider the constitutionality of affirmative action or determine its validity under federal civil rights legislation, in a way that sheds light on the constitutional issues. Moreover, I assess these decisions both in terms of the structural grammar of equality and of the conceptions of distributive and compensatory justice developed in chapter 1.

1. The Logical Progression from Segregation to Affirmative Action

Ideally, the spheres of education and employment are, with rare exceptions, spheres of assimilation in which the effect of differences in race or sex ought to remain completely neutral.[1] Absent a history of first-order discrimination, equality of opportunity could be satisfied by implementing color- and gender-blind constitutional principles. Once a state has practiced official racial segregation, however, a mere return to colorblindness may not be sufficient to lead to integration. This is clearly demonstrated by the aftermath of *Brown*. Merely lifting legal barriers or relying on voluntary measures did not lead to school integration. States therefore had to pursue integration through affirmative race-conscious remedies, such as race-related assignments to particular schools.[2] Further, to offset the competitive advantage of the beneficiaries of unequal elementary and secondary education, it may be necessary to grant a preference in the competitive educational and employment arena to blacks who were denied an equal elementary or secondary school education. Viewed from this perspective, affirmative action is arguably but a preference designed to offset other unjustified preferences, and to restore fair competition.

From the overall standpoint of assuring equality of opportunity, there may be an unbroken logical progression from segregation to affirmative action. Nonetheless, shifts in the balance of equalities and inequalities encountered along the path to full assimilation give rise to several vexing and controversial issues. Segregation permits association of inequality with inferiority.[3] Repeal of state-supported segregation, on the other hand, establishes formal equality. But to the extent that formal equality preserves inequality of opportunity, color-blind policies would merely perpetuate the inequalities caused by a prolonged period of segregation.[4]

Color-conscious policies adopted by a state to promote public school integration, on the other hand, may treat all the groups who are subject to them equally. Thus, if both black and white children are transported away from their own neighborhood in order to integrate a school system, both racial groups are treated equally. Nevertheless, if blacks seek integration and whites oppose it, equal treatment and lot-regarding equality are likely to be accompanied by subject-regarding inequality. Moreover, assuming that some but not all whites, and some but not all blacks, must be transported outside of their neighborhood to achieve integration, then inequalities will arise within each group.

Consistent with the goal of public school integration to provide each child with an equal education, desegregation does not exclude any child from a free public education. Further, the subject-regarding inequalities arising out of differences in preferences and expectations are arguably justifiable. A black person's preference for integration is a preference for not being treated as an inferior, which deserves priority over a white person's preference for attending a neighborhood school, for reasons of convenience or of racism. Finally, inequalities between individual members of the same racial group may be justified so long as the means of selection employed to determine particular school assignments are consistent with the postulate of equality. This follows from the fact that equal treatment of each individual within each racial group would make it impossible as a practical matter to achieve integration.

Unlike color-conscious policies used to integrate public school systems, preferential university admissions or public employment must exclude some individuals in order to include others. Further, there is another important distinction between school integration and affirmative action. School desegregation is a direct and complete remedy for school segregation—it provides the desired integration that segregation blocks and eliminates the evil of school segregation—whereas preferential treatment is often neither a direct nor a complete remedy. Indeed, preferential treatment seems to be a direct remedy only if the wrongful exclusions it seeks to offset occurred at the university admissions or job hiring levels. If the exclusions occurred at the level of elementary or secondary school, however, the remedy may be both indirect and incomplete. It is indirect if the university or employer has not done anything to deny an applicant an equal opportunity, and it is incomplete because it does nothing to eliminate the source of the problem, which is located at the elementary and secondary school level.

Finally, there is an apparent difference in the way the processes of school desegregation and affirmative action cast the relationship between the individual and the group, respectively. Both of these must take group characteristics into account. Affirmative action, however, would seem to invert the specific relationship between individual and group compared to the relationship found in school desegregation. In the context of school desegregation, group characteristics are invoked for purposes of facilitating the achievement of individual-regarding equality. Racial assignments are thus made, but only because they seem necessary to insure an equal education in an integrated school system for every child. Affirmative action, by contrast, appears to single out individuals for special treatment for purposes of promoting group-regarding equality. Thus, when a less well qualified member of one group is preferred over a better-qualified member of another group, these individuals may not seem to be considered in their own right, but rather as representatives of the respective groups to which they belong. From this, it may be tempting to conclude that, whereas in school desegregation the group is subordinated to the individual, in affirmative action, on the contrary, the individual is subordinated to the group.

In sum, the step from race-conscious remedies in the context of school desegregation to the race-conscious practices associated with affirmative action may correspond to a single step in the logical progression from segregation to assimilation. Nevertheless, this single step cannot be taken without raising a number of difficult issues. Chief among these are the place of affirmative action in the context of the relation between the aims of distributive justice and those of compensatory justice, the relation between preferential treatment and the rights of innocent third parties disadvantaged by its implementation, and the justification for affirmative action consistent with constitutionally permissible parameters for the relationship between the individual and the group. With these issues firmly in mind, we now turn to an examination of the Supreme Court's affirmative action cases.

2. *Equal Protection and Affirmative Action*

Starting with its 1978 decision in *Bakke,* the Supreme Court has handed down before 1990 ten decisions squarely addressing the legitimacy of affirmative action. In these cases the Supreme Court addressed the issue of the legitimacy of affirmative action in various different contexts, including public university admissions, employment hiring, promotions and layoffs, and public work contracts. Also, the Court has scrutinized both race-based and gender-based affirmative action plans. Taken together, what is most remarkable about these ten decisions, however, is their failure to establish authoritatively or clearly the constitutional boundaries of affirmative action.[5] Indeed, in none of the cases where the constitutionality of affirmative action was addressed has a majority on the Court joined together in a single opinion.[6] Nevertheless, since the Court's decision in *Bakke,* two distinct positions have emerged. The first, advanced by Justice Powell in that case, interprets equal protection as requiring that the same protection be given to every person regardless of race.[7] The second is perhaps best captured by Justice Blackmun's statement in *Bakke* that "in order to treat some persons equally, we must treat them differently."[8] The first position promotes equal treatment, or marginal equality. The second position stresses equal results, or global equality, even if that requires imposing or tolerating marginal inequalities.

Each of these positions tends to go hand in hand with a different constitutional test and a different conception of justice. Justices who adhere to the marginal equality position generally link equal treatment to the strict scrutiny test and to acceptance of affirmative action as constitutional only when it serves narrowly compensatory goals[9]—that is, when it is provided by an actual wrongdoer to redress the harm inflicted upon actual victims.[10] Thus, notwithstanding certain statement to the contrary, no justice has in fact strictly adhered the maxim that "the Constitution is color blind."[11] Proponents of the global equality position, on the other hand, are willing to allow preferential treatment so long as it meets the less stringent intermediate scrutiny test and is consistent with legitimate objectives of distributive justice or with aims that are at least in part distributive.[12]

The issue of the constitutionality of affirmative action first reached the Supreme Court in the 1974 case of *DeFunis* v. *Odegaard,* which involved a challenge to a preferential program favoring minority applicants for admission at a state university law school. The Court, however, refused to hear the case on the merits on the grounds that it was moot. The constitutionality of preferential treatment was raised again in 1978, in *Regents of the University of California* v. *Bakke.* This time the issue was addressed, but by only five of the justices. These justices agreed that affirmative action is constitutional under certain circumstances, but agreed on little else.

Two years after *Bakke,* in *Fullilove* v. *Kluznick,* the entire Supreme Court for the first time squarely addressed the constitutionality of affirmative action programs, and six of the justices held the programs involved there to be constitutional. Moreover, since *Fullilove,* there have been seven additional Supreme Court decisions bearing on the constitutionality of affirmative action. Not until *City of Richmond* v. *J. A. Croson Co.* decided in 1989 did a majority on the Court even agree on the constitutional standard applicable in affirmative action cases. In that case a majority of justices for the first time adopted the strict scrutiny test for race-based affirmative action. As we shall see below, however, the five justices who settled on that test did not agree on what it actually requires in the context of affirmative action. Accordingly, although *Croson* could signal an important turning point in affirmative action jurisprudence, the new order that it announces may well be more apparent than real.

3. The Supreme Court Affirmative Action Cases

A. The Bakke Decision

In *Bakke* the plaintiff challenged the University of California at Davis' medical school's special admissions program, which was designed to assure the admission of a specified number of black and other minority applicants. Under that program, sixteen of the one hundred places in the first-year medical school class were set aside to be filled with minority applicants.[13] All minority and nonminority candidates could compete on an equal basis for the remaining eighty-four places (276, 289, 305). Alan Bakke, a white applicant to the medical school, was rejected. In both 1973 and 1974, when Bakke applied, "applicants were admitted under the special program with grade point averages, MCAT scores, and benchmark scores significantly lower than [his]." Bakke alleged that the special admissions program violated his rights under the equal protection clause, as he had been rejected because of his race (276–78).

There were several purposes for Davis' special admissions program, some distributive, others at least partially compensatory. One purpose was to integrate the medical profession, a distributive goal. A second purpose was to counter discrimination, a broadly compensatory and perhaps also distributive goal. The third purpose, to increase the number of physicians willing to work in underserved areas, reveals a sensitivity to cultural differences and an awareness of the reality of segregated residential patterns. The final purpose, different in kind from the others, was to "obtain the educational benefits that flow from an ethnically diverse student body" (306).

Bakke provides a prime example of the divisiveness and fragmentation that has characterized the Supreme Court's handling of affirmative action cases. Not only did the Court in *Bakke* fail to produce a majority opinion, but it did not even manage to muster a single majority in support of its decision. The justices in *Bakke* were divided essentially into three groups: one group of four who, as already mentioned, altogether refused to address the constitutionality of affirmative action; another group of four who embraced the global equality position and formulated a fairly broad constitutional justification for affirmative action; and Justice Powell, the architect of the marginal equality position, whose pivotal decision made him side in part with the first group of four and in part with the second. The first group of four justices felt that it was unnecessary to reach the constitutional issue raised in *Bakke* because it was of the opinion that the Davis dual admissions program violated statutory law. The second group of four justices, on the other hand, felt that the Davis dual admissions program was constitutional. Finally, Justice Powell sided with the latter four justices in as much as he felt it necessary to reach the constitutional issue, and as he concluded that affirmative action is constitutional under certain circumstances. Because he thought that the affirmative action plan at stake in *Bakke* was overly broad to pass constitutional muster, however, he sided with the first group of four for the proposition that Alan Bakke had been wrongfully denied admission to the Davis Medical School.

According to Justice Powell, the Davis dual admissions program violated Alan Bakke's equal protection rights. He found it particularly objectionable that, because of his race, Bakke was completely foreclosed from competing for admission to any of the sixteen medical school places set aside for minority applicants. In Justice Powell's view, Bakke, an innocent individual, was being asked, because of his race, to bear the brunt of redressing group grievances that were not of his making (298). Emphasizing that the equal protection of individuals, not groups, is the concern of the Fourteenth Amendment, Justice Powell declared that Bakke could not be burdened for the benefit of a group unless this was necessary to accomplish a compelling state interest (299, 309–10). And absent prior discrimination by Davis involving some statutory or constitutional violation, Justice Powell was unwilling to find the requisite compelling state purpose.

Justice Powell's opinion, however, does not flatly reject the use of racially based preferential treatment in state university admissions in the absence of wrongdoing by the entity providing affirmative action.

While he rejects rigid quotas absent such wrongdoing, Justice Powell indicates that preferential treatment can be constitutional, if it is used to promote diversity among the student body and if it guarantees that each applicant regardless of race shall receive individual consideration with respect to each of the places that the state university has decided to allocate.

Consistent with Justice Powell's *Bakke* opinion, admissions programs such as the one at Davis can only be constitutionally acceptable and satisfy the strict scrutiny test if they fit within the paradigm of compensation—that is, if they involve an actual wrongdoer compensating his actual victims. Indeed, not only does Justice Powell assert that a state university must be a wrongdoer to establish an admissions quota, but he intimates that the beneficiaries of such quota must be "actual" victims rather than merely victims of "societal discrimination"—that is, discrimination occurring within a domain of allocation or sphere of interaction other than that within which the contested affirmative action plan is designed to operate (307–10).

In contrast to the narrow compensatory departure it allows from the equal treatment principle, Justice Powell's marginal equality position tolerates an extensive distributive departure for purposes of fostering student diversity. Justice Powell expresses his approval of the Harvard admissions plan, which, unlike the Davis plan, is supposed to give full consideration to each individual applicant, with race counting as one among the many factors weighed to arrive at admissions decisions. As the justices joining Justice Brennan's opinion in *Bakke* indicate, however, the differences between the Harvard and Davis plans may be more a matter of form than of substance (324). To the extent that the racial factor is not sufficiently quantifiable, it can be easily manipulated to yield the same proportion of minority students as an inflexible quota would. Accordingly, Justice Powell's broad approval of distributive affirmative action could be used to achieve what he seeks to prevent through his narrow toleration of compensatory admissions quotas.

In general, the reasons behind Justice Powell's toleration of departures from the equal treatment principle for both compensatory and distributive purposes are not sufficiently articulated to justify the particular lines he draws between constitutionally permissible and impermissible affirmative action. From the standpoint of compensatory justice, any departure from the equal treatment principle by an advocate of the marginal equality position should be justified, but Justice Powell fails to provide any satisfactory reason why he draws the line at the paradigm of compensation. Since Davis instituted its preferential admissions voluntarily, it is difficult to understand Justice Powell's insistence that such a plan is unconstitutional unless provided by an actual wrongdoer. Moreover, given the historical setting in which *Bakke* arose, it is difficult to understand from the victims' standpoint, why the Constitution should distinguish between "actual" victims and victims of "societal discrimination."

By limiting the constitutionally permissible compensatory benefits of affirmative action to actual victims, Justice Powell forecloses the possibility of using preferential medical school admissions as a remedy for discrimination elsewhere in the state system. Yet, from a practical standpoint, as Justice Brennan points out, it is precisely those applicants to Davis' medical school who have been denied an equal education at the elementary and secondary school levels, and who have thus been denied the necessary tools to achieve means-regarding equality of opportunity sufficient to compete effectively for medical school admissions, who are most deserving of receiving preferential treatment.

Justice Powell's broad acceptance of distributive race-conscious university admissions programs, on the other hand, is based on his belief that a state university's goal of a diverse student body amounts to a compelling state purpose (315, 319). Whether that belief is justified, particularly in the case of a medical school, is certainly subject to debate. In any event, once race is accepted as a proper factor to consider for purposes of achieving student diversity, it is susceptible to manipulation for restricting entry by members of certain groups. Thus, for example, if a relatively high proportion of Asians would gain admission to medical school based solely on a competitive admissions process, a state university could limit the number of its Asian medical students under the guise of pursuing a more diverse student body.

Unlike Justice Powell, the four justices who joined Justice Brennan's opinion did not resort to a mechanical application of the antidiscrimination principle. Actually, although the Brennan group applied an intermediate level of scrutiny to the classification involved in Bakke, their adherence to the antidiscrimination principle was more a matter of form than of substance.[14] The four justices acknowledged that *Bakke* did not fit neatly into the "prior analytic framework" (358), and having embraced the global equality position, they concentrated on the nature of the classes affected by the special admissions program rather than on the classification involved.[15] This approach enabled them to conclude that, when confronted with unequal needs and unequal conditions, equal protection can go beyond equal treatment.

The class disadvantaged by Davis' special admissions program was that of white applicants, like Bakke. According to the Brennan group, however, the different treatment accorded to that class did not relegate its members to the position of inferiors or saddle them with any social stigma (357). Moreover, as Justice Brennan clearly stated, the ultimate purpose of the special admissions program was the institution of equal opportunity for all, a purpose that cannot be achieved by neutrality or equal treatment because of the disparate effects of past and present discrimination (369).

Establishing equality of opportunity is a distributive goal, but it does not by itself provide a sufficient constitutional justification for the preferential treatment accorded by Davis. According to the four justices, it is not enough that minorities are chronically underrepresented in the medical profession—which is indicative of the fact that their prospects of becoming physicians are much lower than those of whites—such underrepresentation must be causally linked to past state discrimination. Thus, in the opinion of the four justices, a state is constitutionally entitled to adopt a race-conscious preferential treatment program to "remove the disparate racial impact . . . [produced by] past discrimination (369). Insofar as the constitutionality of affirmative action depends on the proof of past discrimination, it appears to require a compensatory component. However, insofar as it depends on the existence of a plan to combat present competitive disadvantage—particularly since it is permissible for such a plan to grant preferential treatment to individual members of the discriminated group who have not themselves experienced such discrimination—it seems to contain a distributive component (363). Although, as envisaged by the Brennan group, an affirmative action plan must combine compensatory and distributive elements, such a plan is arguably neither plainly compensatory nor plainly distributive. Indeed, such a plan does not have to provide for compensation of actual victims of discrimination, or prefer an actual victim over another member of the preferred group who may have only experienced societal discrimination or who may have never personally confronted direct discrimination.

Besides conflating distributive and compensatory concerns, Justice Brennan's opinion deflates the issue of the innocent white victim of preferential treatment. Thus, Bakke may feel that Davis' dual admission program cost him a place in the entering class at the medical school. As Justice Brennan sees it, though: "There is a reasonable likelihood that, but for pervasive racial discrimination, [Bakke] would have failed to qualify for admission even in the absence of Davis' special admissions program (365–66). If this argument is correct, then Bakke obviously lacks a legitimate claim, as he has no right to keep the ill-gotten benefits of invidious past discrimination. But since it is conceivable that a white applicant rejected under an affirmative action plan would have succeeded absent the plan and absent past discrimination, the issue of the innocent white victim remains genuine.

The interplay of equalities and inequalities surrounding a preferential treatment plan, such as Davis', that attempts to remedy the present effects of past discrimination is highly complex. The past discrimination consisted of unequal treatment because of race; more specifically, a state sponsored denial of formal equality of opportunity to blacks. Indeed, as Justice Brennan indicates, at one time there were penal sanctions for anyone attempting to educate blacks (371). Such past discrimination deprived blacks of the means to compete on an equal footing with whites, dramatically reducing their prospects of success.

Mere termination of state-sponsored discrimination restores formal (means-regarding) equality of opportunity, but tends to perpetuate prospect-regarding inequality of opportunity and group-regarding as well as individual-regarding inequalities of result. Preferential treatment, on the other hand, establishes both means-regarding and prospect-regarding inequality of opportunity for individuals. In addition, it promotes prospect-regarding equality of opportunity for groups and group-regarding equality of result.

In the last analysis, the Brennan group's opinion in *Bakke,* which accords constitutional legitimacy to preferential treatment designed to remedy the present effects of past discrimination, may establish an apparently fair and attractive standard, but it fails to provide a sufficiently comprehensive justification in support of that standard. Further, the opinion does not advance any satisfactory proposal for dealing with the problem of the innocent white victim or for determining the proper constitutional balance between individual-regarding and group-regarding concerns.

B. The Weber Decision

In the 1979 case of *United Steelworkers* v. *Weber,* the Supreme Court upheld by five to four a private employer's voluntary racial quota under Title VII of the Civil Rights Act of 1964. *Weber* did not raise any constitutional equal protection issues and did not address what Title VII requires.[16] The principal issue in *Weber* was whether Title VII *forbids* a private employer from voluntarily adopting a racial quota to remedy a racial imbalance in its workforce (199–200). Nevertheless, the case sheds further light relevant to the constitutional issues raised by affirmative action, particularly as a consequence of the Court's examination of statutory language forbidding an employer "to discriminate against any individual . . . because of such individual's race."[17] The justices that joined Justice Brennan's majority opinion interpreted the above language from the perspective of the global equality position, whereas the dissenting justices' approach was clearly anchored in the marginal equality position.

Although the affirmative action in *Weber* was characterized as being "voluntary," it was, in fact, hardly so. Indeed, the employer instituted the plan pursuant to a collective bargaining agreement with the union representing both its black and white employees (198–99).[18] Moreover, the employer had already been subject to prosecution for violations of federal laws in connection with its racially discriminatory practices at several of its plants other than the one involved in *Weber*. Thus, as one commentator observes, "the employer in *Weber*, whatever its other motivations, hoped that the race-conscious training program would divert attention from the fact that it had long been engaged in discriminatory employment practices that violated federal law."[19]

Prior to the adoption of the employer's affirmative action plan, because of exclusion of blacks from craft unions, only 1.83 percent of the skilled craftworkers at the plant were black, even though the workforce in that plant's geographical area was 39 percent black. Pursuant to the affirmative action plan, instead of hiring already trained outsiders, the employer established a training program to prepare its own workers to fill craft openings. Selection of trainees was made on the basis of seniority, with the proviso that 50 percent of the new trainees had to be black until the percentage of black skilled craftworkers approximated 39 percent. Weber, a white worker rejected for the training program, although he had more seniority than several of the black employees who were accepted, brought class action alleging that the plan violated Title VII (198–99).

In upholding the validity of the plan, Justice Brennan, writing for the majority, stated, "The purposes of the plan mirror those of the statute. Both were designed to break down old patterns of racial segregation and hierarchy. Both were structured 'to open employment opportunities for Negroes in occupations which have been traditionally closed to them'" (208, quoting remarks of Senator Humphrey). Accordingly, Justice Brennan's opinion legitimates the racial quota involved in *Weber* on primarily distributive grounds. What he endorses as statutorily permissible is a race-conscious practice, the purpose of which is to bring about equality of opportunity in the employment of skilled craftworkers. Although the 50 percent quota requires an interim equality of result in the pursuit of equality of opportunity, Justice Brennan makes clear that Title VII permits the race-conscious pursuit of equality of opportunity not of equality of result—in this case group-regarding equality of result. As Justice Brennan points out, the plan "is not intended to maintain racial balance, but simply to eliminate a manifest racial imbalance" (208).

The plan's focus on eliminating racial imbalance gives it a remedial purpose bearing traces of a backward-looking compensatory concern. Moreover, while there can be no doubt in the context of *Weber* that there has been systematic wrongdoing harming a significant number of blacks, the plan does not fit within the paradigm of compensation, either on the side of the wrongdoer or on that of the victim. The employer was guilty of wrongdoing at other plants, but no proof of such wrongdoing had been established regarding the plant affected by the quota. On the other hand, whereas a large number of blacks had been wrongfully excluded from the skilled crafts trade because of their race, the beneficiaries of the quota were not necessarily chosen from among those who had been victimized.

Requiring proof of wrongdoing before permitting a quota like that in *Weber* is undesirable, as it leads to an unnecessary proliferation of litigation while thwarting wrongdoers who voluntarily seek to remedy their wrongs. On the other hand, a purely forward-looking distributive approach appears deficient in that it would not permit a sufficient distinction between quotas providing marginal inequalities designed to eliminate inequalities of opportunity attributable to racism and those that foster such marginal inequalities to promote group-regarding equalities of result in employment. Like his approach in *Bakke,* Justice Brennan's opinion in *Weber* ultimately relies on a justification of affirmative action that is in part compensatory and in part distributive. Nothing in his opinion in *Weber* indicates, however, how these two concerns should be reconciled or how the compensatory concern may be met, in spite of the above-mentioned significant deviation from the paradigm of compensation.

C. The Fullilove Decision

Unlike in *Bakke,* in *Fullilove* v. *Klutznick* the constitutionality of affirmative action programs had to be squarely faced. By a majority of six to three, the Supreme Court upheld the constitutionality of an affirmative action program enacted by Congress to remedy present inequalities arising from the continuing effects of past discrimination.[20] In addition, the Court addressed the issue left unresolved by Bakke: the harm preferential treatment causes to innocent nonminority competitors (484–85). Finally, in upholding Congressional authority to enact affirmative action programs, the Court emphasized Congress' constitutional mandate to achieve "equality of economic opportunity" (490). Notwithstanding these developments, however, the court fell far short of providing a full-blown picture of the constitutional dimensions of affirmative action.

Fullilove involved a challenge to the "minority set-aside" provision of the Public Works Employment Act of 1977, enacted by Congress to alleviate national unemployment (456–57). The act provided for the distribution of federal funds to state and local governments for public works projects. The minority set-aside provision declared that no grant would be made for any "local public works project" unless at least ten percent of such grant would be expended for minority business enterprises ("MBE"). Under this scheme, ten percent of the funds allocated for a project would have to be expended in procuring services or supplies from MBEs (456–57). Moreover, within this framework, MBEs were to be awarded contracts even if their bids were not the lowest, provided that their higher bids merely reflected attempts to cover increased costs due to the present effects of past discrimination (474).

In assessing the burden of the set-aside on innocent nonminority businesses, Chief Justice Burger, writing for the Court, stated: "It is not a constitutional defect in this program that it may disappoint the expectations of nonminority firms. When effectuating a limited and properly tailored remedy to cure the effects of prior discrimination, such 'a sharing of the burden' by innocent parties is not impermissible" (484). The chief justice went on to observe that the actual burden on innocent nonminority businesses was light, as they were excluded from competing in what amounted to 0.25 percent of overall construction contracting opportunities (484–85*n*.72). In his concurring opinion, Justice Powell also emphasized the lightness of the burden on nonminorities. Moreover, using a balancing test, he concluded that the government interest in enacting the set-aside provision outweighed any "marginal unfairness" to the innocent nonminority businesses (514–15).

Because of the lightness of the burden on nonminority contractors, the issue of the innocent victim of preferential treatment was resolved without difficulty in *Fullilove.* This, however, leaves open the question whether a balancing test is appropriate when an innocent victim has suffered more than a marginal injury. Indeed, it seems quite reasonable to tolerate a 0.25 percent reduction in the prospects of success of nonminority businesses, if that is necessary in order to achieve a worthwhile government purpose. But the same may not be true in a case in which an innocent nonminority person's prospects of success would be reduced, for example, by forty percent. Yet, it is conceivable that, even in the latter case, application of the balancing test would lead to validation of preferential treatment. For example, the government interest in compensating blacks who have been systematically excluded from public employment may plausibly be deemed to outweigh an innocent white person's interest in not having his prospects of obtaining public employment reduced by forty percent. But nothing in Justice Powell's opinion in *Fullilove* indicates whether there are any constitutional limits to balancing government interests against the harms that preferential treatment inflicts upon innocent members of nonpreferred groups.

The affirmative action plan approved in *Fullilove* appears to be distributive in nature. The purpose of Congress was to increase the number of minority businesses who are awarded public works contracts. As interpreted by the Supreme Court's majority opinion, however, the affirmative action plan involved in *Fullilove* was so narrowly circumscribed as to be arguably but the functional equivalent of a compensatory scheme. Indeed, under this interpretation, the minority set-aside applied only to those who were actual victims of discrimination, and the preference it granted was narrowly tailored to compensate only for those increased costs of doing business that could be attributed to the effects of past discrimination (474). Under these circumstances, the partial setting aside of the general distributive principle of awarding contracts to the lowest bidders could be justified in terms of the need to provide compensation for past violations of distributive rights. In short, because of the particular facts involved and the Court's interpretation of the preferential treatment before it, the decision in *Fullilove* leaves the constitutional contours of affirmative action vague and uncertain.

D. Affirmative Action and Layoffs: The Stotts and Wygant Decisions

Six of the seven affirmative action cases decided by the Supreme Court following *Fullilove* presented the issue of the validity of preferential treatment in the context of public employment. In four of these cases, the Court upheld the affirmative action plan involved; in the remaining two, *Stotts* and *Wygant,* which both involved race-conscious preferences in the context of layoffs, however, the Court struck down the affirmative action plans before it.

Layoffs are usually the byproduct of a shrinking economy. Frequently, as cutbacks in production are called for, some workers must be laid off, and this is customarily carried out in an order of reverse seniority, whereby the employer must dismiss workers with less seniority before laying off others who possess greater job seniority.

The use of seniority as a shield against layoffs is also apt to foil the achievement of the distributive goals sought to be realized through the implementation of affirmative action plans. Let us assume, for example, that, within one year, through the use of preferential hiring an employer has increased the proportion of blacks in his work force from 0 to 10 percent. Suppose now, that the next year, because of a recession, the employer has to lay off 10 percent of his workforce. It is clear in that case that, if layoffs must proceed strictly in an order of reverse seniority, no blacks will be able to keep their jobs. To avoid such results, several affirmative action plans have provided for some modification or suspension of the rule that layoffs must adhere strictly to the order of reverse seniority. That, however, inevitably leads certain more senior non-minority workers to lose jobs that they would have kept but for the affirmative action plan. Moreover, losing one's job seems to amount to a substantially greater injury than merely failing to obtain a position for which one competes.

The clash between the remedial aims of affirmative action programs and the workings of the seniority system is the principal issue raised in

Firefighters Local Union No. 1784 v. *Stotts*. In *Stotts* the issue was whether the aims of a remedial affirmative action plan could take precedence over the dictates of an established seniority system in the face of mandatory layoffs. The case arose in the context of a statutory dispute under Title VII and of a dispute concerning the terms of a consent decree.[21] Although the constitutionality of the affirmative action plan was not at issue, the Supreme Court's decision in *Stotts* sheds some interesting new light on the issue of harm to the innocent third party and on the relation between the individual and the group. *Stotts* involved a consent decree entered into by the city of Memphis and its fire department, after becoming defendants in a class action suit alleging racial discrimination in the department's hiring and promotion practices. The consent decree mandated an affirmative action plan setting hiring goals to make the proportion of blacks in the department consistent with the proportion of blacks in the total local population. After the affirmative action plan went into effect, a budget deficit made it necessary for the department to lay off some of its employees. In accordance with the seniority system in effect, the layoffs were to be made according to a "last hired, first fired" formula. Since a relatively large proportion of blacks had been recently hired, the layoffs would have undermined the goals sought to be achieved by means of the affirmative action program. To avoid this result, the consent decree was modified, and an amended layoff plan adopted. According to this new plan, the reverse seniority order of layoffs had to be suspended in part, to protect the jobs of blacks who held certain defined classes of positions. As a consequence of this, some nonminority employees with more seniority were laid off, while blacks with less seniority kept their jobs (565).

The Supreme Court held that the modified layoff plan was impermissible. The Court pointed out that the purpose of the consent decree had been to provide a remedy for the past hiring and promotion practices of the fire department. Furthermore, noting that Title VII protects bona fide seniority systems, the Court emphasized that it was "inappropriate to deny an innocent employee the benefits of his seniority in order to provide a remedy in a pattern or practice suit such as this" (575). On the other hand, however, the Court also made clear that actual victims of past discrimination "may be awarded competitive seniority and given their rightful place in the seniority roster." Finally, the Court added that even an actual victim may not be entitled to be awarded a position similar to that wrongfully denied in the past, if the only way to make such a position available were to have an innocent nonminority employee laid off (579).

The affirmative action plan involved in *Stotts* had a distributive purpose, namely to readjust the distribution of fire fighter positions so as better to approximate the likely racial composition that the fire fighter force would have had absent any "practice and pattern" of discrimination. Consistent with this, the core of the Supreme Court's decision in *Stotts* is that, when an affirmative action plan has a distributive purpose, the seniority rights of innocent nonminority employees take precedence over the implementation of the plan, even in the face of past discrimination by the very governmental entity that has instituted the plan. On the other hand, however, the Court's decision recognizes that, when preferential treatment is accorded as compensation to an individual who has been an actual victim of past discrimination, then the latter's compensatory rights take precedence over the seniority rights of innocent employees.

The distributive aims of the *Stotts* plan appear to be much more group-regarding than individual-regarding. As stated in the dissenting opinion of Justice Blackmun, the main purpose of the affirmative action plan in *Stotts* was to provide a remedy for the discriminated-against group as a whole rather than to any of its individual members (612–16). Accordingly, the distinguishing feature of the race-conscious hiring goals set in *Stotts* is that "no individual member of the disadvantaged class has a claim to [the relief] and individual beneficiaries of the relief need not show that they were themselves victims of the discrimination for which the relief was granted." Carrying this analysis over to the layoff situation, the principal consideration would appear to be the group-regarding one of preserving the plan's contemplated proportions of blacks and whites. Consistent with this, as Justice Blackmun indicates, no individual black employee has any right against being laid off so long as the percentage of black representation of the fire fighter force is maintained (613).

While *Stotts* raised without fully resolving the issues of the relation between the individual and the group and the problem of the innocent third party in layoff situations in the context of the Civil Rights Law, *Wygant* v. *Jackson Board of Education* addresses these same issues in the context of the equal protection clause. *Wygant* arose out of the implementation of a layoff provision designed to maintain the percentage of minority teachers in the Jackson public school system. This layoff provision was added to the collective bargaining agreement between the Jackson, Michigan, Board of Education and the union representing the teachers in the Jackson public schools, because of racial tension in the community that extended to its public schools.[22] According to the added provision, layoffs were to proceed in the customary order of reverse seniority except that at no time was there to be a greater percentage of minority teachers laid off than the percentage of minority teachers employed at the time of the layoff. Accordingly, when layoffs became necessary more senior tenured nonminority teachers were laid off while less senior nontenured minority teachers were allowed to keep their jobs (270–71).

The lower federal courts held that racially preferential layoffs were permissible under the equal protection clause as an attempt to remedy "societal discrimination" by providing "role models" to minority school children. These lower courts therefore upheld the constitutionality of the added layoff provision (272). In another five to four decision, the Supreme Court reversed, and found the layoff provision unconstitutional. Again, no majority on the Court could agree on any single opinion.

The plurality opinion by Justice Powell focuses on two important issues: whether societal discrimination provides sufficient constitutional justification for the adoption of a race-conscious affirmative action plan, and whether the layoff provision implemented by the Jackson School Board imposes an unconstitutional burden on "innocent" nonminority teachers. With respect to the first of these issues, Justice Powell reiterated the position he took in *Bakke* to the effect that "societal discrimination" is too "amorphous" as a basis for a valid affirmative action plan (276). Moreover, the purpose of the affirmative action plan, including the contested layoff provision, in *Wygant* was not compensatory, but rather to provide "role models" for minority students in the Jackson public schools (274). Applying the strict scrutiny test, Justice Powell concluded that the school board's use of a race-conscious layoff provision to provide role models to its minority students in order to counteract the effects of societal discrimination violated the equal protection clause (283–84).

As is the case with all affirmative action plans designed to remedy the present effects of past conduct, the *Wygant* plan had both a backward-looking and a forward-looking component. Justice Powell's opinion finds the *Wygant* plan wanting because of both its backward-looking and forward-looking objectives. Although there was evidence of past discriminatory practices by the Jackson Board, there was no formal finding to that effect. Accordingly, under the marginal equality position adopted by Justice Powell in *Bakke,* the board was not sufficiently responsible for past discrimination to justify, from a constitutional standpoint, its assumption of a duty of compensation. In accordance with the paradigm of compensation, the board could not be singled out as the source of the past evil sought to be remedied through affirmative action. Because the board is not more responsible for societal discrimination than other institutions and persons, under Justice Powell's conception of strict scrutiny, it cannot set out to remedy the effects of such societal discrimination through an affirmative action plan.

If the board were *compelled* to assume a disproportionate share of the responsibility for societal discrimination under the guise of some compensatory duty, one may be inclined to agree with Justice Powell's analysis. But since the board *voluntarily* agreed to implement an affirmative action plan to eliminate the lingering effects of past societal discrimination, it seems arbitrary to prevent the board from carrying out that plan, unless it is demonstrated that the board's past conduct squarely places it within the paradigm of compensatory justice.

While Justice Powell adheres to the paradigm of compensation on the side of the wrongdoer, unlike in *Bakke*, in *Wygant* he intimates that equal protection does not foreclose departing from the paradigm on the side of the victim. Indeed, according to Justice Powell's opinion in *Wygant*, if an affirmative action plan is implemented by a wrongdoer its beneficiaries may include persons who are not "actual" victims (277–78). No justification, however, is offered for this deviation from the position adopted by Justice Powell in *Bakke*. Ultimately, both his position in *Bakke* and that in *Wygant* announce that the strict scrutiny test under the equal protection clause tolerates departures from the equal treatment principle. But it remains unclear why these departures should be accepted from the standpoint of the marginal equality position, or whether either of these departures is more susceptible to justification under that position than the other.

Justice Powell also found constitutional fault with the forward-looking objective of the board's affirmative action plan. In its broadest terms, this objective can be characterized as being essentially distributive in nature. The immediate purpose of the disputed layoff provision was to preserve the ratio of minority to nonminority teachers in the Jackson public schools. The ultimate purpose of the board's affirmative action plan, however, was to maintain a sufficient number of minority teachers in the Jackson public schools to continue affording a sufficient number of positive role models for minority students. Moreover, the justification for role models was presumably that the latter would be able to motivate and inspire minority children to succeed in their studies as well as their nonminority counterparts. Thus, the ultimate purpose of the board's affirmative action plan was apparently the promotion of equality of result in public school education or of fair equality of opportunity in relation to the competition for places and positions for which the completion of a high school education is a prerequisite.

The core of Justice Powell's objection to the role model rationale appears to be that the role model objective of the board's plan is not sufficiently directly related to any remedial purpose. If *remedial* is understood in a narrow compensatory sense, then it is undeniably true that focusing on providing adequate role models for minority students is not likely to "make whole" minority teachers who were denied employment in the Jackson public schools because of first-order racial discrimination. On the other hand, however, the role model objective may be arguably justified within a narrow compensatory framework, if it is accepted as a means to make up for the pedagogical and psychological harm suffered by minority students as a consequence of racial discrimination in the past hiring of public school teachers. Indeed, if the lack of a sufficient number of minority teachers in the past has stunted the educational development of minority students, then providing a sufficient number of role models may lead to the redress of the injury experienced by such minority students.

As to the second broad issue that Justice Powell addresses in his opinion in *Wygant*, namely, the constitutionality of the burden imposed by the contested layoff provision on "innocent" nonminority employees, his views closely follow, and elaborate upon, those of the majority in *Stotts*. The most noteworthy aspect of Justice Powell's pronouncements concerning the burden on innocent third parties in *Wygant* relates to his comparison of the relative burdens imposed by race-conscious hiring goals and race-conscious layoff provisions, respectively. Apparently applying the balancing test he announced in his *Fullilove* opinion, Justice Powell concludes in *Wygant* that the burden on innocent third parties in layoffs is much heavier than its counterpart in hiring. Consequently, he finds that the heavy burden on innocent nonminority employees imposed by the layoff provision involved in *Wygant* is constitutionally impermissible.

Two separate arguments underlie Justice Powell's conclusion. The first is that, in hiring cases, the burden on innocent individuals is "diffused to a considerable extent among society generally," while in layoff cases, such burden falls entirely upon the shoulders of a small number of individuals (282–83). The second argument, in turn, is that, whereas hiring goals often foreclose but one of several opportunities, layoffs more typically leave those who have lost their job without reasonable immediate prospects of finding suitable comparable alternative employment (283–84).

Justice Powell did not elaborate on his first argument. Upon further reflection, however, this argument does not seem well grounded. Preferential treatment in hiring does not have primarily a diffuse effect on society at large, but rather definite sharply defined negative consequences for a small number of individuals: the applicants who would have succeeded in their objective but for the preferential treatment accorded to certain other applicants. If the applicants who are preferentially treated are qualified, affirmative action in hiring is not likely to lead to any dramatic decrease in efficiency, and is thus unlikely to impose any significant burden on society at large. Accordingly, the injury to innocent third parties attributable to preferential hiring seems as sharply concentrated on a small number of individuals as is that stemming from preferential layoffs.

Justice Powell's second argument seems better grounded than his first, but it is questionable whether it should be given as much weight as he appears to give to it. Customarily, the university or job applicant has many more opportunities than the employee who is about to be laid off. The typical university applicant, for instance, usually applies to more than one university, and rejection by one of these because of preferential admissions does not mean that the same applicant will not be accepted by a comparable institution. On the other hand, layoffs tend to occur in times of economic contraction when job opportunities are dwindling. A relatively senior nonminority employee who loses her job as a consequence of a layoff is therefore unlikely to find a comparable position and, if the economy is in the midst of a serious downturn, may not have reasonable prospects for any kind of employment.

Differences between hiring and layoff victims, however, need not be as dramatic. It is significant, for example, that the "more senior" nonminority fire fighters laid off in *Stotts* joined the force on the same day as the "less senior" minorities who kept their jobs.[23] More generally, the most likely nonminority victims of race-conscious layoff policies are not the presumably less mobile and less easily employable most senior employees, but rather those with relatively little seniority. On the other hand, while university applicants may typically have several different opportunities, the same may often not be the case for job applicants who have developed certain specialized skills or who seek government employment. Thus, for example, a candidate who applies for a fire fighter job and who is unsuccessful because of a preferential hiring scheme may be left without any comparable job opportunity within the municipality where he resides. In short, whereas generally layoff plans may tend to leave their victims with fewer opportunities than those possessed by the victims of preferential hiring plans, in certain circumstances race-conscious layoffs and hiring goals may be equally destructive of certain employment opportunities.

In their dissenting opinion in *Wygant,* Justices Marshall, Brennan, and Blackmun emphasize that, while layoffs are unfair, this does not necessarily render all race-conscious layoff practices unconstitutional (296). For these justices the constitutional question presented in *Wygant* is a narrow one: assuming that a race-conscious hiring plan is constitutional, can a race-conscious layoff plan designed to preserve the results achieved through the hiring plan also be constitutional (300)? Adhering to the global equality position and stressing that the purpose of the affirmative action plan in *Wygant* was to ameliorate the present effects of past discrimination, these justices concluded that the disputed layoff provision did not offend the Constitution (303).

The principal focus of the dissenting opinion written by Justice Marshall is the tension between the need to preserve the gains obtained through the preferential hiring plan and to minimize the inevitable unfairness associated with a race-conscious layoff plan. It is obvious that a "last hired first fired" layoff policy would destroy the faculty integration achieved through the preferential hiring plan designed to remedy the absence of minority teachers resulting from the past discriminatory practices of the board and the Jackson community as a whole. On the other hand, layoffs are undoubtedly unfair, in the sense that they are undeserved (307). And they are undeserved because they do not depend on the quality of the performance of the laid-off employee but rather on circumstances beyond the latter's control.

Justice Marshall criticizes Justice Powell for overlooking the critical fact that any layoff policy, whether or not race-conscious, inevitably causes harm to innocent employees who undeservedly lose their jobs (307). From Justice Marshall's perspective, it is not *because* it is race-conscious that a layoff practice injures innocent employees, but rather because any layoffs inevitably harm innocent persons. Moreover, Justice Marshall also stresses that the challenged layoff provision emerged as a modification of "contractual expectations that do not themselves carry any connotation of merit or achievement." In other words, since the original collective bargaining agreement between the Jackson Board and the teachers' union contained a layoff provision adopting the reverse seniority order rather than tying layoffs to the relative merits or achievements of individual teachers employed in the Jackson public schools, the modification of such a layoff provision along race-conscious lines did not contravene any equal opportunity rights or expectations. As Justice Marshall states, the modified layoff provision "does not interfere with the 'cherished American ethic' of 'fairness in individual competition' . . . depriving individuals of an opportunity that they could be said to deserve" (309–10).

Consistent with Justice Marshall's analysis, one may certainly contend that any layoff plan based on seniority rather than on relative achievement or productivity would violate certain equal opportunity rights. Indeed, if job hiring should conform to the principle of equality of opportunity it seems consistent to insist that the same principle should apply to layoffs. In *Wygant,* however, the layoff plan based on seniority was adopted pursuant to a collective bargaining agreement. Accordingly, it seems legitimate to argue that whatever putative equal opportunity rights may have originally existed with respect to layoffs were voluntarily waived upon entering into the labor contract. Furthermore, as mentioned earlier, modification of the layoff provision contained in that labor pact to further the aims of an existing affirmative action plan would not appear to revive previously voluntarily extinguished equal opportunity rights.

If the above analysis is correct, it would seem to follow that race-conscious layoffs are ultimately *less* objectionable than race-conscious job hiring. Assuming adherence to the principle of equality of opportunity, it is arguably unjust to deviate from that principle in order to hire more minorities. On the other hand, layoff provisions based on seniority, though not in accordance with the principle of equal opportunity, may nevertheless be deemed not unjust, to the extent that they reflect a voluntary forfeiture of certain equal opportunity rights. From the standpoint of the principle of equality of opportunity, moreover, a modification of a seniority-based layoff plan to include certain race-conscious considerations does not appear to make the amended layoff plan any more unjust than its original counterpart. To be sure, the amended layoff plan may be more objectionable than the original one, because making race a factor can itself be deemed unjust. In that case, the race-conscious layoff plan may be as unjust as the race-conscious hiring plan from the standpoint of racial justice, but the former would remain less unjust than the latter from the standpoint of equality of opportunity.

It is plausible to argue, however, that layoffs based on seniority bear some relation to equal opportunity rights. Although layoffs based on seniority are not likely to increase additive efficiency, they may contribute to an increase in compositive efficiency.[24] Indeed, the expectation that the longer one stays at one's job the less likely it will be that one will lose that job may promote the same sense of fairness and stability as the expectation that one will not lose one's job merely because a more qualified candidate has suddenly emerged. And if this intuition is correct, layoffs based on seniority may be viewed as an integral part of an overall scheme governed by the principle of equality of opportunity.

If layoffs based on seniority foster compositive efficiency, Justice Marshall's emphasis on the lack of equal opportunity implications associated with the move from seniority-based layoffs to preferential layoffs is clearly misplaced. Accordingly, too, the move from seniority-based to preferential layoffs would seem to be at least as unjust under the equal opportunity principle as the move from competitive to preferential hiring. And under these circumstances the crucial issue once again would appear to be whether the use of race with respect to hiring and/or layoffs could be justified consistent with adherence to the principle of equal opportunity.

There is a striking contrast between the opinions of Justice Marshall and Justice Powell in *Wygant* concerning the calculation of the actual harms attributable to preferential layoffs—a calculation that is crucial to the proper functioning of the balancing test announced by Justice

Powell in *Fullilove.* As will be remembered, according to this balancing test, the state's interest pursued through an affirmative action plan must be weighed against the harms that such plan would cause to innocent members of the nonpreferred group. According to Justice Powell's analysis, the harm experienced by a person who is laid off must be weighed against the relevant government interest. Moreover, consistent with this analysis, since layoffs generally impose greater harms than the failure to succeed in the competition for a scarce position, a government interest that, under the balancing test, justifies preferential hiring may not be sufficiently weighty to legitimate preferential layoffs.

Viewing the matter from Justice Marshall's perspective, on the other hand, it is important to remember that all layoffs cause harm to those who lose their jobs because of them, regardless of the order in which they are carried out. Accordingly, the harm to be weighed in applying the balancing test is not the overall harm suffered by the average victim of a layoff but the excess harm that such a victim experiences because of the preferential nature of a given affirmative action layoff plan. Provided a race-conscious layoff plan is not intended to cast any racial group as inferior, the excess harm caused by the move from a seniority-based to a racially based layoff plan is arguably limited to an increase in the prospects of losing one's job through a layoff. Indeed, the protection that a seniority-based layoff plan offers is the gradual decrease in the prospects of losing one's job to a layoff. The more seniority one accumulates, the less likely it becomes that one will be laid off. But by introducing race as a factor in determining the orders of layoff, one increases the prospects of layoff for nonminority employees. Because no one knows at the time that a layoff plan is established or modified whether at some future time he or she will be laid off, the injury that a nonminority employee is likely to suffer due to the imposition of a race-conscious layoff plan would appear to be limited to an increase in the degree of insecurity about maintaining one's job in the future. Moreover, ordinarily, such increased insecurity should be proportional to the *increase* in the prospects of being laid off *attributable* to the adoption of a race-conscious layoff plan.

Whether the increased job insecurity experienced by nonminority employees pursuant to the adoption of a preferential layoff plan constitutes a greater harm than the decrease in the prospects of success of nonminority applicants pursuant to the implementation of a preferential hiring plan seems difficult to determine in the abstract. Actually, even if one knew the actual figures by which the prospects of job loss are increased and by which the prospects of success in the competition for scarce positions are decreased by an affirmative action plan, it might still be difficult to ascertain the relative harms of preferential layoffs and preferential hiring. Let us assume, for example, that we have a preferential hiring plan that reduces the prospects of success of nonminorities by 10 percent, and a preferential layoff plan that increases the nonminority employees' prospects of being laid off also by 10 percent. Are these changes in prospects likely to cause identical harms? If not, which of the two is likely to cause greater harm? The answers to these questions are not self-evident, but it seems fair to assume that *some* hiring plans are likely to produce greater harm than *some* layoff plans. Thus, if a hiring quota reduces the prospects of success of nonminority applicants by 40 percent, it would appear that in all likelihood it would cause more harm than a preferential layoff plan that increases nonminority prospects of layoff by one percent.

Acceptance that certain preferential layoffs may cause as much harm as, or less harm than, certain preferential hiring plans would have important consequences for the constitutional balancing test. First, where preferential hiring and layoffs cause innocent parties the same degree of harm, any government interest that tips the balance in favor of the affirmative hiring plan ought to do the same for the layoff plan. Second, where the hiring plan causes greater harm, a government interest not weighty enough to sustain it might be sufficient to tip the constitutional balance in favor of the layoff plan. In conclusion, consistent with Justice Marshall's analysis in *Wygant,* a preferential layoff plan may be as constitutionally valid as, or more or less valid than, a preferential hiring plan, depending on the particular circumstances involved.

Justice Stevens also filed a dissenting opinion in *Wygant.* This opinion is particularly noteworthy because of its endorsement of the proposition that an affirmative action plan may be constitutional even if its justification is a purely forward-looking one. As one commentator has pointed out, concentrating on forward-looking justifications may produce important advantages, such as reducing the appeal of protests concerning the windfall benefits affirmative action bestows on nonvictims, and of claims of injustice against innocent third parties (Sullivan 1986, 97). Furthermore, Justice Stevens squarely endorses the ideal of building an integrated society (ibid., 98), embraces the global equality position, and proposes a criterion whereby legitimate uses of race-conscious policies can be distinguished from those that are constitutionally objectionable.

According to Justice Stevens, the constitutionality of the *Wygant* layoff plan turns on the answers to these two questions: first, does the board's affirmative action plan advance the public interest in educating children for the future? And, second, if the answer to the first question is in this affirmative, does this public interest and the manner in which it is pursued justify the adverse effects that the preferential layoff plan imposes on the group that is disadvantaged by it (313)?

Justice Stevens' emphasis on the quality of future public education evinces a purely forward-looking concern relating to the state's distribution of educational goods. Noting that education "is the very foundation of good citizenship," Justice Stevens appears to assume, without much elaboration, that affirmative action in the service of the purely distributive aim of providing an improved public education is in principle constitutionally defensible (315, 315*n.8*). Moreover, Justice Stevens stresses that, if a forward-looking affirmative action plan advances the purpose for which it has been put into effect, and if certain procedural constraints are observed, this plan would be valid provided that the public interest that it promotes justifies the adverse effect that the plan is bound to have on the group it disadvantages (317).

In Justice Stevens' view, the ultimate goal in race relations is the complete elimination of racial considerations from all governmental decision-making processes. Since American society is far from achieving this assimilationist ideal, however, Justice Stevens believes that it is reasonable for a school board to conclude that a racially integrated faculty would be better able to provide greater educational benefits to its racially mixed student body than would an all white faculty (320). Accordingly, Justice Stevens concludes that the end sought to be achieved through the *Wygant* affirmative action plan is constitutionally valid. But this does not necessarily entail that this plan as the means to that end is itself constitutional. Justice Stevens believes nevertheless that a race-conscious plan can be a constitutional means to a color-blind end. Moreover, the criterion that Justice Stevens proposes for use to determine when race conscious policies are constitutionally permissible is one based on the contrast between *inclusionary* and *exclusionary* decisions based on race (316). Essentially, according to this criterion, the use of race-conscious policies for purposes of *excluding* a racially disadvantaged group from some desirable benefits is constitutionally illicit. Conversely, the use of such policies with a view toward *including* members of a racially disadvantaged group in the class of those eligible to receive certain coveted benefits should be constitutionally permissible.

Focusing on the layoff plan in *Wygant,* Justice Stevens asserts that there is a "critical difference" between *excluding* a minority faculty candidate because of her skin color and *including* more minorities on a school's faculty for the same reason (316). Furthermore, he explains that

> The exclusionary decision rests on the false premise that differences in race, or in the color of a person's skin reflect real differences that are relevant to a person's right to share in the blessings of a free society. . . . [T]hat premise is "utterly irrational." . . . Nevertheless, the fact that persons of different races do, indeed, have differently colored skin, may give rise to a belief that there is

> some significant difference between such persons. The inclusion of minority teachers in the educational process inevitably tends to dispel that illusion whereas their exclusion could only tend to foster it. The inclusionary decision is consistent with the principle that all men are created equal; the exclusionary decision is at war with this principle. One decision accords with the Equal Protection Clause of the Fourteenth Amendment; the other does not. (316)

Although inclusionary race-conscious policies may not treat any person as an inferior, they may nevertheless significantly harm those whom they must displace or leave aside to make room for those whom they seek to benefit. Justice Stevens is aware of this issue, and the constitutional test he advances in *Wygant* purports to deal with it by balancing the race-conscious policy involved against the public interest sought to be promoted by that policy. Applying this test to the facts in *Wygant,* Justice Stevens concludes that the public interest in integrated education outweighs the harm caused to innocent nonminority employees by the preferential layoff plan. In arriving at that conclusion, Justice Stevens' appraisal of the harm caused by the preferential layoff plan involved in *Wygant* closely parallels that of Justice Marshall (319–20).

Comprehensive plans, like those at stake in *Stotts* and *Wygant,* which include preferential hiring as well as preferential layoffs, can be viewed both in terms of group-regarding equality of result and individual-regarding (prospect-regarding) equality of opportunity. Focusing on the latter, to the extent that the ratio of black-to-white employees in a firm is to remain equivalent to the proportion of blacks-to-whites in the population at large, then the prospects of each black person to obtain and maintain a position with that firm are the same as those of each white person. Under those circumstances, an affirmative action plan used to achieve and maintain a given racial proportion produces equal prospects of success for each member of society regardless of race. Moreover, from the standpoint of maintaining one's job, a preferential layoff plan, such as the one in *Wygant,* provides individual black employees with the same prospects of being laid off as their individual white counterparts. In the last analysis, therefore, forward-looking distributive preferential layoff plans can promote prospect-regarding equality of opportunity for the individual as well as group-regarding equality of result.

The numerous opinions filed in *Stotts* and *Wygant* provide several important insights concerning the many difficulties surrounding the constitutionality of affirmative action layoff plans. Nevertheless, these two cases leave the core questions raised by affirmative action unresolved. In particular, they fail to provide a clear and coherent constitutional demarcation between compensatory and distributive aims, concerning the relation between the individual and the group, and relating to the limits on placing burdens on innocent third parties.

E. Numerical Goals as Remedy for Persistent Egregious Discrimination and Evasion of Remedial Court Orders: The Sheet Metal Workers Decision

Local 28, Sheet Metal Workers' Intern. Ass'n v. *E.E.O.C.*, decided by the Supreme Court in 1986, addresses the issue of the validity of the use of race-conscious remedies under Title VII and under the Constitution in a case of extreme resistance against all efforts, including judicial decrees, to put an end to systematic racial discrimination designed to exclude blacks and Hispanics from union membership. A majority of the Court held that race-conscious remedies, including the use of numerical goals, were appropriate under the circumstances. Once again, however, no majority of the Court joined in any single opinion on the most important statutory and constitutional issues raised by the case.

The Sheet Metal Workers' union in general, and Local 28, in particular, had a long history of racial discrimination and of systematic exclusionary practices designed to deny membership to minorities. The union, founded in 1888, provided for the creation of "white local unions." One of them was Local 28, which was established in 1913. Although the International Union formally repealed all racial restrictions in 1946, Local 28 flatly refused to admit any blacks until 1969.[25]

Local 28 ran an apprenticeship program that was a prerequisite to union membership. Union membership was, in turn, necessary to secure employment with contractors in the New York City Metropolitan area. Local 28's systematic exclusion of blacks and Hispanics from its apprenticeship program created an "impenetrable barrier for nonwhite applicants." This prompted New York State to take action against Local 28 in 1964, and led to a state court order commanding the adoption of race-neutral procedures for selecting apprentices (427*n.*2).

As Local 28 was refusing to comply with the state court's order, the federal government sued in federal district court in 1971 to enjoin Local 28 from "engaging in a pattern and practice of discrimination against black and hispanic individuals" (428). The district court concluded that Local 28 had excluded nonwhites through a variety of discriminatory practices, including requiring an entrance examination and the completion of an academic program not related to job performance, and providing union funds to subsidize special training sessions for friends and relatives of union members, with a view toward better preparing them for the apprenticeship examination. In addition, the court determined that at various times Local 28 had restricted the size of its membership rather than grant access to nonwhites (429–30). Finding that Local 28 had engaged in repeated "bad faith" attempts to prevent or delay all attempts to integrate its membership, "The court established a 29% nonwhite membership goal, based on the percentage of nonwhites in the relevant labor pool in New York City." The union was supposed to reach this goal by 1981 (432).

In 1982, Local 28 was held in civil contempt for failure to implement the procedures designed to remedy its discriminatory practices. By 1982 Local 28 had achieved a nonwhite membership of 10.8 percent in spite of the 29 percent goal. After further failures in compliance, the federal district court entered a second civil contempt order against Local 28 in 1983 (434), and established a 29.23 percent minority membership goal to be met by 1987. On appeal, the Circuit Court of Appeals for the Second Circuit upheld the district court, and found the 29.23 percent minority membership goal proper because of Local 28's "long continued and egregious racial discrimination" and because it would not "unnecessarily trammel on the rights of any readily ascertainable group of non-minority individuals" (437). The Supreme Court affirmed the Second Circuit's decision.

Writing for a plurality, Justice Brennan emphasizes that the purpose of Title VII of the Civil Rights Act is to provide equal employment opportunities. With this in mind, Justice Brennan notes that in some cases it might be enough to end discriminatory practices in order to open up the competition for scarce positions in accordance with the principle of equality of opportunity (448). In other cases, particularly when there is a long history of discrimination, however, it may be necessary to provide some form of preferential remedy in order to make meaningful equality of opportunity possible. In the latter cases, as Justice Brennan observes,

> affirmative race-conscious relief may be the only means available "to assure equality of employment opportunities and to eliminate those discriminatory practices and devices which have fostered racially stratified job environments to the disadvantage of minority citizens." . . . Affirmative action "promptly operates to change the outward and visible signs of yesterday's racial distinctions and thus, to provide an impetus to the process of dismantling the barriers, psychological or otherwise erected by past practices." (450)

Moreover, Justice Brennan maintains that in the context of ongoing discrimination by an employer who has failed to institute race-neutral hiring procedures, preferential hiring to meet certain numerical goals may be the best compromise between two unacceptable alternatives: a flat prohibition against all hiring or further toleration of racially discriminatory job hiring procedures (450–51).

Justice Brennan insists that the affirmative action plan in *Sheet Metal Workers* is not inconsistent with the Court's holding in *Stotts* to the effect that preferential treatment can only be legitimately used as make-whole relief for actual victims of past first-order discrimination (472–75). Justice Brennan explains that "this limitation on *individual* make-whole relief does not affect a Court's authority to order race-conscious affirmative action. The purpose of affirmative action is not to make identified victims whole, but rather to dismantle prior patterns of employment discrimination and to prevent discrimination in the future" (emphasis in original; 476). Consistent with these statements, it seems that Justice Brennan agrees that Title VII prohibits the use of affirmative action for the distributive purpose of achieving equality of result through the establishment of a racially balanced union membership. On the other hand, he believes that Title VII permits the use of affirmative action for the distributive purpose of achieving equality of opportunity, but not as part of any compensatory scheme that would allow preferential treatment of nonvictims.

Further, Justice Brennan stresses that the affirmative action plan in *Sheet Metal Workers* is designed to provide collective not individual relief. In his own words, "Such relief is provided to the class as a whole rather than to individual members. No individual is entitled to relief, and beneficiaries need not show that they were themselves victims of discrimination (477). Collective relief, moreover, can arguably be justified in the context of the facts in *Sheet Metal Workers*. Indeed, candidates for apprenticeship with the union were generally recruited through informal contacts with insiders. Thus, a large number of candidates were the friends or relatives of union members and apprentices, and since the overwhelming majority of insiders were white, the prevailing informal procedure for the recruitment of candidates was unlikely to lead to increased nonwhite union membership. One logical way to remedy this situation would seem to be to set temporary numerical goals designed to increase the number of nonwhite insiders. That would presumably eventually automatically lead to a desirable increase in the recruitment of nonwhite candidates for union membership (477).

The collective relief approved by Justice Brennan does not necessarily exalt the group at the expense of the individual. It is a plausible argument that the ultimate aim of the remedial use of affirmative action in *Sheet Metal Workers* is to provide some kind of individual-regarding equality of opportunity to achieve union membership regardless of race. Because of the prevailing artificial exclusion of nonwhites, and because of the operative practice for attracting apprenticeship candidates, however, the use of group-regarding preferential treatment appears to be a prerequisite to the achievement of equal opportunities for individuals.

Justice Brennan's decision in *Sheet Metal Workers* seems justified in part on distributive grounds, and in part on compensatory grounds. The group-regarding relief designed to eliminate the lingering effects of persistent discrimination and to lead to individual-regarding equal opportunities clearly seems to pertain to the domain of distributive justice. On the other hand, insistence on the requirement that the union have engaged in past first-order discrimination appears to back the claim that compensatory considerations justify imposing on the union the burden of carrying out the affirmative action plan decreed by the lower courts.

It is not clear, however, what connection there is, if any, between these compensatory and distributive considerations. Be that as it may, the most important point to emerge from Justice Brennan's opinion in *Sheet Metal Workers* is that preferential treatment may be, on occasion, the only means to put a prompt and meaningful end to a persistent practice of *ongoing* first-order discrimination.

F. Preferential Promotions: The Vanguards and Paradise Cases

Resistance to full racial integration of the workforce can form at various junctures. Thus, if hiring discrimination is eliminated and if minorities begin to find a place within the workforce, those bent on pursuing exclusionary practices at any cost may concentrate on denying minority employees opportunities for promotion. When this happens, minorities may gain entrance to the workforce but are relegated to remain in subordinate positions. If the mere removal of existing impediments to minority promotions does not remedy this situation, it seems logical to resort to the use of preferential promotions.

In the *Vanguards*[26] and *Paradise*[27] cases, the Supreme Court evaluated the legitimacy of preferential race-conscious promotion plans benefiting individuals who were not the actual victims of past first-order discrimination. In both cases a majority on the Supreme Court upheld the validity of a preferential promotion scheme involving numerical targets.

Vanguards centered on the validity under Title VII of a consent decree requiring race-conscious promotion quotas and numerical goals. Cleveland's Fire Department had engaged in a "historic pattern of discrimination." As a result of litigation in 1973, the department increased its hiring of minorities. But through discriminatory promotions practices that included an examination said to be biased against minorities, the use of seniority points, and the manipulation of retirement dates to insure that minorities would not head promotion lists when higher positions became available, the department inhibited minority advancement beyond the lowest ranks within the hierarchy (505). Against this backdrop in 1980, the Vanguards, an organization of minority firefighters, brought a lawsuit against the city of Cleveland claiming, among other things, racial discrimination in the promotion practices of the Fire Department (504). This lawsuit eventually led to a consent decree providing that a fixed number of already-approved promotions be awarded to minorities and that, for a limited period of time, a certain percentage of future promotions be reserved for minorities.

The legal question raised in *Vanguards* is a narrow one: does Title VII authorize the consent decree approved by the district court? In the course of answering in the affirmative, however, the majority on the Supreme Court shed some light on the issue of the effect of preferential promotions on innocent nonminority employees, which is relevant both to statutory and to constitutional analysis. The purpose of the preferential promotions approved in *Vanguards* was remedial in nature. Moreover, such promotions were not limited to actual victims of racial discrimination in hiring or promotion (516). Nevertheless, the Court's majority did not find it unreasonable to impose a racial quota in promotions for a period of four years. The majority found that, although the nonminority firefighters adversely affected by preferential promotions were themselves innocent from any wrongdoing, they had benefited from the effects of past discrimination, and that it was hence not unjust to make them bear some of the burden of the remedy. Also, the majority emphasized that the preferential promotions plan in *Vanguards* did not require the hiring of unqualified blacks or the discharge of any white fire fighter and did not impose any insurmountable impediment to the promotion of nonminorities (515).

In *Paradise*, the Supreme Court decided, in a five-to-four decision, that a preferential promotions plan benefiting minority individuals who were not actual victims of past first-order discrimination could be justified under the equal protection clause.[28] Moreover, although the majority did not agree on a single opinion, the plurality opinion and the concurring opinions shed some additional light on the weight to be accorded to the burdens imposed by preferential promotion plans on innocent employees who would have been promoted but for the operation of such a plan.

What gave rise to the *Paradise* litigation were the various systematic discriminatory practices of the Alabama Public Safety Department. In 1972, a lawsuit was brought in federal district court against the department for blatant and persistent systematic discrimination of blacks in hiring. No black state trooper had ever been employed by the department in the thirty-seven years that the department's patrol had been in existence. The district court found this conduct to have violated the Fourteenth Amendment, and ordered the department to hire one black trooper for each white trooper joining the force, until blacks would constitute 25 percent of the state trooper force. The district court also enjoined the department from engaging in any future first-order discrimination with respect to, among other things, hiring and promotions. Moreover, the district court made it clear that the temporary 50 percent hiring quota it had imposed was meant to eradicate the present effects of past discrimination (154–55).

In 1974, the plaintiffs returned to the district court for further relief, as the department had artificially restricted the size of the force in order to avoid hiring more blacks. Also, the department experienced a highly disproportionate rate of attrition for blacks hirees because of its deliberate selection of blacks who were not the best qualified among the black candidates on the eligibility roster, and of its social and official discrimination against blacks at its trooper training academy. Finally, the department provided whites with preferential treatment in testing and training, while subjecting blacks to harsher discipline (156–57).

In 1977, the plaintiffs had to return to district court to obtain further relief, this time on promotions. For the thirty-seven years prior to the 1972 litigation, not a single black trooper had been on the department's Force. After losing in court, the department reluctantly began hiring black troopers, but by 1978 not a single black was included among the 232 state troopers who held the rank of corporal or any higher rank. Under these circumstances, in 1979, the parties entered into a consent decree, according to which the department agreed to develop within one year a fair promotions procedure that would have no adverse impact on blacks seeking promotion (158).

Further court proceedings took place in 1981 and 1983 because of the department's continuing failure to implement a fair promotion procedure (159–60). By the end of 1983, the district court, finding the department's failure to be intolerable, decided that 50 percent of all promotions had to go to blacks until 25 percent of the troopers with the rank of corporal and 25 percent of those with higher ranks were black—the 25 percent figure corresponding to the percentage of blacks in the relevant labor market (163, 179).

In reaching its decision, the district court remarked that the effects of past discrimination in the department "will not wither away of their own accord" and that "without promotional quotas the continuing effects of this discrimination cannot be eliminated." Finally, the district court stressed that the promotion quota which it was imposing was "flexible," "temporary," and "specifically tailored" to eliminate the present effects of past discrimination. In support of this, the court pointed out that the department could unilaterally terminate this quota at any time, by simply adopting acceptable promotion procedures (163–64). The Court of Appeals affirmed the 1983 district court decision.

In his plurality opinion, Justice Brennan concludes that the promotion quota is legitimate under the Fourteenth Amendment, and that it even satisfies the strict scrutiny test (166). Moreover, Justice Brennan views the promotion quota as being remedial rather than punitive (170*n.20*), and as a means to eradicate the present effects of present and past discrimination (166–71).

From the standpoint of the department, the promotion quota in *Paradise* seems to be compensatory in nature. From the perspective of the blacks who stand to be promoted as a consequence of it, on the other hand, the quota may be viewed as either compensatory or distributive. It seems compensatory to the extent that the blacks it would benefit are most likely those denied promotions because of the department's racist practices. To the extent that no particular black trooper has a right to a promotion, however, the quota may seem distributive. Further, from the perspective of society at large, the quota seems to be clearly distributive. Indeed, integrating the state trooper force may in part be justified by considerations of compositive efficiency. The hiring and promotion of black troopers may well restore community trust in law enforcement, encourage citizen cooperation, and ease racial tensions through the assignment of black troopers in black neighborhoods (167*n.18*).

According to Justice Brennan, in establishing the promotion quota, the district court properly balanced all the collective and individual interests at stake, including those of white troopers eligible for promotion (185). Among the collective interests at stake, one can mention those of white and black troopers as groups, those of the community served by the troopers, and those of society in having its judicial decrees upheld. The most important individual interests affected, on the other hand, were those of the department and those of individual black and white troopers, including those eligible for promotion. Taking the interests of black and white troopers as groups, it appears that the promotion quota is fair inasmuch as it provides each of these two racial groups with the proportion of positions within the trooper hierarchy that it most likely would have obtained absent all first-order discrimination. Further, from the perspective of the community served by the troopers the promotion quota seems desirable to the extent that it enhances compositive efficiency.

Turning to the individual interests involved, the promotion quota clearly seems beneficial to individual black troopers. Indeed, the promotions quota increases their individual prospects of success at being promoted to a higher rank. Moreover, to the extent that the discriminatory practices of the department unjustly diminished the prospects of success of individual blacks, their newly increased prospects of success may be viewed as a means to the eventual redress of past injustices. From the perspective of whites—and particularly of innocent white troopers otherwise eligible for promotion—however, the quota results in a substantial decrease in the prospects of promotion. Accordingly, the legitimacy of the promotional quota in *Paradise* ultimately turns on the nature of the burden that it imposes on innocent white troopers.

Both Justice Brennan's plurality opinion and Justice Powell's concurring opinion conclude that the burden imposed by the promotion quota in *Paradise* on innocent white troopers is constitutionally acceptable. Noting that the quota is temporary in nature, Justice Brennan places great significance on the fact that it imposes no absolute bar to white advancement as 50 percent of those promoted are white (182). Moreover, both Justices Brennan and Powell stress that the denial of a promotion imposes a lesser harm than either a layoff or the refusal of a future employment opportunity because of a preferential hiring plan (182, 188–89). In fact, in Justice Powell's opinion, the promotion quota in *Paradise* is merely likely to *delay* the promotions of certain white troopers (189).

One may object that the fact that a lost or delayed promotion is likely to cause a lesser harm than a lost job or job opportunity should not be dispositive of the constitutionality of a promotion quota such as that in *Paradise.* Consistent with the preceding analysis of the preferential layoffs in *Wygant,* it may be argued that the relevant inquiry is not whether a lost promotion is less painful than a layoff or a lost job opportunity. Instead, what is important is whether the difference between the burden imposed by a race-conscious promotion policy and a color-blind one is a constitutionally tolerable one.

According to the Court's majority in *Paradise,* the burden imposed by the promotion quota on innocent white troopers was constitutionally permissible. Moreover, this conclusion is buttressed by Justice Stevens' assertion in his concurring opinion that though "innocent," the white troopers were the "beneficiaries of the past illegal conduct" of the department (193*n.*2). As Justice Stevens sees it, although the white troopers in *Paradise* were innocent in the sense that they were not personally responsible for the institution and implementation of the department's racially discriminatory and exclusionary practices, they nevertheless benefited from the prolonged absence of real competition from black candidates for promotion (193).

White troopers who joined the department during the time that no blacks were hired for the trooper force benefited from the reduction in competition for entry-level trooper positions. Indeed, some among these white troopers would undoubtedly not have been hired had there been no discrimination against blacks. If these white troopers were eligible for promotion prior to the time the department began hiring blacks, they enjoyed greater opportunities for promotion than they would have absent first-order discrimination. Whites who were hired after the department ended hiring discrimination and who received, or were eligible for, a promotion prior to the institution of the promotions quota also clearly enjoyed a benefit attributable to the department's discriminatory practices. Some of these white troopers obtained promotions that they would not have received otherwise; the remainder benefited from a significant increase in prospects for a promotion, attributable to the advance elimination of all potential competition from black troopers.

In the last analysis, in many cases the benefits reaped by "innocent" white troopers clearly seem to justify the imposition on them of the burdens produced by the implementation of a remedial promotions quota. Moreover, even if no benefits are involved—as in the case of white troopers hired after the promotions quota went into effect—the burden imposed by preferential promotions seems significantly lighter than that imposed by preferential hiring or layoffs. That fact alone, however, is not sufficient to justify the conclusion that preferential promotions are constitutional. Although that conclusion may well be ultimately warranted, the Court in *Paradise* fails to provide the necessary justification.

G. Women and Affirmative Action: The Johnson Case

In *Johnson* v. *Transportation Agency Santa Clara County, California*, the Supreme Court addressed for the first—and thus far the only—time the issue of the legitimacy of affirmative action plans that provide for preferential treatment of women. *Johnson* arose in the context of Title VII, but its importance extends well beyond the confines of statutory interpretation. Indeed, although the constraints imposed on affirmative action by Title VII differ from those that issue from the Constitution, there is a substantial overlap between the relevant statutory and constitutional criteria applicable to preferential treatment plans put into effect by public employers.[29] Accordingly, the six-to-three decision in *Johnson* upholding under Title VII the validity of a preferential promotions plan favoring women sheds important light on the constitutionality of affirmative action plans designed to benefit women.

The litigation in *Johnson* arose out of the voluntary affirmative action plan unilaterally promulgated by the Transportation Agency of Santa Clara County (619). The Agency decided to implement its plan, which included among other features preferential promotions favoring women, because of its conclusion that the mere prohibition of discrimination would not be sufficient to remedy the effects of past practices and to permit the achievement of an equitable representation of women on its workforce (620). Specifically, the agency's plan provided that in making promotions in "traditionally segregated job classifications" in which women are "significantly underrepresented" the agency is authorized to consider the sex of a qualified applicant as one among several relevant factors (622). At the time the plan was adopted, women represented approximately 36 percent of the county's workforce, but only 22 percent of the agency's employees (621). Moreover, none of the skilled craft worker positions at the agency were held then by women. In 1979, there was an opening for the promotional skilled craft position of road dispatcher. Twelve county employees applied for promotion to road dispatcher, including the plaintiff, Johnson, and Joyce, the woman who was eventually awarded the promotion (623).

Nine of the twelve applicants, including Joyce and Johnson, were deemed qualified for the job and were interviewed by a two-person board. Seven of the nine scored above 70 in this interview and were thus certified eligible for selection by the appointing authority. Johnson's score of 75 earned him a tie for the second highest score, while Joyce ranked next with a score of 73. The board recommended that Johnson be promoted, but before any final action was taken, Joyce contacted the agency's affirmative action office and expressed her fears that her application would not receive a disinterested review. As no woman had ever before been employed as a road dispatcher, the coordinator of the affirmative action office recommended to the agency director that Joyce be promoted (623–24). The agency director, who had also reviewed the board's recommendation that Johnson be promoted, finally decided that Joyce ought to be promoted. He subsequently explained that his decision had been based on the consideration of several factors, among which Joyce's sex was but one (625).

The chief importance of the Supreme Court's decision in *Johnson* lies in its approval for the first time of an affirmative action plan designed to provide preferential treatment to women. The Court's majority opinion is remarkable, however, for its virtually complete silence on the issue of whether affirmative action plans favoring women ought to be regarded differently than those that favor racial minorities. Indeed, the majority opinion does not explicitly deal with any of the following important questions: whether the assimilationist ideal accepted by the Supreme Court in relation to distinctions based on race should be applied without qualification to gender-based differences; whether—assuming legitimation of the assimilationist ideal with respect to gender-based differences—past practices having a discriminatory effect on women justify the pursuit of affirmative action plans that favor women; and, assuming a positive answer to the last question, whether affirmative action is likely to display the same virtues as a remedy in the context of gender-based first-order discrimination as it arguably has in that of racial discrimination.

According to Justice Brennan's majority opinion, the legitimacy of an affirmative action plan favoring women does not hinge on proof of past first-order discrimination by the public employer using preferential promotions. The validity of such a plan, however, does appear to depend on the existence of some kind of first-order discrimination against women. Accordingly, Justice Brennan indicates that preferential treatment of women is warranted under Title VII if it is pursued for purposes of eliminating the effects of sex discrimination in the workplace (632). Moreover, at least in the eyes of the three dissenting justices, what the majority of the Court has approved in *Johnson* is the use of preferential treatment of women to overcome the effect of "societal attitudes" that have limited the entry of women into certain types of jobs (664).

Because of "societal discrimination," there was a paucity of women in traditionally segregated job categories, and the agency set out to remedy this imbalance. As a benchmark for assessing its progress in eradicating the effects of such discrimination, the agency set the long-term goal of having a workforce that mirrors the percentage of women in the area labor force (621–22). Justice Brennan noted that there were "strong social pressures" against women pursuing certain types of jobs and that in some areas there were not enough women with the requisite skills (634*n.12*). In view of this, he felt that the agency was justified in setting flexible annual short-term goals designed "to provide a more realistic indication of the degree to which sex should be taken into account in filling particular positions" (635). The goal established by the agency for openings in the skilled craft workers job category for the year 1982 was to award 3 of the 55, or 6 percent, of the expected openings to women. According to the Court's majority, this goal was modest and flexible, and it imposed a minimal intrusion on the legitimate expectations of male employees, who could still count on being awarded 94 percent of the available skill craft positions (638–39*n.15*). Finally, emphasizing that Joyce's sex was only one of the factors that were weighed in arriving at the decision that led to her promotion over Johnson (637), the majority noted that notwithstanding the "small dent" that Joyce's promotion made on the numbers, it had a much larger impact inasmuch as it communicated encouragement to other women to consider the possibility of "non-traditional" employment (637*n.14*).

A major issue not addressed by the Court's majority is whether job segregation along gender lines ought to be automatically associated with first-order discrimination, as racial segregation in jobs most likely would. This issue was addressed, however, in Justice Scalia's dissenting opinion. According to Justice Scalia, it is wrong to attribute the same meaning to the job segregation involved in *Johnson* as to that found in a case such as *Weber,* where blacks were systematically excluded from certain positions. In Justice Scalia's own forceful words,

> It is absurd to think that the nationwide failure of road maintenance crews, for example, to achieve the Agency's ambition of

> 36.4% female representation is attributable primarily, if even substantially, to systematic exclusion of women eager to shoulder pick and shovel. It is a "traditionally segregated job category" *not* in the *Weber* sense, but in the sense that, because of longstanding social attitudes it has not been regarded *by women themselves* as desirable work. (Emphasis in original; 688)

To the extent that women themselves may not desire certain kinds of jobs, job segregation according to gender does indeed seem to be different than its racially based counterpart. Arguably, however, this difference should mark the beginning, not the end, of the relevant inquiry. Justice Scalia is certainly aware of this, but nonetheless expresses considerable doubt that social attitudes that lead women away from certain jobs are reprehensible in the way that first-order discrimination is (688). If one believes that such social attitudes are legitimate, then it seems justified to reject affirmative action as a means to reverse the consequences that naturally flow from the expression of these attitudes. Indeed, if these social attitudes draw significant normative support from nearly unanimously accepted nonassimilationist values, then attempts to alter these attitudes may entirely lack in justification.

On the other hand, there may be strong support for the view that social attitudes which tend to channel women away from certain jobs are not only as pernicious as first-order discrimination, but in one sense even more harmful. Whereas first-order discrimination is generally manifest for all to see, and its effects well known, the evils attributable to sexist social attitudes are often concealed, and their effects not readily perceived even by their victims. Accordingly, the evil consequences of sexist social attitudes may be easier to perpetuate than those of first-order discrimination. Affirmative action appears to be uniquely suited to break up the vicious cycle created by the exclusion of women from certain jobs which leads them not to seek such jobs and which, in turn, apparently justifies their continuing exclusion from these jobs. For one thing, the very institution of a preferential hiring or promotions plan favoring women poses a dramatic challenge to the sexist social attitudes sought to be altered. It forces these attitudes into the open and challenges their proponents either to justify them—as part of their efforts to refute the legitimacy of affirmative action—or to reconsider them. For another thing, such a preferential hiring or promotions plan forces employers to hire or promote the few women who, like Joyce, already possess the requisite skills to fill traditionally segregated positions. As mentioned by Justice Brennan, hiring someone like Joyce is likely to have an important symbolic and communicative impact. It lets both employers and prospective female employees know that women are suited to fill traditionally segregated positions, and it generally undermines the presuppositions behind sexist social attitudes. Thus, for example, if myths concerning women's physical and psychological attributes lend apparent justification to the conclusion that women do not belong on the police force, then the most effective way to refute these assumptions may be to have female police officers who perform all their professional duties with skill and competence. In short, in certain cases at least, affirmative action arguably provides the best means toward a speedy and effective breakdown of stereotypical sexist social attitudes.

Even if affirmative action is effective in altering sexist social attitudes, the question remains whether preferential treatment can be given satisfactory legal and constitutional justification when used to combat stereotypical social attitudes. Unlike in the context of first-order discrimination, merely sharing with a vast portion of society certain stereotypical attitudes arguably does not justify charging any particular agent of allocation with an individualized duty of compensation. Indeed, certain stereotypical attitudes may be widespread and even embraced by a significant number of the members of the group that is stereotyped. Accordingly, it seems unfair to impose a duty of compensation on a select number of employers who are no more responsible for perpetuating gender-based stereotypes than anyone else. In other words, inasmuch as the ideal of assimilation is nearly always applicable in the context of race, any affirmative action plan designed to remedy the effects of violations of that ideal presumably includes a compensatory component. On the other hand, if the ideal of assimilation is not likewise operative in the context of gender, then gender-based affirmative action plans designed to remedy the effects of anti-assimilationist policies may not be performing any compensatory function.

Affirmative action plans that favor women, however, can be given legal and constitutional justification even if they lack a compensatory purpose. As will be remembered, Justice Stevens offered a purely forward-looking constitutional justification of affirmative action in *Wygant*. According to Justice Stevens, an affirmative action plan is constitutional if it is used in the pursuit of a valid (distributive) state purpose, if it is *inclusionary* rather than *exclusionary*, and if the benefits it creates outweigh the burdens it imposes on innocent third parties.[30] Some affirmative action plans favoring women satisfy this test, as does the preferential promotions plan in *Johnson*. Indeed, the purpose of that plan was to remove an impediment that prevented women from obtaining distributive justice at the workplace. Moreover, the plan was designed to increase the representation in the workforce of women like Joyce, and not to exclude men like Johnson, or to stigmatize them or cast them as inferiors. Thus, the plan was inclusionary rather than exclusionary. Finally, to the extent that it set a modest short-term hiring and promotion goal of 6 percent, the benefits produced by the plan in *John-*

son easily outweigh the burden that it imposed on a relatively small number of innocent male employees—the temporary postponement of certain promotions.

There is also another possible distributive justification for affirmative action in favor of women, which is not purely forward-looking. As already indicated, one of the most noteworthy aspects of the majority opinion in *Johnson* is its conclusion that a public employer need not have engaged in first-order discrimination to be able to adopt an affirmative action plan that is legitimate under Title VII.[31] This justification apparently does away with the necessity of a compensatory requirement without thereby abandoning the demand that a valid plan have a backward-looking component. Accordingly, affirmative action could be justified as a means to rectify the present effects of past conduct even if it fulfills no compensatory purpose. Consistent with this, preferential treatment may be as justified in the context of a shift in the prevailing distributive norms as in that of violations of a single distributive norm. Therefore, women whose opportunities have been handicapped as a consequence of the projection of repudiated social attitudes would seem as deserving of preferential treatment as the minority victims of past first-order discrimination.

Even if this last argument is deemed persuasive in the context of Title VII, it is likely to encounter stiff opposition in that of the Constitution. Indeed, under Justice Powell's marginal equality position, both in its *Bakke* and *Wygant* formulations, legitimate deviations from the equal treatment principle require proof of wrongdoing by the public entity dispensing preferential treatment. Moreover, even under the global equality position taken by the Brennan group in *Bakke,* constitutional affirmative action must at least in part be compensatory, albeit that the public entity providing preferential treatment need not itself have been a wrongdoer.

Neither Justice Powell's nor Justice Brennan's above-mentioned position have thus far received any comprehensive justification. It is therefore fair to inquire whether it would be constitutionally defensible to waive the compensatory requirement in the case of a *voluntarily* implemented affirmative action plan that is *both* backward- and forward-looking. In other words, the question is whether, all other things being equal, the same affirmative action plan would become unjust only because, instead of being carried out by a guilty employer, it is carried out by one who is an innocent volunteer.

The most logical answer to this question is a negative one. The compensatory requirement with respect to the employer clearly seems justified primarily out of concern for the rights of the latter. While it may be unjust to require one who is innocent to "pay" for the damages caused by another, it does not seem unjust to allow a volunteer to assume the burdens of compensation. Moreover, particularly where the actual wrongdoer is out of reach, it actually seems *desirable* to encourage such voluntary undertakings.

An otherwise legitimate affirmative action plan designed to remedy the present effects of past first-order discrimination should not lose its validity simply by virtue of being run by an innocent volunteer. Similarly, a voluntarily implemented affirmative action plan in favor of women, in the context of stereotypical social attitudes rather than overt first-order sex discrimination, should not be deemed necessarily illegitimate. To determine whether it may be legitimate, however, requires further elucidation. As will be remembered, in the case of an affirmative action plan meant to remedy the present effects of past first-order discrimination, considerations of compensatory justice are likely to concern not only the employer who runs the plan, but also the group or the individuals who are to benefit from it. On the other hand, whereas women have undoubtedly been the victims of first-order discrimination, one of the key assumptions made for purposes of this discussion in light of Justice Scalia's opinion in *Johnson* is that the gross underrepresentation of women in certain job categories is not the result of first-order sex discrimination.

Let us compare the case of a black job applicant disadvantaged because of deliberate violations of continuously valid distributive norms with that of a female job applicant who suffers from a similar fate in the context of a shift in the applicable distributive norms. The principal disadvantage experienced by both the black and the woman in question appears to be exactly the same: a significant diminution in the prospects of obtaining certain desirable jobs. Moreover, in both cases, an affirmative action plan designed to remedy the present effect of past practices presumably accomplishes the same thing: it raises the prospects of success of its intended beneficiaries to where they would have been but for the past practice giving rise to the plan.

From a strictly forward-looking perspective it does not seem to make any difference whether an individual lacks the tools needed in the competition for certain jobs because of a racially motivated deprivation of a decent education or because he has squandered numerous readily available educational opportunities. Nor does it seem to matter from this perspective whether a group's lower prospects of success stem from subjection to pervasive first-order racial discrimination or from some freely chosen collective course of action voluntarily endorsed by a vast majority of the members of the group, such as a decision for religious reasons to forgo certain publicly available educational opportunities.[32] In view of this, insistence on some backward-looking justification for a valid affirmative action plan may be invoked to avoid legitimating preferential treatment for those who freely choose to forgo or to squander opportunities that were once fully available to them.

Based on this analysis, preferential treatment in favor of women whose opportunities are reduced as a consequence of widely repudiated social attitudes seems as constitutionally legitimate as preferential treatment of blacks or women whose opportunities have decreased because of first-order discrimination. Indeed, in both cases, the decrease in the prospects of success linked to the relevant specified past practice is not attributable to the voluntary conduct of present members of the disadvantaged group.[33] Moreover, in both cases the means-regarding inequality of opportunity sought to be remedied is the consequence of past social and political practices. In the case of blacks, it is racial discrimination, segregation, and the projection of demeaning stereotypes; in that of women, it is the pervasive dissemination of social attitudes that portray women as ill suited to carry out various kinds of responsible jobs.

The Supreme Court's decision in *Johnson* upholds the legitimacy of affirmative action to combat gender-based job segregation attributable to societal discrimination but largely fails to address the crucial question of whether, from a legal or constitutional standpoint, preferential treatment in employment ought to be treated differently according to whether it favors women or blacks. On the other hand, *Johnson* does make an important contribution to the jurisprudence of affirmative action in general, as a majority on the Court approves the voluntary institution of a gender-based affirmative action plan by a public employer who has not engaged in first-order discrimination. Finally, consistent with the analysis conducted above, in the context of voluntary public employer participation, it appears that affirmative action in favor of women can be justified to remedy the present effects of past social practices to the same extent as affirmative action in favor of blacks, even assuming that the competitive disadvantages of women are not, strictly speaking, attributable to first-order discrimination.

H. A Constitutional Turning Point: The Croson Case

In its 1989 decision in *City of Richmond* v. *J. A. Croson Co.* a majority on the Supreme Court for the first time has settled on a single standard—the strict scrutiny test—to determine the constitutionality of affirmative action based on race.[34] *Croson* therefore marks an important turning point. The Court's decision declared unconstitutional a minority business enterprise (MBE) set-aside program devised by the Richmond, Virginia, City Council (717–20). The holding and tenor of the Court's opinion stand in sharp contrast with the Court's decision in *Fullilove*, where virtually identical federally mandated set-asides were found to be constitutional. Although the two cases are technically distinguishable,[35] and although it is certainly too early to assess the full impact in *Croson*, the clear change in direction signaled by the holding in *Croson* seems likely to strike a major blow against long-standing concerted efforts to narrow the economic gap between black and white entrepreneurs.

At the core of the *Croson* controversy is the minority set-aside provision of the Richmond municipal public works contract ordinance. To place this ordinance in its proper context, it is important to keep in mind that as the "cradle of the Old Confederacy" (757; Blackmun, J., dissenting), Richmond stands as a symbol of the sad history of slavery, racial discrimination, and segregation that cast blacks as inferiors and systematically deprived them of the most basic rights and benefits enjoyed by whites. Well into the 1970s, Richmond stood as a vivid epitome of the stubborn persistence of racial "apartheid" (748; Marshall, J., dissenting) in all too many municipalities throughout the United States. Through the official acts of its governing officials, Richmond, among other things, deliberately diluted the voting rights of its black residents, mounted stiff hurdles against school desegregation, and sanctioned pervasive housing discrimination (748).

Juxtaposed to this all-too-negative picture of Richmond, however, is a much more positive and hopeful one of more recent vintage. Not only have blacks now come to share political power with whites in Richmond, but members of both races have "joined hands" to deal constructively with controversial matters (753; Marshall, J., dissenting). For example, since 1975, Richmond has outlawed discrimination by the city and by private parties in the award and performance of public contracts (751; Marshall, J., dissenting). Thus, the *Croson* controversy is embedded in a sequence of events marking the transition between two eras.

This is not to say that Richmond has achieved racial equality. The construction industry, in particular, had been particularly resistant to racial integration, with minorities almost completely left out. This phenomenon, however, was not unique to Richmond. The construction industry had been notorious in its exclusion of blacks on both a statewide and nationwide basis (714). The problem in Richmond was therefore both similar to, and part of, a much broader national problem. Not surprisingly, the solution sought by Richmond was along the same lines as that adopted earlier by Congress.

While Richmond's 1975 outlawing of discrimination in public contracts removed formal barriers to participation by minorities, it did not bring about racial integration in the city's construction industry (726). In 1983, when Richmond enacted its ordinance mandating the preferential set-asides, the city's population was 50 percent black, but only 0.67

percent of its prime construction contracts had been awarded to MBEs in the five years preceding adoption of the ordinance (714). Against this background, the city enacted an affirmative action plan ("the Plan") requiring contractors awarded city construction contracts to subcontract a minimum of 30 percent of the total dollar amount of each contract to MBEs (712–13).

The Plan was supposed to be "remedial" in nature and was enacted for a limited duration of five years "for the purpose of promoting wider participation by minority business enterprises in the construction of public projects" (713; quoting Richmond, Virginia, city code §12-158a). Adoption of the Plan came after a public hearing, at which a member of the city council testified to widespread "race discrimination and exclusion on the basis of race" in the construction industry (714; quoting statement of councilperson Marsh). In addition, participants at the hearing introduced the statistics concerning the disparity between Richmond's black population and the number of city contracts awarded to MBEs, and noted the virtually complete lack of MBE membership in local construction trade associations (714).

Superficially, *Croson*'s contribution to the constitutional jurisprudence of affirmative action seems to be simple and clear: for the first time a majority of justices on the Court agreed that race-based preferential treatment can be justified under the equal protection clause only if it meets the strict scrutiny test. Upon more probing consideration, however, the picture that emerges is anything but clear. First, although six of the justices found the Plan to be unconstitutional, only five agreed that the strict scrutiny test provided the correct judicial standard.[36] Of those five, moreover, only four—a mere plurality—agreed on what would satisfy strict scrutiny in the context of race-based affirmative action—that is, compensation to actual victims of past discrimination, even if not undertaken by the actual wrongdoers (729). The fifth justice in this group, Justice Scalia, had a more narrow conception of strict scrutiny and argued that it would only be satisfied when compensation is undertaken by actual wrongdoers (287; Scalia, J., concurring).

The dissenting justices rejected adoption of the strict scrutiny test in favor of the more lenient intermediate scrutiny test (243; Marshall, J., dissenting). They also noted that, in prior affirmative action cases, the justices disagreed on the appropriate standard of review but always took a practical approach (245; Marshall, J., dissenting). Finally, notwithstanding their contention that the strict scrutiny test "is strict in theory but fatal in fact" (752; Marshall, J., dissenting; quoting *Fullilove* v. *Klutznick* [1980], Marshall, J., concurring), the dissenters sought to demonstrate that, contrary to the majority's conclusions, the Plan involved in *Croson* met even the requirements of strict scrutiny.

Notwithstanding their disagreements on several other matters, all nine justices seem to agree in *Croson* on the proper conception of constitutional equality at the highest levels of abstraction. They all believe that the equal protection clause is designed to uphold the equal worth, dignity, and respect of every individual regardless of race (720–21; Stevens, J., concurring at 730; Scalia, J., concurring at 736–39; Marshall, J., dissenting at 750). Moreover, in spite of their differences on the legitimacy of color-conscious means, all the justices share the notion that the ultimate fulfillment of constitutional equality lies in the establishment of a truly color-blind society (727). Also, several justices reiterate that it is a central purpose of the equal protection clause to constitutionalize the principle of equality of opportunity (720–21). Yet, for all these points of convergence, the disagreements concerning the proper constitutional standard by which to assess affirmative action evince a failure on the part of all the justices to make necessary connections between different levels of abstraction and to promote a satisfactory resolution of the continuing split over the two conflicting judicial positions articulated in *Bakke*.

Because of Justice Scalia's refusal to join her opinion on this point, Justice O'Connor's views on strict scrutiny are only shared by a plurality of justices. Her analysis is firmly anchored in the marginal equality position articulated in *Bakke*.[37] Justice O'Connor specifies that race-based affirmative action can meet the strict scrutiny test if it is "remedial" in nature (721). A remedial race-based affirmative action plan serves a compelling state interest if it is compensatory in nature, and if it is properly circumscribed to benefit only actual victims of discrimination. Such a plan need not, however, be carried out by a wrongdoer in order to remain constitutional so long as a nonwrongdoer assumes a duty of compensation voluntarily (727–29).

Justice O'Connor's conception differs from that of Justice Powell in *Bakke*,[38] on whom she relies as a proponent of equal treatment (721; quoting *Regents of University of California* v. *Bakke* [1978] at 298), and from that expressed in his plurality opinion in *Wygant*,[39] which she joined. As we have seen, in his opinions in *Bakke* and *Wygant*, Justice Powell stresses that, in order to be constitutionally permissible, compensatory affirmative action must be dispensed by a wrongdoer.[40] In his opinion in *Wygant*, however, Justice Powell specifies that compensatory affirmative action provided by a wrongdoer does not cease being constitutional if its benefits extend beyond "actual" victims of racial discrimination.[41] Accordingly, in *Bakke* Justice Powell equates constitutional compensatory affirmative action with the paradigm case of compensatory justice, while in *Wygant* he equates it with a model that differs from the paradigm on the side of the victim but not on that of the wrongdoer. In short, the two opinions by Justice Powell in *Bakke* and *Wygant* and Justice O'Connor's opinion in *Croson* yield three different models of constitutionally permissible compensatory affirmative action.

Although all three models are predicated on adoption of the marginal equality position announced in *Bakke,* they cannot be reconciled or comprehensively evaluated on the basis of the conception of constitutional equality that emerges from the Supreme Court's affirmative action decisions. All three models implicitly acknowledge the validity of limited departures from equal treatment, but it is not clear whether the particular departure associated with any one of the three models is more consistent with the governing principle of equal treatment. Therefore, from the perspective reflected in Justice O'Connor's opinion in *Croson,* no principled determination can be made between compelling and noncompelling compensatory affirmative action.

Embracing a much broader conception of what counts as "remedial," Justice O'Connor asserts that a city like Richmond has a compelling interest in preventing the expenditure of its tax dollars in furtherance of private racial discrimination:

> If the city could show that it had essentially become a "passive participant" in a system of racial exclusion practiced by elements of the local construction industry, we think it clear that the city could take affirmative steps to dismantle such a system. It is beyond dispute that any public entity, state or federal, has a compelling interest in assuring that public dollars, drawn from the tax contributions of all citizens, do not serve to finance the evil of private prejudice. (720)

Thus, if the construction industry is dominated by white-owned businesses that systematically refuse to deal with MBEs or to hire black candidates of employment, then a municipality would have a compelling interest in instituting a set-aside provision reserving some of its public construction contract work for MBEs.

This latest compelling state interest is in a broad sense "remedial," in that it is designed to rectify the effects of objectionable past or present private practices. Unlike the previous compelling interest advanced by Justice O'Connor and discussed above, however, the interest now under consideration relates to a distributive rather than a compensatory use of affirmative action. Indeed, on the assumption that public authorities have had no hand in the institution and maintenance of private racially discriminatory practices in the construction industry, the government would have no compensatory duty toward any of the victims of such private discrimination. Further, institution of the set-aside would not lead to exaction of compensation from the private wrongdoers, in the sense of divesting them from unjust gains already realized or forcing them to make any of their victims "whole." Nor would such a set-aside necessarily serve to compensate actual victims of private discrimination, because it presumably draws no distinction between victim and nonvictim MBEs. On the other hand, through implementation of the set-aside, the government would prevent the use of public funds in furtherance of a private scheme in the construction industry designed to prevent minorities from receiving any significant share of the available construction business.

Thus, although distributive in nature, the compelling state interest in not having public funds used to further private racial discrimination is not purely forward-looking. It aims to thwart the derivation of future distributive benefits traceable to the exploitation of advantages gained by past wrongdoing. Justice O'Connor's opinion does not furnish a theoretical nexus between her relatively narrow conception of constitutionally permissible compensatory affirmative action and her relatively broad conception of constitutionally permissible distributive affirmative action. At a practical level, however, those two conceptions are linked inasmuch as they both condition the constitutional legitimacy of affirmative action on the existence of past or ongoing racial discrimination. Therefore, consistent with Justice O'Connor's analysis, affirmative action, whether it is compensatory or distributive, can only be constitutional if it is "necessary" to remedy wrongs caused by past or ongoing discrimination.

Justice O'Connor's opinion fails to provide an overall framework that would reconcile her vision of what makes race-based affirmative action a necessary means toward a compelling state end with some coherent vision of constitutional equality. Her conception of strict scrutiny as articulated in *Croson* leaves many important questions unanswered. Moreover, Justice O'Connor's refusal to uphold the constitutionality of the Plan seems at odds with her relatively broad tolerance of distributive affirmative action. Actually, she only manages to reconcile the two by combining an exceptionally stringent causal requirement with a completely abstract and acontextual grasp of the relevant facts.

The dissenting justices, for their part, embrace the global equality position articulated in *Bakke* and reject the propriety of subjecting racial classifications favoring blacks to the strict scrutiny test (752; Marshall, J., dissenting). The dissenting justices advocate adoption of the intermediate scrutiny test in the context of affirmative action favoring blacks (743; Marshall, J., dissenting) but nonetheless offer a demonstration that the Richmond Plan, placed in its proper historical, social, and political context, does satisfy the requirements imposed by that test.

According to Justice Marshall's assessment, the Plan in *Croson* clearly satisfies the strict scrutiny test. In his view, Richmond can advance two compelling interests for enacting the Plan. The first is the city's interest in "eradicating the effects of past racial discrimination" (743; Marshall, J., dissenting). Even assuming that racial discrimination in Richmond is a thing of the past, the city still has, in Justice Marshall's judgment, a compelling interest to remove "barriers to competitive access, which had their roots in racial and ethnic discriminations, and which continue today" (743; Marshall, J., dissenting; quoting *Fullilove* v. *Klutznick* [1980] at 478; Powell, J., concurring). In other words, so long as equality of opportunity is not fully realized in the competition for public works construction contracts due to lingering effects of past discrimination, Richmond has a compelling interest to intervene in that competition, through affirmative action if necessary, in order to level the field of competition. Further, in this context, preferential treatment of blacks who are not "actual" victims of racial discrimination would be justified as a "necessary" means to end disproportionate opportunities for success deriving ultimately from past racist practices. Therefore, preferential treatment of nonvictims, which Justice O'Connor considers to be inadmissible under strict scrutiny, satisfies Justice Marshall's interpretation of that test (754–55; Marshall, J., dissenting).

The second compelling interest singled out by Justice Marshall in *Croson* is also considered compelling by Justice O'Connor. This is Richmond's interest in preventing city funds from being spent in ways that reinforce and perpetuate the effects of private discriminatory practices in the public works construction industry (744; Marshall, J., dissenting; 720; O'Connor, J.). In spite of their agreement that this interest is compelling, Justices O'Connor and Marshall are led to opposite conclusions largely on the basis of their respective assessments of the relevant facts and circumstances present in *Croson*.

In the last analysis, the majority's adoption of the strict scrutiny test as the applicable standard by which to determine the constitutionality of race-based affirmative action does not introduce any significant new measure of clarity or stability to the confusing status of preferential treatment plans under the equal protection clause. As we have seen, besides being inherently indeterminate, strict scrutiny means different things to different justices, and there is no majority agreement in *Croson* on what it requires. Nevertheless, all the conceptions of strict scrutiny elaborated in *Croson* share the following least common denominator: to satisfy the strict scrutiny test, it is necessary to establish a causal nexus between past or ongoing racial discrimination and a resulting present injury or disadvantage.

In contrast to their disagreements concerning the applicable constitutional standard, the justices in *Croson* do agree on the principal facts. Yet, paradoxically, the bitter split between the Court's majority and the dissenters ultimately revolves more around the proper interpretation of commonly accepted facts than around disputes concerning constitutional doctrine. Indeed, acceptance of the same principal facts leads to diametrically opposed conclusions concerning the meaning and existence of compensable discrimination, the causal links between such discrimination and a compensable injury or disadvantage, and suitable remedies to redress the injury or eliminate the disadvantage. Moreover, these opposite conclusions are traceable to reliance on contrasting modes of interpretation.

The first of these—to which I will refer as the atomistic mode of interpretation—is a more discrete mechanical mode of interpretation relying on the disconnection of facts from the context in which they are embedded and on the recombination of such disconnected facts into mechanistic causal chains made up of direct and linear links. The second mode of interpretation—which I will refer to as the ecological mode of interpretation—is more holistic and systemic in nature, approaching social facts and events in terms of the interaction between individuals, groups, and their social, political, and historical environment. Moreover, under an ecological mode of interpretation, causal relationships need not be direct or linear. Instead, they may be indirect and multifaceted, as they are shaped by the historical sequence of adaptations and disruptions that characterize the interactions between human actors and their intersubjective environment.

The contrast between these two modes of interpretation is particularly useful in the context of *Croson* because it helps explain the sharp division between the Court's majority and the dissenters concerning the key issues of racial discrimination and its relation to the disproportionately small number of MBEs awarded public construction contracting work. The majority's emphasis on "amorphous" societal discrimination (722–23), and the supposed absence of an unbroken direct causal link between such discrimination and the infinitesimally small number of MBEs engaged in public construction contracting work (723–26), clearly exemplifies the atomistic mode of interpretation. In contrast, the dissent's focus on the voluminous historical record of official discrimination (740–43, 746; Marshall, J., dissenting) and on the interrelationship between numerous race-conscious and seemingly race-neutral practices (752) reflect the ecological mode of interpretation.

Viewing the matter from the standpoint of the atomistic mode of interpretation, as does Justice O'Connor, it is difficult in the factual setting of *Croson* to extract any direct causal links. Although Justice O'Connor acknowledges "the sorry history of both private and public discrimination in the country," she then reduces it in Richmond's case to the label "societal discrimination," which in her view does not warrant imposing a "rigid racial quota" in the award of public construction contracts (714). This is because two different sets of relevant factual considerations conceivably lead to a break in the mechanistic causal chain the would otherwise directly link the admitted "sorry history" of discrimination to the virtually complete lack of MBEs in public construction contract work in Richmond prior to the institution of the Plan. The first of these factual considerations relates to the enactment in 1975 by Richmond of a city ordinance prohibiting "both discrimination in the award of public contracts and employment discrimination by public contractors," and to the lack of evidence concerning violations of this ordinance (726*n.3*).

The second set of relevant factual considerations relates to the existence of nonracial factors that may account for the lack of success by MBEs in the competition for Richmond's public construction contracts. Among these nonracial factors, Justice O'Connor mentions "deficiencies in working capital, inability to meet bonding requirements, unfamiliarity with bidding procedures, and disability caused by an insufficient track record," all of which she believes are likely to affect anyone seeking to establish a new business, regardless of race (724). Finally, Justice O'Connor speculates that perhaps today's imbalance may be due ultimately to black entrepreneurs' disproportionate attraction to industries other than construction (726). In short, Justice O'Connor appears to disconnect salient occurrences from one another and from the broader context in which they emerge, and to accept the existence of causal links between such occurrences only if every other plausible alternative must be ruled out.

Justice Marshall, in contrast, adopts the ecological mode of interpretation and reaches diametrically opposed conclusions concerning discrimination, its effects, and the need for affirmative action. For him, racial discrimination is not merely the product of certain separable and clearly definable acts with fully circumscribed and readily recognizable effects. Instead, when placed in its proper context, discrimination, according to Justice Marshall, "takes a myriad of 'ingenious and pervasive forms' " (745; Marshall, J., dissenting [quoting *Regents of University of California* v. *Bakke* (1978) at 387; Marshall, J., concurring in part and dissenting in part]).

From the standpoint of Justice Marshall's contextual approach, the juxtaposition of Richmond's massive pre-1975 official racial discrimination, of the systematic nationwide and local private discrimination in the construction industry, of Richmond's 1975 antidiscrimination ordinance, and of the fact that by 1983 only 0.67 percent of the city's public construction contracting work went to MBEs, clearly points to the conclusion that the present-day racial imbalance is the effect of past (and present) invidious discrimination. Indeed, when placed in its proper historical context, Richmond's 1975 race-neutral antidiscrimination ordinance does not break the causal chain that leads from past systematic discrimination to subsequent grossly disproportionate racial imbalance in the construction industry. Instead, the antidiscrimination ordinance has the effect of largely freezing the racial imbalance attributable to the outlawed pre-1975 practices (751; Marshall, J., dissenting). While adherence to the ordinance may prevent the imbalance from worsening through further purposeful exclusion, it does nothing to rectify the imbalance as it stood in 1975. Thus, if—as is the case in *Croson*—construction trade associations have virtually no black members (714), race-neutral public contracting practices alone are not likely to lead to an increase in MBE participation. That result might not seem unjust if the paltry minority representation among Richmond's contractors were truly simply a matter of choice. But, when placed in context, the disproportionately small number of blacks seeking to join the construction industry, contrary to Justice O'Connor's suggestion (726), is not a matter of mere predilection. It is rather a reflection of the long experience of humiliation and rejection that has made blacks reluctant to enter what they justifiably perceive as a hostile environment.

Justice Marshall also rejects Justice O'Connor's suggestion that since certain nonracial factors may have contributed to the failure of MBEs to obtain a greater proportion of Richmond's public construction contracts, available race-neutral remedies must be exhausted before turning to affirmative action. According to Justice Marshall, race-neutral remedies, such as loosening bonding requirements or simplifying bidding procedures, have not led to significant improvements for MBEs when used in the past (751; Marshall, J., dissenting). Moreover, one might add, from a contextualist standpoint, that the seemingly race-neutral factors invoked by the Court remain so only when viewed in isolation. In the context of systematic racial discrimination, these factors take on another light, as they are likely to exacerbate the relative disadvantages experienced by victims of racism. As an illustration, the inability of an entrepreneur to meet bonding requirements may not be unjust if it is the consequence of unwise past business practices on his part rather than of racial oppression. Accordingly, loosening bonding requirements for all enterprises instead of instituting a set-aside for the victims of racial oppression may be an overbroad remedy, providing a competitive windfall for certain nonminority entrepreneurs without placing the victims of racism in the competitive position in which they would have been absent discrimination.

If it is constitutionally legitimate for Richmond to do whatever is required to eradicate racial discrimination and its lingering effects in all public construction contracting work, then a strong argument can be made that recourse to the ecological mode of interpretation is amply justified. More generally, the ecological mode of interpretation seems to go hand-in-hand with the global equality position, while the atomistic mode of interpretation seems more compatible with the marginal equality position. In the last analysis, therefore, the justification of each of these modes of interpretation would seem to depend on that of the respective position with which it is associated.

Croson is a case of considerable importance, but not necessarily for the reasons that are apparent initially. Settling, for the first time, on a single judicial test for the determination of the constitutionality of race-based affirmative action is undoubtedly noteworthy. *Croson*'s principal importance, however, may in the long run lie elsewhere. What is most remarkable about the Supreme Court's decision in *Croson* is the stark contrast between the apparent simplicity and clarity of the legal test that the Court embraces and that test's inability to account coherently for the complexities inherent in the controversy that it purports to resolve. Accordingly, far from bringing lasting order to the constitutional debate over affirmative action, *Croson* only manages to overcome hopeless fragmentation by systematically decontextualizing whatever stands in the way of its single-minded resolve to reach its ultimate legal conclusion. Thus, although the majority in *Croson* opts for the marginal equality position, it certainly fails to make a persuasive case for it.

The ten Supreme Court decisions considering the legitimacy of affirmative action reviewed in the course of the preceding analysis provide an incomplete and inconclusive picture of the constitutional virtues and vices of preferential treatment because of race or gender. This is due, in significant part, to the sharp divisions among the various justices on the Court. These divisions have led to several affirmative action decisions without majority opinion, and to a consequent frequent lack of judicial guidance concerning the legitimate scope and limitations of affirmative action beyond the very narrow confines of the particular factual settings in an individual case. In particular, members of the Court are sharply divided on what ought to count as a sufficient constitutional justification for affirmative action.

At one end of the spectrum, one finds Justice Stevens, who has embraced a purely forward-looking distributive justification of affirmative action. Next, is the more narrowly drawn forward-looking justification endorsed by Justice Powell In *Bakke.* According to that justification, while quotas in university admissions are impermissible, counting race as one of many factors is permissible for purposes of fostering racial diversity among the student body. A much broader justification of affirmative action that is both forward- and backward-looking is that announced by the Brennan group in *Bakke,* to the effect that preferential treatment including quotas is constitutionally permissible if used to remedy the present effects of past first-order discrimination. This justification involves both a compensatory and distributive component, although as argued in the course of the discussion of the *Johnson* case, it may, under certain circumstances, be based exclusively on distributive considerations. Finally, at the other end of the spectrum are the differing narrowly compensatory justifications articulated by Justices Powell, O'Connor, and Scalia.

While the various justifications endorsed by members of the Court span from narrowly compensatory to broadly distributive, the Court's opinions fail to provide a coherent account of the relationship between the compensatory and distributive components of justifications, such as that of the Brennan group in *Bakke*. Further, while some of the justices seem willing to consider as legitimate only individual-regarding equalities affected by affirmative action, others, at least implicitly, appear to place significant weight on group-regarding equalities that might have a bearing on the distribution of individual equalities. None of the Court's opinions, however, provide a satisfactory account of the proper constitutional balance between group-regarding and individual-regarding interests, in light of the fact that it is the individual who is the subject of equal protection under the law.

Finally, the Court's decisions provide extensive treatment of the issue of the burden that affirmative action plans impose on "innocent" third parties. Preferential layoffs place the heaviest burden on the latter, followed respectively by preferential hirings and by preferential promotions. Consistent with this, the Court has struck down preferential layoffs in *Stotts* and *Wygant,* while on occasion approving both preferential hiring and preferential promotions. Despite this extensive treatment, however, the Court's resolution of the innocent third party dilemma has thus far been superficial. Layoffs are inherently more painful than the failure to be hired or promoted, but that is almost beside the point when determining the legitimacy of an affirmative action plan. Instead, what is important is whether the difference in burden between preferential layoffs, hiring, and promotions and their respective race-neutral or gender-neutral counterparts is constitutionally tolerable. And on this last issue the Court provides very little guidance. Ultimately, the Supreme Court has not offered a fully coherent satisfactory solution to any of the three major issues discussed above. Nevertheless, the extensive, if partial and fragmented, record of the Supreme Court on these three issues suggests possible avenues of justification for affirmative action plans. In Part Three, I shall attempt to explore these possibilities in light of the philosophical insights concerning affirmative action examined in Part One.

PART THREE

Equality, Difference, and Consensus: Toward an Integrated Conception of the Justice of Affirmative Action

CHAPTER EIGHT

The Limitations of the Major Liberal Philosophical Conceptions of the Justice of Affirmative Action

In Part One of this book, I undertook a critical review of the principal arguments that can be made from the standpoint of liberal philosophy for and against affirmative action. In Part Two, I explored the constitutional dimensions of affirmative action under the equal protection clause as interpreted by the Supreme Court. These inquiries lead me to conclude that liberal philosophy has thus far failed to provide a persuasive systematic account of affirmative action and that the Supreme Court has yet to articulate a sufficiently comprehensive constitutional doctrine capable of bringing principled order and consistency to affirmative action cases arising under the equal protection clause. In Part Three, I seek to develop an integrated philosophical and constitutional conception of the justice of affirmative action consonant with adherence to the postulate of equality. On the philosophical front, I argue that the deficiencies encountered in the libertarian, contractarian, utilitarian, and egalitarian approaches to affirmative action can be overcome through recourse to a dialogical process involving a reversal of perspectives and the suppression of power-dominated strategic communication. In doing so, I rely, in part, on Kohlberg's concept of justice as reversibility and on Habermas' communicative ethics. On the constitutional front, I elaborate on the consequences following from the conclusions reached in Part Two and argue that the antidiscrimination principle should be replaced by a mediating constitutional principle relying on substantive equality and designed to emulate the dialogical process.

Before attempting to construct an integrated philosophical and constitutional conception of the justice of affirmative action, however, we must examine more systematically why none of the intermediate philosophical conceptions traditionally associated with liberal theory succeeds in providing a satisfactory account of the justice of affirmative action. In this chapter, I concentrate on those limitations in the libertarian, contractarian, utilitarian, and egalitarian conceptions of justice that arguably make them inadequate as vehicles for the determination of the scope of the justice of affirmative action in the context of contemporary American society. As we shall see, these various liberal conceptions of justice do not all suffer from the same particular limitation. Nevertheless, all of them ultimately fail to maintain the kind of equilibrium between autonomy and welfare and between identity and difference that concrete compliance with the postulate of equality would require.

First, I briefly outline the role of the relation between individual autonomy and welfare in the context of liberal conceptions of justice and of the interplay of identity and difference in the context of the relation between the races and the sexes consistent with adherence to the postulate of equality. Then I focus on the respective deficiencies of the four liberal conceptions of justice examined in Part One which, I argue, prevent them from sustaining a proper balance between autonomy and welfare and between identity and difference.

1. Justice, Autonomy and Welfare, and Equality as Identity and as Difference

A. Autonomy and Welfare

As will be remembered, the postulate of equality is founded on the moral autonomy of the individual and on her freedom to devise and pursue a suitable life plan. Autonomy, however, is not worth much without welfare.[1] Unless an individual can achieve a minimum of welfare, she cannot exercise her rights of autonomy. On the other hand, while welfare is essential for meaningful autonomy, the pursuit of welfare may also interfere with or curtail individual autonomy. For example, the welfare state, through public interest regulation, taxation, income redistribution, and the imposition of limitations on the enforceability of private contracts, may significantly limit the sphere of individual autonomy.

Devising an optimal equilibrium between individual autonomy and welfare poses a central problem for liberal conceptions of justice. Moreover, while it is beyond the scope of the present analysis to examine or justify this point in any detail,[2] the four conceptions of justice discussed in Part One can be interpreted as four different prescriptions for striking an optimal balance between autonomy and welfare. To be sure, some of these conceptions, such as the libertarian, seem much more concerned with autonomy than with welfare; others, such as the egalitarian, on the contrary, appear much more interested in welfare than in autonomy.

Nevertheless, one can conceive for each of these conceptions a plausible context in which such conception would foster the requisite equilibrium between autonomy and welfare. Thus, libertarians may concentrate on autonomy because they believe that in a society of autonomous individuals a sufficient degree of welfare will be automatically achieved. Egalitarians, on the other hand, may be predominantly concerned with welfare because they are convinced that without the equal allocation of certain goods many individuals would lack meaningful autonomy.

To the extent that each of the four liberal conceptions of justice operating at a middle level of abstraction can be interpreted as striking some plausible equilibrium between autonomy and welfare, all of them are susceptible to satisfying the more abstract postulate of equality. At lower levels of abstraction, however, these middle-level conceptions may not seem equally suited to promote the requisite balance between autonomy and welfare. For example, if one settles on some particular, fairly concrete conception of autonomy or welfare, one may be more inclined to accept some middle-level conceptions of justice than others. Or, in the light of actually prevailing social, political, and economic relationships, the type of equilibrium between autonomy and welfare conceivable under a particular middle-level conception of justice may appear to be practically unfeasible. Thus, if the requisite equilibrium under the libertarian criterion of justice depends on the assumption of the economic self-sufficiency of the individual, then that criterion might well seem inadequate in the context of an economy marked by a high level of interdependence. Let us assume, for example, that, in a society where individuals are largely economically self-sufficient, Nozick's entitlement theory of justice, discussed in chapter 2, guarantees the highest possible degree of individual autonomy compatible with an acceptable level of welfare for all. In a contemporary industrial economy marked by a substantial lack of self-sufficiency, however, Nozick's theory may seem inadequate because it is indifferent to questions of welfare. As one critic has stated, Nozick's criterion of justice "licenses a system in which the wealthy and their successors can maintain economic and legal privileges indefinitely and in which the less well-off are caught in an endless cycle of relative deprivation" (Pettit 1980, 101).

The justice of affirmative action also depends on *where* and *how* one draws the line between autonomy and welfare concerns. Again, if individuals are truly economically self-sufficient, distributive affirmative action in employment would not appear to make any sense, and even the prohibition against first-order discrimination would seem largely superfluous. Indeed, under those circumstances, affirmative action and the prohibition against first-order discrimination in the economic arena would arguably constitute unwarranted intrusions into the sphere of individual autonomy. On the other hand, in the context of a highly interdependent economy, the prohibition against first-order discrimination in employment may be defended as a necessary element of liberal justice, and affirmative action in employment as a plausible requirement of distributive justice.

To the extent that the justice of affirmative action depends on the historical, social, political, and economic circumstances of the groups singled out for preferential treatment, it is not sufficient to consider the legitimacy of affirmative action from the standpoint of the middle-level conceptions of justice. It is also necessary to evaluate middle-level conclusions in terms of relevant, more concrete, historically grounded factors. Thus, a comprehensive assessment of the arguments concerning affirmative action made from the standpoint of a middle-level conception of liberal justice requires further examination in terms of relevant concrete factors likely to be present in a society like ours. In particular, as I attempt to demonstrate in the next sections of this chapter, viewed in terms of contemporary American society, each one of the four middle-level conceptions of justice examined in Part One fails to strike a satisfactory balance between autonomy and welfare. And, at least in part because of this failure, none of them provides an ultimately persuasive account of the justice of affirmative action.

B. Identity and Difference

The question of the proper relationship between identity and difference cuts across all levels of abstraction, from that of the principle of formal justice to that of every ordinary legal classification. Moreover, from the standpoint of justice, the important question is not so much what constitutes identity or difference. Rather, it is which differences ought to be taken into account and which disregarded in the allocation of rights, duties, benefits, and burdens. As pointed out in chapter 1, the postulate of equality disregards several differences—for example, physical, mental, educational—in the course of establishing a moral identity among all individual subjects. Also, throughout the previous discussion, it was assumed that, at least in the sphere of employment allocation, differences in race and gender ought to be ideally disregarded. And consistent with this ideal, the sphere of employment allocation ought to be a sphere of assimilation.

In other contexts, the issue of which differences ought to count and which should be disregarded is much more controversial. For example, in the context of the constitutionality of affirmative action, proponents of the marginal equality position are only willing to take racial differences into account for very narrowly defined compensatory purposes, whereas proponents of the global equality position are willing to consider racial differences for much broader remedial purposes. And in the event that a completely color-blind constitutional principle were adopted, then racial differences would have to be totally disregarded by every law and practice coming within the sweep of the Constitution.

Because differences in race and gender have been historically exploited to subjugate members of certain races and women and to treat them as inferiors, it may seem wise to err on the side of disregarding such differences and of prescribing equal treatment. Indeed, there has been a general tendency to treat those who are different as though they are inferior (Todorov 1982, 152). But there has also been a corresponding tendency to associate identity with equality (ibid.), in the sense of mandating conformity and the repudiation of cherished differences as a precondition for treatment as an equal.[3]

In the context of the dynamics between identity and difference, the link between equality and identity is merely the other side of the coin that links difference with inferiority or inequality. This can be illustrated by comparing the metaphor of the master and the slave with that of the colonizer and the colonized. The master treats the slave as inferior *because* he is different—whether the slave be different because of his race, because he belongs to a vanquished enemy, or, at the higher levels of abstraction of Hegel's *Phenomenology of Spirit,* because he is the other who confronts the self of the master.[4] On the other hand, the colonizer does not treat the other as inferior because the latter is different. Instead, the colonizer treats the other as an equal but forces the other to abandon that which makes the other different. Thus, the Spanish conquistadors did not enslave the Indians whom they colonized. They forced them to renounce their religion and to embrace Christianity.[5]

In light of this dynamic between identity and difference, the purpose behind the prohibition against taking certain differences into account can be circumvented by imposing one's own values on others. Thus, for example, in a bilingual society one may equally frustrate the legitimate aspirations of the linguistic minority by discriminating against them and treating them as inferior or by forbidding all discrimination but forcing everyone to learn and use the dominant language. Accordingly, to avoid this possibility, differences should be disregarded only insofar as that is necessary to prevent subordination. And conversely, equalization and identity of treatment should be permitted only so long as they are not used to suppress genuine differences for purpose of imposing dominant values.

Consistent with these observations, a particular difference may have to be disregarded for some purposes but taken into account for others. For example, a difference in religious affiliation appears in most cases irrelevant and should therefore be disregarded in the context of job allocation. On the other hand, such difference should be taken into account where that would facilitate religious expression and promote diversity without interfering with the religious or cultural aspirations of others. In general, a sphere of activity with respect to which a particular difference should be disregarded can be called a "sphere of assimilation," while one in which a particular difference should be taken into account can be referred to as a "sphere of differentiation."

It is obvious that the conception of the justice of affirmative action is likely to change depending on how certain relevant differences are divided into spheres of assimilation and spheres of differentiation. For example, if racial differences should never be acknowledged—that is, if for all conceivable purposes racial differences ought to fall into spheres of assimilation—then presumably race-based affirmative action would never be just. On the other hand, if a particular middle-level conception of justice inadequately accounts for relevant differences, or improperly carves out spheres of assimilation and spheres of differentiation, then its treatment of affirmative action is likely to be ultimately deficient.

2. *The Limitations of the Libertarian Position*

Libertarians may be perceived as subordinating welfare considerations to individual autonomy expressed in terms of freedom of choice.[6] As already mentioned, however, the libertarian position may also be interpreted as requiring the achievement of an optimal equilibrium between individual autonomy and welfare. Consistent with this interpretation, it is significant that even Locke and Nozick concede that there may be circumstances under which the exercise of property rights may be legitimately curtailed to secure a minimum of individual welfare for all.[7]

Even if the libertarian grants absolute lexical priority to individual property rights and freedom of choice in the belief that it will lead to an optimal equilibrium between autonomy and welfare, it is doubtful that he could be persuaded of the necessity of adopting laws prohibiting first-order discrimination. We have reviewed in chapter 2 the arguments which the libertarian is likely to make in support of that position. What remains to be elucidated is why the libertarian's refusal to outlaw first-order discrimination clashes with the demands of the postulate of equality in the context of contemporary American sociopolitical realities.

It is important to emphasize that the libertarian's refusal to outlaw first-order discrimination is not per se violative of the postulate of equality. Indeed the libertarian's refusal does not stem from racism, sexism, or any other position that holds that some human beings are inherently inferior to others. Rather, the libertarian's refusal is predicated on the belief that laws prohibiting first-order discrimination would unduly interfere with the individual's broadly defined Lockean property rights.

Notwithstanding their acknowledgement that there may be circumstances under which it would be appropriate to limit somewhat the exercise of individual property rights, both Locke and Nozick remain confident that the unfettered exercise of individual property rights is best suited to promote the maximum of individual autonomy compatible with the maintenance of a sufficient amount of individual welfare. In Locke's vision each individual is capable of self-sufficiency, provided only that no one interferes with her appropriations.[8]

Unlike Locke, Nozick seeks to justify adoption of the libertarian position in the context of a contemporary society characterized by a free market economy. In such a society the individual can no longer be viewed properly as being self-sufficient, but must rely primarily on carrying out contractual exchanges with others in order to reach a sufficient level of personal welfare. Consistent with this, Nozick recasts the libertarian ideal in the slogan "from each as they choose, to each as they are chosen" (Nozick 1974, 160). In keeping with the libertarian tradition, Nozick thus emphasizes that the individual has no positive duty to other individuals or to society as a whole and that others likewise have no positive duty toward the individual, including no duty to select any particular individual as a partner in contractual exchange. As we have already seen, an obvious consequence of this position is that any regulation prohibiting first-order discrimination would be illegitimate as it would unduly restrain individual freedom of choice.

To the extent that individuals in the Nozickean universe are not self-sufficient, it would seem to be much more difficult for a contemporary libertarian than for his Lockean counterpart to refute the claim that rejection as a contractual partner because of race or gender undermines the dignity and self-respect of those who become the victims of discrimination. Indeed, in the context of a fully developed market economy, it is not possible to cut loose from others and to fulfill one's ambitions and potential in isolation. Therefore, when the individual's welfare depends on the proliferation of contractual exchanges, the mere refusal to deal with someone on the basis of race or sex may frustrate the victim's ability to reach the requisite equilibrium between autonomy and welfare.

As I pointed out in chapter 2, Nozick acknowledges that it would be "disturbing" if transfers of individual holdings through contractual exchanges were "arbitrary."[9] Relying upon his belief in the "invisible hand" quality of competition in a free market economy, however, Nozick concludes that contractual transactions in a capitalist society are by and large rational. Accordingly, in a free market setting in which rational individuals seek to maximize profits, and in which they are subject to the "invisible hand" mechanisms of unfettered competition, the vast majority of contractual exchanges will depend exclusively on purely economic considerations regardless of the race or gender of prospective contractors. And, to the extent that rational economic interests are capable of restraining racism and sexism in the economic marketplace, prohibitions against first-order discrimination may well loom as unnecessary intrusions that would interfere with the maximization of freedom.

Lockean self-sufficiency and Nozickean free market competition among purely economically motivated individuals may arguably provide sets of conditions that reconcile the refusal to prohibit first-order discrimination with genuine adherence to the postulate of equality. Neither of these two models of interaction, however, accurately depicts the processes of intersubjective conduct prevalent in contemporary American society. Actually, even assuming that Nozick's free market vision is essentially correct, and that economic actors possess a complete rationality of means, blanket toleration of first-order discrimination would still be pernicious in present-day American society. Indeed, as mentioned in chapter 2, in a society characterized by pervasive racism, the purely rational exercise of one's economic self-interest in maximizing profits may compel the practice of exclusion because of race. Thus, the owner of a hotel who is only interested in deriving the greatest possible profit from his business may have a purely economic interest in refusing service to blacks in order not to lose a much more numerous and much wealthier white clientele.[10] Under such circumstances, even a completely racially neutral free market mechanism with a fully operative invisible hand device could serve to perpetuate entrenched racism.

Further criticisms of the adequacy of the libertarian position are based on the conviction that the Nozickean model is fundamentally flawed in that it disregards many of the most important features of contemporary property relations. First, one may reject the Nozickean model by challenging the conclusion that modern markets are guided by a benevolent "invisible hand." Second, even if such an invisible hand mechanism were operative, one may be persuaded that contemporary property-based relationships lead to great imbalances of power among various participants in the market which are bound to upset the requisite equilibrium between individual autonomy and individual welfare.

In the absence of an invisible hand mechanism, granting lexical priority to private property rights would arguably lack justification. Under such conditions, the maintenance of Lockean property rights may well lead to extreme disparities in wealth, placing a large number of deprived individuals at the mercy of those who control a disproportionate share of society's economic resources. Thus, there would be in all likelihood deprivations or diminutions in individual autonomy and welfare that would upset the requisite equilibrium between autonomy and welfare. Further, to the extent that a disproportionate number of blacks and women are among the most deprived members of a society marked by large disparities in wealth and by pervasive racism and sexism, the strict preservation of Lockean property rights would contribute to perpetuating the status of blacks and women as inferiors. In other words, in such a society, Lockean property rights may be used as weapons by those who are determined to perpetuate racism and sexism.

Even in the presence of invisible hand mechanisms, there is an important lack of analogy between the individual contractor who is the prototypical protagonist of the atomistic market economy and the large modern corporate employer. In the case of the individual contractor it is arguably important to protect the complete freedom to choose with whom to deal because such freedom is inextricably linked with that individual's privacy interests. Similar considerations of privacy do not seem to apply, however, in the case of the large corporate employer. This follows either from the conclusion that realization of a corporation's right to autonomy does not require the kind of associational privacy that is important to individuals, or from the belief that large corporations are bound to set aside considerations of privacy in the course of pursuing their business interests.

The conclusion that the protection of the genuine property interests of the large corporation does not require the recognition of full associational privacy rights is based on an analysis of the typical structure of the large corporation with thousands of employees. Ownership of such a corporation is likely to be spread among a large number of shareholders who are not involved in the corporation's day-to-day management, and who are unlikely to care much about the corporation's ordinary operations, except to the extent that the latter might affect the corporation's profitability. Unlike the individual owner of a family-sized business who must work closely with a handful of employees, therefore, the shareholders of a large corporation are unlikely to have any personal contact with the corporation's employees. And absent such personal contact, the corporate shareholder's enjoyment of her corporate ownership property rights would not seem to depend on any genuine associational privacy interest regarding the selection or treatment of corporate employees.

In contrast to the shareholders, corporate management is bound to have numerous contacts with the corporation's employees. To the extent that management does not have ownership interests in the corporation, however, one may argue that it has no genuine Lockean property rights with respect with the employment positions that the corporation is empowered to allocate. Moreover, even if management is viewed as the representative entrusted with the property interests of shareholders, it should not be allowed to claim as legitimate a right to first-order discrimination in hiring that the shareholders themselves could not properly claim. Keeping in mind that it is unlikely that management of a large corporation would have a close personal working relation with most of the employees, it would be difficult for management to seek to justify first-order discrimination solely on the basis of its legitimate associational privacy interests. Management would therefore have to appeal to other aspects of the corporate owners' property rights to justify its discriminatory policies.

Even if arguably the corporate owners could justify squandering corporate assets as a legitimate exercise of their Lockean property rights, however, the corporate managers could not do the same because of their fiduciary duties toward the corporate owners. In other words, because corporate management has an obligation to advance the profit-making interests of the corporation's owners, a manager does not enjoy the same freedoms as one who runs a business that she owns. Thus, for example, whereas the latter may have a perfect right to hire exclusively on the basis of nepotism, the corporate manager arguably has a duty to the corporation's owners to refrain from engaging in the same practice to the extent that it would be deleterious to the corporation's profitability. Consistent with this analysis, arguably, management has an obligation to conduct the corporation's hiring activities in accordance with the dictates of formal equality of opportunity. Indeed, to the extent that the individual identity (as opposed to the individual qualifications) of those who work for the corporation is of little concern to corporate management, there seems to be no legitimate reason to allow those in management to embrace the libertarian mantle of property and privacy rights for the sole purpose of furthering the goals of racism and sexism.

The libertarian's refusal to ban first-order discrimination in the private sector makes that position difficult to reconcile with the postulate of equality in the context of contemporary advanced economies. To the extent that the libertarian position defends broad Lockean property rights regardless of consequences, it fails to address fundamental welfare concerns. The libertarian position should also be considered inadequate if it advocates broad Lockean property rights in the erroneous belief that contemporary economies are regulated by "invisible hand" mechanisms. Finally, even if such a belief in invisible hand mechanisms proves to be justified, contemporary toleration of first-order discrimination in the private sector would not. This is because of the significant differences between contemporary corporate employment practices and the exchange practices typical of classical market economies.

There is also a second major reason why the libertarian position appears inadequate in the context of contemporary American society. This reason is practical rather than purely theoretical. In a nutshell, it is that strict compliance with the libertarian position would require an undesirable departure from the status quo. Indeed, in contemporary American society all but the smallest private agents of allocation are required by law to refrain from engaging in first-order discrimination against blacks and women in their hiring and promotion practices. Thus, the state, through the implementation of civil rights laws, affords blacks and women some rights of equality of opportunity. Strict compliance with a Nozickean libertarian position, however, would presumably require repeal of such civil rights laws. Furthermore, arguably such a repeal would not only take away existing equal opportunity rights from blacks and women but it would also have the effect of conferring renewed legitimacy to the treatment of black and women job applicants as inferiors.[11] And to the extent that acceptance of the formal equal opportunity requirements imposed by civil rights laws is widespread, their repeal, even if not unjust, would be unwise. Indeed, it would most likely reopen deep-seated wounds that the civil rights laws have at least partially healed, and renew the bitter conflict that preceded the enactment of the civil rights laws.

3. *The Limitations of the Egalitarian Position*

As discussed in chapter 5, egalitarians are prone to reject equality of opportunity in favor of equality of result. Thus, whereas libertarians may consider that adherence to equality of opportunity would place too strong a constraint on individual autonomy, egalitarians are likely to feel that satisfaction of demands of equality of opportunity is insufficient to secure individual welfare. Notwithstanding this important difference, the egalitarian position is ultimately likely to prove inadequate for the same reason as the libertarian: they both fail to secure the kind of equilibrium between autonomy and welfare that is required by the postulate of equality. In addition, at least certain versions of the egalitarian position would seem particularly prone to thwart difference and diversity.

According to the extreme egalitarian position, justice requires the achievement of lot-regarding equality of result.[12] Literal compliance with this requirement, however, would appear to necessitate a ceaseless process of redistribution that would inevitably produce pervasive invasions of privacy and continuous interference with expressions of individual autonomy. Moreover, as pointed out in chapter 5, the extreme egalitarian places too much emphasis on envy, with the deleterious consequence of almost completely stamping out the development of individuality and individual creativity. With its single-minded pursuit of lot-regarding equality, the extreme egalitarian position is prone to do away with all vestiges of difference and diversity and to reduce equality to complete identity. And the sacrifice that this would require in individual liberty and autonomy would be so great that it would, as a practical matter, place the extreme egalitarian at odds with the postulate of equality.

Strict and comprehensive adherence to lot-regarding equality of result is likely to lead to such unattractive consequences that it is doubtful that one could find many genuine extreme egalitarians. Subject-regarding equality of result, on the other hand, presents a seemingly much more palatable alternative. Indeed, it lacks the leveling dimension of its lot-regarding counterpart and is, accordingly, in principle at least, in a position to afford sufficient protection to difference and individual diversity.

Subject-regarding equality of result would most probably satisfy the postulate of equality, but, as discussed in chapter 5, its realization may be problematic. First, even assuming a general agreement concerning what it requires, it may be impossible for society to bring about subject-regarding equality for everyone. For example, while not all members of society are likely to covet the same job, it is quite conceivable that a scarcity of desirable positions would make it impossible for each individual to obtain the position which is best suited to advance his or her life plan.

Second, realization of subject-regarding equality of result may remain a sometimes undesirable or overly utopian goal. As pointed out in chapter 5, some subjectively defined needs may be highly repugnant. Moreover, unless subjective needs can be adequately communicated and claims concerning the importance of particular needs verified, subject-regarding equality of result may well be practically unmanageable.

Third, adoption of a mixed lot- and subject-regarding equality of result can lead to the solution of some of the above problems, but is likely to create problems of its own. For example, depending on how broad a domain is to be governed by lot-regarding equality of result, there may be substantial imbalances between individual autonomy and welfare. Furthermore, to the extent that certain important needs are objectively defined and subjected to lot-regarding equality of result, this version of egalitarianism is likely to trample unduly on genuine differences.

In the last analysis, not all of these problems are necessarily insoluble.

As I shall argue in the next chapter, through use of a dialogical process and by means of switches in perspectives, it is possible to obtain certain insights into the relative importance that certain goods may acquire in relation to different individual life plans. Accordingly, it would be possible for an egalitarian who advocates subject-regarding equality of result to provide a satisfactory ranking of the needs of different individuals. Nevertheless, the egalitarian's position would still have to be deemed unsatisfactory to the extent that it calls for the achievement of subject-regarding equality of result above all else. Indeed, as I will argue in the next chapter, not all individual life plans necessarily stand on the same footing. And to the extent that they do not, treating them as though they do would most likely upset the proper relationship between identity and difference. Accordingly, the pursuit of subject-regarding equality of result can sometimes, but by no means always, be justified.

4. The Limitations of the Utilitarian Position

Upon first impression, the utilitarian criterion of justice appears to be more attractive than its libertarian and egalitarian counterparts. Indeed, utilitarians apparently sacrifice neither identity nor difference, neither integration nor differentiation. Utilitarians take individual identity into account by counting each individual but not counting any individual more than once, and by taking each individual's preferences into full account in the calculus of utilities. Moreover, utilitarians fully acknowledge individual differences, by taking each individual's preferences at face value and by refusing to rank preferences in terms of their nature or their object. Finally, utilitarians provide integration through the aggregation of all individual preferences for purposes of determining society's net aggregate preferences and of validating the distribution of goods that is best suited to satisfy such net aggregate preferences.

Although it does provide for some integration and differentiation, the utilitarian position ultimately falls short inasmuch as it fails to foster the kind of equilibrium between autonomy and welfare that must be maintained in order to satisfy the postulate of equality. The integration made possible by the utilitarian is arguably too crude. It aggregates individual preferences, taking into account their degree of intensity but not the identity or the particular perspective of the subject of such preferences. Accordingly, utilitarian integration is achieved only through the decontextualization of all the particular preferences sought to be aggregated. On the other hand, while the utilitarian respects difference in the sense of acknowledging and counting all the particular preferences of each person, the process of differentiation set in motion by the calculus of utilities proves equally inadequate. Indeed, such process considers difference purely in the abstract—that is, as though the individual preferences through which a person is set apart from others are severable from one another and from the totality of other attributes possessed by their owners.

Thus, for example, if the intensity of a destitute person's desire for a decent home and shelter were no greater than a millionaire's desire for some additional luxuries, utilitarianism would not dictate that the desire of the former be given priority over that of the latter. To be sure, utilitarianism considers the destitute person and the millionaire as equals and treats their respective preferences as being of equal weight because of their equal intensity. Utilitarianism fails, however, to provide the means to establish that a preference for the basic necessities of life ought to be given priority over an equally intense preference for luxuries, no matter how superfluous. Accordingly, utilitarianism seems incapable of affording sufficient substantive protection to individual autonomy, dignity, and respect.

For our purposes, two consequences of utilitarianism's failure to provide satisfactory mechanisms of integration and differentiation are particularly important: first, the failure to rule out the legitimacy of first-order discrimination; and second, the failure to provide adequate support to the inherent dignity of the person.

The utilitarian's inability to convincingly rule out the legitimacy of first-order discrimination was discussed in chapter 4 and need not be repeated here. There, is however, a further argument which a utilitarian might advance in support of the claim that utilitarianism can be conceived so as to foreclose the legitimacy of first-order discrimination. This argument is not purely theoretical but is at least in part practical and dependent on the validity of certain empirical assertions about our society. It is based on an argument advanced by Hare in an attempt to demonstrate that utilitarianism cannot fairly be interpreted as being compatible with the maintenance of slavery.[13] The crux of Hare's argument is that, while it is possible to *imagine* circumstances under which slavery would maximize utilities, the principal virtue of utilitarian moral theory lies in its ability to afford practical guidance in light of the actual circumstances prevailing in our own social reality. Furthermore, argues Hare, in a society such as ours, the utilitarian must reject slavery because it is bound to result in much more misery than good. Along similar lines, a utilitarian could argue that while one could undeniably *imagine* circumstances under which first-order discrimination would maximize utilities, such cannot be the case in the context of our own society.

Even if one generally accepts Hare's argument and agrees with his assessment of slavery, it does not follow that the above utilitarian argument concerning first-order discrimination is equally persuasive. The reason for this is ultimately an empirical one. Indeed, it seems fair to assume that in a society like ours, with its extensive manifestations of racism and sexism, and its numerous instances of polarization along racial and gender lines, there could be realistic and entirely plausible situations in which toleration of first-order discrimination would lead to less strife and overall unhappiness than its prohibition. Moreover, particularly in a case where a community is comprised of a large majority of whites and a small minority of blacks, the greater the intensity of the hatred between the races, the more likely it would seem that the toleration of first-order discrimination would lead to the greater happiness of a greater number than its prohibition. Consistent with this, following Hare's brand of utilitarian theory would certainly not foreclose the legitimacy of tolerating first-order discrimination.

The second major criticism of the utilitarian position is the very familiar one that it does not afford sufficient protection to the inherent dignity of the person as the subject of moral choice. This criticism has been made so often by many, including Rawls, that it need not be restated in any detail here. In a nutshell, the main thrust of this criticism, as articulated by Rawls, is that "utilitarianism does not take seriously the distinction between persons" (Rawls 1971, 27). By differentiating persons in a purely formal way and by integrating individual preferences as if they were disembodied entities, the utilitarian disregards the integrity and dignity of the person as a historically situated actor interacting with other similarly situated actors. In particular, because of its single-minded concern with the determination and achievement of the overall welfare, utilitarianism does not afford sufficient protection to individual rights or autonomy.

5. *The Limitations of the Contractarian Position*

Like its utilitarian counterpart, the contractarian position proposes means to achieve an integration of individual perspectives without sacrificing the process of differentiation. The contemporary contractarian position, as articulated by Rawls and Goldman, however, appears to accord greater respect than does utilitarianism to the equal autonomy of each individual. Indeed, in Rawls' words, "each person possesses an inviolability founded on justice that even the welfare of society as a whole cannot override" (Rawls 1971, 3). Consistent with this, the contractarian maintains that individuals are not merely to be counted, but that their consent must be secured before they can legitimately be expected to conform to social norms. As we have seen, it is to emphasize the importance of such unanimous consent that Rawls resorts to the hypothetical social contract device. Each contractor brings his or her perspective to bear on the bargaining process that precedes formation of the hypothetical social contract. The aim of the bargaining process is to arrive at common principles (integration) that are compatible with each contractor's individual perspective (differentiation) (ibid., 11–12). The operating principle designed to lead from the multiplicity of individual perspectives to the adoption of common principles, moreover, is the norm of reciprocity, which requires each individual to recognize every other individual as having a life plan of his or her own.[14] Applying the norm of reciprocity, the contractarian expects to discover the common principles that will promote equal respect for each individual and the kind of social cooperation best suited to maximize each individual's opportunity to pursue his or her own life plan without infringing on another individual's equal opportunity to do the same.[15]

Based on the assumption that no rational person is willingly likely to accept being cast as an inferior because of race or sex, the contractarian—unlike the utilitarian—can systematically reject the legitimacy of first-order discrimination through application of the norm of reciprocity. But this does not mean that the contractarian position leads to successful integration while preserving a sufficient degree of differentiation. As we shall see, contractarians can successfully block the move from equality to inferiority but only at the price of reducing difference to identity.

One of the significant virtues of contemporary contractarian theory is the realization that use of the contract device in the context of prospective contractors who are fully aware of their social, political, economic, and historical position is merely bound to reproduce existing power relationships and patterns of domination. In this context, imposition of the Rawlsian veil of ignorance is crucial to prevent would-be hypothetical contractors from exploiting superior social position or greater natural assets to obtain a more favorable deal. But whereas the veil of ignorance may insure that the common principles adopted by hypothetical contractors are not a mere reflection of superior bargaining power, by the same token it seems bound to lead to common principles that do not properly account for differences. Focusing on Rawls' original position behind a veil of ignorance, common principles emerge only after all differences in life plans and in natural and social assets have been set aside. Under these circumstances, common principles are reached, not from a diversity of perspectives that incorporates the multitude of existing individual differences, but from the mere abstract identity that equalizes all individual perspectives after having neutralized all the possible sources of individual differences.

The veil of ignorance's reduction of each individual contractor to an abstract ego shorn of all difference renders the contract-making process a monological rather than a dialogical one. Ordinary contracts that involve a real bargaining process reflecting the differing interests and objectives of the individuals involved are the product of a dialogical process leading to the specification of contractual terms that are mutually agreeable. If no real differences exist between abstract subjects seeking to reach a hypothetical contract, however, the need for dialogue completely disappears. Indeed, since all abstract egos are essentially interchangeable, a rational decision concerning legitimate common principles can be reached monologically by any one of them.

The above objection against the use of abstract egos to generate common principles through a hypothetical contract is undoubtedly serious. Upon closer scrutiny, however, there is a further objection which is potentially even more damaging. Moreover, while this latter objection appears to be equally applicable to Rawls and to Goldman, it can be put into a somewhat sharper focus when examined in the context of Goldman's limited veil of ignorance.

If one looks closely at the notion of an abstract ego, it should become apparent that the greater the suppression of differences, the less likely it would seem that any concrete common principles could emerge *except to the extent that all individuals possess certain universal attributes, objectives, and dispositions.* Now, for the sake of argument, let us assume that there are no such universal attributes and the like shared by all individuals. In that case, the abstract ego (the ego that remains after all differences have been removed) would encompass nothing more than the bare fact of individuality (the fact that the ego in question is in principle capable of differentiation). From that fact alone, however, it would seem impossible to derive any common norms with substantive content, let alone any universally acceptable principles of justice.

Failure to recognize this limitation does pose an additional serious problem, in that not only is differentiation generally suppressed, but certain differences—that is, certain attributes possessed by some but not by others—become privileged above all others and are allowed to contribute disproportionately to the shaping of society's common identity. Thus, not only is difference generally sacrificed for the sake of preserving equality as identity, but identity itself is ultimately recast as conformity with a particular perspective. And for the many who do not happen to share this perspective, this means that formal equality can only be purchased by submitting to the values of others, or, in other words, that the price of identity is adoption of the values promoted by a colonizing other.

Goldman's hypothetical contract concluded behind a limited veil of ignorance provides a particularly clear illustration of this last problem. As we have seen, Goldman postulates that his contractors do not know their race, sex, or social position. For the sake of simplicity, let us focus only on race and sex, and let us stipulate that there is no such thing as a universal race or sex. That means that a person is either a man or a woman and either nonwhite or white. Moreover, while we can *imagine* a universe in which persons would have no race or gender (or all persons have the same race and gender), in such a universe both first-order discrimination because of race or gender and affirmative action would be completely ruled out. Accordingly, such a universe would be of little use to someone like Goldman who seeks to determine whether, and under what circumstances, affirmative action may conform with commonly acceptable principles of justice in the context of our own society. But if every person must be either man or woman and either white or nonwhite, what could it possibly mean to operate behind a veil of ignorance that makes persons lose awareness of their race or gender?

One possible answer is that while race and gender cannot be eliminated, they can be treated as differences that need not be taken into account in devising common principles. Under this assimilationist view, race and gender would be acknowledged but would play a role, in the context of normative discourse, which would be no greater than that actually likely to be played by eye color.[16] Accordingly, the disregard of differences of race and sex required by the veil of ignorance could be conceivably satisfied through the hypothetical contractors' adoption of a perspective that is essentially indifferent concerning a person's race or gender.

Many objections can be raised against this last proposal. First, arguably, assimilationism is but one perspective among many, and therefore, its adoption by the hypothetical contractors would lead to an unwarranted privileging of one perspective over many others that appear to be equally respectable. Because of this, not only would a large number of persons be deprived of the opportunity to bring their individual perspective to bear on the selection of common principles, but they would also in some sense be forced to adhere to a perspective with which they did not agree.

Second, it seems clear that, in the United States at least, race has not been merely a matter of skin pigmentation and that differences between the sexes have not been solely confined to the realm of physical characteristics. Instead, the historical trajectory of race and gender relations in the United States has led to the emergence of profound divisions manifested in vastly differing perspectives, often grouped along racial- and gender-based lines. For example, given the long history of racial discrimination and oppression, the perspective of blacks is likely to be significantly different from that of whites in a number of important respects, but particularly concerning questions of racial justice.

One important consequence that follows from having race- and gender-based differences that run deep enough to shape antagonistic perspectives is that hypothetical contractors in search of common normative principles cannot simply rid themselves of all traces of race or sex. Indeed, while such contractors operating behind a veil of ignorance may usefully forget the identity of their particular skin pigmentation and of their physical gender-based attributes, they would nonetheless be incapable of shedding the constraints of their racially and sexually informed individual perspective. In other words, to the extent that blacks and whites, and men and women, have different, and to some degree antagonistic, perspectives; and that there can be no perspective that is constituted completely independently of its subject's race or sex; the hypothetical contractors would seem to have no other choice but to adopt a race- and gender-specific perspective. Thus, a hypothetical contractor may not know if he or she is black or white, or a man or a woman, but such contractor cannot escape having either a white or a nonwhite perspective, as well as either a masculine or a feminine perspective.

Because the removal of race and gender identity behind Goldman's partial veil of ignorance is only skin deep, it risks unwittingly giving privilege to the perspective—the vision, system of beliefs, and cultural biases—of one race and gender over that of other races and that of those who belong to the opposite gender. Further, if Goldman's hypothetical contractors share the perspective of white males, any hypothetical agreement that they may reach would run a high risk of imposing as common principles certain norms issued from the dominant perspective of the very group that is most responsible for the proliferation of race- and gender-based inequities. Accordingly, while Goldman's partial veil may serve to remove the superficial trappings behind racism and sexism, it may well also reinforce (albeit in a completely unintended way) the more deeply entrenched yet much more difficult-to-discern systematic networks of attitudes, perceptions, and beliefs that underlie the obdurate persistence of substantive race and sex inequalities.

In sum, the purpose of Goldman's partial veil undoubtedly is to provide a more inclusive subject capable of forging common normative principles designed to deal with racial and sexual inequalities. Because of contractarianism's failure to account sufficiently for differing perspectives, however, Goldman's partial veil ultimately risks leaving the task of generating common norms as the preserve of an exclusive subject. And to the extent that white males are that exclusive subject, Goldman's scheme may ultimately lead to the perpetuation of the status of nonwhites and women as the outsiders, as society's "others,"[17] who are relegated to the subordinate position of those who must always play by rules that they have not had an opportunity to shape.

The contractarian position is more successful than the utilitarian in foreclosing the legitimacy of first-order discrimination. On the other hand, contemporary contractarianism proves ultimately unsatisfactory because of its failure to properly account for differences and because of its inability to coordinate a multiplicity of divergent perspectives. Moreover, to the extent that perspectives cannot be fully abstracted in the course of constructing the abstract ego of hypothetical contractors, the contractarian is likely to give privilege to one particular perspective over all others. Also, insofar as the dominant perspective is more likely to yield views and values that appear to be universally valid—that is, that seem to be valid regardless of anyone's own particular perspective—it seems almost inevitable that the contractarian will end up giving privilege to that position. In the last analysis, contemporary contractarianism fails because, while it appears to be dialogical in nature, it is in fact monological.

In conclusion, all four conceptions of justice considered in this chapter have shortcomings and limitations that render them unsuitable to provide a definitive or comprehensive assessment of the justice of affirmative action. Both the utilitarian and contractarian positions, because of their greater emphasis on combining integration and differentiation—and perhaps to a somewhat lesser degree the egalitarian position that is committed to subject-regarding equality of result—however, possess certain particularly attractive features. These features ought to be incorporated in any alternative conception of justice that might be adopted because of its superior ability to coordinate the multiplicity of individual perspectives without sacrificing the differences that ought to count. With this in mind, I now turn to the task of formulating such an alternative conception of justice.

CHAPTER NINE

Justice as Reversibility, Equality, and the Right to Be Different

To overcome the shortcomings of the positions criticized in chapter 8, one must find suitable means to coordinate the multiplicity of individual perspectives encountered in society without compromising the differences that distinguish each from the others. Moreover, one ought to retain from the contractarian perspective the requirement that the means selected be in some meaningful sense mutually consensual in nature. Likewise, from the utilitarian perspective, one ought to preserve the requirement that all individual preferences be taken into account.

In this chapter, I argue that adoption of a dialogical process involving a reversal of perspectives according to the principle of justice as reversibility satisfies these requirements. In order to relate the dialogical process that I propose to the monological positions examined above, I begin by taking another look at the reversal test discussed in chapter 3. Then, I briefly consider the progression from nonreciprocity to reciprocity, and from reciprocity to reversibility. After that, I compare the characteristics of justice as reversibility with those of contractarian and utilitarian of justice. Further, as we shall see, the success of justice as reversibility depends on the availability of a dialogical process capable of fostering the kind of communicative interaction necessary to make genuine reversals of perspectives possible. Accordingly, I attempt to delineate the broad outlines of such dialogical process, drawing upon Habermas' theory of communicative ethics and upon his concept of the ideal speech situation. Finally, I argue that justice as reversibility provides better means than alternative conceptions of justice to coordinate perspectives without leveling differences, and that it is therefore best suited to satisfy the requirements following from the postulate of equality.

1. *The Reversal Test Revisited*

As discussed in chapter 3, the reversal test can play a useful role in determining whether a particular form of unequal treatment is compatible with the requirement of the postulate of equality that each person be treated as an equal. As used by Goldman, in the context of race or gender relations, the role switch mandated by the reversal test is supposed to indicate whether unequal treatment is a function of legitimate role differences or of invidious discrimination on account of race or gender.[1] Use of a limited role switch that does not involve a reversal of perspectives, however, is likely unwittingly to give privilege to one perspective to the exclusion of others just as deserving of attention.

This last point is perhaps best understood in terms of the criticisms against the contractarian use of the veil of ignorance device made in chapter 8. As we saw there, using the veil of ignorance so as to render individual contractors unaware of their own race or gender does not remove race- or gender-related differences from the original position. Similarly, a limited role switch may lead those involved to imagine that they possess different racial or sexual identities but does not lead to the adoption of the particular perspectives associated with such identities. Accordingly, a limited role switch is likely to produce only partial insight into the plight of the other. And, to the extent that such limited role switch is undertaken from the dominant perspective, it would promote that perspective while giving the impression of taking full account of the needs and aspirations of others.

To illustrate, let us suppose that prolonged institutional racism has deprived blacks of a basic education and demoralized them to the point that they now suffer from a severe lack of motivation. Under those circumstances, a white who imagines that he is black but does not adopt a black perspective might well conclude that all that *he* would need as a black would be the opportunity to make up his educational deficiencies so that he could compete on an equal footing with whites. From his own perspective as a highly motivated and competitive individual, he cannot appreciate the important role that lack of motivation is likely to play in shaping the perspective of blacks. And because of this, our white person is unlikely to address the issue of lack of motivation satisfactorily. More important, however, because he has imagined that he was black, and on that basis reached a conclusion concerning what society owes its black members, our white protagonist is likely to become frustrated that remedial education does not put unmotivated blacks on a competitive par with whites. And precisely because he made the effort to imagine what it would be like if *he* were black, and conceived a solution for what *he* considers to be the problem confronting blacks, our white protagonist may well become inclined to blame blacks for the failure of *his* proposed solution. Not able to understand why blacks would not avail themselves of the opportunities that *he* (imagining himself to be black) would, he might conclude that it is only because of some "cultural deficiency" that blacks cannot overcome their disadvantages.[2] Thus, the limited role switch, while initially promoting sympathy for the plight of the disadvantaged other, at the end is prone to reinforce the suppression or subordination of alternative perspectives.

A complete role switch including a reversal of perspectives, on the other hand, might prove to be a useful tool against the undue privileging of any particular point of view. Indeed, being forced to acknowledge not only the claims of others but also the importance of these claims from the standpoint of their claimants might check the tendency to suppress the perspectives of others and to promote one's own point of view as though it were (or should be) universally shared. Absent a reversal of perspectives, ego may switch places with alter but continue to accord to alter's claims—now imagined to be ego's—much less importance than alter does. Consistent with this, ego may readily agree to deny alter's claims while sincerely maintaining that such denial does not affect alter's treatment as an equal. The reversal of perspectives, however, opens the door to a weighing of competing claims, in terms of the relative importance of each such claim from the individual perspective of the person who interposes it. And this, in turn, makes it possible to continue the pursuit of equality while maintaining a much higher degree of differentiation. Thus, in the context of a switch in perspectives, ego would not only recognize as legitimate those claims of alter that ego would be prepared to justify from ego's own perspective, but also those other claims of alter that ego would only see fit to accept upon adoption of alter's own perspective.

Whereas the reversal of perspectives provides the means to rank otherwise incommensurable competing claims, it cannot alone bring about schemes of distribution that would automatically satisfy the requirements imposed by the postulate of equality. To illustrate this, let us imagine a conflict between a racist's claim that there ought to be a complete separation of the races and the claim of a member of a racial minority to the effect that there ought to be full racial integration of all public facilities. Let us suppose further that the racist is sincere and that his claim for complete separation between the races is based on a religious ideology to which he fervently subscribes. The member of the minority group, on the other hand, while committed to racial integration, is not as intensely focused on it as the racist is in promoting segregation. Through reversal of perspectives, the member of the minority group therefore ought to realize that segregation is more central to the fulfillment of the racist's life plan than is integration in her own life plan. Accordingly, if justice required nothing more than that priority be given to claims that achieve a higher rank pursuant to an application of a reversal of perspectives test, then the claim to segregation should prevail over the conflicting claim to integration. More generally, so long as justice is thus dependent exclusively on the outcomes of the reversal of perspectives test, claims requiring the subordination of others may sometimes legitimately prevail over conflicting claims made from a perspective committed to the treatment of all persons as equals. Because of this, the reversal of perspectives standing alone cannot satisfy the constraints imposed by the postulate of equality. Thus, while the reversal of perspectives may be a necessary means, it is by no means a sufficient means, toward the achievement of an optimal degree of integration and differentiation in the context of adherence to the postulate of equality.

2. *From Reciprocity to Reversibility*

Even if the reversal of perspectives provides the best means fully to account for differentiation, it falls short as a criterion of justice because, consistent with the postulate of equality, justice cannot consist in merely maximizing recognition or expression of difference. While stressing difference is particularly important in light of the tendency to reduce equality to identity and to give privilege to one perspective above all others, the indiscriminate promotion of difference for its own sake is likely to lead to division and fragmentation, and eventually to the loss of any sense of overall community. Indeed, if justice were to consist *exclusively* in upholding every person's right to be different, it would promote separation rather than integration, as it would encourage each person to stress that which makes him or her different from others rather than that which is shared in common by all members of society. Taken to its logical extreme, moreover, emphasis on the right to be different would, paradoxically, devalue difference itself. This is because the greater the unchecked proliferation of difference, the less differences would be celebrated as enriching and the more each person or group would perceive the differences pursued by others as threats to that person's or group's own right to be different.

It is only against a common core of identity that differences can ultimately enrich rather than impoverish individuals who seek self-fulfillment in a community. Common identity, however, can take many different forms, some of which undoubtedly would be hostile not only to the expression of legitimate differences but also to the notion that all individuals are entitled to equal dignity and respect. Thus, for example, some forms of patriotism may promote a common identity through the suppression of legitimate differences, while absolute monarchy may likewise strongly uphold national identity without granting any right to equal respect. It is essential for adherents to the postulate of equality to find a core of common identity that does not lead to the suppression of legitimate differences or to the denial of equal respect. Such common identity can be achieved, moreover, through implementation of the norm of reciprocity.

The norm of reciprocity has been said to be universal, but one finds great disparity in its various concrete formulations (Gouldner 1973, 242). Nevertheless, all such formulations can be understood as requiring some kind of exchange of equivalents.[3] The difficult questions are to determine what "equivalence" means in a particular context and what ought to count as being the equivalent of any given thing offered in exchange. Moreover, the relative status of the persons entering into an exchange relationship may also have a bearing on the determination of whether the things exchanged can be deemed equivalent. Thus, it could be argued that a small token of recognition from a highly ranked official ought to be considered, in some sense, to be the equivalent of a much larger token from a lowly ranked member of society.

Notwithstanding these various possibilities, adherence to the postulate of equality constrains the range of acceptable meanings that may be legitimately ascribed to the concept of reciprocity. Specifically, because of its counterfactual stipulation that all individuals are equal qua individuals, the postulate of equality precludes acceptance of exchanges of patently unequal tokens as capable of satisfying the kind of equivalence required by the norm of reciprocity. Further, the particular equality stressed above all by the postulate of equality is that which extends to all individuals in so far as they are viewed as the subjects of moral choice. Consistent with this, reciprocity can be conceived as apt to delimit a common identity through the mutual recognition of individuals as autonomous subjects of moral choice.

The counterfactual equality underlying this latter conception of reciprocity is an equality among abstract egos. In other words, the equality that I am referring to here is one that is stipulated as transcending all the differences—including those in race, sex, abilities, talents, social position, cultural background, degree of moral rectitude, and fundamental belief systems—that may be invoked to distinguish one historically situated concrete ego from another. With this distinction firmly in mind, it is now possible to provide a more specific account of the mutual recognition that the norm of reciprocity might be construed to require in the context of adherence to the postulate of equality. Such mutual recognition is as abstract egos standing free from particular spatiotemporal determinations, but endowed with the capacity to exercise moral choice (regardless of whether the concrete persons standing behind these abstract egos are *actually* capable of exercising moral choices). Moreover, such mutual recognition as abstract egos promotes a common identity as abstract egos: every individual, no matter how different he or she may be from other individuals in the concrete historical setting in which they all find themselves, is nevertheless identical to other individuals as an abstract ego. In short, reciprocity as mutual recognition between individuals who view each other exclusively as subjects of moral choice produces a conception of equality based on the identity of all abstract egos.

The norm of reciprocity interpreted as requiring equality based on the identity of all abstract egos provides powerful support for the rejection of first-order discrimination on the basis of race or sex. Indeed, arguments purporting to lend support to the treatment of blacks or women as inferiors frequently concentrate on actual or apparent differences that can serve to divide concrete individuals along racial or gender lines. For example, a racist may seek to justify the treatment of blacks as inferiors by arguing that the latter are lazy and irresponsible. Similarly, a sexist may suggest that women ought to be subordinated to men because in his view women are physically weaker and more emotionally unstable than men. One way to counter the arguments of both the racist and the sexist is by making better supported factual arguments that contradict those of the racist and the sexist, and that undermine or invalidate the latter's conclusions. Even if the factual arguments presented by the foes of racism and sexism are deemed to be conclusive, however, it is always possible for the racist and the sexist to turn to other existing or apparently existing differences between the races or the sexes and argue that the latter justify treating blacks or women as inferiors. By invoking the norm of reciprocity and relying on the conception of equality as identity of all abstract egos, however, the foes of racism and sexism can consistently reject the legitimacy of treating blacks or women as inferior without in every instance having to demonstrate that a claimed difference does not actually exist or that an existing one does not warrant the differences in treatment sought by the racist or sexist.

To recapitulate, the norm of reciprocity understood as fostering a common identity and equality among abstract egos must be invoked to overcome the difficulties posed by exclusive recourse to a reversal of perspectives test. While the latter test may suffice to afford the manifold diversity of all concrete egos full expression, it is inadequate to preserve equality or to promote common identity. Mutual recognition as abstract egos, on the other hand, appears to go some way in filling the gap left open by the proliferation of differentiation through application of the reversal of perspectives test. Accordingly, at this point, we seem left with identity and equality among abstract egos and with ever greater differentiation among concrete egos, but with no discernible synthesis between the two.

Abstract egos may appear to be fully disembodied, but the perspective of an abstract ego cannot be merely neutral. As we saw in chapter 8, in the course of our discussion of the shortcomings of the contractarian position, there cannot be a perspective from which all race- or gender-related determinations are purged. By the same token, it would seem to be all the more unrealistic to believe that there could be a perspective cleansed not only of all traces relating to race and sex but also of virtually all other ingredients that contribute to the definition of the particular perspectives of concrete persons. Accordingly, and for the same reasons discussed in chapter 8 in connection with the critique of the contractarian position,[4] the perspective of the abstract ego, while apparently neutral, is actually likely to give privilege to some particular concrete perspective above all others.

Taken by itself, the abstract ego seems very much like the hypothetical contractor of contemporary contractarianism: they both promote equality as identity, they both appear neutral, but they both allow the privileging of the dominant perspective. On the other hand, the process of reversal of perspectives, to the extent that it operates without any constraints, appears to produce outcomes that display the same virtues and vices as those promoted by a pure utilitarian approach: they both accord full recognition to individual differences, they both appear to respect the individuality of each person—utilitarianism, by counting each person as one and no more than one; the process of reversal of perspectives, by taking into account every individual perspective—but ultimately neither of the two allows for a sufficient common identity or for an equality among persons that transcends all differences and all change.

What is needed to overcome these limitations is a position that relies on reciprocity without discarding difference, that makes room for both the abstract ego and the concrete ego, that promotes the virtues of contractarianism and utilitarianism without embracing their vices, and that provides a unifying framework in which equality can simultaneously coexist with identity and with difference. Such a position, moreover, can be constructed through an elaboration of Kohlberg's conception of justice as reversibility. For Kohlberg, justice as reversibility is the culmination of a progression through six stages of moral development that span nonreciprocity to reciprocity, and from the latter to reversibility or, in other words, to a reciprocity of perspectives. In the following discussion, I shall draw upon Kohlberg's theory to account for the passage from nonreciprocity to reciprocity, and from the latter to reversibility.

Like Kohlberg, I am searching for a normative position that allows for the greatest possible integration compatible with the greatest possible differentiation. By placing such a search within the context of adherence to the postulate of equality, I am constrained to limit my choice only among those positions that satisfy the norm of reciprocity understood as requiring the mutual exchange of tokens of equal recognition. Thus, to the extent that the progression through Kohlberg's stages of moral development reveals a *logic* that marks the passage from nonreciprocity to reciprocity, and from the more formal and abstract kinds of reciprocity to more comprehensive ones, which are better suited to encompass integration and differentiation, there appears to be a substantial convergence between Kohlberg's enterprise and my own. On the other hand, I shall not rely on his more controversial hypotheses concerning the correspondence between stages of cognitive development and stages of moral development. Indeed, to the extent that Kohlberg's six stages of moral development are meant to correspond to actual stages of cognitive development, or to reflect how ontogeny recapitulates phylogeny, they remain well beyond the scope of my own inquiry and concerns in this book. In short, while I am interested in Kohlberg's theory in so far as it offers a logic for the passage from nonreciprocity to evermore encompassing forms of reciprocity compatible with adherence to the postulate of equality, I am not concerned with empirical issues relating to the cognitive or moral development of individuals or of the species.[5]

The progression through Kohlberg's six stages of moral development takes us from the nonreciprocity of the first stage to the full reciprocity of perspectives of the sixth (Kohlberg 1981, 148–62 ff.). For our purposes, however, what is most important about this progression is the transition between the fifth stage, which is associated with the moral positions of the utilitarian and the contractarian,[6] and the sixth stage, which is that of justice as reversibility.[7] Brief mention must be made of the transition from nonreciprocity to reciprocity, however, to the extent that it informs the logic that underlies the progression toward justice as reversibility. Accordingly, I shall briefly address this transition, but only in the most general terms. Such general terms, it moreover ought to be emphasized, while capturing the essence of Kohlberg's own analysis, are not ones that he himself explicitly addresses.

From the standpoint of fulfilling the aims of the postulate of equality, it can be shown that there is a clear logical progression from nonreciprocity to reciprocity and from reciprocity to reversibility. The paradigm of a nonreciprocal relationship is that of master and slave, in which the master treats the slave not only as an inferior, but also as though the latter were lacking a perspective of his own. Accordingly, the master does not consider the slave as an alter ego who is entitled to pursue an independent life plan but as a mere instrument who exists to satisfy the master's desires.[8] As an inferior, the slave deserves no recognition, and his only raison d'être, from the master's perspective, is to provide recognition to the master. This recognition is achieved by reducing the slave's legitimate role to being a mere reflection of the master's self-image, and by compelling the slave to devote his full attention to the production of those goods that the master has determined will contribute to the satisfaction of the master's desire.

The nature of actual historical master and slave relationships are likely to differ in various respects from the paradigm case discussed above.[9] Nevertheless, all such relationships remain nonreciprocal to the extent that the master refuses to acknowledge that the slave is entitled to have a perspective of his own, and that the master treats the slave as though the latter did not have any worthy needs, desires, objectives, and aspirations of his own. Such nonreciprocity, moreover, is particularly important not only because it is in sharp contrast with reciprocity, but also because it has figured prominently in the legal and institutional relationships that existed between the class of black slaves and that of their white masters in the United States.[10]

Reciprocal relationships within the confines of the postulate of equality, on the other hand, involve, as already mentioned, mutual recognition, with each person acknowledging that every other person has, and is entitled freely to express, his or her own perspective. In reciprocal relationships, each person is the equal of every other person in the sense that he possesses a separate perspective worthy of the same respect as every other individual perspective. But a distinction must be drawn between reciprocal relationships that involve what may be termed *mere* reciprocity and those that generate a comprehensive form of reciprocity that requires a reversal of perspectives. In the context of mere reciprocity, each person recognizes the equality of every other person as the *possessor* of a separate and independent perspective. On the other hand, when mere reciprocity prevails, it is only from her own perspective that a person can grasp the expressions issued from another person's perspective. Like in the case of the limited reversal test discussed above, ego can apprehend the content of alter's perspective only from ego's perspective, thus imposing the weight of ego's own values on alter's goals and designs. Because of this, mere reciprocity promotes an equality dependent on identity but is incapable of sustaining a more comprehensive equality that would also account for differences.

Although the pursuit of a form of equality that encompasses both identity and difference requires the passage to a more comprehensive type of reciprocity, mere reciprocity is not devoid of virtue. Actually, its very weakness is also, upon further reflection, a source of strength. The failure to grasp the other's needs and aspirations from the latter's perspective, while bound to lead to the suppression of certain differences, is also likely to encourage the expression of one's own perspective and the vigorous pursuit of the goods necessary to the fulfillment of one's own life plan. Those who cannot assert their own perspective are in danger of becoming engulfed by the perspectives of others, and thus ultimately of losing the sense that they possess a separate identity. As indicated by our examination of the process of complete reversal of perspectives, if an individual cannot legitimately pursue interests simply *because* they are her own, then there is a danger that such an individual will have to surrender her autonomy to allow for the satisfaction of the more intensely and passionately felt needs and desires of others. Consistent with these observations, mere reciprocity is valuable not only because it prompts each person to recognize every other person as an equal who possesses a separate perspective, but also because it encourages the kind of individual self-assertion that is likely to promote individual identity and autonomy.

Mere reciprocity marks an important moment in the quest for an optimal equilibrium between identity and difference in the context of the postulates of equality. Mere reciprocity promotes self-identity and mutual identity. But mere reciprocity, by the same token, is unlikely to promote a sufficient level of differentiation wherever one particular perspective is likely to predominate. Indeed, mere reciprocity does nothing to prevent a dominant perspective from suppressing or subordinating alternative perspectives. Because of this, under conditions of significant inequalities between existing perspectives, mere reciprocity is unlikely to lead to the requisite equilibrium between identity and difference. In particular, to the extent that the relationship between the races and between the sexes in the United States is predicated on the historic subordination of blacks' and women's perspectives to those of white males, mere reciprocity is unlikely to promote equality in race and gender relationships.

The inadequacy of mere reciprocity makes imperative a more comprehensive form of reciprocity, if we are to achieve the requisite equilibrium between identity and difference. This more comprehensive form of reciprocity must encompass a switch in perspectives that would make it possible for each person to assess the claims of others from the perspective of the person who makes the claim. This entails reliance on the process of complete reversal of perspectives, but not *exclusive* reliance on it. Individual self-assertion within the constraints of mere reciprocity may not be sufficient to achieve the desired equilibrium between identity and difference in the absence of equality of bargaining power. That does not mean, however, that some measure of such self-assertion is not necessary in order to reach the desired outcome. Indeed, the dominant party in consensual transactions entered into against a background of formal equality (of identity) cannot legitimately hold to his superior position, but this does not justify allowing him to be relegated to the position of a subordinate. Because of this, a reciprocity of perspectives must not suppress individual self-assertion, but only place upon it the minimum of constraints necessary to prevent domination. In the last analysis, the weaknesses of both mere reciprocity and of complete perspective reversals may be overcome through a dynamic confrontation whereby each of these strives to keep the other in check.

With this in mind, let us now turn to Kohlberg's principle of justice as reversibility and determine whether it fosters the requisite equilibrium without unduly constraining the individual's right of self-assertion.

3. Kohlberg's Principle of Justice as Reversibility and the Reciprocity of Perspectives

As conceived by Kohlberg, the concept of reversibility encompasses that of reciprocity but extends beyond it.[11] Reversibility involves not only recognizing that others have their own perspective, but also trading positions with others to become aware of the nature and content of their perspectives, so that each gains a richer understanding of the other's objectives. In Kohlberg's terms, reversibility is a "reciprocity of perspectives."[12]

Justice as reversibility, on the other hand, requires that intersubjective conflicts be resolved by subjecting all the competing claims to each and every one of the perspectives of the individuals involved in the conflict until only the reversible claims survive—that is, the claims that can be justified from all the relevant perspectives.[13] Further, Kohlberg views justice as reversibility in terms of a process of "ideal role-taking" or of the playing of "moral musical chairs."[14] In his own words,

> Moral musical chairs means going around the circle of perspectives involved in a moral dilemma to test one's claim of right or duty until only the equilibrated or reversible claims survive. In 'nonmoral' or competitive musical chairs there is only one 'winning person'. In moral chairs there is only one 'winning' chair which all other players recognize if they play the game, the chair of the person with the prior claim of justice. (Kohlberg 1979, 262)

Kohlberg also offers a somewhat different formulation of what justice as reversibility is supposed to achieve, which is couched in terms of ideal role-taking:

> (a) The decider is to successively put himself imaginatively in the place of each other actor and consider the claims each would make from his point of view.
> (b) Where claims in one party's shoes conflict with those in another's, imagine each party to trade places. If so, a party should drop his conflicting claim if it is based on nonrecognition of the other's point of view. (Ibid., 263)

The notion of justice as reversibility, as Kohlberg points out, is already at work in Rawls' original position behind the veil of ignorance.[15] Rawls' original position, however, is reversible only in a purely formal sense. Indeed, as I discussed in chapter 8, the effect of the veil of ignorance is to remove from each individual that which makes his or her own perspective different from that of others. What remains is a single perspective that all individuals in the original position share. Hence, although the individual perspectives in the original position are fully reversible, the elimination of all differences makes reversibility essentially trivial. Once all differences are removed, reversibility produces no more than an acknowledgement that others possess *a* perspective just as I do.

In Kohlberg's conception, on the other hand, justice as reversibility as the expression of the highest stage of moral development, represents a definite advance over Rawls' contractarian position. Unlike in Rawls' original position, the participants in Kohlberg's procedure must take all differences into account. Thus, any agreement that they may reach after having traded perspectives would appear to be suited to respect relevant differences as well as relevant identities. In short, upon initial consideration at least, Kohlberg's conception of justice as reversibility appears to possess all the virtues of Rawls' contractarian theory, with the added advantage of satisfactorily accounting for all relevant differences.

Upon further consideration, there is an ambiguity in the notion that each claimant who enters into Kohlberg's dialogical arena possesses a separate perspective. Indeed, does a "separate perspective" refer to a different set of basic religious, political, social, and economic beliefs—that is, to a different ideology? Or does it refer instead to a different vantage point within the same ideological perspective?

The distinction between these two possibilities is important, as indicated by the following example. Suppose there is a conflict between one person's claim to a right to life and another's claim to a right to property, such that the satisfaction of either of these two claims can only be achieved through frustration of the other. This is the situation in Kohlberg's own example, which is known as "Heinz's dilemma" (Kohlberg 1979, 259ff.). A is very sick and can only survive if she obtains a very expensive medicine that is the property of B. A cannot pay for the medicine, and B refuses to give it or to lower the price, confident that eventually a rich person will be willing to pay the asking price for it. Now, if A and B both share the belief that life is more important than property, then through a reversal of perspectives B ought to become convinced that he has a moral duty to give the medicine to A. Indeed, since B values life more than property, he should realize that A's need for the medicine has greater priority than his own property needs. On the other hand, if A and B have radically different ideologies such that in A's system of normative beliefs life always has priority over property, while in B's, the contrary happens to be the case, a reversal of perspectives would not yield a satisfactory solution to the conflict. While both A and B would be able to "see" it from the other's perspective, justice as reversibility could offer no reason for either of them to subordinate his or her own claim to that of the other.

To the extent that the viability of justice as reversibility may depend on the acceptance of certain universally applicable normative principles and on the rejection of any broad-based ideological differences, one may object that the process of reversibility is largely superfluous. Pursuant to this objection, which is similar to that made by Dworkin against Rawls' use of the hypothetical social contract device,[16] what ultimately determines legitimate normative rights and duties are universally applicable principles, and not the process of reversing perspectives. And, if this is true, the process of reversibility would not only be unnecessary but it could also be misleading in so far as it might conceal that it is the acceptance of universal principles, and not the trading of individual perspectives, that justifies taking a particular ethical stance.

Upon closer scrutiny, however, it should become apparent that the very requirement to recognize relevant differences makes the process of perspective reversals necessary to the full development of the implications flowing from the postulate of equality. Thus, although the postulate of equality leads to the exclusion of certain perspectives and certain differences, it also demands commitment to the greatest possible inclusion and accommodation of remaining perspectives and differences. Moreover, such inclusion is arguably much less likely to be achieved through the monological expression of a single voice than through dialogical exchanges in the process of perspective reversals among proponents of diverse perspectives.

Restricting perspective reversals to those who share a common core of fundamental values certainly appears more likely to lead to consensus than keeping the process open to representatives of the most widely diverging ideological viewpoints. But such consensus need not be merely among persons who already share the same perspective *ex ante,* that is prior to the implementation of any perspective reversal. Indeed, there can be certain genuine differences in perspective—beyond simple differences in vantage point within a commonly shared collective perspective—among proponents of the postulate of equality. This follows from the fact that the postulate of equality requires the acceptance of diverse moral, political, and religious ideologies, so long as these do not impinge upon any individual's equal right to moral autonomy.

Alternatively, one may argue that the process of reversal of perspectives is not superfluous even if adherence to the postulate of equality were incompatible with the preservation of a multiplicity of perspectives. In other words, even if the *collective* perspective of all adherents to the postulate of equality is the same, their *individual* perspectives are not, to the extent that each of them is free to pursue a life plan that does not interfere with the equal opportunity of others to do likewise. In short, recognizing that others have life plans of their own is not the same as understanding the order of priorities established from the standpoint of a particular life plan. And to be able to achieve such an understanding, one cannot simply rely on common values, but must also endeavor to grasp the point of view of the individual who puts forth the priorities in question.

Taking into account the above modifications and qualifications, Kohlberg's conception of justice as reversibility can be adapted and transformed into a suitable vehicle for the promotion of justice in the context of the postulate of equality. As indicated in the course of the previous discussion, the principal objectives sought are the achievement of the fullest possible measure of integration compatible with the maintenance of the highest possible degree of differentiation through an optimal equilibrium between identity and difference; and the encouragement of individual self-assertion within limits required to avoid subordination. As also discussed, moreover, neither mere reciprocity nor an unlimited reciprocity of perspectives is ultimately likely best to promote the postulate of equality. But a reciprocity of perspectives that is limited—in the sense of not including all perspectives rather than in that of requiring only a partial reversal of included perspectives—may provide the best means to achieve the objectives identified above.

To justify this last claim, one must explain both how the contemplated reciprocity could be limited in a fair and principled manner and how it could operate without introducing any significant problems of its own. Turning to the first of these tasks, it would appear that reciprocity can be limited by defining it as mutual recognition among all those who subscribe to the postulate of equality and who genuinely respect the integrity of the perspectives of others. In other words, this kind of reciprocity requires mutual recognition as equals and mutual recognition of the integrity of the other's perspective. Thus, if mere reciprocity entails mutual recognition of persons as *possessors* of a separate perspective, in the kind of reciprocity under consideration, there is mutual recognition of the other's *need to maintain the integrity of his or her own perspective.* Mere reciprocity among possessors of separate perspectives permits broad-based competition limited only by the need to preserve everyone's right to compete under uniformly applicable rules, but reciprocal recognition of the integrity of perspectives requires greater restrictions on individual self-assertion in order to preserve the integrity of every perspective. On the other hand, whereas an unlimited reciprocity of perspectives may suppress self-assertion to the point of fomenting undue subordination, reciprocal recognition of the integrity of perspectives is likely to avoid this pitfall by excluding from consideration (at least to the extent that they appear to be irreconcilable) the perspectives of those who refuse to respect the integrity of the perspectives of others.

To set the distinctions between nonreciprocity, mere reciprocity, and reciprocity of perspectives in sharper focus, one may find it useful to imagine nonreciprocal relationships as being between enemies or between superior and subordinate; merely reciprocal ones, as relationships between competitors abiding by common rules of competition; and more fully reciprocal ones, involving a reciprocity of perspectives, as relationships involving a certain fiduciary component. Fiduciaries are agents who owe a duty of loyalty to their principals, and who must act in the best interests of their principals rather than merely dealing with them at arms' length. The fiduciary component I have in mind here, however, would be much more limited. It would impose essentially a negative rather than a positive duty. Thus, pursuant to this fiduciary duty, each person would be obligated to yield otherwise valid claims whenever this would be necessary to preserve the integrity of the perspective of another in a way that does not threaten the integrity of perspective of anyone else.

With these distinctions in mind, we might say that the limited reciprocity of perspectives advocated here requires that one treat everyone who is not an enemy threatening one's life or autonomy as at least a competitor. Further, one would have to treat those who respect the integrity of the perspectives of others as more than competitors, by yielding certain benefits as a fiduciary would, in the limited circumstances described above. Finally, to determine when one must yield otherwise valid claims to those with whom one shares a commitment to the reciprocity of perspectives, one ought to rely on the reversal of perspectives.

It is plain, from the preceding discussion, that the limited reciprocity of perspectives advocated here can be implemented in an orderly and comprehensive manner. Also, we have seen how it solves the problems posed by mere reciprocity of perspectives. Upon further examination, it should also become apparent that a limited reciprocity of perspectives is unlikely to produce any new significant problems of its own. Since the limited reciprocity of perspectives does not discard the requirements of mere reciprocity, and since it limits the process of complete reversal in such a way that no ego is obligated to defer to any alter who does not respect the integrity of that ego's perspective, it seems unlikely that a limited reciprocity of perspectives would significantly adversely affect any identity interest protected by mere reciprocity.

On the other hand, the picture with respect to unlimited reciprocity of perspectives appears to be far less clear. Indeed, it may seem at first that the move from unlimited to limited reciprocity of perspectives inevitably requires some overall reduction in difference. But even if this were conceded, such reduction would not have to give rise to any significant problem. This is because the objective of proponents of the postulate of equality is not the mere proliferation of difference for its own sake, but the achievement of the greatest possible difference consistent with the preservation of an adequate sense of individual identity for all. Furthermore, if one looks at the matter more closely, one may conclude that an unlimited reciprocity of perspectives would not necessarily lead to the coexistence of a greater number of differences. In fact, such an unlimited reciprocity is ultimately no more suited than a limited one to accommodate incompatible differences. Both these forms of reciprocity must deny recognition to some differences. The essential distinction between them is that unlimited reciprocity favors more intensely asserted differences, whereas limited reciprocity gives precedence to those differences that are least likely to interfere unduly with self-assertion and individual identity. In short, regardless of whether the limited reciprocity of perspectives is likely to lead to the recognition of a smaller number of differences than would its unlimited counterpart, it does not appear to raise any significant problem that might be avoided by sticking to unlimited reciprocity.

4. The Three Faces of Justice as Reversibility

Justice as reversibility relying on a limited reciprocity of perspectives—to which I will refer as "justice as reversible reciprocity"—provides systematic means to deal with different kinds of conflicting claims. Some of these claims, such as those that are incompatible with the postulate of equality and advanced by individuals who do not respect the integrity of the perspective of others, deserve to be completely disregarded. For example, the claim of a religious fanatic who believes it to be his divine mission to establish a racially segregated society to preserve racial purity, to force others to convert to his religion and to give up the right to make moral decisions for themselves, ought to be given no recognition whatsoever, no matter how genuine or sincere his belief might be. To the extent that this is possible without compromising the moral autonomy of others, such a religious fanatic ought nevertheless to be accorded the respect owed to everyone as the possessor of a perspective—particularly, since every person can conceivably change his or her perspective.[17] But when it comes to considering conflicting claims through the reversal of perspectives, the above-mentioned claim of the religious fanatic must simply be left out.

A. Justice as Reversibility as the Functional Equivalent of Contractarian Justice

With respect to a certain class of claims, justice as reversibility operates as the functional equivalent of the contractarian criterion of justice. Paradigmatic of this class are certain fundamental claims asserting entitlements to relationships that comply with the requirements of mere reciprocity. An example of such a claim would be the assertion of the right not to be treated as a slave. It is not necessary to understand the actual perspective of anyone who claims the right not to be treated as a slave. All that is required to ascertain the validity of such a claim is evaluation of it in terms of a mere reciprocity standard, such as Goldman's limited reversal test, according to which competing claimants trade positions but not perspectives. For this reason, as applied to the class of claims under consideration, justice as reversibility can be said to operate as the functional equivalent of the contractarian criterion of justice. By the same token, any claim that can only be satisfied if someone is treated like a slave does not deserve recognition because it is flatly inconsistent with the postulate of equality. Consistent with these observations, justice as reversibility, just like the contractarian criterion of justice, brands as inherently unjust all forms of first-order discrimination leading to the treatment of their victims as inferiors.

B. Justice as Reversibility Proper

Another class of claims includes those that are made from a perspective that is compatible with the postulate of equality and that recognizes the integrity of the perspectives of others. To the extent that two or more of the claims belonging to this class are in conflict with one another, it is only through a complete reversal of perspectives that justice as reversibility can ascribe any legitimate order of priority among them. Also, conflicting claims belonging to this class may either be made from different vantage points within the same perspective or from altogether different perspectives.

To illustrate the first of these alternatives let us consider the following example. Two mothers, each with a sick child, place conflicting claims to obtain a scarce medicine which is in such short supply that there is only enough of it to cure one of the two children. Moreover, one of the children has a milder case of the disease, and she will eventually recuperate fully even without taking the medicine, but not without going through a period of substantial pain and suffering. The other child, on the other hand, has a much more severe case of the disease and might well die if she does not get the medicine.

The two mothers share the same perspective for all purposes relevant here. They both believe that saving the life of a sick child ought to be a mother's highest priority and that relieving the pain and suffering of a sick child would be her next highest priority. Despite sharing the same perspective, however, they both have different vantage points insofar as each mother views the order of priorities just described in terms of her own child.

At the level of mere reciprocity, each mother will acknowledge the right of the other to press a claim for the medicine—that is, will recognize the other as a legitimate competitor for the scarce medicine. But the mother of the child with the milder case of the disease will continue to press her own claim because the pain and suffering of her own child will cause her much greater distress than the prospect of the other woman's child dying. At the level of the reciprocity of perspectives, however, through a complete reversal of positions, each mother can accurately assess the predicament of the other by imagining that both sick children are her own. In that case, it seems clear that each mother would want the medicine for the child who is otherwise likely to die. Accordingly, justice as reversibility would require that the claim of the mother whose child is sicker be given priority over that of the other mother. With the kind of claims involved here, therefore, justice as reversibility requires that some claims be satisfied at the expense of the others. To the extent that all claimants agree to abide by the outcome of the complete reversal of perspectives, there ought to be a consensus among all competing claimants concerning the order of priority of their respective claims.

As an example of conflicting claims in the context of different perspectives rather than different vantage points we may imagine the following situation. Two persons, A and B, have conflicting claims to a single bottle of wine, under circumstances in which no other bottle is likely to become available for a number of weeks. From the standpoint of mere reciprocity, both A and B are entitled to compete for the bottle of wine, with the winner having a legitimate right to keep it. And this would hold true even if we stipulate that A, who is a profoundly religious person who needs the wine in order to be able to perform an important ritual, lost out in the competition to B, who is an agnostic hedonist who enjoys drinking good wine. From the standpoint of a reciprocity of perspectives, however, if the pleasure that B anticipates to derive from the bottle of wine is less important relative to the fulfillment of his life plan than is the performance of the ritual involving wine relative to the realization of A's life plan, then both A and B should agree that A's claim to the bottle of wine ought to prevail over B's. Accordingly, given the impossibility of having all their respective claims satisfied, justice as reversibility requires that they agree that claims that are more important relative to the perspective of one of them be given priority over claims that are less important relative to the perspective of the other. Moreover, through the implementation of a complete reversal of perspectives, they ought to reach a consensus concerning which claims ought to be given priority over conflicting claims.

C. Justice as Reversibility as the Functional Equivalent of Utilitarian Justice

There is a subclass of the claims belonging to the last class for which the complete reversal of perspectives does not yield an order of priorities. Moreover, the conflicting claims within such a subclass may involve either different vantage points within the same perspective or different perspectives. Conflicting claims within the same perspective belong to the subclass in question if, after submission to the reversal of positions test, none of the claims involved emerges as superior to any of the remaining claims. Conflicting claims issuing from different perspectives, on the other hand, should be included in the subclass under consideration if, after application of the complete reversal of perspectives test, none of these emerges as being more important relative to the perspective to which it is associated than any other conflicting claim is relative to the different perspective to which it is associated.

To illustrate this, let us assume that a municipality enjoys a fixed revenue surplus that everyone agrees ought to be used to provide public recreational facilities. The choice lies between building a swimming pool or tennis courts. Some residents would prefer the swimming pool; others, the tennis courts. Further, let us suppose that all the residents share the same basic perspective and that they all ascribe the same importance to recreational activities but that, from the vantage point of some, swimming is the preferred form of recreation, whereas, from that of others, tennis is. Under these circumstances, if each resident switched places with every other resident, they would all realize that individual preferences for a swimming pool are no more intense than those for tennis courts. Accordingly, each resident would be justified in concluding that the preferences of others are not entitled to any greater deference than her own preference.

In situations of this kind, justice as reversibility does not require according priority to any of the conflicting claims. Indeed, refusal to grant such a priority would not deny recognition to the integrity of all the perspectives (or vantage points within the same perspective) involved. To the extent that all the relevant claims stand on an equal footing, and that none is more important than any other from the standpoint of maintaining the dignity of any individual, justice as reversibility would arguably be satisfied by a resolution of conflicts among such claims on the basis of calculations of net preferences or net utilities. To return to our last example, the requirements imposed by justice as reversibility would be met if the municipality put the matter to a vote of its citizens and proceeded to build the recreational facility preferred by a majority. Accordingly, in cases such as this, justice as reversibility can be said to operate as the functional equivalent of the utilitarian criterion of justice.

Insofar as reversibility operates as the functional equivalent of the contractarian criterion of justice, it may be ultimately monological in that it does not require grasping the perspective of another person. On the other hand, both justice as reversibility proper and as the functional equivalent of the utilitarian criterion of justice are dialogical in that they depend on communication as the means for one person to be able to understand the point of view and the overall perspective of another. With respect to the latter, moreover, although the calculation of net preferences may not itself be dialogical in nature, the prior necessary determination of whether all the relevant conflicting claims should stand on an equal footing can only be made through a reversal process that is inherently dialogical.

5. Habermas' Communicative Ethics and the Possibility for the Undistorted Communication of Perspectives

The success of justice as reversibility depends on the accurate communication not only of individual claims but also of the particular point of view that gives shape to such claims. In some cases, such as the one involving the two mothers with sick children, a high level of understanding of the perspective of another can be achieved with a minimum of communication. Since each of the mothers involved knows how it feels to be the mother of a sick child, it does not take that much for her to imagine what it would be like if she were the mother of the other woman's child. In other cases, in which the perspectives of the conflicting claimants have much less in common to begin with, however, communication about each other's perspective is likely to be much more difficult. Thus, for example, a white person who has never experienced racial discrimination, and who does not know how it feels to the member of a readily identifiable minority group, may not understand what systematic racial discrimination means from the perspective of a black victim.

The need for adequate communication is particularly acute whenever the nature of another's perspective is not readily deciphered. Yet difficulty in communication stems not only from the inability to articulate one's innermost thoughts and beliefs, but also from distorting factors, such as deception and self-deception. Because of this, it is necessary to determine next whether communicative interaction may be sufficiently stripped of distortion to fulfill the dialogical needs of justice as reversibility.

The problem of systematically distorted communication and the possibility of undistorted communication figure prominently in Habermas' theory of communicative ethics. Among the types of communicative distortions considered by Habermas are those caused by power, ideology, deception, and self-deception—all of which have played an important role (and are likely to continue to do so) in communication between the races and between the sexes. On the other hand, by means of a counterfactual device that he terms the "ideal speech situation," Habermas provides us with a critical tool designed to expose communication distortions and to indicate the directions in which a normatively oriented reconstructed dialogue relying on undistorted communication would lead. The dialogical model for the validation of normative claims presented by Habermas' communicative ethics requires consideration of all conflicting claims and of all different perspectives. Accordingly, this dialogical model not only appears to be fully compatible with the requirements of justice as reversible reciprocity but also seems particularly well suited to specify the practical conditions that must obtain to insure the viability of this conception of justice. Moreover, both justice as reversible reciprocity and communicative ethics depend on the achievement of a consensus among all the participants in a relevant dialogical exchange.

Because of its stress on distorted communication, its construction of a dialogical model for the settlement of conflicting claims, and the distinction it draws among different kinds of interests—namely, common, generalizable, and particular interests—Habermas' theory of communicative ethics deserves further examination here. Indeed, such examination may well shed additional light on some of the important issues left unresolved in the course of our previous discussion of justice as reversibility. But to see how this might be accomplished it is first necessary to present a brief sketch of some of the most salient features of Habermas' conception of communicative ethics.

A major strength of communicative ethics, which is essentially reconstructive in nature, lies in its outstanding suitability as a tool for critical analysis. In Habermas' assessment of social relationships, traces of power, ideology, deception, and self-deception are embedded in the normative structures that actually regulate intersubjective dealings at a given time. These traces play an important role in the preservation and perpetuation of relationships of domination, pursuant to which certain persons or groups wield greater power and authority, and others possess less control and autonomy, than seems justified based on the particular state of prevailing material conditions. Moreover, not only do these traces affect the configuration of existing operating norms, but also they seem bound to permeate all forms of social interaction, including communication and the social processes leading to the formation and transformation of individual and collective self-images.

Against this background the tasks of communicative ethics loom as essentially twofold: first, communicative ethics must identify and expose the traces identified above and the forces that lie behind them; and, second, it must counterfactually reconstruct the universe of intersubjective relationships as though these traces and forces were completely neutralized and discarded. Expressed somewhat differently, as conceived by Habermas, the counterfactual reconstruction envisaged as the second task should be guided by the following question:

> How would the members of a social system, at a given stage in the development of productive forces, have collectively and bindingly interpreted their needs (and which norms would they have accepted as justified) if they could and would have decided on organization of social intercourse through discursive will-formation, with adequate knowledge of the limiting conditions and functional imperatives of their society? (Habermas 1975, 113)

It should be added that both of the tasks serve a predominantly critical purpose. Indeed, both the exposure of forces that lie behind illegitimate forms of domination and the counterfactual reconstruction of the universe of social relationships vividly underscore the inadequacy of prevailing norms and modes of intersubjective interaction.

Through the performance of its twofold tasks of exposure and reconstruction based on dialogue, communicative ethics appears to be particularly well suited to advance the aims of justice as reversible reciprocity. Indeed, what prevents one person from being able to appreciate the perspective of another may frequently be traceable to differences in power and ideology or to instances of deception and self-deception. Moreover, once the causes of such failures in appreciation have been identified and set aside, it ought to be possible, at least in principle, to coordinate all existing perspectives by means of the dialogical process of the reversal of perspectives. The coordination of perspectives, thus obtained, should permit, in turn, the elaboration of a system of normative principles which would facilitate the reconstruction of intersubjective relationships in a way that accords all individual perspectives equal dignity and respect.

On the other hand, the Habermasian presupposition that traces of power, ideology, deception, and self-deception are embedded in operative normative structures and permeate communicative interaction and the formation of self-images rings especially true in the context of race and gender relations. Not only, for example, are racial and sexual stereotypes promoted respectively by the racist and the sexist, but they also are often likely to figure prominently in the formation of the self-image of the victims of racism and sexism. It seems obvious that the use and the ideological reinforcement of negative stereotypes should serve the racist's and the sexist's aim to perpetuate their domination over their respective victims. The more one is convinced that blacks are lazy and irresponsible or that women are emotionally unstable and weak, the more one may feel confident in asserting that it is justified for white males to occupy positions of power and to play dominant roles in society. It seems much less obvious, however, why the victims of racism and sexism may be prone to incorporate features of negative stereotypes into their respective self-images. Nevertheless, the phenomenon of false-consciousness, by which the victim embraces, at least in part, the ideology of his oppressor, is by no means unfamiliar in the context of race and gender relationships. Indeed this phenomenon has even received judicial recognition, as evidenced by Justice Marshall's observation that "members of minority groups frequently respond to discrimination and prejudice by attempting to dissociate themselves from the group, even to the point of adopting the majority's negative attitudes towards the minority."[18] Thus, there may be circumstances under which the presumption that blacks are lazy and irresponsible is so strongly maintained and institutionally reinforced that it has no practical chance of being effectively refuted. Under such circumstances, a black individual may well increase the opportunities to improve his lot by internalizing (through, among other things, self-deception) the racist presumption and by convincing himself that he is an atypical member of his racial group.

Also of much relevance to an evaluation of the legitimacy of affirmative action is that the Habermasian presumption concerning distortions in communication attributable to unequal power relationships seems particularly appropriate in the context of hierarchical employment relationships. It seems indeed unlikely that communications between employees and employers who have discretion concerning employee salaries, promotions, and firings would tend to be completely open and frank. Let us assume that an employer asks a group of employees whether they have any complaints about their work. It may well be that they do, and that they have aired these among themselves, but that they will keep them concealed from the employer for fear of losing their jobs or of subjecting themselves to other forms of reprisal. Under such circumstances, moreover, there may be a significant amount of deception or self-deception on the part of both the employer and the employees. For instance, the employer may know of the employees' fears and merely communicate with the latter to convey the (false) impression that management "cares." Or the employer may seek to communicate, fully expecting no significant employee complaints, in order to reassure himself (regardless of what the facts really are) that all employment relationships are harmonious. Finally, the employees may take management's inquiry as an indication of real concern, and nevertheless suppress their grievances in order to generate a more positive image of their employment situation. In all these cases, however, it seems fair to assume that unequal power relationships have distorted the communications between employer and employees.

To grasp more fully the place that systematically distorted communication occupies within Habermas' theory of social action, it is necessary to refer to the important distinction that he draws between communicative action and strategic action. In the broadest terms, communicative action is defined by Habermas as action oriented to reaching an understanding; strategic action, as action oriented to the actor's success (Habermas 1979, 41). Habermas maintains that strategic action may be pursued openly or in a concealed manner. As an example of openly strategic action, one can cite a tennis game in which both the players and the spectators are fully aware that each player is playing the game in order to win. Latently strategic action, as conceived by Habermas, involves either manipulation or systematically distorted communication, or both (ibid., 209). Moreover, Habermas distinguishes between the two as follows: "Whereas in systematically distorted communication at least one of the participants deceives *himself* about the fact that the basis of consensual action is only apparently being maintained, the manipulator deceives at least one of the *other* participants about his own strategic attitude in which he *deliberately* behaves in a pseudoconsensual manner" (emphasis in original; ibid., 210).

Viewed from the standpoint of justice as reversible reciprocity, the deception involved in manipulation and the self-deception inherent in systematically distorted communication clearly pose a serious threat to the integrity of the process of the reversal of perspectives. To illustrate this last point, let us assume a discussion among certain blacks and whites concerning whether justice as reversibility would legitimate the use of affirmative action to redress the present effects of past racial discrimination. Let us suppose, further, that from the perspective of blacks oriented toward reaching an agreement concerning what would be *just* under the circumstances, affirmative action would loom as the most suitable means to redress the present effects of past discrimination. Nonetheless, one of the black participants in the discussion may sincerely claim that he does not believe that affirmative action would be just under the circumstances. That black participant would be the victim of self-deception, however, if the actual reason for his claim were that he believed that because of his superior talents the availability of affirmative action would tend to devalue his performance in the eyes of whites, thus reducing his ultimate chances of success in a white-dominated society.

The preceding example also illustrates how self-deception and systematically distorted communication may undermine the dialogical process designed to lead to justice. Indeed, if the white participants in the above-mentioned example are entitled to take the black participant's claim that affirmative action is unjust *from his own perspective* at face value, they would gather important support in their efforts to reach an agreement that rejects affirmative action. If even some blacks believe affirmative action to be unjust, then whites who oppose it from the standpoint of their own interests may gain an important bargaining advantage in the deliberations over the justice of affirmative action. Accordingly, unless the self-deception is unmasked, the process designed to lead to justice as reversibility would be seriously compromised.

In Habermas' view, the purpose of communicative ethics is to settle questions of justice by means of communicative action (White 1988, 48–49). Merely submitting these questions to a dialogical process ostensibly oriented toward reaching a consensus, however, as we have seen, does not insure success. Marked inequalities in the distribution of power may impose external constraints on dialogue to the extent that it tends to inhibit some of the participants in the discussion from presenting certain of their claims. Latently strategic action through deception and self-deception is also likely to impose internal constraints on communication, and thus distort the dialogical process in such a way as to lead to the production of a false consensus (Benhabib 1986, 284). To overcome these difficulties, Habermas introduces the concept of the "ideal speech situation."

The ideal speech situation is a counterfactual, the ultimate aim of which is to make it possible to arrive at a rational consensus based exclusively on the force of the better argument (MacCarthy 1978, 306). Moreover, it is important to stress that the ideal speech situation must insure "not only unlimited discussion but discussion that is free from distorting influences, whether their source be open domination, conscious strategic behavior, or the more subtle barriers to communication deriving from self-deception" (ibid.). Use of the ideal speech situation, however, raises at least two vexing problems. The first concerns the practical feasibility of eliminating the various distortions that are apparently inevitably present in all actual dialogues. The second relates to the reconstruction of dialogues after they have been purged of all distortions. Is such a reconstruction truly dialogical, and is it capable of accurately capturing the diverse perspectives of the various participants? Or is it ultimately monological much in the same way as Rawls' original position behind the veil of ignorance?

While difficult, the first of these problems is not insurmountable. To be sure the distortions discussed above are substantial and not always easy to detect. They are also numerous, and, accordingly, distortion-free communication is bound to remain an ideal. Nevertheless, measures can be taken to reduce distortions significantly, perhaps sufficiently to make justice as reversibility a practically workable standard. Thus, although manipulation and deception cannot always be detected, they frequently are. In the long run, manipulators and deceivers may act in ways that are inconsistent with their professed normative principles. Moreover, the deceptions of claim makers ostensibly engaged in communicative action can be kept in check by having the latter's claims compared with those of persons who appear to be similarly situated, and by disregarding those claims that seem to be completely out of line. Distortions resulting from the dominance or superior power of the person to whom the claim is made, on the other hand, can be minimized by imagining what the same claim maker would say to an equal. For example, in the case of a communication between employees and their employer, one can check the claims actually presented by employees to the employer against the grievances that employees discuss with their peers. Finally, even instances of false consciousness can be detected, and thus discounted, particularly if one assumes that, consistent with the postulate of equality, it is suspicious for individuals to act as though they were not entitled to equal dignity and respect. Thus, for instance, if a member of a persecuted racial minority embraces the negative stereotypes propagated by racists, it seems fair to presume that this represents an instance of false consciousness.

All instances of self-deception cannot be thus ferreted out, however, inasmuch as it is possible for there to be controversy concerning what constitutes false consciousness in a given set of circumstances. For example, when a woman maintains that the proper role for women is confined to being a housewife and mother, this may be interpreted plausibly as an expression of false consciousness in a male-dominated society. But many, including women, in the nineteenth century thought that the role of women as housewives and mothers was divinely ordained.[19] This raises the question of whether a nineteenth-century woman who embraced the above perspective was displaying false consciousness or whether she was merely expressing a legitimately held religious belief. It is, of course, possible to maintain that the religious beliefs in question were themselves part of an ideological apparatus designed to reinforce an established male-dominated social order. Nevertheless, a theory of justice based on the premise that all individual perspectives are, at least prima facie, entitled to equal respect ought not to be lightly invoked to discredit sincerely held religious beliefs.

Given the constraints imposed by the postulate of equality, the only legitimate means to uproot self-deception and false consciousness appears to be through persuasion in a fair and open-ended dialogue. Moreover, whereas self-deception embodied in religious beliefs may be particularly difficult to identify and to eliminate, the task is somewhat less onerous in the context of justice as reversible reciprocity, to the extent that only those religious perspectives that acknowledge the integrity of other perspectives are due consideration for purposes of the application of the reversal of perspectives test. In our last example, the issue raised may be nearly impossible to settle in the abstract but more manageable when it arises in a concrete historical setting. Thus, if an overwhelming majority of women fervently believe that it is their religious duty to fulfill the roles of mother and housewife, it is hard to imagine that fair and open dialogue would convince any significant number among them that they are the victims of self-deception. On the other hand, if women are sharply divided on the issue, and if the religious tradition involved is being seriously challenged as biased against women, then it seems more likely that a substantial number of women would eventually become convinced that they had been the victims of deception or self-deception.

Completely undistorted communication can only remain an ideal, but a sufficient number of distortions can be identified and isolated so as to render justice as reversible reciprocity workable. Because some distortions are unlikely to be completely removed, justice as reversible reciprocity must remain an imperfect procedure. Accordingly, any result to which it leads is always subject to further revision, for subsequent removal of additional distortions revealed in the course of ongoing dialogues.

The second problem posed by the ideal speech situation concerns the reconstruction of dialogues once the distortions found in actual communication have been identified and removed. If such reconstruction were truly a collective effort jointly conducted by all participants, then it would be carried out through an *actual* dialogue. Otherwise, the reconstruction of dialogues must be, at least in part, hypothetical. But a hypothetical reconstruction seems immediately open to attack as lacking a genuinely dialogical character, much along the same lines as Rawls' hypothetical social contract concluded by parties who find themselves in an original position behind a veil of ignorance.

A hypothetical reconstruction of actual dialogues—involving, among others, participants who refuse to abandon beliefs and claims based on distortions—must be conducted by someone whose function it is to decide which fragments of actual discourse to include and which to exclude, as well as which components of hypothetical discourse to include, in the reconstructed dialogue. Arguably, through the introduction of fragments of hypothetical discourse, the reconstructor can shape the hypothetical dialogue according to the biases of his own perspective, thus reducing an apparently dialogical process into a monological one. Moreover, by deciding which beliefs and claims are to be allowed expression in the reconstructed hypothetical dialogue, the reconstructor can predetermine the outcome of such dialogue, and insure that it accords with ex ante premises concerning what justice ought to require.

In order to determine whether this last problem can be satisfactorily solved, it is necessary to take a closer look at the role of communicative action in the context of communicative ethics, and at the relation that they both may bear to justice as reversible reciprocity. According to Habermas, communicative action taking place under conditions that make it possible for a rational consensus to be reached exclusively on the force of the better argument provides a procedural means to arrive at a just resolution of conflicting claims. In other words, Habermas maintains that the dialogical structure and properties of communicative action are generative of a procedure that, if followed, leads to the satisfaction of certain minimal requirements of justice of a universalistic ethics (White 1988, 23). Moreover, Habermas claims universal validity for his concept of rationality (Habermas 1984, 138). Accordingly, the dialogical process engendered by communicative action is supposed to yield a rational consensus concerning what justice requires under a given set of circumstances. In short, those who are committed to a communicative action can be led through dialogue to adopt what they all "can will in agreement to be a universal norm" (Habermas 1982; 257) according to which they can settle their differences in a just manner.

Habermas' recourse to communicative action as the basis for a universalistic ethics, and his insistence on the possibility of universal rationality, have led to harsh criticism.[20] Indeed, even if the possibility of undistorted communication were conceded, it seems arbitrary to maintain that norms are just *because* they are the product of an agreement among participants engaged in communicative action. Further, even if we accept this last proposition, it seems gratuitous to suppose that the dialogical process involved in communicative ethics would have to lead to a rational consensus among initially antagonistic participants.

It is difficult to accept the claim that communicative ethics is universally valid. Indeed, there are numerous circumstances under which dialogue and the reaching of a genuine consensus would not produce any legitimate norms. For example, in the context of an ethical system where valid norms are believed to be divinely prescribed or logically deducible from certain fundamental premises, neither the presence of communicative action nor the reaching of a completely uncoerced consensus would have, strictly speaking, any effect on the determination of the validity of moral norms. If it is up to God to decide which ethical norms ought to be adopted by a just society, then no consensus reached among mere mortals could confer legitimacy on any proposed ethical norm.

But it is unnecessary to determine, for our purposes, whether a Habermasian could successfully meet these criticisms. A proponent of justice as reversible reciprocity can avoid the difficulties that apparently beset Habermas' conception, without having to give up the dialogical process in the generation of valid norms and just outcomes. As pointed out in section 3, from the standpoint advocated here, the reversal of perspectives sought to be accomplished through the implementation of a dialogical process is neither meant to be unlimited nor thought to be independently justified. Thus, as we have seen, the perspectives of those who refuse to recognize the integrity of the perspectives of others are excluded from the process of the reversal of perspectives. Further, it is not the mere *fact* that a particular ethical outcome emerges from the dialogical process that accounts for that outcome's justice or legitimacy. Indeed, no outcome can be just unless it conforms with the postulate of equality. Nevertheless, the dialogical process is not superfluous, but necessary to produce an optimal balance between identity and difference.

Since the dialogical process itself plays an indispensable role in the determination of normatively valid outcomes, it seems particularly urgent to settle whether an actual dialogue or a hypothetical one, or else some combination of the two, would be best suited to satisfy the aims of justice as reversible reciprocity. Habermas asserts, somewhat paradoxically in light of his invocation of the ideal speech situation, that only an actually carried out dialogue can yield a legitimate normative outcome in the context of communicative action (Habermas 1982, 257). At least from the standpoint of the theory advocated here, however, actual dialogues are problematic in that they are not only likely to include deception and self-deception but also points of view that are altogether inconsistent with the postulate of equality. On the other hand, as we have seen, hypothetical dialogues are also unsatisfactory insofar as they allow for reconstructions of dialogues that predetermine outcomes in accordance with the perspective and the biases of the reconstructor.

One way to solve this problem would be to combine actual and hypothetical dialogues in such a way as to minimize the shortcomings of both. This could be accomplished by limiting reconstruction to the essentially negative task of removing those fragments of discourse that are the expression of deception, self-deception, or disregard for the postulate of equality. As thus limited, the reconstructor could not, in principle, introduce, withdraw, and rearrange fragments of discourse at will in order to reshape the debate to suit his or her bias. Thus, for example, a reconstruction of a debate between the races or between the sexes would have to include fully the various positions, arguments, and claims actually advanced by blacks and whites or by men and women, except to the extent that these are either inconsistent with the postulate of equality or the product of deception or self-deception.

Two serious objections can be raised against reconstructing dialogues on the basis of a combination of actual and hypothetical dialogue fragments. First, limiting the role of the reconstructor to a negative one does not ultimately solve the problem posed by reliance on a hypothetical dialogue, to the extent that the removal of deception and self-deception from actual discourse is so broad and ill defined a task as to afford the reconstructor sufficient latitude for introducing his or her bias into the reconstructed debate. Second, unless one is willing to accept Habermas' controverted belief in the universal validity of rationality, there appears to be lacking a legitimate criterion for the determination of which, among all the contested claims, are the most persuasive.

These objections, however, are not insurmountable. Even if one rejects the validity of Habermas' conception of universal rationality, suitable guidance for the determination of normatively justified dialogical outcomes is possible. Indeed, as already discussed in the course of the last section, the reversal of perspectives by means of a dialogical process in the context of justice as reversibility is supposed to be carried out according to clearly circumscribed normative criteria. These criteria are provided, moreover, by the postulate of equality and by the norm of reciprocity, interpreted as requiring the mutual recognition of the integrity of each other's perspective. Provided only that the possibility of the intersubjective communication of claims and perspectives is accepted, the inclusion in, or the exclusion from, the relevant dialogue of particular claims and points of view should be determined exclusively by reference to the dictates of the postulate of equality. On the other hand, the resolution of conflicts among those claims that are included in the dialogue is supposed to be made in accordance with the priorities established pursuant to the application of the norm of reciprocity as interpreted above.

A further limitation on the reconstructor's ability to abuse his role is a function of the distinction between the formulation of a life plan and the implementation of means designed to contribute to the realization of such a life plan. Whereas it is possible for deception and self-deception to affect both of these endeavors, consensus concerning relevant distortions appears to be much more likely in the context of implementation of life plans than in that of their formulation. Although the formulation of life plans is constrained by a horizon of possibilities delimited by prevailing material conditions, it nevertheless appears to retain an irreducible measure of individuality attributable to the subjective make-up of its author. Thus, a reconstructor may have good grounds to believe that a particular life plan bears a substantial imprint of distortion that has markedly reduced its author's perceived horizon of possibilities—as in the above example involving women who perceived their own legitimate role as being confined to mother and housewife. This notwithstanding, however, the reconstructor must consider whether the life plan in question is ultimately the product of some idiosyncrasy of its individual author rather than the product of the distortion.

On the other hand, this problem seems much more likely to occur in cases of apparent distortions affecting the implementation of already-formulated life plans. This is because the implementation of means would appear to be subject to a criterion of limited rationality that leaves little room for irreducible idiosyncratic variations. This criterion, it should be emphasized, does not rely on any concept of universal rationality, but only on the possibility of a limited rationality of means. In accordance with such a limited rationality criterion, once a particular end has been formulated, it should be possible to determine which means would be the most likely to promote the end in question consistent with the requirements of justice as reversible reciprocity.

To illustrate this point, let us return to the example of the black person who rejects the legitimacy of affirmative action, apparently based on self-deception. Also let us first suppose that the person in question offers as a reason for his rejection the fact that he has formulated a life plan that establishes as a goal separate nationhood for American blacks. Under these circumstances, it might be nearly impossible for a reconstructor to argue persuasively that the life plan in question is a product of self-deception. On the other hand, however, let us imagine that the same black person formulates a life plan that requires him to obtain the material and other benefits associated with competitive employment in our present-day social setting. In this case the reason offered for the rejection of the legitimacy of affirmative action is, let us say, that affirmative action is unjust because it devalues the achievements of blacks who would have succeeded absent any preferential treatment. Here, unlike in the previous case, however, the reconstructor seems to be in good position to determine independently whether affirmative action would constitute a just means toward the achievement of the ends that our black protagonist has set for himself pursuant to the dictates of his life plan. With a sufficient understanding of the life plan involved and of the objectives shaped by such a life plan, the reconstructor can reasonably assess whether affirmative action would promote these objectives consistent with equal dignity and respect for all and with reciprocity concerning the integrity of perspectives. And on that basis the reconstructor would seem to have reasonable grounds to determine whether our black protagonist's rejection of affirmative action as unjust is the product of self-deception.

In summary, while there does not seem to be any foolproof method to avoid abuses in the reconstruction of dialogues for purposes of assessing normative claims, the above examination reveals that such abuses can be sufficiently checked to preserve the integrity of the dialogical process involved. Indeed, the possibility for abuse seems reduced to manageable proportions provided that the reconstructor's task is limited to the removal of fragments of discourse which introduce distortion into the dialogical process, and that one assumes the existence of a limited rationality of means in the pursuit of objectives set by formulated life plans. Moreover, since certainty cannot be achieved, all reconstructions should remain open to challenges and to further discussion. But placed within these constraints, a reconstruction based, in part, on actual dialogue and, in part, on hypothetical dialogue can serve both the critical and the constructive requirements of justice as reversible reciprocity.

Before closing this section, we turn to the objection that it is arbitrary to suppose that communicative action would lead a group of antagonistic claimants to a rational consensus establishing an order of priority among their claims. This objection has been anticipated, and met, at least in part, in section 3. As will be remembered, I argued there that the exclusion, from the reversal of perspectives process, of those ideologies and perspectives that do not allow for recognition of the integrity of other perspectives substantially increased the likelihood that a consensus could be reached concerning the just resolution of competing claims. Nevertheless, further light can be shed on this issue through a critical examination of the distinction that Habermas draws between "generalizable interests" and "particular interests," and of his claim that communicative action can only lead to a genuine consensus through the assertion and interpretation of generalizable interests (Habermas 1975, 108).

For Habermas, a "generalizable interest," as opposed to a "particular interest," is a need that "can be communicatively shared," a "common interest" that "all can want" (ibid.). Habermas claims that we can distinguish particular interests from generalizable interests through the principle of universalization, which has to be satisfied by the latter, but not by the former (ibid.). As interests that all can want, generalizable interests, through application of the principle of universalization,[21] make it possible for those engaged in communicative action to discover "what all can will in agreement to be a universal norm" (Habermas 1982, 257). In other words, through an exchange of roles that corresponds to the ideal role-taking invoked by Kohlberg, the participants in communicative action will, according to Habermas, reach a consensus and only adopt norms that satisfy the following condition: "that the consequences and side-effects for the satisfaction of the interests of *every* individual, which are expected from a *general* observance of the norm, can be accepted with good reason by *all*" (emphasis in original; ibid.).

In short, communicative action, through the ideal speech situation that is supposed to purge all distortions from the dialogical process, leads to the emergence of commonly shared generalizable interests.[22] Moreover, through application of the principle of universalization, these generalizable interests become, according to Habermas, the basis upon which a genuine consensus can be reached concerning universally applicable norms.

To the extent that Habermas' communicative ethics makes just outcomes dependent on the promotion of interests that pass a reversal of perspectives test, it seems indistinguishable from the sixth stage of Kohlberg's theory of moral development—that is, the stage of justice as reversibility. There is, however, an important difference between the two theories. Unlike Kohlberg, Habermas is not satisfied with taking needs, wants, and interests as he finds them, but insists that they are themselves subject to transformation through dialogue. Habermas himself draws attention to this difference between his theory and Kohlberg's. In his own words,

> If needs are understood as culturally interpreted but ascribed to individuals as natural properties, the admissible universalistic norms of action have the character of general, moral norms . . . . This corresponds to Kohlberg's stage 6. Only at the level of [communicative ethics] can need interpretations themselves—that is, what each individual thinks he should understand and represent as his "true" interests—also become the object of practical discourse. (Habermas 1979, 90)

From the standpoint of meeting the objection that the dialogical process is unlikely to yield a consensus, an important consequence follows from an acceptance of Habermas' assertion that individual interests can be dialogically transformed and redefined. Initially antagonistic individual claims could be harmonized through the transformation of underlying needs and interests, so as to assure a meaningful consensus.

This possibility appears to deprive the objection under consideration of significant force. But it may only be attainable at too high a price. If one takes a closer look at Habermas' proposed dialogical transformation of individual interests, one may wonder whether it does not ultimately depend on a systematic suppression of individual interests in order to make room for supposedly more universal and more encompassing collective interests.[23] This disturbing latter possibility is enhanced, moreover, by the problematic nature of Habermas' concept of generalizable interest, which he fails to define adequately.[24] In particular, it is not clear whether, in Habermas' understanding, generalizable interests are confined to collective interests held in common by the members of an identifiable group—such as the common interest that all the citizens of a country may have in the proper military defense of their national territory—or whether they are also supposed to include individual interests that can (or must), in some sense, be made acceptable to all.

Wherever one may ultimately draw the line between particular and generalizable interests, Habermas' claim concerning the transformation of individual interests through dialogue remains problematic to the extent that it depends for its validity on a universal rationality. In the absence of workable criteria of universal rationality, it would seem as difficult to distinguish "false" needs and interests from "true" ones as it would be to stamp out all distortions from every individually formulated life plan. This difficulty, however, need not lead to a complete rejection of the very notion that individual interests may be transformed through dialogue. Indeed, not only does that notion sound highly plausible, but it could also be useful in formulating utopian positions emerging within the horizon of possibilities circumscribed by prevailing material conditions, which would provide a powerful basis for the critical assessment of actually asserted interests and existing theories and institutions relying on such interests.

Moreover, the notion of the possibility of a dialogical transformation of interests arguably underlies certain important feminist critiques of male-dominated institutions and interests, including, as we shall see in the next section, Carol Gilligan's celebrated challenge of the very premises underlying Kohlberg's moral theory. Accordingly, any assessment of the justice of affirmative action that relies on justice as reversibility would remain incomplete unless it addressed the possibility of the dialogical transformation of needs and interests. In sum, Habermas' notion of the dialogical transformation and shaping of needs and interests can serve a useful critical function in the context of certain *discussions*, provided that it is not invoked for the purpose of discarding actual interests from relevant discourses or of shaping the "reconstruction" of existing needs and interests that would otherwise be left intact.

Further, the distinction between particular and generalizable interests is important in itself inasmuch as it furnishes the divide that Habermas uses to separate the proper domain for genuine *consensus* from that for genuine *compromise*. In the most general terms, a consensus can be said to be an agreement concerning something that all want, while compromise can, by contrast, be characterized as an agreement concerning something that at least some do not want, but that all are willing to accept. Particularly where the possibilities for consensus are considered to be relatively dim, it is important to ascertain whether a compromise—and what kind of compromise—might be accepted as being just.

According to Habermas, a compromise can only be accepted if it fulfills the following two conditions: first, there is a "balance of power among the parties involved"; and second, the interests subject to negotiation are nongeneralizable (Habermas 1975, 112). The implementation of the first of these conditions is almost self-explanatory: without it, communicative ethics might have to accept as legitimate actual contracts that only the libertarian would deem to be just and other kinds of contracts that might satisfy a contractarian but that would fall short of justice as reversibility. The need for the second condition, on the other hand, may not be as self-evident but is equally important. Indeed, even assuming that compromise and consensus may, in principle, allow for a similar degree of differentiation, by definition a compromise makes for less integration than a consensus. Moreover, if a consensus is possible, the reaching of a mere compromise would appear to indicate that the dialogical process required by communicative ethics has not been completed, or that it has not been sufficiently rid of distortions.

Whether affirmative action can ultimately be justified, in the context of the contemporary American scene, in terms of a compromise or of a consensus, is a question deferred until the next chapter. Nevertheless, to the extent that it seems plausible that affirmative action may only be deemed legitimate as a matter of compromise, the above distinction drawn by Habermas and the constraints imposed by his two conditions for the legitimacy of compromise might prove to be fruitful. Indeed, if it turns out that affirmative action can only be accepted as a compromise, then unless this can be demonstrated to be a "genuine compromise"—in Habermas' sense of the term—such an acceptance could not count as a legitimate justification consistent with justice as reversible reciprocity.

It is important that the kind of compromise contemplated here is a compromise concerning normative principles and not a compromise limited to the settlement of conflicting claims. Unless this distinction is kept firmly in mind, one is likely to confuse the kind of compromise contemplated by Habermas with the entirely different kind of compromise that might be involved in the course of applying justice as reversibility, insofar as it is the functional equivalent of the utilitarian criterion of justice. In the latter case, while one may speak of a "compromise" in the sense that all participants accept a settlement of their conflicting claims in accordance with the dictates of a utilitarian calculus, there is no compromise concerning applicable normative principles. Actually, after having realized, through the reversal of perspectives, that none of the competing claims is more important from the perspective of its owner than is any other from that of its owner, all the claim makers are presumed to reach a genuine consensus. Pursuant to that consensus, all such claim makers communicate to each other their conviction that the principle of utility provides the fairest and most satisfactory means to settle claims that cannot otherwise be ranked in any compelling order of priority.

In the Habermasian kind of compromise, on the other hand, there is no agreement concerning principles, except in the broadest and most abstract of senses, in which it can be said that engaging in communicative action itself presupposes adherence to certain general intersubjective normative principles. Indeed, strictly speaking, consistent with the definitions provided by Habermas, in the context of purely particular nongeneralizable interests, one cannot generate universally applicable normative principles—that is, normative principles that all participants in communicative action would want. Therefore, Habermasian compromises would appear to be proper either where no applicable intersubjective normative principle is recognized as legitimate or where there is a clash between several proposed principles and no dialogical means to reconcile them.

Finally, use of the Habermasian distinction between consensus and compromise does not depend on the discovery of the exact meaning that Habermas attaches to the concept of generalizable interest. Such use, however, does require that some workable means be found to distinguish between interests that would make consensus possible and interests to which compromise can give legitimate expression. One way to accomplish this is by preserving Habermas' distinction between interests that all can want and all other interests, but by further stipulating that collective as well as individual interests can qualify as interests that all can want. Indeed, all may want something because they each have an individual interest in it, or because they all have a common interest in it as a group. On the other hand, interests—whether they be individual or common to particular groups within society—that cannot be wanted by all the participants in communicative action can apparently only lead to compromise.

In conclusion, there is no way to guarantee that the submission of conflicting claims to the dialogical process associated with communicative action and with justice as reversible reciprocity will lead to the emergence of a genuine consensus. Admittedly, rejecting Habermas' presumption of universal rationality, and curtailing the exploitation of the possibility for the discursive transformation of actual interests as a means to reconstruct stated interests, may well lead to an overall decrease in the likelihood of reaching genuinely consensual agreements. Nevertheless, by combining the admissibility of Habermasian compromises with the exclusion from the process of perspectives that refuse to acknowledge the integrity of other perspectives, it would appear that the odds for the possibility of a just resolution in accordance with the principle of justice as reversible reciprocity would be relatively high. In the last analysis, however, whether such a just resolution is possible in any particular case depends ultimately on the prevailing actual circumstances, the interests asserted, and the perspectives advanced by the various participants in the dialogical process designed to produce a just resolution of a given conflict. In any event, with respect to the particular conflicts that underlie the debate over affirmative action, I shall argue in the next chapter that the dialogical process involving a reversal of perspectives does establish the legitimacy of affirmative action in certain sets of circumstances.

6. Justice as Reversible Reciprocity is Best Suited to Maximize Integration and Differentiation in Accordance with the Postulate of Equality

Justice as reversible reciprocity is suited to promote justice in accordance with the postulate of equality while maintaining an equilibrium between identity and diversity, and between integration and differentiation. Accordingly, justice as reversible reciprocity possesses the same virtues held respectively by its contractarian and its utilitarian counterparts without sharing their respective vices. Although it may not yield a resolution for every conflict, when justice as reversible reciprocity does lead to such a resolution—whether it be by means of a consensus or of a genuine compromise—it does so in a way that allows for as much individual autonomy to pursue one's own life plan as is compatible with efforts to eliminate relationships of domination.

Through the institution of a dialogical process, justice as reversible reciprocity furnishes a procedure that, if properly followed, can lead to the just resolution of disputed claims. Given the proper context of its application, however, this procedure can neither yield justice in the absence of a conception of the good, nor operate as a successful vehicle for the establishment of pure procedural justice. To be sure, the postulate of equality, the norm of reciprocity, and the limited pluralism that they seek to institute do not project a fully elaborated conception of the good or a universally applicable determination of the good life. Nevertheless, they do impose at least a negative conception of the good, to the extent that they posit as illegitimate any particular conception of the good that rejects or disregards equal respect, the integrity of the perspectives of others, the desirability of a limited pluralism in the choice of individual life plans, or the virtue of settling conflicts through undistorted dialogue. Moreover, as specifically applied to affirmative action, the constraints flowing from this negative conception of the good do not of themselves lead to any specific answer, but they do foreclose acceptance of first-order discrimination or suppression of the points of view of minorities and women from the arena of public discourse.

As a consequence of this, any conclusion reached concerning the justice of affirmative action pursuant to the principle of justice as reversible reciprocity is bound to be ultimately dependent on the acceptance of certain values that are rejected by racists, sexists, and those who assert the right to suppress the discourse of all those with whom they disagree (as opposed to that of those who would suppress the discourse of others). This limitation certainly restricts the circle of those who may be drawn into the dialogue. But since these exclusions only affect persons who reject the validity of the postulate of equality, they pose no significant problem that could not be equally raised in connection with the libertarian, contractarian, utilitarian, or egalitarian conceptions of justice.

On the other hand, justice as reversible reciprocity does not lead to purely procedural justice both because of the above mentioned restrictions concerning participation in the dialogical process and because the actual dialogue, once commenced, is itself not free from constraints. As previously indicated, it is not the mere fact that the relevant dialogical process has taken place that insures the legitimacy of its outcome. Instead, this process only leads to legitimate outcomes if certain potential participants are excluded and if actual discourses are reconstructed to the extent necessary to purge them of distortions. Moreover, the exclusions and the reconstruction involved cannot be achieved through the mere implementation of some procedure, but require, as we have seen, reference to substantive standards and principles.

Although it is not purely procedural, justice as reversible reciprocity does remain procedural to a significant extent. Because it fosters a limited pluralism, the criterion of justice as reversibility cannot determine just outcomes ex ante but must rely on the workings of an undistorted dialogical process. Thus, within the constraints imposed by the needs for exclusions and for reconstruction, justice as reversible reciprocity is capable of dispensing procedural justice—albeit imperfect procedural justice[25] inasmuch as completely undistorted communication and transformation of needs in an environment free of all domination are bound to remain ideals. In the last analysis, to the extent that it is imperfect procedural justice, justice as reversible reciprocity makes for less than complete certainty. This, however, appears to be the inevitable consequence of attempting to account for the full complexity of actual intersubjective dealings and to accommodate as many differences as are compatible with equal respect for all and with reciprocal recognition of the integrity of the perspectives of others. Finally, the fact that justice as reversible reciprocity yields imperfect procedural justice is further mitigated by the open-ended nature of the dialogical process on which it depends. Since all the resolutions of conflicts emanating from the dialogical process are always open to revision based on further discussion, the imperfect procedural justice produced by justice as reversible reciprocity is unlikely to lead to the permanent enshrinement of oppressive institutions and relationships.

Justice as reversible reciprocity is arguably better suited than the libertarian, contractarian, utilitarian, or egalitarian perspective to strike a proper balance between individual-regarding and community-regarding concerns. By requiring reciprocal recognition among abstract egos, justice as reversible reciprocity allows for a sufficient degree of individual self-assertion to thwart subordination of the individual to the collectivity. Moreover, by granting widespread recognition to the differences that set concrete egos apart from one another, justice as reversible reciprocity accounts not only for the individual in the abstract but also for his or her individuality. On the other hand, by promoting consensus, by giving it privilege over mere compromise, and by generally stressing the importance of dialogue and of reaching agreements, justice as reversible reciprocity encourages the expression of common interests and the realization of commonly held objectives.

Even if we assume unanimous agreement with the preceding observations there remains a seemingly formidable objection to the ability of justice as reversible reciprocity to satisfy the postulate of equality, particularly in those contexts that are most relevant to the legitimacy of affirmative action. According to this objection, which is raised by Carol Gilligan against Kohlberg's theory of moral development, the very conceptualization of questions of ethics in terms of a debate concerning conflicting claims to rights is fundamentally deficient as it completely ignores the moral perspectives of women.[26]

The main thrust of Gilligan's critique of Kohlberg can be briefly reformulated as follows. The dialogical model set up in accordance with justice as reversibility to resolve moral conflicts is inherently biased against women, not because it refuses them access but because the price of their admission is the suppression of the feminine voice and the reformulation of women's needs, interests, and values in accordance with the constraining limitations of masculine discourse. Specifically, Gilligan maintains that there is a profound difference between the psychological makeup of men and women. Whereas men establish their identity through separation, competition, and achievement, women develop theirs through intimacy, attachment, care, and self-sacrifice (Gilligan 1982, 12, 73–74, 132). Whereas men seek independence, women strive for connection and interdependence (ibid., 21). Moreover, as a consequence of these differences in psychological makeup, Gilligan argues that women are likely to develop a conception of ethics that contrasts sharply with that of men. In Gilligan's view, men's ethics are oriented to rights, equality, and fairness; women's to responsibilities, equity, and the recognition of differences in need among "concrete others" (ibid., 164).

Consistent with these contrasts stressed by Gilligan, the principle of justice as reversibility does not exclude expression of the individual needs, interests, or desires or women. But it does systematically decontextualize them, and thus it arguably poses a greater threat to the integrity of feminine perspectives than would a mere exclusion of their claims. Indeed, justice as reversibility gives the impression of treating women as full partners in the dialogical process. But the very structure of that process forces women to suppress their more fundamental differences in order to obtain a degree of recognition that poses no threat to the dominance of masculine perspectives. In short, justice as reversibility makes it possible for an individual claim advanced by a woman to be given priority over a competing claim made by a man, but it forecloses what is much more important from a feminine perspective—namely, in Gilligan's own words, the replacement of "the hierarchy of rights with a web of relationships" (ibid., 57).

If achieving equal dignity and respect does not require giving up masculine separation for feminine connection, then Gilligan's critique can be used to challenge not only the legitimacy of justice as reversibility but also that of the postulate of equality. This, however, would have most disturbing implications for the position that I have articulated in this chapter, for it would logically require that the determination of the justice of affirmative action in favor of women be made from a perspective that is seemingly irreconcilable with fundamental feminine needs, interests, values, and aspirations. Indeed, if masculine and feminine perspectives are on a collision course, and if the former but not the latter embraces the postulate of equality, then, in accordance with the principles espoused in the preceding sections of this chapter, the dialogical process designed to resolve the conflict concerning the justice of affirmative action could legitimately exclude feminine viewpoints from consideration.

If masculine and feminine perspectives were completely irreconcilable, then there would appear to be cause for utter despair, and affirmative action would be, needless to add, entirely superfluous. But such utter despair and pessimism are certainly not warranted based on Gilligan's own assessment of the differences between the masculine and the feminine moral outlooks. Indeed, Gilligan's vision is not of separate spheres of morality, one driven by the search for equality and fairness, the other, by a quest for connection and interdependence. Rather, her vision and her hope is for a morality that encompasses both the masculine and the feminine and that integrates rights and responsibilities as the complementary poles of a broadly inclusive ethico-political perspective.[27] Moreover, as we shall see, so long as one does not consider that hope to be vain, the recognition of feminine perspectives does not threaten either the legitimacy of the postulate of equality or that of justice as reversible reciprocity as buttressed by the Habermasian assumption of the dialogical transformability of individual needs and interests.

If one concedes that no satisfactory reply to Gilligan's objection can be made from the standpoint of Kohlberg's own moral theory and conception of justice as reversibility, it does not follow that the dialogical model for the resolution of normative conflicts must be necessarily biased against feminine perspectives. Indeed, if one assumes the possibility of the discursive transformation of needs and interests, it seems, in principle, as likely for women to convince men of the benefits of greater connection and interdependence as it is for men to persuade women of the virtues of competitive achievement and independence. Moreover, once one allows for the transformation of needs and interests, the dialogical process need not be oriented toward the resolution of conflicting claims to rights. As a consequence of dialogue between the sexes, it may as well be oriented or reoriented toward the reconciliation of conflicting responsibilities.

It may be further objected, however, that given the current status of the relationship between the sexes, putting masculine and feminine perspectives on an equal footing would only serve to perpetuate existing patterns of male domination. According to this objection, masculine perspectives stressing separation, independence, competition, and achievement are not merely reflections of the different psychological makeup of men. They are also apt to promote the legitimacy of existing systems of distribution of wealth and power which have allowed men to reach dominant positions and which, because of this, are likely to perpetuate male domination.

This last objection can be met by proponents of a Habermasian dialogical model through recourse to the notion of undistorted communication. To the extent that masculine perspectives are (consciously or unconsciously) used strategically for purposes of buttressing structures of domination, they would distort the dialogical process required by communicative ethics, and ought therefore be left out of the reconstructed dialogue designed to lead to just outcomes. On the other hand, unless a particular masculine perspective is inherently inextricable from structures of male domination, it ought not be completely excluded from the relevant reconstructed dialogue. Generally, masculine perspectives insofar as they are undistorted and accord recognition to the integrity of feminine perspectives ought to be included with the latter in the dialogical process that is expected to lead to the resolution of ethical conflicts.

In principle at least, justice as reversible reciprocity is capable of leading to consensuses or genuine compromises that promote neither male nor female domination. However, given both the utopian and the critical dimensions that are peculiar to the notion of the dialogical transformability of needs and interests, there arises a problem that has a significant impact on the legitimacy of gender-based affirmative action. This problem concerns the *timing* of transformations of transformable needs and interests, and is particularly acute when such a transformation can only be expected to take place over a very extended period of time. In the latter situation, there may be a difficult dilemma regarding whether to hold out for a consensus until the relevant interests have been fully transformed, or whether to reach an interim consensus or compromise on the basis of partially transformed, or yet to be transformed, interests. Moreover, although this dilemma may have strategic implications, it is not primarily a dilemma concerning strategic action but rather one regarding what would satisfy justice at a particular point in time.

To illustrate both how such a dilemma may arise, and how its resolution may affect a determination of the legitimacy of gender-based affirmative action, let us consider the following example. Suppose that feminist critics of a contemporary male-dominated society conclude that a completely just order consistent with the horizon of possibilities delimited by prevailing material conditions cannot be achieved until all the existing interests in separation, competition, and individual achievement are transformed into interests in interdependence, mutual cooperation based on care for others, and communal harmony. Such a transformation cannot be completed, however, after a short number of dialogues, but would require several decades, or perhaps even several generations to become accepted by all concerned. That is to say, that while the dialogical process may presently be capable of removing the distortions attributable to male dominance, it cannot, in the absence of a lengthy process, transform the interests informed by undistorted masculine perspectives into interests representative of undistorted feminine perspectives.

Moreover, let us also assume that existing institutions at our male-dominated society are used to perpetuate first-order discrimination against women over and above whatever inhibitions they may place on the expression and realization of feminine perspectives. Thus, whereas the allocation of scarce employment positions is otherwise carried out through a fair competition among applicants, women applicants are forced to compete on an unequal basis. If the dialogical search for justice would focus on existing interests, provided only that they are rid of distortions, a consensus would undoubtedly emerge on the proposition that first-order discrimination against women is unjust and that it ought to be, therefore, remedied. Moreover, let us also stipulate that all participants in the dialogical process would agree that gender-based affirmative action would provide the most just means to rectify the wrongs inflicted by first-order sex discrimination in employment.

In that case a proponent of a feminine perspective confronts the following dilemma: whether to endorse affirmative action and the elimination of first-order sex discrimination in employment for now or whether to hold out, in the hope that at some future date competition in employment will be replaced by mutual care and cooperation. If competition itself is deemed unjust then, whether or not it may be fair, it ought to remain arguably unacceptable. On the other hand, if the elimination of competition in employment would require a revolution in attitudes, beliefs, needs, interests, and modes of production, and if consensus on any of those issues is most unlikely except in some far-off future, then it may seem reasonable to concentrate first on putting an end to first-order discrimination.

Viewing the matter from the standpoint of communicative action, no negative implication ought to follow from a present agreement to remedy the effects of first-order sex discrimination in employment. This follows from the fact that justice as shaped by communicative action is both contextual (it depends on the actual conflicts and actual possibilities of the participants in the dialogical process) and open ended (it is always subject to further revision pursuant to the outcome of future dialogues). Accordingly, it is not inconsistent to claim that, given existing interests, justice presently requires that competition in employment be totally rid of the effects of first-order sex discrimination, while maintaining that, in the longer term, justice demands a steady transformation of existing interests so as to make possible a consensus that competition in employment ought to be eliminated.

Consistent with the above analysis, even if affirmative action cannot play a legitimate role in the long run, considerations of justice might still require its adoption in the short term. More generally, the clash between short-term and long-term interests can itself be subjected to the dialogical process, just as can the issue of whether particular needs and interests ought to be transformed. Accordingly, in the last analysis, the feminist critique of Kohlberg's theory does not undermine the legitimacy of justice as reversible reciprocity as buttressed by the transformability of needs and interests.

In conclusion, the relative virtues of justice as reversible reciprocity seem superior to those libertarian, contractarian, utilitarian, and egalitarian conceptions of justice. Moreover, justice as reversible reciprocity can apparently overcome the most significant objections likely to be launched against it. With this in mind, I now turn to a detailed examination of whether, under what circumstances, and to what extent justice as reversible reciprocity may legitimate affirmative action consistent with the constitutional constraints discussed in previous chapters.

CHAPTER TEN

Toward an Integrated Philosophical and Constitutional Justification of Affirmative Action

Based on the adoption of justice as reversible reciprocity as the applicable criterion of justice, we are now in a position to determine the conditions under which affirmative action may be deemed to be constitutionally permissible and just. These conditions are fairly limited but nevertheless important.

In section 1, I argue that affirmative action is justified if one embraces the principle of equality of opportunity that permeates American ideology and the constitutional values emanating from the equal protection clause. Moreover, I argue that affirmative action can be justified in terms of a unified conception of compensatory and distributive justice.

In section 2, I take a final look at affirmative action in terms of the relationship between the individual and the group. Although purely group-related justifications of affirmative action must be rejected as inconsistent with the postulate of equality, group affiliation remains relevant for purposes of assessing the legitimacy of individual-regarding affirmative action plans.

In section 3, I address what is probably the most difficult problem confronting proponents of the justice of affirmative action who subscribe to the postulate of equality. That problem is commonly referred to as that of the "innocent white male" who apparently must bear the brunt of the burden of preferential treatment extended to blacks and women. Finally, in section 4, I attempt to define the nature and scope of a constitutional justification of affirmative action that is consonant with justice as reversible reciprocity. There are compelling reasons for adopting the position taken by the Brennan group in *Bakke,* but they are not necessarily the reasons advanced in that case. Moreover, I argue that justice as reversible reciprocity requires rejection of the antidiscrimination standard in favor of an approach based on substantive equality.

1. The Nexus between Affirmative Action, Equality of Opportunity, and a Unified Conception of Distributive and Compensatory Justice

Affirmative action can be justified only in those sociopolitical contexts in which adherence to the postulate of equality leads to the embrace of the ideal of equality of opportunity. Where equality of result can be ultimately achieved because there is no scarcity in the goods to be allocated, on the other hand, affirmative action would be pointless—in the sense that it would serve no legitimate purpose to prefer some over others, if all could receive the good they desire.

Before taking a closer look at the nexus between affirmative action and equality of opportunity, it is necessary to determine what kind of equality of opportunity is likely to be justified from the standpoint of justice as reversible reciprocity, in the context of scarce jobs and places at universities. As discussed in chapter 3, according to the contractarian criterion of justice, fair means-regarding equality of opportunity is warranted because it neutralizes advantages relative to social position without interfering with the individual's use of her natural talents and capacities. The reason for the contractarian's refusal to interfere with the use of natural talents, moreover, as it will be remembered, is that it would violate the dignity and the integrity of the individual. On the other hand, as mentioned in chapter 5, the egalitarian criterion of justice specifies that a person no more deserves his natural assets than the social advantages thrust upon him. Consistent with this, the egalitarian maintains that no one is entitled to any special reward or additional benefit on account of possessing superior natural assets. Because of this, the egalitarian may opt for prospect-regarding equality of opportunity in job allocation.

Short of pursuing a transformation of needs and interests that would lead to the consensual elimination of competition in the allocation of scarce positions, a proponent of justice as reversible reciprocity should arguably be attracted to a position that falls somewhere between the contractarian and the egalitarian positions. This position adopts the contractarian notion that individuals should be entitled to exploit their superior natural assets to the extent that that would redound to the benefit of all. It also borrows the egalitarian concept that an individual should not be rewarded because of possessing superior natural assets.

Participants in the dialogical process associated with justice as reversible reciprocity would arguably allow for differences in natural talent to count in the allocation of scarce positions to the extent that this would produce added benefits for all and permit those with greater talents to fulfill their potential. Indeed, equal dignity and respect would seem to require that each one be allowed to develop and make constructive use of her natural talents and capacities. And from the standpoint of the reversal of perspectives, a person without a certain particular talent should come to realize the importance that the development and expression of that talent is likely to have to one who is actually endowed with it. For example, through the reversal of perspectives, a person who is uninterested in music and tone-deaf ought to understand the importance that developing musical skills and putting them to use is likely to have to a musically gifted person.

Unlike a contractarian, however, a proponent of justice as reversible reciprocity would not sanction the disparities in power, wealth, and prestige associated with the allocation of desirable positions to those with the greatest natural assets. If the winners in the competition for scarce employment acquired benefits *intrinsically* related to performance on the job—that is, the further development of one's talents and the satisfaction derived from actually contributing to the common welfare of the community—then a consensus should be reached concerning the legitimacy of using differences in natural talents to allocate scarce positions. In that case, moreover, any egalitarian appeal to prospect-regarding equality of opportunity in the allocation of jobs should be rejected as based on envy and on the desire to suppress enriching differences. By the same token, however, even if allocating scarce jobs to the most talented contributes to the benefit of all, *extrinsic* rewards such as power and wealth do not appear to be justified. Indeed, such extrinsic rewards do not themselves redound to the benefit of all and are likely to promote relations of domination. Hence, a consensus should be reached concerning the adoption of the principle of fair (global as to all social assets) means-regarding equality of opportunity as the means to allocate scarce positions, provided that the external benefits currently associated with success—that is, greater power and wealth—are kept in reasonable check. This could be achieved, in part, by reducing disparities in salaries, and, in part, by emulating Michael Walzer's suggestion that achievement in one sphere of interaction, such as the business world, should not lead to the acquisition of disproportionate power in another, such as the political arena.[1]

Keeping the preceding observations in mind, let us return to our inquiry into the possible nexus between equality of opportunity and affirmative action. It may be difficult at first to detect any connection between the two. Indeed, a purely future-looking system of allocation based on fair means-regarding equality of opportunity appears to exclude the use of affirmative action. If one imagines using this norm to set up a system for allocating scarce jobs, one would be primarily concerned with preventing socially relative advantages from playing a significant role. This may be accomplished through the redistribution of wealth and the distribution of educational assets. But from the purely forward-looking distributive perspective presently under consideration, preferential treatment based on race or gender appears to run directly counter to equality of opportunity—an impression that undoubtedly accounts for much of the opposition against affirmative action.[2]

It may be objected that this last conclusion ignores Goldman's contractarian justification of affirmative action under distributive justice in the case of chronic poverty and lack of motivation, which was discussed in chapter 3. But a system of allocation run from the beginning according to the dictates of fair equality of opportunity is not likely to yield any chronic poverty. Indeed, in such a system mechanisms of equalization would insure that no member of society is relegated to poverty. Therefore, where chronic poverty is encountered it is in all likelihood the result of another system of allocation. Conversely, if a system based on fair equality of opportunity must confront chronic poverty, that system is not likely to be, strictly speaking, exclusively forward-looking. In short, a system based on fair equality of opportunity that must eliminate the evils of chronic poverty has to be, in part, backward-looking.

Any justification of affirmative action consistent with fair equality of opportunity therefore must be, at least in part, backward-looking. Moreover, the most obvious such justification involves compensation of an actual victim of past discrimination. Thus, when a person's right to an equal opportunity to compete for a scarce place or position has been violated, the best means of compensation would be to provide that person with a competitive advantage in a subsequent competition for the same, or a similar, position that is commensurate with the competitive disadvantage suffered in the previous competition. As argued convincingly by Goldman, and as discussed extensively in chapter 3, such compensation is not only just under the applicable norms of compensatory justice but also essential to preserve the integrity of a distributive system based on equality of opportunity. In the strongest case for compensation, the victim would be accorded the same position or the most nearly equivalent position available from the agent of allocation responsible for the violation of the victim's right. As discussed at greater length in preceding chapters, compensation in the above case satisfies both the libertarian and contractarian criteria of justice. In addition, subject to qualifications based on its impact on third parties to be discussed in section 3 below, compensation in the above case is consistent with the distributive and compensatory aims of fair means-regarding equality of opportunity, and apparently satisfies justice as reversible reciprocity.

Such compensation can also be justified under the equal protection clause—or more specifically under the strict scrutiny test applied to racial classifications pursuant to the antidiscrimination principle, which was criticized above in chapter 6. Indeed, applying the strict scrutiny test, compensation of an actual victim of first-order racial discrimination represents a "compelling state interest," while preferential treatment, where required to make the victim whole, clearly amounts to a "necessary means." Because of this, the use of affirmative action by a wrongdoer for the purely compensatory purpose of making actual victims whole has the unanimous support of the present Supreme Court.[3]

If an agent of allocation who is not a wrongdoer voluntarily undertakes to compensate an actual victim, the legitimacy of using preferential treatment does not appear weakened. Indeed, so long as the focus remains exclusively on the parties who dispense and receive compensation, no injustice occurs where a non-wrongdoing person voluntarily undertakes the burden of compensation—assuming, of course, that the burden involved falls exclusively on the volunteer. The only conceivable objection might be that allowing a volunteer to assume the burden of compensation might in effect relieve the actual wrongdoer from the obligation to compensate, and thus provide the latter with an unjust windfall benefit. This objection, however, can be easily met, by simply stipulating that the volunteer's deed does not relieve the wrongdoer of the obligation to provide compensation. Moreover, to ensure that the victim does not receive double compensation, the wrongdoer may be directed to discharge his compensatory obligation in a way that does not directly benefit the already-compensated victim, such as by conferring a benefit on the volunteer or on the community as a whole.

From the perspective of a victim discriminated against at the job level or at the university application level, affirmative action in the strict compensatory sense described above may provide the best possible measure of compensation. For other victims of past discrimination, however, such a narrowly circumscribed form of affirmative action is of little help. Thus, for example, a black person who received an inferior public school education because of racial discrimination is likely to suffer a significant handicap in the competition for scarce positions. In this case, compensation in kind, namely a superior public school education or its equivalent, may be inadequate. This would be particularly true if the education in question would require several years of study and the job applicant were an adult who needed to earn a living in order to support a family.[4] On the other hand, simply awarding this person the position she seeks, on a preferential basis, may seem inappropriate because, unlike the case of the person discriminated against at the job-seeking level, there is no reasonable assurance that the victim of past discrimination (at the public school level) would have secured the job but for the discrimination.

Pervasive discrimination at the educational level deprives some members of society of important tools needed in the competition for jobs, and thus, like discrimination at the job-seeking level, undermines the integrity of any distributive scheme relying on equality of opportunity. Moreover, such integrity is undermined both because of a loss in legitimacy, stemming from the denial of an equal opportunity to certain members of society, and of a loss in efficiency, because of the removal of talented individuals from the marketplace for jobs because of a lack of adequate tools. In the case of a qualified job applicant who was denied the job because of discrimination, giving that individual the job (or a similar job) in compensation is unlikely to disrupt seriously the efficiency of the system of distribution. In the case of those who were denied tools necessary to compete successfully for jobs because of discrimination, however, granting them jobs in compensation could have a serious impact on the efficiency of the system of distribution and therefore could worsen the already partially impaired functioning of that system.

From the standpoint of the distributive system's efficiency, it might seem preferable to foreclose compensating victims of past educational discrimination with jobs for which there are other persons who are more qualified. From the standpoint of that system's legitimacy, however, it may be inadequate to rely entirely on some other form of compensation, such as monetary damages. Indeed, the award of such damages, even if coupled with better educational programs for subsequent generations, may relegate too many members of the discriminated-against group for too long to subordinate positions, and thus fail to ameliorate their sense of self-respect or to increase their confidence in the system.[5] What is needed is a way to reintegrate the victims of past discrimination into the mainstream of society—which entails receiving a share of the jobs allocated by society—without having to grant to individual victims jobs that they would not have obtained even if they had never experienced any discrimination.

One of the principal evils of invidious discrimination in education is that it deprives its victims of the means to compete on an equal footing with others for scarce jobs. In other words, the means-regarding inequality of opportunity brought about by a segregated—and thus inferior—public school education results in the institution of a prospect-regarding inequality of opportunity in the marketplace for jobs. The present injury stemming from past discrimination is *the diminished prospect of getting a competitive position.* Accordingly, the best way of presently making these victims of past discrimination whole is increasing their prospects for obtaining competitive positions to the point where their prospects would have been, absent any past discrimination.

To the extent that competitive disadvantages are the product of social as opposed to natural causes, the principle of fair means-regarding equality of opportunity requires that they be eliminated. Otherwise, scarce job allocations could not be exclusively a function of differences in natural talents and efforts. Moreover, diminished prospects for some inevitably means increased prospects for others. In such a case, affirmative action seems particularly well suited to bring everyone's prospects to where they most likely would have been but for the discrimination. Suppose, for example, that systematic racial discrimination results in diminishing the prospects of success of blacks by 10 percent while increasing that of whites by a corresponding amount. In that case, preferential treatment improving the prospects of success of blacks by 10 percent ought to bring the probabilities of success of both blacks and whites where they should have been absent racial discrimination.

Whenever a deficiency in means, whether educational or otherwise, is attributable to a violation of a right, affirmative action designed to eliminate the reduction in prospects of success corresponding to such deficiency in means is compensatory in nature from the standpoint of the victim. On the other hand, such affirmative action may or may not be compensatory from the standpoint of the agent of allocation who dispenses it. So long as the latter is either an actual wrongdoer or a volunteer, however, affirmative action designed to accord a preference in one sphere (say, public employment) to a victim of discrimination in another sphere (say, public education) appears to be just as legitimate as affirmative action used in the strict compensatory sense described above.

Notwithstanding this last conclusion, preferential treatment in one sphere for a victim who has suffered a deprivation in another sphere has encountered much stiffer constitutional resistance than its more narrowly circumscribed counterpart. There may be several reasons for this, including that the former is much more likely than the latter to give the impression that it operates as a distributive rather than a compensatory device. Preferential treatment designed to improve the prospects of success of a class of victims does operate on, and have a direct effect on, the sphere of distribution. Accordingly, such preferential treatment seems quite different from more conventional forms of compensation, such as the payment of monetary damages. Moreover, it is by no means self-evident that increasing someone's future prospects of success constitutes a genuine compensation for having wrongfully deprived that person of certain means of success in the past. Nonetheless, altering prospects of success through preferential treatment in order to wipe out the effects of a wrongful deprivation of means, and thus to put victims of such deprivation in the position in which they would have been absent any wrong, does constitute a legitimate means of compensation.

Legal causation is another reason for greater constitutional resistance to preferential treatment in a sphere other than that directly disrupted by discrimination. There is no question but that there is a direct link between wrong, injury, and compensatory remedy in the case of an applicant who won the competition for a job, was nonetheless refused the job because of race or sex discrimination, and is at a later time awarded that job as compensation. The existence of such a link is far less clear, however, in the case of a job applicant who is treated fairly at the job competition level but who has been deprived of significant educational tools because of wrongs perpetrated in the sphere of public education. This should not settle the matter against compensation, but rather lead to further inquiry concerning how much uncertainty should be tolerated by a constitutionally acceptable principle of compensation, and concerning who shall bear the added burdens produced by the existence of such uncertainty.

In cases of first-order discrimination, the degree of uncertainty associated with causation involving the level of job allocation exclusively is likely to be much smaller than that relating to causation linking the level of education to that of job allocation. It is certainly highly speculative to assert that, but for an inferior education, a person would have won the competition for a certain kind of job. It seems much less open to debate, however, that an inferior education is bound to diminish someone's prospects of success in the competition for jobs. When a wrong has been as persistent and as pervasive as racial discrimination and segregation in the public school systems of many of the American States—and when the disparities between the percentage of whites in relation to the total white working population holding certain coveted employment positions and that of blacks in relation to the total black working population holding similar positions are glaring—it seems beyond serious dispute that the wrong in question is the cause of a substantial reduction in the prospects of success of blacks in the employment market. Under these circumstances moreover, it seems reasonable to presume that the measure of the reduction in the prospects of success of blacks is roughly equivalent to the difference between the ratio of blacks with desirable employment to the total number of blacks in the workforce and that of whites with such desirable jobs to the total number of whites in the workforce. Based on that presumption, the compensatory function of preferential treatment would be to raise the prospects of success of blacks until they become roughly equivalent to those of whites.

Even conceding that racial discrimination in education leads to a decrease in the prospects of success of blacks (and to a corresponding increase in the prospects of success of whites), it may be objected that the above presumption is too uncertain to serve as the basis for providing compensation. In general, where compensation can only be achieved by temporarily suspending or interrupting the functioning of an essentially just system of distribution, it seems unfair to extend it to cases involving uncertain wrongs and harms. However, as discussed in chapter 3, in the context of long-lasting systematic first-order race discrimination involving public school segregation, the validity of distributive claims of whites who win the competition for scarce jobs is as uncertain as the validity of compensatory claims of blacks who assert a right to have their prospects of success raised so as to approximate those of whites. In view of this, the objection against affirmative action because of causal uncertainty loses much of its force.

While it may be rational to assume that the disparity between the proportion of whites and the proportion of blacks who hold certain desirable jobs is attributable to the effects of first-order racial discrimination, it is of course possible that at least part of this disparity is ultimately due to some other cause. This mere possibility certainly should not foreclose the constitutionality of using affirmative action as a compensatory device. Indeed, in the case of long-standing, massive, and systematic wrongs such as those perpetrated against American blacks, it seems warranted to adopt a rebuttable presumption that existing discrepancies in prospects of success are the result of first-order racial discrimination. This would leave it up to the party who opposes preferential treatment to demonstrate the existence of factors other than racial discrimination that could explain all, or part, of the relevant discrepancy. Moreover, given the prevalence of sex discrimination in the United States, a similar presumption seems justified in the case of women. Under other circumstances, however, where first-order discrimination against a group is substantially less pervasive and systematic, a similar presumption might not be warranted.

In sum, affirmative action in the sphere of job allocation for the benefit of victims of wrongful deprivations in the sphere of education is compensatory (from the standpoint of the victim, at least) rather than distributive. Because such affirmative action is compensatory, it should be viewed as consistent with the principle of equality of opportunity. Accordingly, such affirmative action should be constitutionally permissible to the extent that the equal protection clause constitutionalizes the principle of equality of opportunity.

Not only wrongful deprivations of educational assets but also willful interference with, or withholding of, other social assets may lead to reductions in the prospects of success in the sphere of job allocation, and thus call for compensatory affirmative action. In particular, pervasive and deeply rooted prejudice, negative stereotypes, demeaning treatment, and a constant stream of indignities experienced on a daily basis are likely to produce in their victims negative self-image, low self-esteem, chronic lack of motivation, and despair. Because of this, these victims' prospects of success in the job market are likely to decline substantially. Preferential treatment in the sphere of job allocation is, therefore, warranted in accordance with the principle of equality of opportunity as a means of compensation designed to make whole the victims of these practices or attitudes. Accordingly, such preferential treatment should be constitutionally permissible.

Justices who maintain that race-based affirmative action must satisfy the strict scrutiny test to be constitutionally acceptable have rejected the legitimacy of using preferential treatment in connection with societal discrimination—that is, discrimination aimed at a sphere of interaction other than that with respect to which affirmative action is sought. Once it is understood that societal discrimination may be pernicious and that it may seriously curtail equal opportunity rights, however, the need to compensate the victims of such discrimination clearly seems compelling. It seems just as compelling as some of the compensation schemes that the justices who embrace strict scrutiny have already found to be compelling.[6] Ultimately, the crucial fact is whether first-order discrimination is systematic and pervasive and whether it has significantly violated equal opportunity rights. Provided it deprives its victims of means to compete, the precise point of contact between discrimination and its victim does not seem terribly relevant.

Finally, another reason why societal discrimination may not appear to warrant compensation has to do with the kind of causal link that can be established between its perpetrators and its victims. As we have seen, in the course of our discussion of the *Croson* case, justices on the Supreme Court have resorted to two distinct modes of causal interpretation. The atomistic model of interpretation associated with the marginal equality position accepts as valid only direct, unbroken mechanical causal links. The ecological model of interpretation embraced by advocates of the global equality position, on the other hand, allows for the recognition of much more complex and context-specific patterns of causation. Given the uncertainty of distributive rights as a consequence of the massive and multifaceted racist and sexist assaults on equal opportunity rights, there seems to be ample justification for embracing the ecological mode of interpretation in affirmative action cases—or at least in affirmative action cases involving a non-wrongdoer who voluntarily agrees to dispense a remedy for past wrongs.

As mentioned in the course of the discussion of the *Johnson* case in chapter 7, an affirmative action plan can be backward-looking and yet be purely distributive even from the standpoint of its beneficiaries. Consistent with adherence to the principle of fair means-regarding equality of opportunity, if past social practices, not unjust when implemented, deprived certain members of society of social assets possessed by all others, then the resulting disparity in means may create a corresponding discrepancy in prospects that can only be eliminated within a reasonable time through the temporary institution of preferential treatment. In that case, affirmative action is remedial, not compensatory, in that it is not designed to rectify any past wrong. Moreover, from a philosophical standpoint, if distributive justice requires that allocations of scarce goods be made in accordance with the principle of fair means-regarding equality of opportunity, and if the latter equality is only within present reach through preferential treatment, the distributive use of affirmative action to close certain unacceptable gaps in prospects would seem to be amply warranted.

In spite of its philosophical justification, the purely distributive use of affirmative action may be problematic from the standpoint of constitutional practice. Even if the achievement of fair means-regarding equality of opportunity is deemed to be constitutionally desirable, some of the practical steps necessary to its full realization appear to be objectionable. Thus, a full equalization of all social assets might require, among other things, taking children away from their families to instill in them certain motivational values, as well as other social and educational attitudes that they would not otherwise obtain, eliminating certain cultural and religious traditions that discourage the acquisition of certain social assets needed to be able to succeed in the competition for scarce jobs, and providing certain social and educational assets to those who have deliberately squandered previous opportunities to obtain them.

Because of the degree of coercion and of state intervention that it is likely to require, the achievement of full fair global (with respect to social assets) means-regarding equality of opportunity does not appear to be constitutionally desirable. In some cases, somewhat lesser means may be preferable to the loss of a precious liberty or to the compromise of strongly held moral or religious principles. Moreover, if a person's competitive inequality is directly attributable to the voluntary election of a particular life plan, then it seems fair to assume that he has freely chosen to forfeit claims to full equality of socially relative means. Thus, for example, if the members of a given religious sect voluntarily decide to forgo the pursuit of state-sponsored and freely allocated available educational opportunities capable of furnishing important tools in the competition for scarce jobs, then they ought not to be heard to complain that they lack full equality of opportunity in the job market.[7] Generally, if because of a free choice of life plan, a person's socially relative means are reduced, and correspondingly his prospects of success are diminished, that person would seem to lack a legitimate claim under distributive justice to have his prospects brought to par through affirmative action.

Since the implementation of affirmative action is ordinarily not without social costs, justice as reversible reciprocity opposes its use to wipe out deficits in prospects attributable to genuinely voluntary choices to forgo available opportunities to acquire social or educational assets. Moreover, through use of the reversal of perspectives tests, it should be possible to distinguish between choices that are genuinely freely made and those that are not. Thus, one who passes up an opportunity to acquire an educational asset in order to pursue a religious objective that is paramount from the standpoint of her life plan should be treated differently from one who is so demoralized by chronic poverty that he believes that the educational asset in question is not worth pursuing.

Insofar as equal protection constitutionalizes fair means-regarding equality of opportunity, it justifies the purely distributive use of affirmative action to remedy those deprivations of social and educational assets that are not the product of a genuinely free choice to forgo available opportunities in order to pursue more important priorities set by one's life plan. Accordingly, constitutional equality, as thus conceived, would be satisfied not by strict equality of socially relative means but rather by the substantial *equalization* of those means consistent with the preservation of fundamental values, such as the autonomy of the family and the freedom to define one's life-plan in accordance with one's religious beliefs.

Adoption of the above criterion of constitutional legitimacy may produce difficult line-drawing problems. Nevertheless, such a criterion does justify the distributive use of affirmative action for women provided that they currently suffer from a deficit in socially relative means resulting from unequal treatment that was arguably not unjust at the time that it was dispensed. Even assuming that their mothers and grandmothers were satisfied with a distributive arrangement that almost completely excluded women from the market for desirable jobs, it does not follow that today's women should be deemed to have voluntarily accepted the disadvantages traceable to the unequal treatment of their mothers and grandmothers. Rather, these disadvantages are thrust upon the contemporary woman, as the unavoidable imprints of a past over which she had no control. Therefore, according to the constitutional criterion proposed above, affirmative action in favor of women is clearly permissible if designed to eliminate the differences in prospects attributable to socially caused deficits in means.

Purely distributive affirmative action, even if adequately backward-looking, would fail to satisfy a constitutional equality predicated on adherence to formal equality of opportunity. This follows from the fact that formal, as opposed to fair, equality of opportunity does not legitimate the equalization of socially relative means. Moreover, consistent with the prevailing judicial interpretation of the Fourteenth Amendment as imposing negative rather than positive duties on the state,[8] it is not surprising that only Justice Stevens has indicated a willingness to legitimate the purely distributive use of affirmative action.[9] Nevertheless, there is nothing inherent in the equal protection clause that makes the constitutionalization of fair means-regarding equality of opportunity inappropriate.

In the last analysis, while affirmative action can legitimately serve the aims of compensatory or distributive justice, it remains an imperfect procedure. This follows from the fact that the improvement of prospects through preferential treatment only makes sense for those who already possess the minimal qualifications necessary to perform satisfactorily in the academic program or job for which they are applying. Favoring those who are not thus minimally qualified, on the other hand, would not only be completely inefficient but would also be self-defeating. Indeed, awarding positions to those who are incompetent to handle them seems unlikely to lead to the integration (or reintegration) of those who have experienced past deprivations of socially relative assets into the mainstream of society. Therefore, while affirmative action cannot benefit all those who have suffered from past socially relative deprivations, it remains useful by making it possible for those who are minimally qualified to eliminate the deficits in prospects attributable to such deprivations.

Although an imperfect procedure, affirmative action may nevertheless have a substantial role in promoting the aims of compensatory or distributive justice. In significant part, how substantial a role it might play depends on the size of the pool of minimally qualified candidates who have experienced past socially relative deprivations. In low- and medium-skill occupations, that pool is likely to be large, while in high-skill occupations, it seems bound to be rather small. Therefore, in the context of low- and medium-skill occupations—which happen to be the kind of occupation involved in a large number of the affirmative action cases discussed in chapter 7—affirmative action, either alone or in combination with the provision of short-term training, is likely to play a major role in wiping out disadvantages caused by past socially relative deprivations.

In the context of compensatory justice, one may object to an affirmative action program that can only be expected to make whole a small fraction of the class of those who have suffered similar wrongful deprivations. Moreover, this objection has two distinct prongs: first, affirmative action might benefit the most talented at the expense of the least talented; second, affirmative action compensates poorly if it does nothing to redress the injuries of a large portion of the victims subjected to the same social wrongs. Both of these criticisms have already been considered and found to be ultimately unpersuasive in chapter 3. For now, therefore, suffice it to reiterate that the favoring of the most talented over those who are less talented is not, strictly speaking, the product of affirmative action, but that of equality of opportunity on which affirmative action is parasitic. Further, with respect to the second criticism, affirmative action's failure to provide a remedy to all those who are entitled to compensation should only be objectionable if affirmative action is meant to be the exclusive means of compensation. But, if it is acknowledged that the use of affirmative action does not eliminate the need to put into effect other means of compensation for those victims whom it cannot make whole, then the second criticism loses its force. Indeed, affirmative action makes some victims whole but does not prevent compensation for other victims.

2. *Affirmative Action and the Relation between the Individual and the Group*

It should be apparent that equality of opportunity for groups is not an end in itself. Instead, its pursuit is subordinated to the goal of restoring individuals' prospects to what they would have been had no social deprivation taken place. Hence, notwithstanding any initial impression to the contrary, affirmative action does not ultimately subordinate individual concerns for purposes of establishing group-regarding equality. On the contrary, it merely uses group-regarding equality as a means of restoring means-regarding equality of opportunity for the individual.

Even conceding this, one may still object that granting preferential treatment to an entire group, such as blacks or women, unduly exalts the group at the expense of the individual and that compensatory preferential treatment should be dispensed to wronged individuals rather than to the groups to whom they belong. Further, not all blacks or all women have been the victims of "actual" discrimination—in the sense that they have not been directly confronted by a rejection based on race or gender in the sphere of education or of job allocation. Conversely, not all victims of discrimination are either black or women. Consistent with this, race-based and gender-based affirmative action appears to be both overinclusive and underinclusive and to provide windfall benefits in the distributive sphere to certain blacks and certain women who were not actual victims of discrimination.

This objection can be met with two arguments: the first supports the conclusion that race-based and gender-based affirmative action are not overinclusive; the second, that they are not underinclusive. But before turning to those arguments, it is necessary to take a further look into the relationship between the individual and the group.

As discussed in chapter 3, a strong argument can be made that American blacks and American women are not entitled to compensation as a group because they lack a sufficient separate corporate group identity to justify it. The inappropriateness of group compensation does not entail, however, the illegitimacy of individual compensation based on group affiliation. In other words, the lack of justification for nondistributive compensation to the group does not foreclose the legitimacy of distributive compensation to (all) the (members of the) group. Accordingly, the question becomes whether all blacks or all women can be said to be legitimately entitled to compensation because of their group affiliation.

The answer depends on the conception that one has of the proper relationship between the individual and the group. From the standpoint of an extreme individualism, the group's relationship to the individual is likely to be regarded as being essentially antagonistic, with the group and its collective objectives standing as obstacles to the fulfillment of individual aims. But conceiving of the group primarily as the antagonist of the individual seems unduly confining and narrow. Indeed, group affiliation and group-related concerns may play an important part in an *individual's* pursuit of *her own* life plan. For example, it is certainly consistent with a conception of the individual as the subject of moral choice and as responsible for defining her own life plan for a particular person to place affiliation to a religious group among her top priorities. Accordingly, if illicit persecution of the religious group in question jeopardizes that person's affiliation (or the value of such affiliation), it is reasonable to argue that she should be entitled to individual compensation on account of the injury to her group affiliation interests. Thus, if bigots set a house of worship afire, the religious congregation affected might be entitled to nondistributive group compensation for its collective injury, and each worshiper to compensation for the individual injury to her religious affiliation rights.

No individual is independent from all groups, and there can be no individual rights except in the context of organized groups, such as political communities.[10] Because of this, it is unrealistic to expect that neat lines could be drawn between individual-regarding and group-regarding concerns. Actually, an individual's pursuit of her life plan is as likely to involve voluntary association with groups as it is to produce confrontation with group-regarding aims. Moreover, some actions are clearly individual-regarding, such as the reckless pursuit of pleasure regardless of its effects on the welfare of the community; others are unmistakably group-oriented, such as risking or sacrificing one's life to defend one's country against a military attack. But in most cases, determining whether a particular action should be considered primarily individual-regarding or group-regarding depends on the particular circumstances involved and on the perspective from which such action is sought to be justified. Thus, for example, collective worship may be viewed as a group-regarding activity from the perspective of a religious group and as individual-regarding from the standpoint of the individual who considers group worship as a means to fulfill her own life plan.

Nevertheless, since the equal protection clause, as well as the postulate of equality, extends to individuals rather than groups, group affiliation may be accorded constitutional relevance only if it can be legitimated from an individual-regarding perspective. Moreover, consistent with the postulate of equality, taking group affiliation into consideration would be justified if it satisfied justice as reversible reciprocity—that is, if the *individual members* of each group, after assuming the identity (including the perspective) of the members of every other group, would reach a consensus that taking group affiliation into account would contribute to the fulfillment of the life plan of at least some of the individuals involved without infringing on the legitimate pursuits of any other individual.

As discussed in the preceding section, justice as reversible reciprocity requires that the allocation of scarce education and employment be made in accordance with the principle of equality of opportunity. From the standpoint of a future-looking distributive system based on equality of opportunity, moreover, group affiliation should be completely irrelevant for purposes of the allocations involved. We have seen, however, that both formal and fair means-regarding equality of opportunity justify the use of preferential treatment for compensatory purposes. In addition, fair means-regarding equality of opportunity legitimates the distributive use of affirmative action to offset past deprivations in social and educational assets. This raises the question of whether distributive concerns may justify using race- or gender-based affirmative action as the means to restore the integrity of a distributive system that is supposed to conform to the principle of equal opportunity. Although race and gender are initially morally neutral, they can become *derivatively* morally relevant as a consequence of racism or sexism.[11] The racist, for instance, by labeling blacks inferior, transforms a morally neutral predicate, namely being black, into an unmistakable mark calling for inferior treatment. Moreover, when racism is as prevalent and as pervasive as it has been in the United States, and when it informs or underlies government policy, as it has for much of the history of the United States, it seems fair to assume that *all* blacks have to one degree or another been the victims of it.[12] Whether racism has systematically deprived them of material assets, or whether it has led to a reduction in motivation, or to harmful distortions in their self-image,[13] it seems reasonable to assume that it has led to some reduction in the prospects of success of all blacks, regardless of whether they have been personally refused a scarce educational or employment opportunity explicitly on account of the race.

A similar argument can be made in the case of women. The sexist casts women as inferiors or as being different and hence unsuited or less suited than men to perform certain tasks and to assume certain responsibilities. Moreover, traditional conceptions of appropriate sex roles may either strongly discourage women from obtaining a higher education and employment or may, through the systematic projection and reinforcement of widely accepted stereotypes, exclude them or steer them away from certain classes of jobs and certain professions. And since sexism and traditional sex roles have had a long and pervasive influence on the shaping of attitudes toward women and on the framing of practices that disadvantage women in the competition for education and for jobs, it is reasonable to assume that every woman in the United States has suffered some reduction in her prospects of success that can be attributed to sexism and to adherence to traditional conceptions of sex roles.

If one accepts that racism and sexism in the United States have had a deleterious effect on the prospects of success of *all* blacks and *all* women, respectively, then neither race-based nor gender-based affirmative action is likely to be overinclusive. That, however, does not preclude such affirmative action from being underinclusive, as there certainly are a significant number of white males who have suffered socially relative material and motivational deprivations. Nevertheless, it seems reasonable to argue that the injuries inflicted respectively by racism and by sexism are sufficiently distinct from other deprivations also resulting in reductions in prospects of success to warrant the conclusion that race-based and gender-based affirmative action need not be underinclusive.

The injuries inflicted by the racist differ from those caused by the sexist, and each of them, in turn, differs from the injuries perpetrated by other forms of group prejudice and stereotype. The racist, for example, is likely to portray blacks as lazy and unreliable,[14] while the sexist may portray women as physically too weak and emotionally too unstable to be suited for certain types of jobs, and the anti-Semite may characterize Jews as cunning and dishonest. Also, the more a particular form of group prejudice is embraced both by nonvictims and victims, the more it is likely to have a deleterious effect on the latter. Thus, if a large proportion of potential employers believe blacks to be lazy and unreliable, black applicants' prospects of employment are bound to decrease. And if both prospective employers and potential women applicants believe that women are physically and emotionally unsuited for certain jobs, it seems inevitable that women's prospects of obtaining such jobs will fall significantly.

All forms of discrimination based on negative group stereotyping are likely to result in the violation of their victims' equal opportunity rights. Yet because different kinds of negative group stereotyping are likely to lead to different injuries, the victims of each such group stereotyping may require a different remedy. In some cases affirmative action may be altogether inappropriate. In others it may be appropriate, but a particular program suited as a remedy for some form of group-based discrimination may not be adequate for others. Thus, racism may adversely affect the prospects of success of blacks differently than sexism is likely to affect those of women. For example, both blacks and women have been the victims of past discrimination in admission to professional schools. In the case of white women, however, such discrimination was not compounded by further deprivations in educational assets attributable to having been forced to attend inferior racially segregated schools. Moreover, while both racism and sexism may have had adverse effects on their victims' motivation, the motivation of blacks to pursue a higher education may have been much more severely affected by racism than that of women by sexism. Accordingly, it would not be surprising if, upon elimination of all racial- and gender-based discrimination in admissions to professional schools, the prospects of success of white women quickly approximated those of white men, while those of blacks continued to lag significantly behind those of whites. And under those circumstances, whereas race-based affirmative action in admissions to professional school would be justified as a means to equalize the prospects of success of blacks, such gender-based affirmative action would be unacceptable if it would raise women's prospects of admission well beyond the point where they would have actually been absent all gender-based discrimination.

On the other hand, one can imagine plausible situations in which gender-based, but not race-based affirmative action would be justified. For example, there may be pervasive sex discrimination, but no racial discrimination, in the allocation of such positions as road dispatcher—the position involved in the *Johnson* case—or truck driver. And, consistent with this, it would be appropriate to implement a gender-based affirmative action plan to equalize the prospects of success of women, but not a race-based affirmative action plan, as black males are in no worse position to obtain a job as road dispatcher or truck driver than are white males.

Because the projection of various negative group stereotypes is likely to lead to distinct injuries requiring different remedies, affirmative action could, in principle, be shaped so that it would not be an underinclusive remedy. If each group injury results in a reduction of individual prospects, a separate, narrowly circumscribed affirmative action plan could be implemented, and then it would be possible to restore full integrity to a system of allocation based on compliance with the equal opportunity principle. Under these optimal circumstances none of the requisite separate affirmative action plans would be either over- or underinclusive.

It may be objected that even if affirmative action for the benefit of the members of one particular group is not underinclusive to the extent that the injury to that group is distinct from other injuries affecting other groups, it may still be underinclusive in that it leaves both members of the benefited group and injured members belonging to other groups without compensation. Thus, a member of the benefited group who lacks the minimal qualifications to handle the goods allocated through the affirmative action plan cannot obtain any meaningful individual compensation through such a plan. Also, while discrimination against blacks may have led to somewhat different injuries than, for example, discrimination against Hispanics, assuming that both kinds of discrimination have produced some diminution in the prospects of success of their respective individual victims, then affirmative action favoring blacks but not Hispanics would appear to remain underinclusive with respect to the latter.

These objections can be met by emphasizing the following: first, that affirmative action, which provides imperfect procedural justice, is not meant to be an exclusive remedy for the injuries resulting from negative group stereotyping; and, second, that affording affirmative action for the members of one group in relation to a particular sphere of allocation is not meant to preclude the legitimacy (or the necessity) of extending preferential treatment to members of other groups, with respect to either the same or other spheres of allocation. Turning to the first of these two points, it is not a convincing argument against affirmative action that it cannot remedy all the injuries inflicted on the individual members of a group singled out for particular forms of mistreatment. If affirmative action is the optimum remedy for a significant portion of the class subjected to the same negative group stereotypes, it should not be discarded simply because it cannot help the remainder of the class. Indeed, a much preferable approach would be to find the best possible means of compensation for those not in a position to benefit from affirmative action and to combine the two remedies so as to provide the best possible compensation for each member of the relevant class. If the two remedies are combined and affirmative action becomes part of an overall program designed to accord each individual member of the relevant group the best available remedy for her injuries, then the overall program would not be underinclusive.

Turning to the second point, the fact that affirmative action for the benefit of one group does not provide any remedy to the wronged members of another group does not make such affirmative action underinclusive, provided that the injuries suffered by the members of the benefited group are sufficiently distinguishable from those experienced by the members of the other group. This is perhaps most obvious when different spheres of allocation are involved. For example, let us assume that sexism has caused a reduction in women's prospects to obtain employment as truck drivers, and racism has caused a comparable reduction in blacks' prospects in obtaining a professional education. If race-based affirmative action, but not gender-based affirmative action is implemented, race-based affirmative action in admissions is not underinclusive because it leaves women injured in relation to another sphere of allocation without a remedy. To be sure, leaving women without a proper remedy may be unjust, but not because they have suffered the *same* injury as the blacks afforded affirmative action. Rather, it may be unjust because the injury suffered by women independently calls for a remedy, or because, though different from that experienced by the blacks who stand to benefit from affirmative action, it is nevertheless equivalent in severity. In either case, as the victims of a separate injury, the women involved require an independent remedy regardless of how narrowly suited a remedy race-based affirmative action may be in the case of blacks.

The same argument applies in cases of different injuries suffered in the same sphere of allocation. If both blacks and Hispanics have been wrongfully excluded from professional education because of group-based prejudices and stereotypes, affirmative action in favor of one but not the other group would not be necessarily underinclusive, provided that the injury suffered by each of these groups were sufficiently different from that suffered by the other. For example, it may well be that because of the unique history of black slavery in the United States and of the particularly vehement discrimination and exclusion experienced by American blacks during most of their history, their injuries are different and more profound than those experienced by Hispanics. In that case, it would seem justified to treat the injuries to blacks separately from those to Hispanics and to institute an affirmative action plan tailored to remedy the injuries to blacks but not those to Hispanics. This, however, would not mean that the injuries to Hispanics should go uncompensated, but only that a different form of compensation—perhaps even a different affirmative action program—would be appropriate. Indeed, if the diminution in prospects of success of black victims was much greater than that of Hispanic victims, then instituting a single affirmative action plan designed to remedy the respective injuries of both groups would either be inadequate to compensate blacks or would provide Hispanics with windfall benefits.

To recapitulate, in the context of a distributive system based on equal opportunity, race- and gender-based group affiliations are supposed to bear no moral relevance regarding the allocation of scarce education and employment. Systematic and prolonged racism and sexism, however, make such group affiliations derivatively morally relevant and may justify individual compensation on the basis of group affiliation as being neither over- nor underinclusive. Moreover, to the extent that race-based or gender-based affirmative action can be used to restore the integrity of a distributive system based on equal opportunity rights, it should be justified under justice as reversible reciprocity.

In view of the preceding analysis, ascribing derivative moral relevance to race and gender in the context of compensatory justice—or of a backward-looking distributive justice in accordance with the principle of fair means-regarding equality of opportunity—is consistent with an interpretation of the equal protection clause as constitutionalizing the principle of equal opportunity. Moreover, the proposition that, for purposes of compensatory justice, it is the racist who frames race as a morally relevant characteristic, has already found constitutional support in the Supreme Court decision in *United Jewish Organizations* v. *Carey.* In that case, arising under Section 5 of the Voting Rights Act of 1965,[15] the Court held that the Constitution permits states to reapportion voting districts so that the percentage of districts with a nonwhite majority approximates the percentage of nonwhites in the county.

The right to vote is a paradigmatic individual right. Each individual has only one vote, and absent any discrimination or unfair procedures, no group of voters has a right to complain that its candidate lost. However, when large numbers of voters vote on the basis of race, and when the state reapportions voting districts with the aim of diluting the impact of nonwhite votes, the process becomes unfairly loaded against nonwhites. Moreover, when nonwhites have been framed in this way as a group for purposes of having the aggregate impact of their votes diluted, each individual nonwhite voter suffers an injury. Indeed, because of discrimination, the prospect that a nonwhite person's vote will contribute to the election of the candidates of his or her choice is unfairly diminished. As a consequence of this, a need for compensation arises, and as the court in *Carey* made clear, a state is not "powerless to minimize the consequences of racial discrimination by voters when it is regularly practiced at the polls."[16]

An apparent irony to *Carey* is that New York's redistricting plan designed "to alleviate the consequences of racial voting . . . and to achieve a fair allocation of political power between white and non-white voters"[17] had the consequence of substantially diluting the voting power of Hasidic Jews, a small and insular group. Upon first impression, it may seem inconsistent to remedy the unfair dilution of nonwhite voting power by diluting the voting power of an innocent insular minority like the Hasidim. Consistent with the proposition that past discrimination causes group affiliation to acquire moral relevance within a sphere of assimilation, however, since the Hasidim were not discriminated against as voters prior to the redistricting, and since the redistricting was not undertaken to discriminate against them, their group affiliation remained morally irrelevant for voting purposes. In view of this, there is nothing inconsistent, in the context of *Carey*, about taking the group affiliations of nonwhites into account while at the same time ignoring those of individual Hasidic voters.

Thus far, the relationship between the individual and the group has been examined in the context of compensation and of remedial assistance pursuant to a partly backward-looking scheme of distributive justice. The individual-group issue also arises in relation to those who are likely to bear the adverse consequences of a particular scheme of compensation or distribution. As discussed in chapter 3, adherence to the postulate of equality precludes allocating the burdens of affirmative action on the basis of some notion of group liability. To the extent that the state itself, or one of its subdivisions, implements affirmative action in the context of constitutional challenges to the practice, however, there seems to be little room for the emergence of problems concerning the relationship between the individual and the group. Moreover, no such problems are likely to arise where a private wrongdoer is charged with the responsibility of setting up an affirmative action plan because of individual culpability rather than group-based liability. On the other hand, regardless of who bears responsibility for administering any particular affirmative action plan, the operation of such a plan is bound to result in the loss of certain otherwise-obtainable benefits by individual members of the group disadvantaged by the plan. This raises the issue of whether these individuals are disadvantaged by affirmative action *because* of their group affiliation and, if they are, whether such a burden is compatible with the postulate of equality and with individual rights in constitutional equality. These issues, which can be encompassed under the rubric of the problem of the "innocent white male," require close examination, for unless they can be resolved satisfactorily they would cast a major shadow on the possibility of bestowing philosophical and constitutional legitimacy on affirmative action.

3. *Justice as Reversible Reciprocity and the Problem of the Innocent White Male*

The difficult problem of the "innocent white male" is raised by the following argument. Even assuming that affirmative action can be legitimated in all other significant respects it is nevertheless unjust because it has a vastly disproportionate adverse effect on a group of white males who cannot fairly be held responsible for the social evils sought to be remedied through affirmative action. This group of white males is made up of those who have never personally undertaken any wrongful action against blacks or women and who would have obtained a coveted scarce educational or employment opportunity but for the implementation of an affirmative action plan.

To appreciate how disproportionate the burden of affirmative action is likely to be on the group of innocent white males identified above, one need only compare it to the burdens that affirmative action is likely to impose on the remainder of society. From a material standpoint, an affirmative action plan implemented by a government entity is likely to impose two kinds of burdens on society as a whole. The first stems from the administration costs incurred in running the plan; the second, from the loss of efficiency resulting from selecting a somewhat less qualified candidate from a victim group over a somewhat more qualified candidate from a nonvictim group to fill a scarce government-allocated position. To the extent that the administrative costs of operating an affirmative action plan are likely to be modest relative to a vast number of government-run programs, the distributive burden traceable to such a plan imposed on each individual taxpayer is likely to be negligible. Further, the distributive cost to each individual member of society attributable to losses in efficiency attributable to affirmative action plans is also likely to be very modest. Actually, in cases involving compositive efficiency, an affirmative action plan may lead to an increase in overall efficiency. For example, an affirmative action plan designed to promote the racial integration of a police department in a racially mixed community may lead to a reduction of racial tensions and to an increase in confidence in the police throughout the community, thus boosting the overall efficiency of the department. On the other hand, even where efficiency is additive, affirmative action is unlikely to produce a sizable negative effect to the extent that it requires the selection of the most qualified available candidate belonging to the victim group over a slightly better qualified member of the nonvictim group. Thus, for example, in the *Johnson* case, where both Johnson and Joyce, the woman who ended up obtaining the job as road dispatcher, were among the best candidates for the job, and where Johnson was only marginally more qualified than Joyce, any resulting loss in efficiency would be in all likelihood virtually insignificant.

The distributive burden imposed by affirmative action on the innocent white male is not only disproportionately heavy, but it also adversely affects interests likely to be crucial in the pursuit of individual life plans. Indeed, affirmative action deprives certain innocent white males of an education, or of an employment position or a business opportunity that he would have otherwise obtained and that he most likely considers important to the fulfillment of his life plan. Accordingly, to overcome the problem of the innocent white male, and to justify affirmative action, notwithstanding the substantial and disproportionate burden that it imposes on the latter, it must be shown to satisfy the requirements of justice as reversible reciprocity. And given the nature of such requirements as articulated in the course of the preceding analysis, this means that affirmative action may be justified in spite of its disparate effects if it does not violate the innocent white male's rights to equal dignity and respect or equal opportunity.

From *Bakke* to *Croson* some Supreme Court justices have viewed race-based affirmative action as discriminating against whites *because* of their race, and have thus lent support to the proposition that affirmative action violates equal dignity and respect rights.[18] As such, affirmative action seems no different than first-order discrimination that singles out blacks because of their race for treatment as inferiors.

Not surprisingly, the justices who subscribe to this view are proponents of the antidiscrimination principle and of the marginal equality position. Further, this view can be justified under a mere reciprocity criterion. Indeed, if it is recognized that all black and white individuals are equals as subjects entitled to choose and pursue their own individual life plans, and if it is accepted that blacks cannot be disadvantaged because of their race, then it follows that as equals whites also should not be disadvantaged because of theirs.

The apparent symmetry between the plight of racially discriminated blacks and innocent whites disadvantaged by affirmative action, however, is purely abstract and superficial. Remedial affirmative action plans, such as those involved in the various Supreme Court decisions discussed above, cannot seriously be considered the product of a racist animus against whites. Consequently, to claim that innocent whites are singled out for disfavorable treatment *because* of their race is unwarranted except from the standpoint of a purely abstract perspective that remains completely ahistorical and acontextual. From a nonstrategic contextually grounded perspective, on the other hand, remedial affirmative action is meant to be inclusionary rather than exclusionary like racism and sexism[19] and intended to make up for societally caused deprivations that have placed blacks and women at a competitive disadvantage. From this perspective, moreover, while innocent white males may be injured by remedial affirmative action, neither the agents of allocation who implement it nor the blacks and women who stand to benefit from the preferences involved are likely to be motivated by any desire to treat white males as inferiors or to deprive them of equal dignity and respect. In short, whereas racism and sexism intend to maintain the members of their targeted groups as outcasts or as inferiors, affirmative action seeks to reinstate those previously excluded because of their group affiliations into the mainstream of society.

Even conceding that affirmative action is fully consistent with the maintenance of a benign intent toward innocent white males, the latter may still become deprived of equal dignity and respect as a consequence of their failure to obtain educational or employment opportunities that would have been theirs but for affirmative action. A person's standing in society, as well as the respect he enjoys, often has much to do with his achievements in education and employment. Failure, on the other hand, may result in loss of standing and of respect. Because of the historical disparities in the treatment of the two races, however, the loss of an educational or employment opportunity is unlikely to have the same effect on a white person and on a black person.

A Marco DeFunis' failure to gain admission at a particular law school, or an Alan Bakke's rejection from medical school, is not likely to subject them to negative group stereotypes or to treatment as unworthy members of society. Moreover, if a disappointed white applicant is forced to abandon a desired career objective, he is unlikely to be stigmatized as a black applicant probably would.[20] Indeed, while society may, on the basis of prejudices nurtured by racism, brand a black person as an inferior because of his failure to succeed in a competition for a scarce position, the same would not occur in the case of a similarly situated white person. By the same token, in the context of sexism, while a woman's failure to obtain a certain position may serve to reinforce negative stereotypes based on gender, the same would be much less likely in the case of a man.

Even conceding that affirmative action neither intends nor produces abridgements of equal dignity and respect rights, innocent white males may still *perceive* the disadvantages foisted upon them by race- and gender-based affirmative action as being unfair and as tending to denigrate their entitlement to equal worth. They may point out that, even if the harms experienced by blacks and women because of first-order discrimination are clearly more substantial than those incurred by white men as a consequence of affirmative action, it does not necessarily follow that the latter are acceptable.

Whether these claims are ultimately valid depends on how they fare in the dialogical process designed to establish what practices may be justified under justice as reversible reciprocity. In order to be in a position to examine this question systematically, however, it is first necessary to determine if the disproportionate disadvantages imposed by affirmative action on innocent white males violates the latter's equal opportunity rights. Indeed, as argued in section 1, justice as reversible reciprocity legitimates the principle of fair equality of opportunity. Accordingly, if affirmative action violates the equal opportunity rights of innocent white males, it cannot be just.

Although affirmative action treats innocent white males unequally, it need not deprive them of any genuine equal opportunity rights. Provided an affirmative action plan is precisely tailored to redress the losses in prospects of success attributable to racism or sexism, it only deprives innocent white males of the corresponding undeserved increases in their prospects of success. Thus, insofar as affirmative action brings the prospects of success of all competitors (and potential competitors) to where they would have been absent racism and sexism, it merely places all competitors in the position in which they would have been if the competition had always been conducted in strict compliance with equal opportunity rights. Consistent with this, remedial affirmative action does not take away from innocent white males anything that they have rightfully earned or that they should be entitled to keep.

As discussed in chapter 3, a distinction can be drawn between different types of benefits thrust upon innocent white males as a consequence of racism and sexism. Some benefits used to develop greater skills and abilities can only be eliminated by preventing their recipients from using their full capacities in the pursuit of their individual life plans. Accordingly, the elimination of these benefits could not be achieved without unduly interfering with the autonomy and the integrity of the person of those who have innocently acquired them.

Increased prospects of success attributable to racism or sexism, however, are not benefits that fall in the same category. Indeed, as pointed out in chapter 3, besides being undeserved, these benefits are separable from other kinds of benefits. Therefore, their elimination can be effectuated without necessarily interfering with personal autonomy or integrity. While one's prospects of success are generally relative to one's skills and abilities, such prospects can be increased or decreased without imposing any constraints on anyone's free use of all the means at his disposal. For example, all other things remaining equal, one's prospects are bound to increase or decrease with the size and quality of the pool of competitors. Similarly, the adjustment of prospects brought about by an affirmative action plan leaves all the other aspects of the competition intact. In the last analysis, the reduction in the prospect of success of an innocent white male does not necessarily violate his right to equal opportunity or personal autonomy and integrity.

Moreover, compensatory affirmative action does not violate the equal opportunity rights of innocent white males even if it does not restore all competitors to where they would have been absent racism and sexism. As indicated in chapter 3, commitment to the principle of equality of opportunity requires according priority to compensatory claims arising from violations of that principle over distributive claims arising under the same principle. To the extent that justice as reversible reciprocity requires adherence to the principle of equality of opportunity, therefore, the compensation—through affirmative action if necessary—of victims of violations of such principle is justified. Moreover, such compensation is not violative of anyone's equal opportunity rights, even if it leads to a distribution of relative prospects among competitors that deviates from that which would have obtained had no violation of equal opportunity rights ever occurred.

Keeping in mind that affirmative action is not intended to abridge the equal dignity and respect rights of innocent white males and that it does not have to violate their equal opportunity rights, we must now turn to a more difficult question. That question is whether affirmative action and the plight of the innocent white male can be reconciled through a dialogical process in the context of adherence to justice as reversible reciprocity. In other words, can the coordination of all relevant perspectives, including that of the innocent white male, yield a genuine consensus or compromise upholding the legitimacy of remedial race- and gender-based affirmative action?

Reconstruction of the dialogical process designed to determine the legitimacy of affirmative action in light of the problem of the innocent white male must proceed on the basis of a presumed general acceptance of certain propositions. Chief among them is the proposition established in section 1 that the spheres of allocation of scarce educational, employment, and business opportunities should be governed by the principle of fair means-regarding equality of opportunity. Moreover, participants in the dialogue are presumed to accept the proposition that the substantial underrepresentation of blacks in education, employment, and business is due to past and ongoing first-order discrimination against them. And, likewise, that similar underrepresentations of women are the product of either first-order sex discrimination or social attitudes and practices which, even if they were not considered unjust when implemented, have resulted in depriving women of fair means-regarding equality of opportunity. Also, participants in the dialogue assume that blacks, women, and white males are genuinely committed to belonging together to a single inclusive community and to the rejection of separatism and the possibility of instituting several mutually exclusive communities.

Given these assumptions, it is possible to follow the thinking of innocent white males through the various stages of reciprocity—starting with mere reciprocity, advancing to limited role reversal, and finally culminating in full reversible reciprocity. The initial position of the participants in the dialogical process would be one that goes beyond the principle of mere reciprocity. All participants would acknowledge universal entitlement to equal opportunity rights and to a right of compensation for violations of such rights. Blacks and women, moreover, might press for extensive compensatory remedies that might promptly put them where they would have been absent first-order discrimination. Initially, white males, operating from a perspective involving a limited role reversal, may agree to the elimination of all first-order discrimination and to the removal of all formal barriers to competition. Indeed, putting themselves, from the standpoint of their own perspective, in the place of black and women victims of first-order discrimination, these white males would presumably conclude that since they would be able to succeed in the competition for scarce educational and employment opportunities absent any formal barriers, so, too, should the blacks and women involved.

On the other hand, from the standpoint of a reciprocity based on a limited reversal of roles, unlike from that of mere reciprocity, innocent white males are unlikely to assert that affirmative action injures them in the same way that first-order discrimination harms its black or women victims. Indeed, white men will be able to understand that the purpose behind remedial affirmative action is different from that of the racist or sexist who engages in first-order discrimination. Moreover, from the stage of reciprocity based on a limited role reversal, white males would acknowledge that blacks and women are entitled to compensation in kind for specific violations of their rights in cases of actual denials of places or positions that they would have obtained but for discrimination. This follows from the capacity of white men to perceive that if one of them had been denied unjustly a position after having won the competition for it, he would feel outraged and would want those who had wrongfully withheld the position to be forced to award it to him. By projecting his own perspective onto a black or a woman, a white man would thus be prepared to accept that blacks and women would be justified likewise in pressing claims for compensation in kind whenever confronted with a similar unjust denial.

Operating from a stage of reciprocity based on limited role reversals, innocent white males would have reason to approve of affirmative action by an actual wrongdoer as compensation in kind for an actual victim, but not of broader remedial uses of affirmative action. In particular, based on their belief that blacks and women should be able to compete on a par with white men once all formal barriers have been removed, innocent white males would have reason to condemn the use of affirmative action to remedy the effects of societal discrimination—that is, discrimination occurring with respect to a sphere of allocation other than that targeted for the institution of preferential treatment. Indeed, within this perspective, in cases of societal discrimination the burden of affirmative action on innocent white males would not only seem disproportionate but also unnecessary. Under these circumstances, affirmative action would be perceived as serving no genuine compensatory purpose, thus affording its beneficiaries an unfair advantage. In the last analysis, the conclusions likely to be reached by innocent white males from the stage of reciprocity based on a limited role reversal are virtually the same as those propounded by the Supreme Court justices who have embraced the marginal equality position. In both cases, affirmative action is legitimate if used for narrow compensatory purposes between actual wrongdoers and their actual direct victims, but illegitimate if it is extended substantially beyond the paradigm of compensation.

Upon reaching the highest stage of reciprocity that involves perspective reversals, innocent white males will be in a position to understand that removal of all formal barriers to competition might not suffice to put blacks or women in the position in which they would have been but for first-order discrimination. Women and blacks, on the other hand, will be able to appreciate that innocent white men do not want to bear the brunt of the burden of redressing the lingering injuries stemming from racism and sexism. The difficult question, however, is whether, after each participant in the dialogical process involving a full reciprocity of perspectives has fully intuited the point of view of every other participant, a genuine consensus or compromise is likely to emerge.

Before being in a position to suggest possible answers to this question, one must focus on the various initial prototypical claims that differently situated participants are likely to bring to the dialogical process. As far as the innocent white males are concerned, since they have the most to lose if competition were to deviate from the principle of formal equality of opportunity, they would have ample reason to insist that affirmative action should not be used as a remedy for the ill effects of racism and sexism. Members of other groups, such as blacks or women, however, do not appear as readily prone to find any single common voice. For example, some blacks—including Justice Marshall—have eloquently argued that the achievement of equal opportunity for blacks requires the use of affirmative action to remedy the lingering effects of racial discrimination.[21] Other blacks, such as the neoconservative scholar Thomas Sowell, have opposed affirmative action[22] and have intimated that the underrepresentation of blacks in the workforce is a result of a lack of commitment to the work ethic rather than to first-order racial discrimination.[23] Further, it does not seem far-fetched to suppose that, if it were not for strategic considerations, there would be many black public voices, at the other end of the spectrum, seeking more radical remedies than affirmative action to bring a more rapid end to the enduring effects of racism.

The spectrum of women's positions is also likely to be very broad. At one extreme, some women wishing to preserve traditional gender-based roles could assert that the workplace should remain primarily a male preserve and that women should devote themselves to the roles of housewife and mother.[24] At the other extreme, on the other hand, would be women seeking a radical transformation of society and the workplace to eradicate all vestiges of male dominance.[25] Inspired by Carol Gilligan's vision discussed in chapter 9, these women would feel justified to claim that male dominance cannot be eliminated unless individualism and competition are replaced by communitarianism and cooperation. In between these two extremes, moreover, would be women who would be satisfied with a fair chance in the existing competition for scarce positions. Some among these latter women would feel that the removal of formal barriers to competition would be sufficient to afford them a fair chance. Others, however, would be convinced that, under prevailing circumstances, only gender-based affirmative action could put women on a competitive par with men.[26]

Focusing first on the spectrum of likely black perspectives, consistent with our initial assumptions, three likely prototypical positions on affirmative action emerge. In the middle is the position that proclaims the legitimacy and desirability of remedial affirmative action. To the right of that position, is one that asserts that affirmative action is an unnecessary remedy; to the left, one that likewise advocates the rejection of affirmative action, but for the reason that it is an inadequate and insufficient remedy to eliminate the lingering effects of racism.

Before examining whether these positions can be reconciled to lead to a genuine consensus or compromise, it is necessary to determine whether any of them should be altogether excluded from the dialogical process by virtue of being essentially strategic in nature. One can make a strong case that a neoconservative position opposing affirmative action, such as that of Sowell, is to a large degree a strategic one. Sowell himself argues that the civil rights policies of the sixties and seventies have threatened democracy and fueled the increasing popularity of white hate groups (Sowell 1984, 90). Retraction from the vigorous pursuit of civil rights for fear of white reprisals, like opposition of affirmative action out of concern that whites will demean the achievements of blacks, is clearly a strategic move, rather than a position oriented toward communicative action. Indeed, it may be in the interests of particular blacks who are likely to succeed, notwithstanding the disadvantages imposed by racism, to promote the status quo instead of opposing it, to the extent that opposition tends to perpetrate racism or its effects. As mentioned in chapter 9, it may be easier for blacks who can succeed following the lifting of formal restraints to project the image that they are exceptions to the widely accepted racial stereotypes, rather than to combat such stereotypes. Thus, for example, in the eyes of one black scholar, "Sowell applies the same stereotypes to the mass of Blacks that white supremacists had applied in the past, but bases these modern stereotypes on notions of 'culture' rather than genetics. Sowell characterizes underclass Blacks as victims of self-imposed ignorance, lack of direction and poor work attitudes" (Crenshaw 1988, 1379). Because of this, concludes the same black scholar, "Sowell exemplifies what may be the worst development of the civil rights movement—that some Blacks who have benefited the most from the formal gestures of equality now identify with those who attempt to affirm the legitimacy of oppressing other Blacks" (ibid., 1379*n.187*).

That positions such as that espoused by Sowell are strategic rather than oriented to communicative action becomes apparent if one compares a successful black's opposition to affirmative action with that of an innocent white male. If affirmative action is deemed legitimate, the innocent white male, but not the successful black, would still have reason to oppose it. This is because the black who can succeed without affirmative action is not any less likely to do so with it, whereas a white who might otherwise succeed may fail only because of affirmative action.

Based on this, a reconstructor seems justified in excluding from the dialogical process the claims against affirmative action of black neoconservatives like Sowell. Of course, such claims would have to be included, if the prospects of success of blacks would not lag behind those of whites in the context of formal equality of opportunity. But if that were the case, then there would not be altogether *any* justification for affirmative action consistent with the equal opportunity principle.

Exclusion of the position espoused by Sowell would mean that black participants in the dialogical process (who believe that the mere lifting of formal barriers to competition would not produce equal opportunity for all blacks) would be divided among the two remaining positions identified above. Some would take the initial position that affirmative action is necessary to put blacks in the competitive position they would have achieved absent racism. Others would counter that affirmative action is insufficient for such a purpose and that a more drastic remedy is indicated. For example, the latter may claim that, in order for blacks to be made whole, it is necessary to change the racial composition of the workforce to reflect what it would have been like absent racism, by, among other things, firing whites from jobs they would not have held absent racism to make room for blacks who would have held them in a color-blind labor market.

Proponents of the latter position may argue that blacks whose initial position is to seek affirmative action are pressing a strategic claim rather than one oriented toward communicative action. According to this argument, advocacy of affirmative action, which represents a slower and less comprehensive remedy, is the product of a compromise reached unilaterally before entering into the dialogical process. In other words, because blacks who feel entitled to a complete remedy fear that whites who occupy the dominant position in society will reject any call for more radical remedies, they limit their initial claims for purely instrumental reasons.

Black proponents of affirmative action may counter this argument by stressing that their initial position is not the product of a strategic retreat but rather of a thoughtful consideration of what would be just consistent with adherence to the equal opportunity principle as viewed from their own perspective. Indeed, it may be plausibly argued that the best way to restore the equilibrium between the integrity and the efficiency of a sphere of allocation in which equal opportunity rights have been systematically violated because of racial discrimination is an affirmative action plan. According to this point of view, moreover, the reason for not pressing for more drastic remedies is not any fear of white opposition, but an independent determination, from the standpoint of a black perspective, that blacks would be better off—both in terms of remedial justice and efficiency—with affirmative action than with more radical remedies.

This last argument is certainly plausible, and therefore, even if it is deemed to be ultimately unpersuasive, the initial claim of certain blacks in favor of affirmative action should be allowed entry into the dialogical process. In the last analysis, even if an initial claim from a black perspective in favor of affirmative action were deemed to be strategic, its erroneous inclusion in the dialogical process would not materially affect the determination of whether affirmative action could be the subject of a genuine consensus or compromise. No such consensus or compromise could be reached without the concurrence of black advocates of remedies more drastic than affirmative action. Accordingly, unless these advocates can be persuaded to embrace affirmative action in the course of the dialogical process, affirmative action could not be legitimated under justice as reversible reciprocity.

If one turns to the likely initial claims of women, any split between those who seek remedial gender-based affirmative action and those who seek more radical remedies should be treated in the same way as the corresponding division among blacks, and for the same reasons. Thus, both women's initial claims to affirmative action and to more radical remedies should find inclusion in the dialogical process. The initial claims of women who oppose affirmative action, either because they seek to preserve traditional sex roles or because they are committed to a profound transformation of society designed to eliminate all vestiges of male domination, however, are more problematic.

Women who advocate the maintenance of traditional sex roles pose a difficult problem for a reconstructor, for it is unclear whether their position can be dismissed as being purely strategic or whether it should be considered as the expression of an unconstrained vision that can be oriented to communicative action. To the extent that this position reinforces patterns of male domination and legitimates the subordination of women, it bears a strong parallel to the black neoconservative position articulated by Sowell. On the other hand, however, to the extent that this position seeks different but equal roles for men and women, and that it may conceivably even combat existing patterns of male domination, it may well deserve a voice in the dialogical process. In practice this position has tended to go hand in hand with inequality between the sexes and the subordination of women.[27] But to the extent that it can conceivably be articulated in a nonsexist manner, a reconstructor should allow it entry into the dialogical process as an initial position.

Women who believe that justice requires a systematic transformation of existing spheres of allocation to eliminate all patterns of male domination may adopt one of two incompatible positions. The first position opposes affirmative action as likely to appease its women beneficiaries, thus reinforcing systemic male domination. The second position, in contrast, does not deem affirmative action to be unjust, on the belief that the current horizon of possibilities precludes any near-term successful profound transformation of social relationships. Actually, this second position may even consider affirmative action to be desirable, inasmuch as it would put more women in a position to launch radical transformations in gender relationships, once this becomes a viable alternative. Further, proponents of the first position may contend that the second position is essentially strategic in nature. Nevertheless, it is plausible to claim that the second position is based not on deception or self-deception but on an accurate assessment of the best interests of women, from a feminist perspective that takes proper account of the limitations imposed by the current horizon of possibilities on the transformability of existing needs and interests. Accordingly, a reconstructor should permit inclusion of both these positions as initial positions in the dialogical process.

An assessment of how all these prototypical initial positions are likely to fare in the dialogical process depends on whether initial intragroup and intergroup differences can ultimately be reconciled. However, it makes sense to begin with the issue of intragroup reconciliation because, whatever the individual life plans of individual members of a group may be, all members of that group who are committed to the postulate of equality share a common interest in not being treated as inferiors and in the removal of the handicaps attributable to having been thus treated.

Submission of the two remaining initial positions launched from the perspective of blacks to the reversal of perspectives test is unlikely to yield a unified black voice. Black proponents of affirmative action may understand why black advocates of more drastic remedies feel that fairness requires prompt and comprehensive compensation. Similarly, the latter may appreciate that the proponents of affirmative action are inclined against more radical remedies because they fear that they would produce an unwarranted loss in efficiency. Even after completing a reversal of perspectives, however, there seems to be no compelling reason for the proponents of either of these positions to yield to those of the other.

Accordingly, this case is to be distinguished from the case in which black proponents of affirmative action are confronted by black supporters of formal means-regarding equality of opportunity. Indeed, in the latter case, the greater efficiency claims of formal equality advocates would have to yield to the affirmative action proponents' justified contention that the integrity of the distributive system requires the restoration of prospects of success to where they would have been but for racial discrimination. In the present case, by contrast, neither of the contending positions would prevent the reinstatement of the integrity of the distributive system. Instead, the disagreement between the respective proponents of these two positions centers on the issue of what would constitute proper compensation for black victims of racial discrimination. Moreover—and this is crucial—those who insist on affirmative action because it is likely to promote greater efficiency do not necessarily take this position because they believe that efficiency should take precedence over compensatory concerns. Rather, they may attach as much importance to the need for compensation as the proponents of more radical remedies, but nevertheless advocate means of compensation that are more compatible with greater efficiency.

It is self-evident that its black proponents would subscribe to a consensus or compromise concerning the legitimacy of affirmative action. From the standpoint of blacks, therefore, the question to be settled by the dialogical process relying on the reversal of perspectives is whether proponents of more radical remedies are eventually likely to become persuaded of the legitimacy of affirmative action—and if the answer is in the affirmative, whether they will reach a consensus or only a compromise.

Submitting the prototypical perspectives of women to the reversal of perspectives test yields results that, to a large extent, parallel those reached in the context of prototypical black positions. Thus, the clash between women whose initial position is to seek formal equality of opportunity and those whose initial position advocates gender-based affirmative action should be resolved in the course of the dialogical process along the same lines as the corresponding dispute among blacks. That is, of course, provided that women, like blacks, cannot expect to overcome within a reasonable time the deficit in prospects of success attributable to first-order discrimination without affirmative action. Similarly, the conflict between those who support affirmative action and those who advocate more radical remedies is no more likely to be worked out in the case of women than in that of blacks. Accordingly, from the perspective of women, an important question to be resolved by the dialogical process is whether advocates of more radical remedies are eventually likely to accept the legitimacy of affirmative action.

Some of the intragroup clashes affecting women, however, have no apparent counterpart in the case of blacks. Women proponents of traditional sex roles, for example, are likely to come into conflict with female advocates of affirmative action. Unlike in the case of blacks, where there appears to be a broad-based consensus (at least among nonseparatists) that the spheres of education and of employment should be spheres of assimilation, female proponents of traditional sex roles may genuinely assert that these spheres should be spheres of differentiation when it comes to gender. The clash between the latter women and female advocates of affirmative action is therefore not a conflict between two groups who have different vantage points within the same ideological perspective. Rather, it is a conflict between groups that subscribe to different ideologies.

It is conceivable that this conflict could be settled by means of mutual accommodation. Female proponents of traditional sex roles could stay away from the workplace and rely on the employment of suitable male relatives to secure economic subsistence. Female supporters of the ideal of assimilation at the workplace, on the other hand, would remain free to compete for employment and to press for gender-based affirmative action in the spheres of education and employment.

It is also conceivable, however, that the respective proponents of these two initial positions would reject mutual accommodation. Advocates of traditional sex roles could contend that gender differentiation in the sphere of employment should be normatively prescribed and that assimilationist efforts relating to the integration of women in that sphere should be actively resisted. Supporters of gender-based assimilation in the workplace, on the other hand, could argue that there is no room for an ideal of differentiation in the sphere of employment and that proponents of such differentiation should be rebuffed because they stand as an obstacle to the realization of equality between the sexes.

Submission of these contending positions to the reversal of perspectives test could yield different results, depending on the relative intensity with which the respective proponents of each of these positions embrace its essential tenets. Thus, if advocates of traditional sex roles strongly object to any deviations from what they consider to be proper gender roles and relationships, the result of the reversal of perspectives test is likely to differ from that which would obtain if they were more tolerant of women who eschewed traditional sex roles without attempting to impose their own views on their sisters.

These likely differences can be sufficiently accounted for by subjecting two different cases to the reversal of perspectives test. The first case involves proponents of both the traditionalist position and the assimilationist position who are initially mutually tolerant; the second, proponents of these respective positions who are initially mutually intolerant. In the case of initial mutual tolerance, the reversal of perspectives test is likely to foment greater mutual understanding and to reinforce an already-present tendency toward mutual accommodation. While traditionalist women will not seek to participate in the workplace, they will not attempt to prevent other women from doing so, or from securing gender-based affirmative action. Under these circumstances, it seems fair to conclude that traditionalist women would be willing ultimately to accept gender-based affirmative action as a matter of compromise, if not as part of a consensus.

In the case of initial mutual intolerance, on the other hand, application of the reversal of perspectives test seems much less likely to lead to mutual accommodation. Traditionalist women's reasons for being intolerant of their assimilationist sisters may include the conviction that the traditionalist position is right and should be therefore adopted by everyone; the belief that tolerance of assimilationism will lead inevitably to the undermining of the traditionalist position; and the fear that assimilationalism in general, and gender-based affirmative action in particular, will lead to a shift in the holding of desirable jobs from men to women, thus jeopardizing the maintenance of the material conditions required to sustain traditional sex roles. Assimilationist women who advocate gender-based affirmative action also may have reasons for being intolerant of their traditionalist sisters. They may be persuaded that traditionalism is a form of false consciousness that serves only to reinforce established patterns of male domination. They may also feel that traditionalism is an obstacle that must be eliminated because it stands in the way of assimilationism and of equality between the sexes. More narrowly, they may fear that the presence of feminine traditionalist voices may be used to buttress resistance against claims for gender-based affirmative action.

Any claim that either of these two positions is right, and should therefore be adopted by all, must be rejected as incompatible with reciprocal recognition of the integrity of the individual perspectives involved. The further claim that the mere presence and spread of assimilationism (or of traditionalism) undermines the preservation of traditionalism (or of assimilationalism), however, cannot be as readily dismissed. If the practice of assimilationism interferes with the fulfillment of traditionalism by spreading an atmosphere that is hostile to it (and vice versa), a reversal of perspectives seems unlikely to convince either the partisans of traditionalism or those of assimilationism to budge from their respective initial positions.

A closer look at these initial positions reveals, however, that they are ultimately illegitimate in the context of a communicative ethics based on justice as reversible reciprocity. Indeed, one of the fundamental tenets of such an ethics is the commitment to remain open to nonstrategic attempts at dialogical persuasion. Proponents of traditionalism and those of assimilationism may find that the constant threat of defections to the opposite camp creates an unstable and potentially hostile atmosphere. It is understandable, therefore, that they should seek to exert greater control over their social environment. But, consistent with a commitment to communicative ethics, such greater control cannot be achieved through the curtailment of open dialogue or through intimidation of those who contemplate switching positions.

To the extent that the assimilationists' intolerance of traditionalists stems out of fear that the latter will lend support to sexism, it is without justification in the context of the dialogical process. Indeed, such fear is purely strategic under the ideal speech conditions of the dialogical process. This is because the existence of women who embrace the traditionalist perspective should not be allowed to carry persuasive weight in any nonstrategic attempt to convince assimilationists not to pursue equality among the sexes in the sphere of employment. Consistent with this, female assimilationists who participate in the dialogical process should not be intolerant of female traditionalists, so long as the latter adhere to the discursive constraints imposed by communicative ethics.

The female traditionalists' opposition to assimilationism and to gender-based affirmative action on the grounds that equality between the sexes in the sphere of employment would undermine the material conditions necessary to the viability of traditional sex roles, however, presents a different kind of issue. Indeed, a traditionalist who respects the integrity of the assimilationist perspective, and who fully understands the reasons for the latter's commitment to gender-based affirmative action, may yet oppose affirmative action as directly inimical to her self-interest. If, through gender-based affirmative action, a large number of women obtain desirable positions that otherwise would have gone to men, female traditionalists, who depend on the earnings of male relatives to sustain their way of life, risk becoming worse off.

The dialogical process does provide a resolution of this last issue. Indeed, joint submission to the reversal of perspectives test of female traditionalists' opposition to affirmative action (as likely to deprive them of the economic support necessary to maintain their way of life) and of female assimilationists' claims to affirmative action prompts the following observations: Affirmative action would increase the likelihood that female traditionalists would become unable to rely exclusively on male relatives for their financial support. The failure to resort to affirmative action, on the other hand, prevents certain women from making up the deficit in prospects attributable to sexism, and thus from achieving fair means-regarding equality of opportunity in the marketplace for scarce employment. Now, let us assume that all other things remain equal, and let us disregard any female traditionalists' claims that are purely parasitic on those of a male relative (on the ground that the clash between women's claims for affirmative action and men's claims against it will be adequately dealt with below). Under these circumstances, it appears that the female assimilationists' claim for affirmative action is likely to be more weighty relative to their life plans than the female traditionalists' claim against affirmative action relative to theirs. From the standpoint of a female assimilationist, affirmative action is tied in with the opportunity to compete on an equal footing, with the equality of respect and dignity associated with not being discriminated on the basis of gender, with the satisfaction to be derived from holding an enriching and fulfilling job, and with the opportunity to obtain goods necessary to the fulfillment of one's life plan. From the standpoint of a female traditionalist, on the other hand, the rejection of affirmative action only appears to be directly linked with the opportunity to acquire the latter goods. Assuming that female traditionalists seek equality of respect and dignity through differentiated sex roles, the equal opportunity rights or the job satisfaction of their male relatives are unlikely to possess much *intrinsic* value from the standpoint of the realization of their own life plans. In short, while for female assimilationists affirmative action may affect both self-respect and security, for female traditionalists it only seems to reduce security. Accordingly, in the context of the dialogical process, female traditionalists should ultimately raise no objections against gender-based affirmative action other than those that might be interposed by the men on whom they have chosen to depend for economic support.

Women who advocate a radical transformation of the sphere of employment to eradicate the vestiges of male domination in the workplace, and who oppose affirmative action as an obstacle to such a transformation, are not likely to reach any consensus or compromise with female proponents of affirmative action. Indeed, the reversal of perspectives is unlikely to bring the position of radical feminists who seek a comprehensive transformation of social relationships any closer to that of female assimilationists who aspire to a fair share of employments under the existing mode of allocation. In an important sense, the position of female advocates of a radical feminization of the workplace is analogous to that of black separatists: they are both committed to rejection of the status quo rather than to seeking justice and accommodation within the framework of its existing institutions. Because of this, like black separatists, women who oppose affirmative action as inconsistent with a program of radical transformation would have no reason to be part of any consensus or compromise on the legitimacy of affirmative action.

To recapitulate, the intragroup reversal of perspectives among women leads to the following results: Female proponents of formal equality of opportunity have no reason to oppose gender-based affirmative action, even if they have nothing to gain from it. Likewise, we have seen that female traditionalists have no legitimate nonstrategic reason of their own—that is, no reason separate from those of men on whom they have chosen to depend for support—for opposing affirmative action. On the other hand, women who oppose affirmative action because they believe that it would hinder the radical transformation that they advocate cannot be expected to be included in any consensus or compromise in favor of affirmative action. That leaves women who advocate the institution of gender-based affirmative action and women who, while committed to the existing mode of employment allocation, nevertheless seek the full integration of women in the workforce through means that are more radical than affirmative action. In the last analysis, given the dialogical interplay between these various positions, from the standpoint of women the key question to be answered in terms of the legitimacy of affirmative action is the same as that which must be addressed from the standpoint of blacks. That question is whether women, committed to the existing mode of employment allocation but who advocate remedies more drastic than affirmative action, are eventually likely to become persuaded of the legitimacy of affirmative action as a matter of consensus or of compromise.

As the result of submitting prototypical intragroup differences to the reversal of perspectives test, the possibility of a consensus or compromise on the legitimacy of affirmative action (among all those who are neither black separatists nor radical feminists seeking an overhaul of existing modes of allocation) depends on the dialogical reconciliation of the following three initial positions in opposition to affirmative action: the initial position of the innocent white male, that of the black assimilationist who advocates remedies that are more radical than affirmative action, and that of the female assimilationist who likewise seeks remedies that are more drastic than affirmative action. As we shall see, such a reconciliation is possible, but only in the form of a compromise rather than a consensus. To explore how this compromise might come about, I shall imagine a plausible dialogue between representatives of these three initial positions and shall refer to them respectively as the "Innocent White Male," the "Radical Black Assimilationist," and the "Radical Female Assimilationist."

Having reached the highest stage of reciprocity—that is, the stage of the reciprocity of perspectives—our three protagonists are capable of fully intuiting the position of their respective antagonists as if it were their own. Accordingly, the Innocent White Male fully understands that his antagonists are impatient in their wish to see the prompt elimination of the adverse effects of racism and sexism. By the same token, the latter are fully cognizant of the Innocent White Male's feeling that he is not responsible for past racial and sex first-order discrimination and that he should not therefore be made to bear the brunt of the compensatory burden for such discrimination.

Based on the above mutual understanding, the Innocent White Male would acknowledge the need for the establishment of fair means-regarding equality of opportunity in the spheres of education and employment but would want to achieve it through the means that are likely to require the smallest possible departure from the status quo. Thus, he might favor the institution of remedial educational and job training programs, but oppose race- and gender-based preferential treatment in education and employment. On the other hand, the Radical Black Assimilationist would recognize the whites' interests in maintaining the present system of education and employment allocation but would insist that blacks be immediately granted their proper place within that system, even if that requires removing whites from positions they currently hold in good standing to make room for blacks who would have been holding similar positions absent past and ongoing racial discrimination. Similarly, the Radical Female Assimilationist would want immediate elimination of the disadvantages attributable to sexism, even at the cost of replacing employed men with unemployed women.

At a relatively high level of abstraction, there is a consensus between all three of our protagonists. Consistent with the analysis carried out in section 1, they all want the competition for scarce education and employment to be governed by the principle of fair means-regarding equality of opportunity. At the more concrete level at which the decision must be made concerning which remedy to implement in order to eliminate the deficits in prospects attributable to racism and sexism, however, no such consensus is apparent. The principal issue that divides our three protagonists is that of timing. The Innocent White Male wants to extend the time over which the remedy should be spread, to spare himself from the painful consequences that an accelerated integration of blacks and women in the workforce would produce. The other two protagonists, however, are in a hurry, and do not want any prolonged deferral of goods to which they feel clearly entitled and which they would be already enjoying but for racism and sexism. Under these circumstances, the best that can be hoped for, therefore, is the reaching of a compromise falling somewhere between the initial position of the Innocent White Male and those of his two antagonists.

Affirmative action offers a middle course between these three antagonistic positions and hence looms as a reasonable compromise. The reversal of perspectives should convince the Radical Black Assimilationist and the Radical Woman Assimilationist that the remedy they initially advocated may produce too painful a disruption in the lives of innocent white males who would have to be forced out of employment positions held for years, and on which they had reasonably come to count for the satisfaction of a substantial portion of their needs and wants. From the standpoint of blacks and women, on the other hand, affirmative action may pave a slower path than initially desired toward a restored distributive equilibrium. Affirmative action would equalize the prospects of present and future black and women applicants to universities and for jobs. It would afford no remedy, however, for those who would have been at a university or in the workforce absent racism or sexism, but who are no longer likely to apply for the university education or job that they would have obtained in a discrimination-free society. This raises the question of whether, for the members of the latter group, the adoption of affirmative action over more drastic remedies is likely to produce a greater disruption relative to their life plans than would loss of employment by the Innocent White Male relative to his own life plan.

There is no clear answer to this question because of the large number of variables involved. For example, the value to a black man of a position that he would be awarded under some more radical remedy but not under affirmative action would appear to depend on whether or not he is sufficiently qualified to discharge it successfully. If he is, the position may contribute substantially to his sense of self-respect and professional satisfaction, as well as to his material needs. If he is not sufficiently qualified, however, the position may make him feel uncomfortable, insecure, and inadequate. Accordingly, not being awarded the position may or may not, depending on his qualifications, have a substantial negative impact on the pursuit of his life plan.

Notwithstanding these variables, it seems fair to assume that not being awarded a position as a consequence of the adoption of a more gradual remedy than the one sought initially is *no worse than* losing one's employment to make room for the victims of others. Moreover, replacing seasoned and well-qualified white male employees with persons who may be insufficiently qualified to handle the position adequately would significantly reduce efficiency, and thus contribute to the detriment of all. Also, the adoption of affirmative action does not preclude awarding other forms of compensation to black and female victims who are not in a position to be or become applicants for scarce university places or employment. In sum, if we add the equivalence of the injuries involved, the inevitable decrease in efficiency, and the possibility of alternative forms of compensation, the reversal of perspectives should persuade the Radical Black Assimilationist and the Radical Female Assimilationist that the move from a radical remedy to affirmative action would constitute a reasonable compromise.

From the perspective of the Innocent White Male, affirmative action should also loom as a middle course between adherence to formal or fair (purely forward-looking) means-regarding equality of opportunity—which would be more favorable to his interests but which would tend to perpetuate existing inequalities attributable to first-order discrimination—and the demand for radical and immediate compensation, which he finds unacceptable. For the Innocent White Male, however, a move to affirmative action is bound to be painful. By raising the prospects of success of blacks and women, affirmative action is bound to lower his own prospects, and thus increase his chances of failure. Failure not only inhibits the realization of a person's life plan, but it is also likely to be painful in its own right.

Against the Innocent White Male's suspicion of affirmative action must be set the fact that, for the Radical Black Assimilationist and for the Radical Female Assimilationist, affirmative action represents the bare minimum of integration into the existing system of allocation compatible with the elimination of the position of blacks and women as inferiors. Moreover, through application of the reversal of perspectives test, the Innocent White Male should become persuaded that the adoption of affirmative action to remedy the effects of racism and sexism at the university and in the workforce would amount to a fair compromise. Indeed, as we shall see, that test indicates that the move from formal equality of opportunity (or fair equality involving less radical means, such as remedial programs) to affirmative action is likely to have less of a negative effect on the integrity of his person and on the pursuit of his life plan than the failure to make such a move would have on the integrity of the person and the life plan of the Radical Black Assimilationist and the Radical Female Assimilationist.

As already pointed out, the Innocent White Male who, because of affirmative action, fails to obtain a position that he would otherwise have secured does not thereby become liable to be treated as an inferior. By contrast, the disproportionately small number of blacks or women at the university or in desirable jobs is often linked to treatment as inferiors. For example, if women are considered too emotionally unstable to hold responsible positions, the general lack of women in such positions may be used as an indication of the validity of the negative stereotype in question. Also, as indicated in our discussion of the *Johnson* case, the award through affirmative action of a road dispatcher job to a woman works not only to her benefit but also to that of other women. Indeed, the very existence of a female road dispatcher who discharges her duties competently belies the validity of the negative stereotype that has prevented other women from obtaining similar jobs.

The Innocent White Male should realize that affirmative action is not intended, nor is it likely, to cast him as an inferior. Nevertheless, his failure to obtain a position that would have been his but for affirmative action will be bound to remain painful. The pain associated with failure to secure a scarce position for which one competes, however, is one that is knowingly accepted by everyone who embraces a distributive system governed by the principle of equality of opportunity. No one knows ex ante whether he will fail to secure a coveted position *because* of affirmative action any more than he is likely to know ex ante whether he will succeed in a fair competition not involving any preferential treatment. Therefore, both with and without affirmative action, the Innocent White Male who enters a competition governed by the equal opportunity principle must accept the prospect of failure. Moreover, while affirmative action increases his prospects of failure, it is by no means the only factor likely to do so. For example, an applicant's prospects of success are bound to diminish as the result of an increase in the size and quality of the relevant applicant pool.

The Innocent White Male should accept that affirmative action, in the last analysis, is likely to cause him no greater harm than a sudden unwelcome increase in the size and quality of the pool of applicants against whom he must compete. Accordingly, the reversal of perspectives test should clearly convince him to settle on remedial affirmative action as a matter of fair compromise. Indeed, the increased prospects of failure that affirmative action imposes on the Innocent White Male seem clearly less significant (in terms of the integrity of his person and the pursuit of his life plan) than do the increases in prospects of success that affirmative action would produce for blacks and women (relative to their own sense of integrity and life plans). In other words, while for the Innocent White Male affirmative action means only a somewhat increased chance of failure, for blacks and women it provides the means to effectuate a transition between inferiority and equality. Moreover, even if affirmative action is responsible for the Innocent White Male's failure to succeed in a particular competition, such as Alan Bakke's failure to gain admission to the University of California at Davis' Medical School, this does not usually amount to anything like an all-or-nothing proposition. For example, the rejection of a Bakke from Davis does not mean that he cannot gain admission to another medical school or pursue another honorable, though less desirable, career that will provide him with respect and with a significant number of goods useful in the pursuit of his life plan. On the other hand, the more pervasive racism and sexism are in a given social setting, the more it would seem that affirmative action could play a key role in the transition of blacks and women from a status of inferiority to one of equality.

Based on this assessment of the reversal of perspectives process, the Innocent White Male, the Radical Black Assimilationist, and the Radical Female Assimilationist should all settle on affirmative action as a reasonable compromise. Moreover, based on the previous analysis of probable intragroup dialogical exchanges, all the participants allowed entry into the dialogical process by the reconstructor, and who are neither committed to separatism nor to a wholesale transformation of existing social and economic institutions, should also accept affirmative action as a means to achieve a fair compromise.

The preceding account of the reversal of perspectives test focused on affirmative action in the contexts of university admissions and job hiring. Therefore, the conclusion that affirmative action represents a reasonable compromise extends at least to these two contexts. Moreover, it seems obvious that, absent truly exceptional circumstances, the failure to obtain a promotion would not result in any greater injury than the failure in the first place to secure a desirable position. Similarly, it seems clear that the relatively insignificant decrease in the prospects of success of white businesses produced by minority set-asides like those involved in *Fullilove* and in *Croson* should be much less onerous than losing in the competition for desirable jobs or university admissions. Accordingly, affirmative action also looms as a fair and reasonable compromise in the context of promotions and in that of minority (or gender-based) set-asides.

The justification of affirmative action under the reversal of perspectives test in the context of layoffs, however, is a much more vexing issue. If a reverse seniority layoff policy is viewed as part of an overall scheme to afford job security to those who perform satisfactorily after having obtained a position, then race- or gender-based affirmative action in layoffs very much resembles forcing white males out of their jobs to make room for blacks and women who are entitled to remedies for the injuries they have suffered at the hands of others. On the other hand, however, layoffs can be viewed as an inevitable consequence of a market-based economy relying on the equal opportunity principle, and the reverse seniority policy as a means of redistributing the prospects of dismissal in a way that deviates from what would be optimal from the standpoint of efficiency. Based on this latter view, affirmative action in the context of layoffs would seem akin to preferential treatment in job hiring. In both cases, the Innocent White Male already faces some prospect of having to confront a dreaded result, and affirmative action merely somewhat increases that prospect.

From the perspective of the Radical Black Assimilationist and the Radical Female Assimilationist, layoffs in the order of reverse seniority would simply undo, in bad economic times, what an affirmative action plan was meant to achieve over a substantial time period.[28] From the perspective of the Innocent White Male, on the other hand, a layoff would be more painful than the failure to obtain a position or a promotion. But even if a layoff were as painful as having one's job unexpectedly taken away to be awarded to a victim of racism or sexism, the Innocent White Male engaged in communicative action would have to recognize that there is an important difference between the two. The possibility of a layoff is something that every potential jobholder in the context of the present system of job allocation should realize and has little choice but to accept when he enters into the competition for scarce positions. By contrast, the Innocent White Male who is a jobholder in good standing has no reason to expect in the context of the present system of job allocation that he will be dismissed to make room for a black or woman victim in need of compensation.

Keeping this important difference in mind, it seems fair to argue that the Innocent White Male's injury attributable to affirmative action is not the loss of his job, but only the added pain traceable to his increased prospects of being laid off as a consequence of departures from the reverse seniority order. Consistent with this argument, the negative significance of the increased prospects of being laid off attributable to affirmative action for the Innocent White Male's life plan is likely to diminish in comparison with the negative significance that the failure to extend affirmative action to layoffs would have on the life plans of the Radical Black Assimilationist and the Radical Female Assimilationist. Indeed, such a failure may well lead to a dismantling of the gains in equality and respectability brought about by race- and gender-based affirmative action in hiring. Because of this, the reversal of perspectives test should persuade the Innocent White Male that a fair and reasonable compromise on affirmative action should extend to layoffs.

There is yet one other potential source of conflict that may thwart the reaching of a compromise concerning the legitimacy of affirmative action. Many different groups may claim entitlement to affirmative action, but given circumstances may only support the award of preferential treatment to some but not all such groups. For example, both the Radical Black Assimilationist and the Radical Female Assimilationist may persuasively contend that their group should benefit from affirmative action. But if, because of a lack in resources, preferential treatment cannot be given to both groups, a compromise between the two groups would appear to be uncertain. Thus, if women's demands for affirmative action are rejected, it may be difficult to imagine why they would readily support preferential treatment for blacks.

Notwithstanding these apparent difficulties, it is entirely conceivable that the reversal of perspectives test could establish an order of priority among conflicting claims of entitlement to affirmative action. And based on that order of priority, it would seem quite plausible that a disappointed claimant would support the ultimate award of preferential treatment to members of a rival group. Thus, for example, if blacks were in much greater need than women to receive preferential treatment in order to successfully complete the transition between inferiority and equality, and if society could not afford to provide affirmative action for both women and blacks, the Radical Female Assimilationist who engages in communicative action would have to endorse the legitimacy of race-based affirmative action, even in the absence of any gender-based counterpart.

In summary, the preceding analysis has established that affirmative action need not violate the rights to equal respect or equal opportunity of those who are disadvantaged by it. Moreover, participation in the dialogical process and submission of conflicting claims to the reversal of perspectives test lead to the conclusion that remedial affirmative action should be legitimated as a matter of compromise. Thus, in the context of widely diverging initial positions, remedial affirmative action provides a mutually acceptable middle ground.

4. *Nature and Scope of the Constitutional Justification of Affirmative Action*

In light of the preceding analysis, the constitutional permissibility of affirmative action should extend well beyond what the majority in *Croson* was willing to accept. Systematic reliance on the postulate of equality and on justice as reversible reciprocity leads to the conclusion that the most justified position on the scope of the constitutional legitimacy of affirmative action thus far expressed on the Supreme Court is that of the four justices who joined Justice Brennan's opinion in *Bakke*. According to that position, which was most recently reiterated in Justice Marshall's dissenting opinion in *Croson*, affirmative action is constitutionally permissible if it is used to remedy the present effects of past first-order discrimination. Moreover, consistent with the constitutionalization of fair (global with respect to social assets) means-regarding equality of opportunity, for which I have argued above in section 1, affirmative action should be permissible under certain circumstances even in the absence of invidious past first-order discrimination. These circumstances are present when the prospects of success of the members of a particular group have been reduced relative to those of the remaining members of society as the result of socially induced deprivations that may not have been unjust when they took place.

Whether purely compensatory, or both compensatory and distributive, or else exclusively distributive, constitutionally permissible affirmative action should be both backward- and forward-looking. It should be backward-looking to allow for distinguishing the deprivations of means that the state should rectify from those that the state should not rectify. Further, constitutionally permissible affirmative action must be designed to put its beneficiaries in the competitive position in which they would have been but for first-order discrimination or other cognizable socially induced deprivation. Indeed, unless it merely makes its beneficiaries whole, affirmative action would lead to violations of the equal opportunity principle by providing such beneficiaries with an undeserved advantage.

On the other hand, constitutionally legitimate affirmative action must be forward-looking because, unless past deprivations have present and future effects, preferential treatment projected into the future would upset rather than promote equality of opportunity. Thus, for example, if one assumes that past racial discrimination caused no diminution in any of its victims' prospects of success, to grant them preferential treatment would give them an undue advantage. This is not to say that such victims should not be entitled to some other form of compensation for their past injuries, but only that, under the circumstances, affirmative action would be unjustified. Finally, constitutionally permissible affirmative action must be forward-looking to make it possible to ascertain whether it is likely to trample on the equal opportunity rights of innocent members of the nonpreferred class by unduly lowering their prospects of success beyond the point at which they would have been but for the relevant past cognizable deprivations.

Provided that all the backward- and forward-looking prerequisites to the constitutional legitimacy of affirmative action are met, it should make no difference whether the state dispenses preferential treatment voluntarily or pursuant to a judicial decree, or whether it does it through the governmental entity responsible for a particular cognizable deprivation or any of its other departments or subdivisions. Indeed, in the context of justice as reversible reciprocity, affirmative action is meant to be neither punitive nor narrowly compensatory, in the sense of fitting within the paradigm of compensation on the side of the "wrongdoer."

As pointed out above in section 1, because of differences between philosophical and constitutional practice, the full equalization of means required for strict compliance with the principle of fair means-regarding equality of opportunity should not be made a constitutional requirement. Instead, the constitutional goal should be the achievement of as complete an equalization of means as is possible without the imposition of unacceptable intrusions of the state into intimate private relationships, such as taking children away from their parents to promote equality in the acquisition of educational assets. If unacceptable intrusions are avoided, however, there seems to be no valid objection to the imposition of a positive duty on the state to promote fair equality of opportunity in the competition for scarce public goods. Moreover, as already indicated, the discharge of that positive duty may require the institution of affirmative action even in the absence of any right to, or duty of, compensation. In short, even in the context of constitutional practice, adherence to the principle of fair means-regarding equality of opportunity justifies purely distributive (though it must be in part backward-looking) affirmative action.

To the extent that fair equality of opportunity requires the imposition of positive duties on the state, it runs counter to the Supreme Court's current interpretation of the Fourteenth Amendment. According to that interpretation, only negative duties—that is, duties to refrain from acting, as opposed to duties to act—are constitutionally imposed on the state.[29] Moreover, consistent with the recognition of only negative constitutional duties as being imposed on the state, the constitutionalization of formal means-regarding equal opportunity, but not that of fair equal opportunity, would be legitimate.

When used to restore the integrity of a distributive system based on formal equal opportunity, positive state duties of limited duration should be constitutionally acceptable even in the face of a vision of constitutional individual rights dependent on the maintenance of negative state duties (of noninterference). As it will be remembered, even Justice Scalia, whose views on the subject are among the most restrictive, has accepted affirmative action as constitutional when its use is strictly confined to cases falling within the paradigm of compensation.[30] Further, the constitutionalization of formal equal opportunity justifies using affirmative action even in cases that do not fit within the paradigm of compensation. Indeed, once it is established that the state has interfered with formal equality of opportunity in a way which produces distortions in relative prospects of success that can only be eliminated within a reasonable time through the imposition of affirmative action, then use of the latter would be justified. And this would hold regardless of whether the state acts voluntarily or through an agency or subdivision other than that responsible for the original interference. What is paramount is that the individual victims of state interference with formal equal opportunity be made whole, rather than that state intervention be restricted so as to conform with the paradigm of compensation.

The constitutionalization of formal rather than fair equal opportunity still affords full justification to the position taken by the four justices who joined Justice Brennan's opinion in *Bakke.* So long as present distortions in relative prospects of success are traceable to past state discrimination, affirmative action is constitutionally permissible if it is designed to place competitors for public goods in the position in which they would be but for such past state discrimination. Moreover, in the context of the American experience with laws interfering with the formal equal opportunity rights of blacks and women,[31] adherence to formal equal opportunity should suffice to afford constitutional legitimacy to a broad range of race- and gender-based affirmative action plans. In sum, there is ample justification for the constitutionalization of fair equal opportunity. But even if only formal equal opportunity were deemed to be constitutionalized, the affirmative action plans involved in all ten affirmative action cases before 1990 decided by the Supreme Court would still pass constitutional muster.

In the context of the constitutionalization of fair means-regarding equality of opportunity, affirmative action to remedy the present effects of past cognizable deprivations of means would meet the requirements of the strict scrutiny test under the antidiscrimination principle. Indeed, the achievement of fair equality of opportunity in the competition for public goods would constitute a "compelling" state interest, and affirmative action would under certain circumstances amount to a "necessary" means. Nevertheless, as previously indicated, the antidiscrimination principle is inadequate as a mediating principle, both because it is too vague in theory—as exemplified by the various inconsistent interpretations it received in *Croson*—and because it is too restrictive in practice, as evidenced by the undue privileging of equal treatment and marginal equality over global equality.

Replacement of the antidiscrimination principle with a mediating principle based on a sufficiently elaborated conception of substantive equality appears to have definite advantages. First, reliance on substantive equality would seem to make for greater consistency and integrity than use of the antidiscrimination principle. Adoption of a mediating principle based on fair means-regarding equal opportunity, for example, is not as open-ended as the antidiscrimination principle on the theoretical level, while being more flexible than the latter on the practical level. The strict-scrutiny test is so indeterminate in theory that it can justify both the result in cases like *Bakke, Wygant,* and *Croson* and the opposite result. The principle of fair equality of opportunity, in contrast, would justify upholding, but not invalidating, the affirmative action plans involved in all ten of the Court's affirmative action decisions rendered to date. On the other hand, from a practical standpoint, fair equality of opportunity affords far greater flexibility than the strict-scrutiny test in the determination of which equalities and inequalities should be deemed constitutionally mandated or permissible. Thus, while strict scrutiny as actually applied has strongly disfavored unequal treatment instituted to promote some global equality, fair equality of opportunity, depending on the particular circumstances involved, is as compatible with equal as with unequal treatment. Accordingly, where the equalization of means requires marginal equality, equal treatment would be justified; but where it requires the achievement of some global equality, unequal treatment would be called for.

Second, adoption of a mediating principle based generally on substantive equality, and particularly on fair equality of opportunity, makes it much more difficult to conceal one's substantive values by remaining behind the mystifying veil of process-based constitutional approaches. Thus, for example, while judicial lip service to equality of opportunity is widespread, it seems highly unlikely that justices who have adopted the marginal equality position articulated in *Bakke* could reconcile their judicial conclusions with a genuine commitment to equal opportunity. Accordingly, once forced into the terrain of substantive equality, the proponents of the marginal equality position frequently would either have to invoke a conception of substantive equality that does not rely on equal opportunity—a risky proposition, given the special place held by the principle of equal opportunity in the American ethos (Rae et al. 1981, 64)—or open themselves to the charge of betraying their own professed values. Indeed, from the standpoint of equal opportunity, stubborn adherence to the marginal equality position and to an overly narrow compensatory framework may appear to be but the means employed to insure the preservation of unfair advantages gained through systematic first-order discrimination. And that is certainly not an attractive prospect for any defender of constitutional equality.

Adoption of fair means-regarding equality of opportunity as the mediating constitutional principle applicable in the context of the equal protection clause justifies a "totality of circumstances" approach to the constitutional legitimacy of affirmative action. Indeed, in the most general terms, the constitutional test for the validity of a particular affirmative action plan should be whether, given the totality of prevailing circumstances, such a plan would be best suited to bring about a fair means-regarding equalization of opportunities consistent with equal respect and dignity and with recognition of the integrity of the individual perspectives involved. Moreover, to provide greater guidance to judges and attorneys engaged in constitutional practice, satisfaction of this test can be made to depend chiefly on meeting the following requirements.

With respect to scarce public goods to be allocated by the state (or any of its agencies or subdivisions), there is a constitutional right to fair means-regarding equality. Further, based on this right, the constitutionality of affirmative action should depend on the following six factors: (1) that there is a class of individuals who, through state action or through cognizable systematic societal action condoned or aided by the state, have been deprived of means (or have not been provided with means awarded to the remaining members of society) on the basis of a morally irrelevant characteristic shared by all the members of the class; (2) that there are present adverse effects traceable to such past deprivation; (3) that the class, taken as a whole, is substantially disadvantaged in the competition for the scarce good which is the subject matter of the affirmative action program, in that the deficiency in means attributable to past cognizable deprivations has resulted in reducing the prospects of success of the individual members of the class; (4) that the affirmative action is reasonably calculated to bring the victims' prospects of success to where they most likely would have been, absent the cognizable past deprivation; (5) that no alternative remedy is likely to bring about the requisite equalization of prospects within the same period of time as would the affirmative action program; and (6) that the burden on an innocent member of a nonpreferred group is limited to a decrease in the prospects of obtaining a good, subject to the affirmative action plan, or an increase in the prospects of losing that good in times of economic contraction, provided that the increase or decrease in prospects involved is reasonably calculated to put the innocent nonpreferred individual in a position that is no worse than that in which he or she would have been but for the cognizable deprivation.

From a practical standpoint, the results reached pursuant to the above six-pronged test are likely to vary substantially, depending on what is taken to count as "cognizable past deprivation," on the kind of causal link between such past deprivation and certain present and future disadvantages that is deemed to be constitutionally sufficient, and on the allocation of the burden of proof to demonstrate the existence of a "cognizable deprivation" and to establish that the requisite causal links are present. Based on the legitimate role reserved for affirmative action in the context of the constitutionalization of fair means-regarding equality of opportunity, however, it is possible to specify further these open-ended terms, and thus to promote greater uniformity of results.

The determination of what should count as a cognizable deprivation takes us back to debate on the Supreme Court concerning whether "societal discrimination" affords a sufficient basis upon which to rest the constitutional legitimacy of affirmative action. As discussed in section 1, when the deprivation that purportedly justifies affirmative action consists in past first-order discrimination, no difference should be made under a constitutional principle based on means-regarding equal opportunity between societal discrimination and discrimination in the same sphere of activity as the affirmative action plan under scrutiny. Indeed, since the purpose of affirmative action is to make up for reductions in the prospects of success attributable to past first-order discrimination, the actual sphere of activity marked by such past discrimination should make no difference provided that reductions in prospects traceable to that discrimination are present in the sphere of activity singled out for affirmative action.

The same reasoning applies even if the past deprivation under consideration does not amount to past state discrimination. Accordingly, "cognizable past deprivation" should be understood to encompass past state discrimination, including societal discrimination, past private discrimination encouraged or condoned by the state, and those deprivations of social and educational assets all of which are neither the results of wrongful acts nor the product of a genuinely free choice to forgo available opportunities to pursue more important priorities set by one's life plan.

Consideration of what should amount to a sufficient causal link between a cognizable past deprivation and a present effect remediable by affirmative action leads back to the clash between the two modes of interpretation encountered in *Croson*. As will be remembered, the majority in *Croson* adhered to the atomistic mode of interpretation, while the dissent adopted the ecological mode. The atomistic mode, which relies on the establishment of direct unbroken mechanical links, is suited to isolate extraordinary departures from the norm that produce sharply defined sequences of effects. On the other hand, the ecological mode seems better suited to capture systemic chains of events that may lack crisply demarcated spatial or temporal boundaries, but which may leave profound and widespread imprints over time. To the extent that the "totality of circumstances" approach is warranted, and that affirmative action is intended to remedy deficits in prospects rather than to exact compensation from particular state wrongdoers, the ecological mode of interpretation clearly seems preferable. This is particularly true in the context of a phenomenon as systematic, widespread, and multifaceted as racial- and gender-based discrimination in the United States. Indeed, the ecological mode of interpretation seems especially fit to reveal the complex network that links the harms caused to the rich panoply of discriminatory practices generated by the racist and by the sexist.

Judicial application of the six-pronged constitutional test proposed above to affirmative action plans, even as further specified by the preceding observations, cannot be either merely neutral or purely mechanical. Indeed, substantive analysis and evaluation are required, as complex webs of equalities and inequalities must be disentangled with the principle of fair means-regarding equality of opportunity serving as a mediating principle. Moreover, as we have seen, the judicial approach to the constitutionality of affirmative action based on a definite conception of substantive equality leads to more determinate results while remaining more flexible than the process-based approaches under the antidiscrimination principle. Nevertheless, although reliance on substantive equality may lead to greater determinacy—in the sense of more clearly opening and closing certain paths leading to a limited number of concrete outcomes—it remains sufficiently indeterminate to afford judges a significant measure of discretion.

Substantive equal protection approaches have been criticized as failing to set limits on judicial activism, thus encouraging judges to invade the province of the legislator.[32] While an attempt at a general refutation of this criticism clearly lies beyond the scope of the present work, I will suggest how commitment to a constitutional mediating principle relying on substantive equality may be compatible with a firm demarcation between the respective provinces of the judge and the legislator.

As discussed in chapter 9, justice as reversibility can be applied to three kinds of situations. Applied to the first of these, justice as reversibility operates as the functional equivalent of the contractarian criterion of justice; applied to the second, it remains sui generis; and applied to the third, it operates as the functional equivalent of the utilitarian criterion of justice. Of these three kinds of situations, the third should be left exclusively to the province of the legislator. Indeed, in this kind of situation, all that justice as reversibility requires is that each person's preference be counted once and no more than once. In this kind of situation, therefore, decisions ought to be made according to the will of the majority, and no room for substantive disagreements with the outcome of the majoritarian process is left to the judiciary.

The justification for affirmative action, on the other hand, depends, as we have seen, on the coordination of various antagonistic perspectives. As a consequence of this, it involves the second kind of situation and requires the application of justice as reversibility proper and of the dialogical process that it requires. Further, to a significant extent, the role of the judge in the adversary system of justice is to coordinate the various perspectives of the litigants before her in order to determine who shall prevail.[33] Accordingly, since issues of affirmative action must be resolved by means of the dialogical process of justice as reversible reciprocity, they constitute substantive issues that seem particularly appropriate for judges to decide.

In sum, in the context of justice as reversible reciprocity, the constitutionality of affirmative action can only be determined in relation to criteria of substantive equality by judges willing to undertake the dialogical task of harmonizing a chorus of genuine but antagonistic clamoring voices. Moreover, when the complexities surrounding the concept of equality are properly accounted for, both philosophy and the U.S. Constitution justify affirmative action to remedy systematic deprivations of equality of opportunity for which the government can be held accountable. Affirmative action is controversial because it seeks to remedy inequalities by means of unequal treatment. It also seems radical because it apparently departs from the ideal of equality of opportunity. Strictly speaking, however, affirmative action is conservative insofar as it is designed to eradicate the effects of first-order discrimination without undermining any overall educational or employment scheme that operates in accordance with the principle of equality of opportunity. Indeed, where formal equality of opportunity would merely perpetuate the effects of first-order discrimination and fair equality of opportunity would provide too slow a remedy to satisfy justice as reversible reciprocity, affirmative action becomes necessary to insure the fair and prompt restoration of a system based on genuine equality of opportunity. Ironically, the sooner affirmative action is allowed to complete its mission, the sooner the need for it will altogether disappear.

Cases

Bradwell v. Illinois, 83 U.S. 130 (1873).

Brown v. Board of Education, 347 U.S. 483 (1954).

Brown v. Board of Education II, 349 U.S. 294 (1955).

Burton v. Wilmington Parking Authority, 365 U.S. 715 (1961).

Castaneda v. Partida, 430 U.S. 402 (1977).

City of Richmond v. J. A. Croson Co., 109 S. Ct. 706 (1989).

Craig v. Boren, 429 U.S. 190 (1976).

Dandridge v. Williams, 397 U.S. 471 (1970).

Defunis v. Odegaard, 416 U.S. 312 (1974).

Deshaney v. Winnebago County, 109 S. Ct. 998 (1989).

Douglas v. California, 372 U.S. 353 (1963).

Dred Scott v. Sanford, 19 How. 393 (1857).

Firefighters Local Union No. 1784 v. Stotts, 467 U.S. 561 (1984).

Fullilove v. Klutznick, 448 U.S. 448 (1980).

Green v. County School Board, 391 U.S. 430 (1968).

Griffin v. Illinois, 351 U.S. 12 (1956).

Harper v. Virginia Board of Elections, 383 U.S. 663 (1966).

Johnson v. Transportation Agency, Santa Clara County, California, 480 U.S. 616 (1987).

Katzenbach v. McClung, 379 U.S. 294 (1964).

Keyes v. School District No. 1, 413 U.S. 189 (1973).

Korematsu v. United States, 323 U.S. 214 (1944).

Kotch v. River Port Pilot Commissioners, 330 U.S. 552 (1947).

Kramer v. Union Free School Dist. No. 15, 395 U.S. 621 (1969).

Local No. 93, International Association of Firefighters v. City of Cleveland, 478 U.S. 501 (1986).

Local 28, Sheet Metal Workers' Intern. Ass'n v. E.E.O.C., 478 U.S. 421 (1986).

Marsh v. Alabama, 326 U.S. 501 (1946).

Palmore v. Sidoti, 466 U.S. 429 (1984).

Personnel Administrator of Massachusetts v. Feeney, 422 U.S. 256 (1979).

Plessy v. Ferguson, 163 U.S. 537 (1896).

Regents of University of California v. Bakke, 438 U.S. 265 (1978).

Railways Express Agency v. New York, 336 U.S. 106 (1949).

Reitman v. Mulkey, 387 U.S. 369 (1967).

San Antonio Independent School District v. Rodriguez, 411 U.S. 1 (1973).

Swann v. Charlotte Meckelenburg Board of Education, 402 U.S. 1 (1971).

Shelley v. Kraemer, 334 U.S. 1 (1948).

Trimble v. Gordon, 430 U.S. 762 (1977).

United Jewish Organizations v. Carey, 430 U.S. 144 (1977).

United States v. Cruikshank, 92 U.S. 542 (1875).

United States v. Paradise, 480 U.S. 149 (1987).

United Steelworkers v. Weber, 443 U.S. 193 (1979).

Wisconsin v. Yoder, 406 U.S. 205 (1972).

Wygant v. Jackson Board of Education, 476 U.S. 267 (1986).

Yick Wo v. Hopkins, 118 U.S. 356 (1886).

Notes

Introduction

1. For the legal scholarship on affirmative action, see generally a symposium: *Regents of the University of California* v. *Bakke* (1978); and *DeFunis* symposium (1975). For a sampling of the extensive legal scholarship on the issue see, e.g., Hooks (1987); Choper (1987); Schwartz (1987); Sullivan (1986); Mishkin (1983); Choper (1981–82); Karst and Horowitz (1979); Tribe (1979); Sandalow (1975); Ely (1974); O'Neil (1971); For a sampling of the philosophical literature on affirmative action see, e.g., Fullinwider (1980); Goldman (1979); Dworkin (1985) and (1977); Nagel (1979); Gross (1978); Cohen, Nagel & Scanlon (1977); symposium on reverse discrimination (1979–80).

2. See, e.g., *City of Richmond* v. *J. A. Croson Co.* (1989) at 746 (Marshall, J., dissenting). (Characterizes the approach taken by the Court's majority as being "disingenuous.")

3. On 2 April 1985, the Justice Department announced that "56 cities, counties and states must modify affirmative action plans so as to end the use of numerical goals and quotas designed to increase employment of women, blacks or Hispanic Americans" ("Justice Dept. Presses Drive on Quotas," *New York Times,* 3 April 1985, sec. A, p. 16, col. 1).

4. See "Deep Racial Divisions Persist in New Generation at College," *New York Times,* Monday, 22 May 1989, sec. A, p. 1; "Poll Finds Blacks and Whites 'Worlds Apart,'" *New York Times,* Thursday, 12 January 1989, sec. A, p. 18; "Racial Differences Found in Care Heart Patients Obtain at Hospitals," Friday, 13 January 1989, sec. A, p. 1.

5. See, e.g., "Ruling on Fire Fighters Is Debated in Alabama" and "Lawmakers Aiming at Reversing Bias Rulings," *New York Times,* Wednesday, 14 June 1989, sec. A, p. 18; "Mayors Deplore Affirmative Action Setbacks," *New York Times,* Thursday, 22 June 1989, sec. A, p. 15.

6. See "Mayors Deplore Affirmative Action Setbacks," *New York Times,* 22 June 1989, sec. A, p. 15.

7. See Thalberg (1980), 138.

8. Compare, e.g., Justice Blackmun's statement in support of the affirmative action program in *Regents of University of California* v. *Bakke* (1978) at 407, to the effect that "in order to treat certain persons equally, we must treat them differently," with Justice Stewart's statement in opposition to the affirmative action program in *Fullilove* v. *Klutznick* (1980) at 526, that "nothing in [the] language [of the Fourteenth Amendment] singles out some 'persons' for more 'equal' treatment than others." Also, compare Reynolds (1987), equality requires repudiation of affirmative action, with Hooks (1987), the achievement of equality requires the use of affirmative action.

9. See chapter 7 *infra.*

10. See, e.g., Minow (1987).

Chapter 1: Definition of Key Concepts and Delimitation of Scope of Analysis

1. Compare Justice Blackmun's statements in Regents of *University of California* v. *Bakke* (1978) at 407 to the effect that "in order to treat certain persons equally, we must treat them differently" with Justice Stewart's dissenting opinion in *Fullilove* v. *Klutznick* (1980) at 526, "Our Constitution is color blind and neither knows nor tolerates classes among citizens" (quoting *Plessy* v. *Ferguson* (1896) (Harlan, J., dissenting).

2. But not all philosophers have accepted the proposition that justice can be equated with equality. See, e.g., Lucas (1980); Stone (1980); and Flew (1978).

3. See note 1, *supra.*

4. *Trimble* v. *Gordon* (1980) at 780.

5. *Trimble* v. *Gordon* (1980); See also Perry (1979) 1027–28.

6. See Rae (1981), 144.

7. See Rae (1981), 47.

8. State action has been interpreted broadly to include allocations by private agents who perform a "public function," see *Marsh* v. *Alabama* (1946), or who have a significant "nexus" with the state. See, e.g., *Burton* v. *Wilmington Parking Authority* (1961).

9. See, e.g., *Burton* v. *Wilmington Parking Authority* (1961).

10. See *Marsh* v. *Alabama* (1946).

11. It is, of course, possible, consistent with logic, that there be constitutional support for affirmative action, but no corresponding acceptable philosophical support for it. This could clearly happen in the case of a constitution explicitly mandating affirmative action in given circumstances. Inasmuch, however, as this is not the case with the United States Constitution, the ramifications of this logic need not be further explored for purposes of the present analysis.

12. See Williams (1971), 116, 137.

13. See Tussman and tenBroek (1949).

14. See Gutmann (1980), 18; Lukes (1973), 125–37.

15. See *Shelley* v. *Kraemer* (1948).

16. See Rawls: "A person's good is determined by what is for him the most rational long-term plan of life. . . . To put it briefly, the good is the satisfaction of rational desire" (Rawls [1971], 92–93).

17. In this connection, see Dworkin (1977), distinguishing between the right to equal treatment and the right to treatment as an equal.

18. See Dworkin (1977), 227.

19. For further discussion of what constitutes an opportunity, see Rosenfeld (1986).

20. See Aristotle (1925).

21. See, e.g., Flew (1978) and Nozick's criticism of Rawls' broad conception of distributive justice as treating goods as though they were "manna from heaven" instead of being historically produced and subject to antecedent claims (Nozick [1974], 199).

22. From the standpoint of subject-regarding equality, by contrast, it is possible that the gain and the loss are not equivalent. Thus, for example, the stealing of an heirloom may represent a much greater loss from the standpoint of the victim than the corresponding gain to the thief, whose benefit is presumably exclusively a function of the use value and/or exchange value of the stolen good.

23. See Lucas (1980), 208, stating that there are some philosophers for whom justice consists simply in keeping one's agreements.

24. See Coleman (1983), 1374.

25. See Greenawalt (1983), 16.

26. 29 C.F.R. Section 1608.3 (c) (1) (1985).

27. 29 C.F.R. Section 1608.3 (c) (2).

28. 29 C.F.R. Section 1608.3 (c) (4).

29. 29 C.F.R. Section 1608.4 (c).

30. Ibid.

31. See EEOC Compliance Manual CCH § 2314 Section 607.15 (1985) "An affirmative action plan must be designed to . . . break down old patterns of . . . hierarchy" and "might include as a goal a gradual restructuring of the production process." An employer may have to eliminate "selection procedures or criteria" that have "an adverse impact on a particular minority group or on women."

Chapter 2: Libertarian Justice and Affirmative Action

1. See Locke (1960), sections 6, 44, 87, 123 and 173; Nozick (1974), 26, 149.

2. See Nozick (1974), 151.

3. See Title II of the Civil Rights Act of 1964, 42 U.S.C. Sections 2000a–2000a–6, prohibiting discrimination in most privately owned hotels and restaurants.

4. See Nozick (1974), 57 ff.

5. See Nozick (1974).

6. See Goldman (1979), 171.

7. See Posner (1979), 171.

8. See Nozick (1974), 158, citing Hayek's conclusion that "in a free society there will be distribution in accordance . . . with the perceived value of a person's actions and service to others."

9. See also Hayek (1979), 151, stating that the power of organizations is much greater than that of the individual and thus may have to be restricted by law in ways in which the individual does not. In particular, organizations must be denied rights to discriminate that are an important attribute of freedom of the individual.

10. See *Regents of University of California* v. *Bakke* (1978) at 371 (Brennan, J., concurring in part and dissenting in part). (Segregation enforced by criminal penalties against private colleges.)

11. See *Yick Wo* v. *Hopkins* (1886). (Race neutral law administered in a racist manner.)

Chapter 3: Contractarian Justice and Affirmative Action

1. See Rosenfeld (1985a).
2. See chapter 1, section 2.
3. See Goldman (1979), 179, 181.
4. See, e.g., *Bradwell* v. *Illinois* (1873). (Woman was refused admission to the Illinois bar and hence prevented from practicing law on account of her sex.)
5. See Goldman (1979), 76–82.
6. Ibid., 80–81.
7. This is based on an example provided by Fullinwider. See Fullinwider (1977).

Chapter 4: Utilitarian Justice and Affirmative Action

1. See Goldman (1979), 141.
2. See Fullinwider (1980), 250.
3. Cf. Fullinwider (1980), 68.
4. See Goldman (1979), 155.
5. See Fullinwider (1980), 88–89.
6. Ibid., 90.
7. See Thomson (1977), 31–33.
8. Ibid.
9. Cf. Fullinwider (1977), 217–20.
10. Dworkin also elaborates an alternative justification of affirmative action which he terms the "ideal approach," but which will not be considered here. See Dworkin (1977), 232ff.
11. See Williams (1971).
12. This example is inspired by the one in Dworkin (1977), 227.
13. See Dworkin (1977), 235.
14. Fullinwider divides jobs into three categories: "high skill" (e.g., pilot), "medium skill" (e.g., plumber), and "low skill" (e.g., janitor) (Fullinwider [1980], 881).
15. See Goldman (1979), 56, 168.
16. As MacIntyre (1977) has sought to demonstrate, utilitarianism itself cannot resolve the question of whether long-term benefits ought to take precedence over short-term ones.
17. See, e.g., J. Bentham: "There is no one who knows what is for your interest so well as yourself" quoted in Pitkin (1967), 198; J. S. Mill, *On Liberty* (1970), 206–07.
18. John Stuart Mill drew a distinction between an individual's "real" and "apparent" interests (Pitkin [1967], 204). He believed that since the individual's "real" interests are often long-range, remote and hard to discern, he or she is often prone to follow narrow and selfish "apparent" interests, even though they cannot ultimately bring him or her as much happiness. As Pitkin points out,

however, Mill's distinction may have certain virtues but is made at the price of contradicting the axiom that the individual is the best judge of self-interest.

Chapter 5: Egalitarian Justice and Affirmative Action

1. See chapter 1.
2. Ibid.
3. The egalitarianism etched by Nagel seems to conform to the third version discussed above. (See Nagel [1979], 90–127).
4. See Nagel (1979), 95; Goldman (1979), 178.
5. See chapter 1.
6. See Nagel (1979), 95; Goldman (1979), 146: Egalitarian advocates randomization in award of position for those who demonstrate a certain minimum level of competence.
7. See chapter 3.
8. See, e.g., Nagel (1979), 94–97; Sher (1979) 85–87.
9. See Nagel (1979), 102; Sher (1979), 85–86.
10. See Nagel (1979), 96.
11. Ibid., 99.
12. Ibid., 101.
13. See Sher (1979), 95.

Chapter 6: Constitutional Equality and Equal Protection

1. A practice is "a complex form of socially established activity that is both made possible and given structure by implicit rules, norms, standards and conventions" (Fallon [1987], 1232). See also MacIntyre (1981), 176–89.
2. By state, I mean both the federal government and/or any of its subdivisions or agencies and the government of any of the states and/or any of its subdivisions or agencies.
3. See, e.g., Gunther (1985), 20.
4. See Greenawalt (1983), 7.
5. See Dworkin (1977), 135–36.
6. See Fallon (1987), 1205–06.
7. See, generally, Greenawalt (1983), 7–10.
8. U.S. CONST. amend. XIV 1.
9. *Trimble* v. *Gordon* (1977) at 779 (Rehnquist, J., dissenting).
10. See, e.g., Dimond (1982), 502; Fallon (1987), 1205, 1244, 1262, 1271; Dworkin (1977), 135; (1985), 298; (1986), 354; and O'Fallon (1979), 31.
11. See Dworkin, "There is no language in the Constitution whose plain meaning forbids affirmative action" (Dworkin [1985], 298).
12. See, e.g., Fallon (1987), 1254.

13. See Dworkin (1986), 362. The framers of the Fourteenth Amendment had a variety of political opinions concerning racial segregation.

14. Cf., e.g., Ely (1980) with Dworkin (1986).

15. See Fallon (1987), 1279.

16. *Shelley* v. *Kraemer* (1948).

17. In addition to Karst and O'Fallon, who were mentioned in the preceding section, other constitutional scholars, such as Dworkin, Baker, and Richards, also elaborate constitutional theories of the equal protection clause that are based on the values embedded in the postulate of equality. See Dworkin (1977), 135, 147; (1986), 362, 381–82; Baker (1983); Richards (1986).

18. Cf. Dworkin's endorsement of the normative proposition that individuals are morally equal as individuals as being valid in the context of political philosophy (Dworkin [1978]).

19. See Dworkin (1977), 133; (1986), 382.

20. See Dworkin (1986), 362.

21. Although several constitutional scholars make reference to it, there is no unanimity concerning the precise contours of the antidiscrimination principle. For a view that differs in several particulars from that elaborated by Fiss, see Brest (1976).

22. See O'Fallon (1979), 51; See also Karst: there is "a widely shared assumption that the equal protection clause lacks substantive content" (Karst [1977], 4).

23. Cf. *Trimble* v. *Gordon* (1977), 780: The "general principle [of equal protection] is that persons similarly situated should be treated similarly" (Rehnquist, J., dissenting).

24. See Tussman and tenBroek (1949).

25. See, e.g., *Railways Express Agency* v. *New York* (1949).

26. See, e.g., *Craig* v. *Boren* (1976).

27. See, e.g., *Korematsu* v. *United States* (1944); *Palmore* v. *Sidoti* (1984).

28. See, e.g., Greenawalt: "in some suspect classification cases, the [Supreme] Court has weighed ends, even though it has not been explicit about what it is doing" (Greenawalt [1975], 565*n.41*).

29. See Sherry (1984), 91–92.

30. See *Regents of University of California* v. *Bakke* (1978), (Brennan, J., concurring).

31. See Fiss (1977), 113.

32. See chapter 1.

33. Ibid.

34. As Walzer states, "The arguments for a minimal state have never recommended themselves to any significant portion of mankind. The political community grows by invasion as previously excluded groups, one after another . . . demand their share of security and welfare" (Walzer [1983], 74).

35. As Dworkin states, "the Constitution cannot sensibly be read as demanding that the nation and every state follow a utilitarian or libertarian or resource egalitarian or any other particular conception of equality in fixing on strategies for pursuing general welfare" (Dworkin [1986], 382).

36. See *Dandridge* v. *Williams* (1970).

37. See, e.g., *Harper* v. *Virginia Board of Elections* (1966); and Gunther: "The 1787 Constitution left it to the states to determine who should have the right to

vote in national as well as state elections" and "The 'Republican form of government' guarantee, Art. IV S. 4 has been held to be nonjusticiable" (Gunther [1985], 811, 811*n*.2).

38. See, e.g., *Griffin* v. *Illinois* (1956).

39. See, e.g., *San Antonio Independent School District* v. *Rodriguez* (1973).

40. See, e.g., *Brown* v. *Board of Education* (1954) at 493: "if the state has undertaken to provide for a basic education," it is a right that must be made available to all on equal terms.

41. Since the interference would either be through the enactment of discriminatory laws or through discriminatory actions taken under the color of law, there would be no difficulty in satisfying the state action requirement of the Fourteenth Amendment. For a judicial statement of that requirement, see *United States* v. *Cruikshank* (1875).

42. As Justice Harlan stated in *Douglas* v. *California* (1963) at 362, "The Equal Protection Clause does not impose on the State 'an affirmative duty to lift the handicaps flowing from differences in economic circumstances.'" (Harlan, J., dissenting; quoting *Griffin* v. *Illinois*, 351 U.S. 12 [1956]).

43. See Maguire: Blacks are treated as the lowest castes of society having "never been accorded their full status of humanity" (Maguire [1978], 883–84).

44. See chapter 3.

45. *Harper* v. *Virginia Board of Elections* (1966).

46. *Kramer* v. *Union Free School Dist. No. 15* (1969).

47. *Griffin* v. *Illinois* (1956).

48. Ibid.

49. *Douglas* v. *California* (1963).

50. *Dandridge* v. *Williams* (1970) at 485.

51. *Douglas* v. *California* (1963) at 362.

52. See Rae et al. (1981), 64: equality of opportunity is the most compelling element of our national ideology.

53. Wilkinson (1975), 985.

54. See, e.g., Wilkinson (1975), 985.

55. *Regents of the University of California* v. *Bakke* (1978).

56. 29 U.S.C. 2000e.

57. Executive Order No. 11, 246, 3 C.F.R. 339, S 101 (1965).

58. See Wilkinson (1975), 984.

59. *Brown* v. *Board of Education* (1954), 495.

60. Ibid., 493.

61. See *Brown* v. *Board of Education* (1955); *Green* v. *County School Board* (1968); *Swann* v. *Charlotte Meckelenburg Board of Education* (1971); *Keyes* v. *School District No. 1* (1973).

62. *Swann* v. *Charlotte Meckelenburg Board of Education* (1971) at 30–31. (Busing is permissible to achieve school integration.)

63. *Kotch* v. *River Port Pilot Commissioners* (1947) at 566 (Rutledge, J., dissenting).

64. As Wilkinson states, "inequality of opportunity simply does not fit neatly on either the higher or lower level of the two-tiered test, as the suspect class compelling state interest formula might imply" (Wilkinson [1975], 984).

65. *Personnel Administrator of Massachusetts* v. *Feeney* (1979) at 265.

66. Ibid.
67. *San Antonio Independent School District* v. *Rodriguez* (1973).
68. Ibid.
69. Ibid., at 23–24.
70. Ibid., at 24.

Chapter 7: The Constitutional Dimension of Affirmative Action

1. By "sphere of assimilation," I mean a sphere of activity within which a particular difference, such as race or gender, ought to be considered as irrelevant, and where it ought to be treated ideally as though it did not exist. See Wasserstrom (1977) discussing racism, sexism, and preferential treatment from the standpoint of an assimilationist ideal.

2. See *Green* v. *County School Board* (1968): *Swann* v. *Charlotte Meckelenburg Board of Education* (1971).

3. See *Brown* v. *Board of Education* (1954) at 495.

4. See *Green* v. *County School Board* (1968). A color-blind plan is insufficient to bring about school integration.

5. See Choper (1987).

6. See, e.g., *United States* v. *Paradise* (1987) (a five-to-four decision with no majority opinion); *Local 28, Sheet Metal Workers' Intern. Ass'n* v. *E.E.O.C.* (1986) (another five-to-four decision with only a plurality opinion on the constitutional issue); *Wygant* v. *Jackson Board of Education* (1986) (another five-to-four decision with no majority opinion); *Fullilove* v. *Klutznick* (1980) (no majority opinion); and *Regents of the University of California* v. *Bakke* (no majority opinion).

7. See *Regents of University of California* v. *Bakke* (1978).

8. Ibid., at 407.

9. A good example is Justice Powell's opinion in *Regents of University of California* v. *Bakke* (1978) at 269–320. In response to the Davis Medical School's argument that its program served the purpose of countering the effects of "societal discrimination," (*Bakke* [1978], 306), Powell stated that the Court has "never approved a classification that aids persons perceived as members of relatively victimized groups at the expense of other innocent individuals in the absence of judicial, legislative, or administrative findings of constitutional . . . violations." (*Bakke* [1978], 307).

10. See Sullivan (1986); see also, e.g., Justice Stewart joined by Justice Rehnquist dissenting in *Fullilove* v. *Klutznick* (1980): preferential treatment may be legitimate to compensate actual victims of state first-order discrimination.

11. See, e.g., Justice Stewart's dissent in *Fullilove* v. *Klutznick* (1980).

12. Representative of this approach is Justice Brennan's opinion in *Regents of University of California* v. *Bakke* (1978) at 355–62. For an endorsement of a purely distributive use of affirmative action, see Justice Stevens' dissent in *Wygant* v. *Jackson Board of Education* (1986) at 313–20.

13. *Regents of University of California* v. *Bakke* (1978) at 305. In this chapter, hereafter cited parenthetically in text by page.

14. See Sherry (1984), 107.

15. Ibid.

16. *United Steelworkers* v. *Weber* (1979) at 199–200. In this chapter, hereafter cited parenthetically in text by page.

17. See 703(a) of Title VII, 78 Stat. 255 as amended, 86 Stat. 109, 42 U.S.C. 2000e–2(a).

18. Days (1987), 461.

19. See Days (1987), 461–62*n*.30, 461.

20. *Fullilove* v. *Klutznick* (1980) at 475, 477–78. In this chapter, hereafter cited parenthetically in text by page.

21. *Firefighters Local Union No. 1784* v. *Stotts* (1984) at 565. In this chapter, hereafter cited parenthetically in text by page.

22. *Wygant* v. *Jackson Board of Education* (1986) at 270. In this chapter, hereafter cited parenthetically in text by page.

23. See Fallon and Weiler (1984), 5.

24. See Fallon and Weiler (1984), 56–57.

25. *Local 28, Sheet Metal Workers' Intern. Ass'n* v. *E.E.O.C.* (1986) at 427*n*.2. In this chapter, hereafter cited parenthetically in text by page.

26. *Local No. 93, International Association of Firefighters* v. *City of Cleveland* (1986). In this chapter, hereafter cited parenthetically in text by page.

27. *United States* v. *Paradise* (1987).

28. *United States* v. *Paradise* (1987). In this chapter, hereafter cited parenthetically in text by page.

29. *Johnson* v. *Transportation Agency Santa Clara County, California* (1987) at 626–27. In this chapter, hereafter cited parenthetically in text by page.

30. *Wygant* v. *Jackson Board of Education* (1986) at 315–16.

31. *Johnson* v. *Transportation Agency Santa Clara County, California,* 480 U.S. 616 (1987) at 632.

32. Cf. *Wisconsin* v. *Yoder* (1972). Based on their constitutional rights to the free exercise of religion, the Amish were exempted from completing mandatory secondary education.

33. Even assuming that in the past all women contributed to the formation of the social attitudes that presently result in the decrease of opportunities for women with respect to certain job categories, daughters and granddaughters cannot be fairly charged with responsibility for the voluntary acts of their mothers and grandmothers.

34. *City of Richmond* v. *J. A. Croson Co.* (1989) at 721–22. In this chapter, hereafter cited parenthetically in text by page.

35. In *Fullilove* v. *Klutznick* (1980), the set-aside was mandated by Congress, which was acting, inter alia, pursuant to its special powers under Section 5 of the Fourteenth Amendment. The opinions of both Justice O'Connor and Justice Scalia in *City of Richmond* v. *J. A. Croson Co.* (1989) at 719–20 and 736–37 lay great emphasis on distinguishing *Fullilove* on the grounds that what is permissible for Congress under Section 5 of the Fourteenth Amendment may be forbidden to state and municipal governments under Section 1. Justices Kennedy and Marshall disagreed with Justices O'Connor and Scalia on this point, however, rejecting the proposition that a law that violates equal protection when enacted by a state could become a guarantee of equal protection if enacted by Congress

(Kennedy, J., concurring in part and concurring in the judgment; Marshall, J., dissenting). Leaving federalism issues aside, the only significant difference between the two plans was that, in *City of Richmond* v. *J. A. Croson Co.* (1989) at 713, there was a 30 percent set-aside, while in *Fullilove* v. *Klutznick* (1980) at 454, the set-aside was 10 percent. However, in *Fullilove* the relevant minority population represented between 15 percent and 18 percent of the total population (Fullilove [1980] at 459), while in *Richmond* it represented 50 percent (*Richmond* [1989] at 722).

36. Justice Stevens joined the majority's holding but did not embrace the strict scrutiny test. Indeed Justice Stevens' concurring opinion appears to rely on an intermediate scrutiny standard. See *City of Richmond* v. *J. A. Croson Co.* (1989) at 732–33 (Stevens, J., concurring in judgment), arguing that the Court must look at characteristics of advantaged and disadvantaged classes that may justify disparate treatment.

37. See *Regents of University of California* v. *Bakke* (1978) at 269–320.

38. *Regents of University of California* v. *Bakke* (1978) at 269–320.

39. *Wygant* v. *Jackson Board of Education* (1986) at 274–77.

40. Ibid.; *Regents of University of California* v. *Bakke* (1978) at 307–09.

41. *Wygant* v. *Jackson Board of Education* (1986) at 277–78.

Chapter 8: The Limitations of the Major Liberal Philosophical Conceptions of the Justice of Affirmative Action

1. "Welfare without right is not a good. Similarly right without welfare is not the good" (Hegel [1971], 87).

2. See Rosenfeld (1985a).

3. See Rosenfeld (1985b), 852–53*n.46* and 865–66, for a more extended discussion of this point.

4. See Hegel (1979), 111–19; Rosenfeld (1989a).

5. See, generally, Todorov (1982).

6. See chapter 2.

7. Ibid.

8. See Locke (1960), 334; Rosenfeld (1985a), 788–89.

9. See chapter 2.

10. See, e.g., *Katzenbach* v. *McClung* (1964). (Federal district court concluded that if Alabama restaurant owner served blacks he would lose substantial business.)

11. See, e.g., *Reitman* v. *Mulkey* (1967). (Repeal of state real estate antidiscrimination law held to violate equal protection clause.)

12. See chapter 5.

13. See Hare (1979).

14. See Rawls (1971), 33.

15. Ibid., 94.

16. See Wasserstrom (1977).

17. See, e.g., Benhabib (1986).

Chapter 9: Justice as Reversibility, Equality, and the Right to Be Different

1. See chapter 3.
2. See Crenshaw (1988), 1379.
3. See Gouldner (1973), 242ff.
4. See chapter 8, section 5.
5. Kohlberg's entire project, grounded on Piaget's genetic structuralism, depends on certain assumptions concerning the process of cognitive and moral development of children and adults, which have been attacked as being empirically unwarranted. I have no occasion to comment on either Kohlberg's claims or the criticisms that they have generated inasmuch as the indication of justice as reversibility as a normative principle in the service of the postulate of equality is not dependent on the empirical validity of Kohlberg's claims.
6. See Kohlberg (1981), 411–12.
7. See Kohlberg (1979), 261ff.
8. Hegel (1979), at 111–19; Rosenfeld (1989a).
9. See, e.g., Binder (1989); Bush (1989).
10. See *Dred Scott* v. *Sandford* (1857); Maguire (1978).
11. See Kohlberg (1979), 265–72; See also Kohlberg (1981), 201–02.
12. See Kohlberg (1979), 266.
13. Ibid., 262; Kohlberg (1981), 166. (Equation of universalizability with reversibility.)
14. Ibid., 267.
15. Kohlberg himself asserts that Rawls' original position behind the veil of ignorance exemplifies the "formalist idea" that moral judgments must be reversible (Kohlberg [1981], 197). It is true that Rawls' original position represents a reversible situation, but it is reversible only in a purely formal sense. The effect of the veil of ignorance is to remove from each individual that which makes his or her own perspective different from that of others. What remains is a single perspective that all individuals in the original position share. Hence, although the individual perspectives in the original position are fully reversible, because all individual differences have been purged, the presence of reversibility remains purely trivial. Indeed, reversibility, in a context where all differences have been removed, amounts to no more than an acknowledgement that others have a perspective just as I do.
16. See Dworkin (1975).
17. Cf. Rawls (1971), 217, on tolerance of the intolerant.
18. *Castaneda* v. *Partida* (1977) at 503 (Marshall, J., concurring).
19. See Tribe (1978), 1061.
20. See, e.g., Lukes (1982); MacCarthy (1982); and Thompson (1982).
21. Universalization is understood by Habermas to be a bridge principle much like the principle of induction (Lukes [1982], 141).
22. See Habermas (1975), 110.
23. Habermas' concept of generalizable interest, which he defines in terms of what all can want, is reminiscent of Rousseau's notion of the general will. According to Rousseau, the general will is the sum of the differences between all

the individual wills, or the "agreement of all interests" that is "produced by opposition to that of each" (Rousseau [1947], 26). Moreover, according to Rousseau's conception, the general will is not simply imposed from the outside but is instead supposed to be voluntarily assumed by each individual in his or her capacity as citizen (ibid., 14, 18). Notwithstanding this, if the individual refuses to give up private interests that conflict with the public interests, Rousseau is unambiguous as to what must then be done. In his own famous words, "whoever refuses to obey the general will shall be compelled to it by the whole body: this fact only forces him to be free" (Rousseau [1967], 18). Thus, from premises that are apparently individualistic in nature, and in spite of the highly voluntaristic character of his theory, Rousseau is lead to embrace positions which, at least in the opinion of some commentators, make him a forerunner of totalitarianism. See Masters (1968), 315.

24. See Lukes (1982), 141.

25. For a definition of "imperfect procedural justice," see chapter 1.

26. See Gilligan (1982), 18.

27. Ibid., 100.

Chapter 10: Toward an Integrated Philosophical and Constitutional Justification of Affirmative Action

1. See Walzer (1983), 19–20.

2. See, e.g., *United Steelworkers* v. *Weber* (1979; Rehnquist, J., dissenting). Title VII's purpose is to promote equality of opportunity, hence it does not permit the use of racial quotas.

3. See *City of Richmond* v. *J. A. Croson Co.* (1989); Rosenfeld (1989b), 1736.

4. See Goldman (1979), 127–28. The time lapse between discrimination in education and job application makes the problem very complex.

5. Cf. *Regents of the University of California* v. *Bakke* (1978; Marshall, J., concurring in part and dissenting in part): "In light of the sorry history of discrimination and its devastating impact on the lives of Negroes, bringing the Negro into the mainstream of American life should be a state interest of the highest order. To fail to do so is to ensure that America will forever remain a divided society."

6. See, e.g., *Fullilove* v. *Klutznick* (1980); *United States* v. *Paradise* (1987).

7. See *Wisconsin* v. *Yoder* (1972).

8. See *Deshaney* v. *Winnebago County* (1989).

9. *Wygant* v. *Jackson Board of Education* (1986; Stevens, J., dissenting).

10. See, e.g., Walzer: Community is the most important good that gets distributed (Walzer [1983], 28–29); and membership in community is distributed by members to outsiders (Walzer [1983], 32).

11. See Bayles (1977), 305.

12. See *Regents of University of California* v. *Bakke* (1978), 387–402 (Marshall, J., concurring in part and dissenting in part).

13. See, e.g., *Castaneda* v. *Partida* (1977).

14. See Bayles (1977), 304.

15. Voting Rights Act of 1965, 42 U.S.C. § 1973.

16. *United Jewish Organization* v. *Carey* (1977) at 167.

17. Ibid.

18. See, e.g., *Regents of University of California* v. *Bakke* (1978); *City of Richmond* v. *J. A. Croson Co.* (1989).

19. See *Wygant* v. *Jackson Board of Education* (1986; Stevens, J., dissenting).

20. See *Regents of University of California* v. *Bakke* (1978), 357–58 (Brennan, J., concurring in part and dissenting in part): Whites are not stigmatized by preferential minority admissions program.

21. See, e.g., Justice Marshall's opinions in *Regents of University of California* v. *Bakke* (1978) and *City of Richmond* v. *J. A. Croson Co.* (1989); see also Hooks (1987).

22. See Sowell (1984), 37–60.

23. See Sowell (1984), 46, 47; See also Crenshaw (1988), 1377.

24. See, e.g., Schlafly (1977); Morgan (1973); Bryant (1976); see also, Andrea Dworkin (1983) for a discussion of the impact of right-wing women.

25. See, e.g., MacKinnon (1987) 3, 32–45 (social relations between the sexes are structured so as to allow for male domination); Scales (1986); cf. Abrahms (1989) (dominant male norms are transformed through integration norms reflecting women's needs and experience).

26. Representative of this view is the approach taken by Justice O'Connor in *Johnson* v. *Transportation Agency, Santa Clara County, California* (1987) at 653, finding that evidence sufficient for a prima facie Title VII action "itself suggests that the absence of women or minorities in a workforce cannot be explained by general societal discrimination alone and that remedial action is appropriate."

27. See, e.g., *Bradwell* v. *Illinois* (1873): (Women can be constitutionally barred from practicing law). See also Schneider and Taub (1982).

28. Cf. *Firefighters Local Union No. 1784* v. *Stotts* (1984; Blackmun, J., dissenting): Layoffs according to a seniority system "would adversely affect blacks significantly out of proportion to their representation."

29. See *Deshaney* v. *Winnebago County* (1989).

30. See *City of Richmond* v. *J. A. Croson Co.* (1989; Scalia, J., concurring).

31. See, e.g., *Brown* v. *Board of Education* (1954); *Bradwell* v. *Illinois* (1873).

32. See Sherry (1984), 98.

33. See, e.g., Hazard (1978), 121: the adversary system is superior because "it is better to have conflicting preliminary hypotheses and supporting proofs presented by the parties so that the judge's mind can be kept open until all the evidence is at hand."

Bibliography

Abrahms, Kathryn. 1989. Gender discrimination and the transformation of workplace norms. *Vanderbilt Law Review* 42:1183.

Aristotle. 1925. *Nichomachean ethics.* Book V. Trans. D. Ross. Oxford: Oxford University Press.

Baker, C. E. 1983. Outcome equality or equality of respect: The substantive content of equal protection. *University of Pennsylvania Law Review* 131:933.

Bayles, Michael. 1977. Reparations to wronged groups. In *Reverse discrimination,* ed. B. Gross. New York: Prometheus Books.

Benhabib, Seyla. 1986. *Critique, norm and utopia: A study of the foundations of critical theory.* New York: Columbia University Press.

Benn, S. I. and R. S. Peters. 1965. *The principles of political thought.* New York: Free Press.

Bennett, Robert W. 1984. Objectivity in constitutional law. *University of Pennsylvania Law Review.* 132:445.

Berger, Raoul. 1977. *Government by judiciary: The transformation of the Fourteenth Amendment.* Cambridge: Harvard University Press.

Berlin, Isaiah. 1977. *Concepts and categories.* New York: Viking Press.

Binder, Guyora. 1989. Mastery, slavery and emancipation. *Cardozo Law Review* 10:1435.

Brest, Paul. 1976. The Supreme Court 1975 term foreword: In defense of the antidiscrimination principle. *Harvard Law Review* 90:1.

Bryant, Anita. 1976. *Bless this house.* New York: Bantam.

Bush, Jonathan. 1989. Hegelian slaves and the antebellum South. *Cardozo Law Review* 10:1517.

Choper, Jesse H. 1981–82. The constitutionality of affirmative action: Views from the Supreme Court. *Kentucky Law Journal* 79:1.

———. 1987. Continued uncertainty as to the constitutionality of remedial racial classifications: Identifying the pieces of the puzzle. *Iowa Law Review* 72:255.

Coleman, Jules. 1983. Moral theories of torts: Their scope and limits. Part II. *Law & Philosophy* 2:3.

Cohen, Marshall, Thomas Nagel, and Thomas Scanlon. 1977. *Equality and preferential treatment.* Princeton: Princeton University Press.

Crenshaw, Kirberle. 1988. Race, reform and retrenchment: Transformation and legitimation in antidiscrimination law. *Harvard Law Review* 101:1331.

Days, Drew S., III. 1987. *Fullilove. Yale Law Journal* 96:453.

Dimond, Paul R. 1982. Strict construction and judicial review of racial discrimination under the equal protection clause: Meeting Raoul Berger on interpretivist grounds. *Michigan Law Review* 80:462.

Dworkin, Andrea. 1983. *Right-wing women.* New York: G. P. Putnam's Sons.

Dworkin, Ronald. 1975. The original position. In *Reading Rawls: Critical studies of a theory of justice,* ed. Norman Daniels. New York: Basic Books.

———. 1977. *Taking rights seriously.* Cambridge: Harvard University Press.

———. 1978. Liberalism. In *Public and private morality,* ed. Stuart Hampshire. Cambridge: Cambridge University Press.

———. 1985. *A matter of principle.* Cambridge: Harvard University Press.

———. 1986. *Law's empire.* Cambridge: Harvard University Press, Belknap Press.

Ely, John Hart. 1974. The constitutionality of reverse discrimination. *University of Chicago Law Review* 41:723.

———. 1980. *Democracy and distrust: A theory of judicial review.* Cambridge: Harvard University Press.

Fallon, Richard H., Jr. 1987. A constructivist coherence theory of constitutional interpretation. *Harvard Law Review* 100:1189.

Fallon, Richard H., Jr., and Paul M. Weiler. 1984. *Firefighters* v. *Stotts:* Conflicting models of racial justice. *Supreme Court Review* 1984:1.

Feher, Ferenc, and Agnes Heller. 1980. Forms of equality. In *Justice,* ed. Eugene Kamenka and Alice Erh-Soon Tay. New York: St. Martin's.

Feinberg, Joel. 1973. *Social philosophy.* Englewood Cliffs, N.J.: Prentice-Hall.

Fiss, Owen. 1977. Groups and the equal protection clause. In *Equality and preferential treatment,* ed. Cohen, Nagel, and Scanlon. Princeton: Princeton University Press.

Flew, Anthony. 1978. Equality or justice. *Midwest Studies in Philosophy* 3: 176–194.

Fullinwider, Robert. 1977. On preferential hiring. In *Feminism and philosophy,* ed. Mary Vetterling-Braggin, Frederick Elliston, and Jane English. Totowa, N.J.: Littlefield, Adams.

———. 1980. *The Reverse discrimination controversy.* Totowa, N.J.: Rowman and Littlefield.

Gilligan, Carol. 1982. *In a different voice: Psychological theory and women's development.* Cambridge: Harvard University Press.

Goldman, Alan. 1979. *Justice and reverse discrimination.* Princeton: Princeton University Press.

Gouldner, Alvin W. 1973. *For sociology: renewal and critique in sociology today.* New York: Basic Books.

Greenawalt, Kent. 1975. Judicial scrutiny of "benign" racial preference in law school admissions. *Columbia Law Review* 75:559.

———. 1979. The unresolved problems of reverse discrimination. *California Law Review* 67:87–129.

———. 1983. *Discrimination and reverse discrimination.* New York: Alfred A. Knopf.

Gross, Barry R. 1978. *Discrimination in reverse: Is turnabout fair play?* New York: New York University Press.

Gunther, Gerald. 1985. *Constitutional law.* 11th ed. Mineola, N.Y.: Foundation Press.

Gutmann, Amy. 1980. *Liberal equality.* Cambridge: Cambridge University Press.

Habermas, Jürgen. 1975. *Legitimation crisis.* Trans. Thomas McCarthy. Boston: Beacon Press.

———. 1979. *Communication and the evolution of society.* Trans. Thomas McCarthy. Boston: Beacon Press.

———. 1982. A reply to my critics. In *Habermas: Critical debates,* ed. John B. Thompson and David Held. Cambridge: MIT Press.

———. 1984. *The theory of communicative action.* Vol. 1. Trans. Thomas McCarthy. Boston: Beacon Press.

Hare, R. M. 1979. What is wrong with slavery. *Philosophy and Public Affairs* 8:103–21.

Hart, H. L. A. 1961. *The concept of law.* New York: Oxford University Press.

Hayek, Friedrich A. 1979. *Law, legislation and liberty: The political order of a free people.* Chicago: University of Chicago Press.

Hazard, Geoffrey C. 1978. *Ethics in the practice of law.* New Haven and London: Yale University Press.

Hegel, G. W. F. 1971. *Philosophy of right.* Trans. T. M. Knox. New York: Oxford University Press.

———. 1979. *Phenomenology of spirit.* Trans. A. V. Miller. New York: Oxford University Press.

Hooks, Benjamin L. 1987. Affirmative action: A needed remedy. *Georgia Law Review* 21:1043.

Karst, Kenneth L. 1977. The Supreme Court 1976 term foreword: Equal citizenship under the Fourteenth Amendment. *Harvard Law Review* 91:1.

Karst, Kenneth L., and Harold W. Horowitz. 1979. The *Bakke* opinion and equal protection doctrine. *Harvard Civil Rights—Civil Liberties Law Review* 14:7.

Kelsen, Hans. 1960. *What is justice?* Berkeley: University of California Press.

Kohlberg, Lawrence. 1979. Justice as reversibility. In *Philosophy, politics and society,* 5th series, ed. Peter Laslett and James Fishkin, 257–72. New Haven and London: Yale University Press.

———. 1981. *The philosophy of moral development: Moral stages and the idea of justice.* New York: Harper & Row.

Locke, John. 1960. *The second treatise of government.* Ed. P. Laslett. Cambridge: Cambridge University Press.

Lucas, John. 1980. *On justice.* Oxford: Clarendon Press.

Lukes, Stephen. 1973. *Individualism.* New York: Harper & Row.

———. 1982. Of Gods and demons: Habermas and practical reason. In *Habermas: Critical debates,* ed. John B. Thompson and David Held. Cambridge: MIT Press.

Lyons, D. 1965. *The forms and limits of utilitarianism.* London: Oxford University Press.

McCarthy, Thomas. 1978. *The critical theory of Jürgen Habermas.* Cambridge: MIT Press.

McCarthy, Thomas. 1982. Rationality and relativism: Habermas's 'overcoming' of hermeneutics. In *Habermas: Critical debates,* ed. John B. Thompson and David Held. Cambridge: MIT Press.

MacIntyre, Alasdair. 1977. Utilitarianism and cost-benefit analysis: An essay on the relevance of moral philosophy to bureaucratic theory. In *Values in the electric power industry,* ed. K. Sayre. Notre Dame, Ind.: University of Notre Dame Press.

———. 1981. *After virtue.* Notre Dame, Ind.: University of Notre Dame Press.

MacKinnon, Catherine. 1987. *Feminism unmodified: Discourses on life and law.* Cambridge: Harvard University Press.

Maguire, Daniel C. 1978. The triumph of unequal justice. *Christian Century* 95:882.

Masters, Roger. 1968. *The political philosophy of Rousseau.* Princeton: Princeton University Press.

Mill, John Stuart. 1970. *On liberty.* Cleveland: Meridan Books.

Minow, Martha. 1987. The Supreme Court 1986 term foreword: Justice engendered. *Harvard Law Review* 101:1.

Mishkin, Paul. 1983. The uses of ambivalence: Reflections on the Supreme Court and the constitutionality of affirmative action. *University of Pennsylvania Law Review* 131:907.

Morgan, Marabel. 1973. *The total woman.* Old Tappan, N. J.: Fleming H. Revell.

Morris, Arval. 1984. Interpretive and noninterpretive constitutional theory. *Ethics* 94:501.

Nagel, Thomas. 1979. *Mortal questions.* Cambridge: Cambridge University Press.

Novak., J., R. Rotunda, and J. Young. 1983. *Constitutional law.* 2d ed. St. Paul, Minn.: West Publishing.

Nozick, Robert. 1974. *Anarchy, state and utopia.* New York: Basic Books.

O'Fallon, James M. 1979. Adjudication and contested concepts: The case of equal protection. *New York University Law Review* 54:19.

O'Neil, Robert M. 1971. Preferential admissions: Equalizing the access of minority groups to higher education. *Yale Law Journal* 80:699.

Perelman, Chaim. 1963. *The idea of justice and the problem of argument.* London: Routledge & Kegan Paul.

Perry, Michael J. 1979. Modern equal protection: A conceptualization and appraisal. *Columbia Law Review* 79:1023.

Pettit, Philip. 1980. *Judging justice: An introduction to contemporary political philosophy.* London: Routledge & Kegan Paul.

Pitkin, Hannah. 1967. *The concept of representation.* Berkeley: University of California Press.

Plamenatz, John. 1956. Equality of opportunity. In *Aspects of Human Equality,* ed. Lyman Bryson, et al. New York: Harper.

Posner, Richard. 1979. The *Bakke* case and the future of affirmative action. *California Law Review* 67:171–89.

Rae, D., D. Yates, J. Hochschild, J. Morone, and C. Fessler. 1981. *Equalities.* Cambridge: Harvard University Press.

Rawls, John. 1971. *A theory of justice.* Cambridge: Harvard University Press.

Rescher, Nicolas. 1966. *Distributive justice.* Indianapolis: Bobbs-Merrill.

Reynolds, William B. 1987. An equal opportunity scorecard. *Georgia Law Review* 21:1007.

Richards, David A., Jr. 1986. *Toleration and the Constitution.* New York: Oxford University Press.

Rosenfeld, Michel. 1985a. Contract and justice: The relation between classical contract law and social contract theory. *Iowa Law Review* 70:769

———. 1985b. Affirmative action, justice, and equalities: A philosophical and constitutional appraisal. *Ohio State Law Journal* 46:845.

———. 1986. Substantive equality and equal opportunity: A jurisprudential appraisal. *California Law Review* 74:1687.

———. 1989a. Hegel and the dialectics of contract. *Cardozo Law Review* 10:1199.

———. 1989b. Decoding *Richmond:* Affirmative action and the elusive meaning of constitutional equality. *Michigan Law Review* 87:1729.

Ross, Alf. 1958. *On law and justice.* London: Stevens & Sons.

Rousseau, Jean-Jacques. 1947. *Social contract.* Ed. Charles Frankel. New York: Hafner.

Sandalow, Terrance. 1975. Racial preferences in higher education: Political responsibility and the judicial role. *University of Chicago Law Review* 42:653.

Scales, Ann. 1986. The emergence of feminist jurisprudence: An essay. *Yale Law Journal* 95:1373.

Schaar, John. 1967. Equality of opportunity and beyond. In *Nomos IX: Equality,* ed. J. Roland Pennock and John W. Chapman. New York: Atherton.

Schlafly, Phyllis. 1977. *The power of the positive woman.* New Rochelle, N.Y.: Arlington House.

Schneider, Elizabeth M., and Nadine Taub. 1982. Perspective on women's subordination and the role of law. In *The politics of law: A progressive critique,* ed. David Kairys. New York: Pantheon.

Schwartz, Herman, 1987. The 1986 and 1987 affirmative action cases: It's all over but the shouting. *Michigan Law Review* 86:524.

Sher, George. 1977. Justifying reverse discrimination in employment. In *Equality and Preferential Treatment,* ed. Cohen, Nagel, and Scanlon. Princeton: Princeton University Press.

———. 1979. Reverse discrimination, the future and the past. *Ethics* 90:81–87.

Sherry, Suzanna. 1984. Selective judicial activism in the equal protection context: Democracy, distrust, and deconstruction. *Georgetown Law Journal* 73:89.

Simon, Robert. 1979. Individual rights and 'benign' discrimination. *Ethics* 90:88–97.

Smart, J. J. C., and B. Williams. 1985. *Utilitarianism: For and against.* Cambridge: Cambridge University Press.

Sowell, Thomas. 1984. *Civil rights: Rhetoric or reality?* New York: William Morrow.

Stone, Julius. 1980. Justice not equality. In *Justice,* ed. Eugene Kamenka and Alice Erh-Soon Tay. New York: St. Martin's.

Sullivan, Kathleen M. 1986. Sins of discrimination: Last term's affirmative action cases. *Harvard Law Review* 100:78.

Symposium. 1975. *DeFunis. Columbia Law Review.* 75:483.

Symposium. 1979. *Regents of the University of California v. Bakke. California Law Review* 67:1.

Symposium. 1979–80. *Ethics* 90:71.

Taylor, Paul. 1973. Reverse discrimination and compensatory justice. *Analysis* 33:177–82.

tenBroek, Jacobus. 1969. *Equal under law.* New York: Collier.

Thalberg, Irving. 1980. Themes in the reverse discrimination debate. *Ethics* 91:138–50.

Thomson, Judith Jarvis. 1977. Preferential hiring. In *Equality and preferential treatment,* ed. Cohen, Nagel, and Scanlon. Princeton: Princeton University Press.

Thompson, John B. 1982. Universal pragmatics. In *Habermas: Critical debates,* ed. John B. Thompson and David Held. Cambridge: MIT Press.

Todorov, Tzvetan. 1982. *La conquête de l'Amérique: la question de l'autre.* Paris: Editions Du Seuil.

Tribe, Lawrence H. 1978. *American constitutional law.* Mineola, N.Y.: Foundation Press.

———. 1979. Perspectives on *Bakke:* Equal protection, procedural fairness, or structural justice. *Harvard Law Review* 92:864.

Tussman, Joseph, and Jacobus tenBroek. 1949. The equal protection of the law. *California Law Review* 37:341.

Walzer, M. 1983. *Spheres of justice: A defense of pluralism and equality.* New York: Basic Books.

Wasserstrom, Richard. 1977. Racism, sexism and preferential treatment: An approach to the topics. *UCLA Law Review* 24:581–622.

Westen, Peter. 1982. The empty idea of equality. *Harvard Law Review* 95:537.

———. 1985. The concept of equal opportunity. *Ethics* 95:837.

Weinrib, Ernest J. 1983. Toward a moral theory of negligence law. *Law & Philosophy* 2:37.

White, Stephen K. 1988. *The recent work of Jürgen Habermas.* Cambridge: Cambridge University Press.

Williams, Bernard. 1971. The idea of equality. In *Justice and equality,* ed. Hugo Bedeau. Englewood Cliffs, N.J.: Prentice Hall.

Wilkinson, J. Harvie. 1975. The Supreme Court, the equal protection clause, and the three faces of constitutional equality. *Virginia Law Review* 61:945.

Index

Abortion, 2
Abstract ego, 243–44, 245; compared to concrete ego, 243; and moral choice, 243; and dominant perspective, 245
Acts of commission, compared to acts of omission, 57
Act-utilitarianism, 36; defined, 113; compared to rule-utilitarianism, 113–14
Affirmative action: defined, 42, 47, 335; as over- and underinclusive, 91, 296, 299–301; limited to tie-breaking situations, 100–01; to provide fair competition, 164, 210, 286, 306, 308, 309, 313, 329, 330; validity under federal civil rights legislation, 172–74; administrative costs, 293, 305; for blacks as distinguished from Hispanics, 302–03; entitlement to, 327. *See* Preferential treatment
Affirmative action programs, 47, 59, 60, 69, 98, 110, 173–75, 339*n.3;* voluntary plans, 169, 172, 179–80, 197, 202–03, 204; to eliminate imbalance, as compared to maintaining balance, 172–73, 199; enacted by Congress, 174, 205; comprehensive plans, 188; remedial court-ordered plans, 189–90, 192, 193, 194; for women, 197, 201; timing of, 322–23; voluntary, as distinguished from court ordered, 329
Agent of allocation, 80, 201, 283, 287, 289; private, 59, 61, 123, 229, 340*n.8;* state as, 60, 155, 156; as actual wrongdoer, 77, 174, 168, 202
Antidiscrimination laws, 54, 212–13
Anti-Semitism, 299
Apartheid, 205
Appellate review of criminal convictions, 158
Aristotle, narrow conception of distributive justice, 30, 31; on compensatory justice, 31
Assimilation: sphere of, 163, 222, 224, 236, 303, 317; process of, 165, 318; defined, 224
—ideal of, 115, 164, 187; and gender, 198, 201, 317–18; as compared to traditionalism (in sex roles), 317–20 passim; and equality of the sexes, 318. *See also* Differentiation
Atomistic mode of interpretation: defined, 211; and the marginal equality position, 213–14, 292, 334
Autonomy, individual, 52, 220, 230, 233, 243, 248, 308; and postulate of equality, 22, 251; zone of, 56; and equality of respect, 145; and egalitarian justice, 220, 221; and libertarian justice, 220, 221, 224; entitlement theory of justice, 221; and self-sufficiency, 221, 225; and contractual exchanges, 225; and contractarian theory, 233. *See* Autonomy and welfare
Autonomy and welfare, 7, 220–22, 224, 226–27, 229, 230, 231

Baker, C. Edwin, 145
Bargaining positions, 65, 69, 72, 156, 234–35, 248, 263
Bill of Rights, 152
Black separatists, 320, 321
Blackmun, Harry A., 166, 178, 182, 339*n.8,* 340*n.1*
Bradwell v. Illinois, 342*n.4*
Brennan, William J., Jr., 169–74 passim, 182, 190–91, 194, 196, 198–202 passim, 283, 328, 330, 341*n.10;* comparison between "Harvard Plan" and preferential admissions in *Bakke,* 169; on justifications for affirmative action, 174,

Brennan, William J., Jr. (*continued*) 191, 214; on equality of opportunity, 190; purpose of Title VII, 190; and purpose of affirmative action, 191

Brown v. Board of Education, 142, 143, 160, 161, 163

Burger, Warren E., 175

Burton v. Wilmington Parking Authority, 340*nn.8, 9*

Circuit Court of Appeals, Second Circuit, 190

City of Richmond v. J. A. Croson Co., 167, 204–15, 292, 326, 331, 334, 339*n.2*

Civil Rights Act of *1964*:

—Title II, 341*n.3*

—Title VII, 159, 172–73, 177, 189–191, 192–93; purpose, 47; and preferential treatment for women, 197, 199, 202

Civil rights legislation, 159, 173, 178, 229. *See also* Civil Rights Act of *1964*

Civil War amendments, 145

Classifications and classes, 170

Coleman, Jules, 32, 36–37, 38

Color-blind policies, 113, 114, 137, 163, 164; and constitutional equality, 143; goal of race relations, 187, 207

Communicative ethics, 7, 219, 239, 258–75 passim, 279, 319; and justice as reversibility, 258, 259, 263, 268, 272, 273; and justice as reversible reciprocity, 259, 260, 262, 265–69 passim, 273, 274–75, 319; ideal speech situation, 259, 263, 271; and the formation of self-images, 260, 261; and reversal of perspectives, 260, 262, 265, 268, 270, 271; and affirmative action, 262, 269–70, 281; principle of universalization, 270, 271; and male domination, 279–80

—and distorting factors: deception, 259, 260, 263, 267, 268; self-deception, 259–70 passim; power, 259, 260, 261, 264; ideology, 259, 260. *See also* Habermas, Jürgen

—and distortions in communications, 259, 261–70 passim; between employer and employee, 261–62, 264

—communicative action, 263, 266, 267, 270, 274, 281, 312, 314, 327; defined, 262; as distinguished from strategic action, 262, 313

—strategic action, 263, 312–15 passim; defined, 262; as distinguished from communicative action, 262

—and reconstructing dialogues, 267–70, 272, 279, 313, 314, 315; hypothetical as distinguished from actual, 265–66, 267, 270

—generalizable interest, 271–72, 274; defined, 270; as distinguished from particular interest, 270

—consensus and compromise, 272–74, 314, 318, 320, 321; defined, 272–73; and affirmative action, 273; and integration and differentiation, 273

Colonizer and colonized, as contrasted with master and slave, 223. *See also* Identity and difference

Compensatory (corrective) justice, 14, 30–40 passim; voluntary compensation, 32, 289, 292, 329; compared to redistribution, 40; and libertarian justice, 57, 59, 61, 62, 63, 64, 286; and contractarian justice, 74, 75–78, 79, 80–81, 82–87, 286; and utilitarian justice, 94, 101; abandonment of compensatory requirement in Title VII cases, 202; and the white male from a standpoint of reciprocity, 310

—and affirmative action, 32, 47, 75–78, 83, 143, 222, 287–95 passim, 311; actual victim, 32–37 passim, 63, 76, 77, 169, 176, 180, 206, 207, 286–89 passim, 311; actual victim

not required, 101, 102, 171; wrongdoer, 169, 179, 192, 206, 207, 287, 311, 329. *See* Group; Justice
—duty of compensation; 201; theory of collective guilt, 86, 88
Competitive disadvantages as a result of past discrimination, 29, 288, 306
Consensus and compromise, 312, 314, 318, 320, 321. *See also* Communicative ethics
Constitution, 100, 158, 189, 197, 223; and political theory, 143
—interpretation of, 135, 137–39, 140, 146, 157; intent of framers, 137, 138, 140, 141, 142, 144; text, 137, 138, 140, 141, 144; constitutional theory, 138, 142, 143, 144; precedent, 138, 143, 144; value arguments, 138–40, 144, 150; sources of values, 139
—constitutional decision making: limitations on judges, 146–47; mechanical balancing, 148
—constitutional scrutiny, 156, 159, 167. *See also* Intermediate level scrutiny; Minimum rationality standard; Strict scrutiny test
Construction industry, exclusion of blacks, 205, 206, 208, 210, 211, 213
Contractual exchanges, 225–26

Dandridge v. Williams, 158
DeFunis v. Odegaard, 166
Desegregation of public schools, 163, 164, 165, 205
Dialogical process, 284, 307, 309–20 passim, 326, 328, 335. *See also* Communicative ethics; Justice as reversibility
Difference: as inferiority, 3, 5, 223, 244, 298; and equality, 6; in natural ability, 120, 131; and utilitarian position, 230, 232; sources of, 234–35; in perspectives, 234, 236, 237, 238, 251; and attributes, 235; race and gender as, 236. *See* Identity and difference
Differentiation, 235, 242, 244, 245, 246, 248, 252; defined, 224; sphere of, 224, 317; and equality, 241; ideal of, and gender, 317. *See also* Integration and differentiation
Discriminatory practices, 189, 190, 193
Distribution: of educational and professional opportunities, 35, 123, 125, 187, 286; according to need as compared to talent, 68–69; of economic and social rewards, 125; of rights, 155
Distributive justice, 14, 30–40 passim, 48, 143, 169, 208, 222, 293; defined, 31; process of distribution as compared to its product, 31, 34; aims of, 35, 36, 161, 165; and affirmative action, 45, 78–79, 91, 221; and libertarian justice, 61, 64; and contractarian justice, 75, 78–79, 89, 90–91, 92; and utilitarian justice, 94; and egalitarian justice, 116, 119, 121, 123, 125, 131; and restoration of prospects of success, 316. *See* Justice
Domain of account: defined, 17; and relationship to domain of allocation, 18
Domain of allocation: defined, 17, 136, 156, 169; and domain of account, 18, 156; and contractarianism, 76; with respect to preferential treatment, 77; and equal protection clause, 155, 156; and state, 155, 157, 159
Domain of equality, 17, 18, 19; defined, 16; distinction between broad and narrow domains, 16; conflict between market liberals and Marxists, 17; and egalitarian justice, 22. *See also* Rae, Douglas
Domain of relevant means, 26
Douglas v. California, 158
Dworkin, Ronald, 12, 104–08, 139–

Dworkin, Ronald (*continued*) 43 passim, 251; and constitutional equality, 144–45
—Alternative utilitarian approach, 104–08; and equal treatment compared to treatment as an equal, 24, 104, 105, 144, 340*n.17*; compared to limited utilitarian argument, 105. *See* Preferences
—and equal treatment, 144; defined, 104

Ecological mode of interpretation, 212; defined, 211; and global equality position, 213, 292, 334
Education: allocation of university admissions, 50, 120; pervasive discrimination in public school education, 87, 103, 160–63 passim, 187, 288; relationship of public school education to higher education and employment, 90, 160, 170, 287–88, 290, 291; use of quotas in university admissions, 126. *See also* Preferential treatment, in education
Efficiency, 35, 121, 125, 139, 181, 184, 288, 305, 314, 315, 316, 323; and libertarian justice, 55, 58, 61; and contractarian justice, 72, 77, 85, 87; and utilitarian justice, 99–100, 108–09; and egalitarian justice, 120, 121
—compositive theory of efficiency, 305; contrasted with additive theory, 99, 305; and reverse seniority layoffs, 184; and preferential promotion plans, 195
Employment: sex or race as a job qualification, 50, 70, 98, 99, 199; entitlement to, 59, 101, 102; and legislation regarding, 159; communication between employers and employees, 261–62, 264. *See also* Preferential treatment, in employment
Entitlement theory of justice. *See* Nozick, Robert
Equal citizenship, 145
Equal Employment Opportunity Commission (EEOC), 47, 341*n.31*
Equalities and inequalities, 20, 21, 135, 156, 164, 171, 311. *See also* Rae, Douglas
Equality, 11; and treatment according to merit distinguished from treatment according to need, 13; and the effect of family values, 26, 293; and competition for scarce positions, 27, 120, 185, 284–90 passim, 330; disputed definition of, 139; and equal protection clause, 144; and voluntary choice, 293–94
Equality of opportunity, 42, 78, 84, 89–90, 119, 120–25 passim, 127, 136, 156, 158, 159, 161–64 passim, 170, 184, 188, 190, 314, 332, 335; defined, 23–24; distinguished from treatment as an equal, 24, 105; and equality of result, 23, 24–25, 117–22, 158–59, 173, 229; inequality of, 66; and competition for scarce positions, 102–03, 190, 210, 293, 325; and equal respect, 102, 309, 328; and inequality of outcomes, 117; and egalitarianism, 117–22; and equal protection right, 157, 160; as distributive goal, 171; economic, 174; and collective bargaining agreements, 183–84; to create a racially balanced union, 191; and equal protection clause, 283, 303; allocation of scarce positions, 284, 285; and affirmative action, 285, 286; and compensation, 291, 308; and groups, 298; and stereotypes, 299; and right of innocent white male, 307–08; and women, 309, 321; and beneficiaries of affirmative action, 329. *See* Fair equality of opportunity; Formal equality of opportunity; Means-regarding equality of opportunity
Equality of respect, 320; and equal protection clause, 145; and postulate of equality, 145

Equality of result, 24, 118, 120, 123, 125, 136, 144, 157, 160, 162, 180, 188, 191, 284; defined, 23–24; preferred under egalitarian justice, 117; and egalitarian justice, 118; and postulate of equality, 118; compared to inequality of result, 119; and prospect-regarding equality of result, 123; and appellate review of criminal convictions, 158; and equal opportunity, 158, 160; lot-regarding compared to subject-regarding, 230; allocation of jobs, 285

Equalization of means, 329, 331

Equal protection clause, 18, 95, 104, 135, 137–39, 142, 143, 145, 147, 156–57, 158, 167, 178, 188, 193, 207, 283, 286; and ideal of equality, 13, 144; and formal justice, 14; state action requirement, 18; and structural grammar of equality, 135; and postulate of equality, 135–36; history, 141; meaning of, 141; and color-blindness, 154; and the individual, 168, 298; departure from equal treatment principle, 170, 180; violation of, 179, 193. *See also* Fourteenth Amendment; Intent of framers

Equal respect, 234, 242, 265, 269, 285; and equal opportunity rights, 102, 309, 328, 332; and equal protection clause, 144; feminine as compared to masculine perspective, 278

Equal treatment, 6, 164, 166, 208, 223, 331; compared to preferential treatment, 3; as distinguished from treatment as an equal, 24, 104, 105, 144, 340*n.17;* in legislation, 141, 149; and equal protection, 170, 209. *See also* Marginal equality

Fair equality of opportunity, 66, 71–74, 91, 156, 180, 286, 307, 331, 332; defined, 28–29; and priority of equalities, 72; compared to formal equality of opportunity, 73, 294, 330, 336; and obligation of the state, 76, 329–30; and distributive justice, 78, 92; and forward-looking affirmative action, 91

Fallon, Richard, 138–40, 142, 143

Feinberg, Joel, 30–31

Firefighters Local Union No. 1784 v. Stotts, 176, 177–78, 181, 188, 191; and group-regarding concerns, 178, 188

First-order discrimination: defined, 4; and equality as exclusive identity, 6; and compensatory justice, 76, 77; motivational or psychological harm caused by, 84, 85, 92, 213, 240, 291; compared to affirmative action, 106, 130, 306; based on idea that group is morally inferior, 146, 225, 298; and equality of opportunity, 163; policies required to combat the effects of, 171; and libertarian refusal to outlaw, 224–25, 226, 228; and contractarian use of reciprocity to reject, 234, 244; and inequalities from, 324

—repudiation of, 4, 14, 122; and court injunction, 194

—and utilitarian theory, 233; justified under utilitarian theory, 99, 100, 108, 232; not justified under Dworkin's utilitarian argument, 106. *See also* Gender-based discrimination; Racial discrimination; Reverse (benign) discrimination; Societal discrimination

Fiss, Owen, 13, 15, 146–54 passim

Formal equality, 6, 228, 235, 248, 316

Formal equality of opportunity, 29–30, 60–64 passim, 156, 159, 228, 229, 313, 316, 330; defined, 28; compared to fair equality of opportunity, 73, 294, 330, 336; and state denial of, 172; and distributive justice, 294; and innocent white male, 311; and gender-based affir-

Formal equality (*continued*) mative action, 321; and positive duties on the state, 330
Formal justice, 14, 21, 147
Fourteenth Amendment, 145, 168; interpretation by present court (negative duties), 294, 330. *See* Intent of framers
Freedom of association, 52–54
Freedom of choice, 53, 224, 399
Freedom of contract, 52, 60, 225; and individual contractor as compared to corporate employer, 227–28
Free market economy, 58, 156, 229, 326; and contractual exchanges, 225–26
Friedman, Milton, 17
Fullilove v. Kluznick, 167, 174–76, 326, 339*n.8;* Powell's balancing test, 175, 181, 184–85, 204
Fullinwider, Robert, 28, 43–44, 94–99 passim, 110–15 passim
Fundamental needs, and lot-regarding equality of result, 118
Fundamental rights, 54, 67, 105, 143, 157, 162; contrasted with derivative rights, 102, 104–05; and intent of framers, 141
Fundamental values, 294

Gender-based affirmative action, 316, 319; to break down stereotypical sexist social attitudes, 201; and compensatory justice, 201–02; compared to race-based, 203; distributive justifications for, 294
Gender-based discrimination, 77, 81, 154, 198, 280; and first-order discrimination, 198–99, 200, 203, 204; in the workplace, 199, 203, 204; compared to race-based, 203–04, 299, 300. *See also* Societal discrimination; Women
Gender-based stereotypes, 201, 298–99
Gender-blind policies, 114, 163
Gender relations, history of, 236–37
Gilligan, Carol, 272, 277–79, 311
Global equality, 15, 158, 166, 168, 170, 172, 182, 186, 209, 331; defined, 19; of opportunity, 23, 27, 28, 120; in education, 28; and remedial purposes to justify affirmative action, 223
Goals of affirmative action, 42; defined, 45; numerical goals, 189, 190, 191, 192
—goals of specific programs, 167–68, 178, 182, 193, 197, 206; backward- and forward-looking components, 179, 180, 324
Goldman, Alan, 28, 32, 35, 53–58 passim, 67–86, 89–93 passim, 101, 111, 119, 120, 121, 157, 233, 235, 286; and awarding jobs to the most competent, 48, 78, 79, 80, 89–90; and reversal test, 70–71, 240–41, 255; and compensation, 75, 157; and distribution, 75, 157;and Nozick's principle of rectification, 75, 76
—and preferential treatment justified for the chronically poor, 78–79; to actual victim, 79–80; and limited veil of ignorance, 236, 237. *See also* Limited (partial) veil of ignorance; Reversal test
Greenawalt, Kent, 42–43, 137, 140
Group proportionment principle, 74; and individual's prospects of success, 74
Group: distributive vs. non-distributive, 82, 85; cohesiveness of, 85, 86; collective relief to, 191; prejudice of, 299
—and relationship to individual, 4, 74, 81–88, 165, 177, 191, 192, 274, 277, 283, 296–304 passim; inequalities between individuals in group, 164; and school desegregation, 164
Group compensation, 81–85, 90, 101, 296; theory of collective guilt, 86, 88; to individual based on group affiliation, 297, 302–03
Group-regarding equality, 74, 174,

188, 191, 192, 215, 296; defined, 15; and equal distribution, 15; contrasted with individual-regarding concerns, 15–16, 165, 172, 177, 178, 191, 192, 215, 277, 296, 297, 304; and inequalities between individuals, 16; and prospects of success, 124; of result and preferential treatment, 172, 173, 188
Gutmann, Amy, 11, 20, 21

Habermas, Jürgen, 7, 239, 258–74 passim, 279. *See also* Communicative ethics
Hare, R. M., 232–33
Harlan, John Marshall, 158
Harvard plan, 169
Hasidic Jews, 303–04
Hayek, Friedrich A., 60–61
Hegel, G. W. F., 223
Hispanics, discrimination against, 189, 301, 302
Hobbes, Thomas, 21, 65
Hypothetical social contract, 234, 235, 251; as compared to real contracts, 235; behind a limited veil of ignorance, 236, 237; and dominant perspective, 237, 238; and abstract ego, 245; compared to reversal of perspectives, 245; and hypothetical reconstruction of dialogues, 265–66

Ideal of equality, 13
Identity, 5, 248; and equality, 5, 6, 235, 242, 244, 245; moral, 22–23; individual, 228; and utilitarian position, 231; society's, 235; and colonizer, 236; as abstract ego, 243–44; and abstract ego as compared to concrete ego, 244. *See* Identity and difference
Identity and difference, 6, 7, 220, 222–24, 230, 234, 242, 245, 248, 252; and mere reciprocity, 247–48; and justice as reversible reciprocity, 275
Individual: and relationship to the group, 4, 74, 81–88, 165, 177, 191, 192, 274, 277, 283, 296–304 passim, 315; prospects of success, 26, 30, 83, 84, 87, 88, 90, 195; and group proportionment principle, 74; needs, 118; and contractarian theory, 233–35; and moral choice, 243, 297; and group affiliation, 283, 296–97
—rights, 95, 100, 104, 143, 144, 152, 160, 224, 233, 297, 303; compared to social utility, 95
Individualism: defined, 20; and self-development, 20
Individual-regarding equality, 16, 168, 188, 215; defined, 15; contrasted with group-regarding concerns, 15–16, 165, 172, 177, 178, 215, 277, 296, 297, 304; and inequalities amongst groups, 16; of opportunity, 188, 191, 192; and group-regarding relief, 191–92; and community-regarding concerns, 277
Inequality: product of social as compared to natural causes, 29, 288; of females as compared to males, 277–78
—of result, 24, 117, 119; and affirmative action 122–28; group-regarding, 172; individual-regarding, 172
—of distribution: and affirmative action, 123
—of opportunity, 66, 159, 160, 174; prospect-regarding, 172
Inferiority and differences, 223. *See also* Identity and difference
Inferiority and equality, 325
Innocent nonminority business, 175, 326
"Innocent white male", 101, 102, 105, 130, 168, 172, 174, 178, 179, 181, 195–97 passim, 283, 324, 394–96 passim; compared to actual victim, 76; and compensation under contractarian justice, 87–88; and utilitarianism, 101, 102, 105; as beneficiaries of first-order dis-

"Innocent white male" (*continued*) crimination or racism or sexism, 103, 171, 193, 196, 197, 308; and preference for status quo, 108; and degree of harm to, caused by preferential program, 196, 199, 201–02, 215; and preferential promotion plans, 196, 326; and role reversal, 309–311, 233; and formal equality of opportunity, 311
—and balancing harm against benefits of preferential treatment, 111, 185, 188, 201, 215, 286; to blacks, 93, 97–98; to society as a whole, 95, 105
—and layoffs, 177, 179, 326, 327; as compared to preferential hiring, 181; as compared to preferential admissions, 182; and preferential promotion plans as compared to hiring plans, 196
—effects on, 193, 307, 323–25 passim; self-esteem of, 97–98, 130, 153, 170; as compared to increase in applicant pool, 103, 325; prospects of success, 185–86, 195, 305, 329
Integration, 188, 205, 245, 246, 252, 324; ideal of, 115; of public schools, 163, 164, 188; as compared to separation, 242
—racial: and color-conscious policies, 164; to reduce racial tension, 305
—in the workplace, 192; obstruction by labor unions, 190; and women, 321. *See* Integration and differentiation
Integration and differentiation, 231–34 passim, 242, 245–46, 252; and hypothetical social contract, 234; and consensus and compromise, 273
Intent of framers, 14, 137; abstract, 141; specific, 141, 142. *See also* Constitution, interpretation of; Fourteenth Amendment
Intermediate level scrutiny, 166; and gender classifications, 151, 154; and racial classifications, 170, 206, 209

Jefferson, Thomas, 159
Johnson v. Transportation Agency, Santa Clara County, California, 197–204, 292, 300, 305, 324
Judicial activism, as compared to province of legislator, 335
Judicial concerns in reviewing affirmative action plans: both compensatory and distributive, 174, 192, 195, 214, 328; both forward- and backward-looking justifications, 202, 203, 209, 214, 304, 328, 330
—compensatory, 180, 181, 195, 215, 286–92 passim, 298, 328; backward-looking concerns, 173, 207, 303, 304
—distributive, 288–94 passim, 298, 328; forward-looking concerns and the chronically poor, 78–79, 90–91, 286; forward-looking justification, 78–79, 91, 94, 108, 116, 126, 174, 179, 180, 186–87, 201, 214, 286, 294, 298; backward-looking concerns, 126, 153, 173, 176–77, 179, 207, 286, 292, 303, 304
Judicial interpretation. *See* Atomistic mode of interpretation; Constitution, interpretation of; Ecological mode of interpretation; Judicial concerns in reviewing affirmative action plans; Judicial review; Supreme Court
Judicial review: and postulate of equality, 146; under mediating principle, 148, 150; and substantive equality, 154
Justice: and relation between distributive and compensatory justice, 31–40 passim, 74–75, 89–93 passim, 135, 157; as contract, 34
Justice as reversibility, 7, 219, 245, 246, 249–52, 256, 259, 275, 335; and utilitarian justice, 239, 257–58, 335; defined, 245, 249; stages,

246; and mere reciprocity standard, 255; and communicative ethics, 258, 259, 263, 268, 272, 273; and affirmative action, 272; biased against women, 277–78, 279
—and contractarian justice, 239, 255, 258; Rawls, 250. *See also* Reciprocity
Justice as reversible reciprocity, 7, 219, 254, 275–78, 281–82, 283, 286, 293, 303, 308, 309, 314, 335; defined, 249; as limited reciprocity of perspective, 254; and communicative ethics, 259, 260, 262, 265, 266, 267, 269, 273, 274–75; and identity and diversity, 275; and postulate of equality, 275, 276, 277; and procedural justice, 275–77 passim; and affirmative action, 276, 280, 309; and dialogical reconstruction, 276, 309, 314, 315, 326; and gender-based affirmative action, 280–83, 319; and substantive equality, 283, 335; dialogical process, 284, 307, 309–17 passim, 335; and equality of opportunity, 284, 298, 308; and intrinsic as distinguished from extrinsic benefits, 285; and innocent white male, 306, 307. *See also* Reciprocity

Kant, Immanuel, 65, 66
Karst, Kenneth L., 143, 145
Kohlberg, Lawrence, 7, 219, 245, 249–50, 252; theory of moral development, 245–46, 270, 272, 277, 279, 281; Heinz's dilemma, 250. *See also* Justice as reversibility
Korematsu v. United States, 152
Kotch v. River Port Pilot Commissioners, 161, 162

Labor unions, 173, 189, 190–93; collective bargaining agreement, 172, 178, 183
Legal causation, 289–90, 292, 333, 334
Legislation, 148, 149; and judicial review, 146; and mediating principle, 147; on racial segregation, 149
Liberal moral theory, 135, 144, 219
Liberal political theory, 135; and ranking of liberty compared to equality, 20; and postulate of equality, 21
Lifting formal barriers to competition, 309–13 passim
Limited utilitarian argument, 100–04; compensatory justification, 101; and theory that job belongs to community, 101–02; in hiring, 102, 109, 110; and preferential treatment, 103; and harm from affirmative action, 109–11
Limited veil of ignorance. *See* Veil of ignorance
Local 28, Sheet Metal Workers' Intern. Ass'n v. E.E.O.C., 189–92
Local No. 93, International Association of Firefighters v. City of Cleveland (Vanguards), 192–93
Locke, John, 16, 21, 56, 66; and self-sufficiency, 225, 226
Lot-regarding equality, 32, 164; compared to subject-regarding equality of result, 23; and identity as compared to difference, 230
—of result, 117, 119, 124, 229, 230; global, 117
Lottery system for allocating scarce goods, 25, 72–73, 121, 125, 127–28; compared to use of affirmative action as a "tiebreaker," 100; compared to quota, 126
Lyons, David, 113

Marginal equality, 15, 27–29 passim, 158, 166, 169, 172, 179, 180, 202, 207, 208, 214, 292, 306, 310, 331, 332; defined, 19; of opportunity, lot regarding, 136; and differences, 222
Market liberals, 17
Marshall, Thurgood, 182, 183, 188, 209–10, 212, 261, 311; on Powell's

Marshall, Thurgood (*continued*) balancing test from *Fullilove*, 184–86; on strict scrutiny test, 206
Marsh v. Alabama, 340*nn.8, 10*
Marx, Karl, 17
Master and slave, 247; as contrasted with colonizer and colonized, 223; paradigm of nonreciprocal relationship, 246
Maximin principle, 66, 68, 72, 74, 84
Means-regarding equality of opportunity, 26, 117, 124, 288, 293; defined, 25; distinguished from prospect-regarding equality of opportunity, 25, 73, 120; marginal, 25–27, 117; and competition for jobs, scarce goods, 27, 73, 170; global, 29, 120; formal, 59, 122, 172, 298, 316, 324
—fair, 29, 74–75, 122, 284–88 passim, 293, 294, 295, 298, 303, 309, 322, 324, 328–34 passim; and contractarian justice, 78, 120; and political events, 158; and prospects of success, 159, 292; and preferential treatment, 172; and women, 309, 320; and distributive affirmative action, 330
Means-regarding inequality of opportunity, 204, 288
Mediating principle in equal protection jurisprudence, 15, 136, 146–47, 154, 219, 331, 332; alternative principle, 332–33, 334
—antidiscrimination principle, 136, 148–53 passim, 170, 219, 283, 287, 331; defined, 147; fit between legislative means and legislative end, 147–50, 152; and postulate of equality, 149, 152; not color-blind, 152, 154; treatment of race-based compared to gender-based legislation, 154; influence in Supreme Court decisions, 161, 306
Mill, John Stuart: distinction between real and apparent interests, 342*n.18*
Minimal state, 52, 55, 61, 62, 63, 155, 156; defined, 60
Minimum rationality standard, 151, 152
Minority business enterprises (MBEs), 174–75, 204–09 passim, 211, 212
Moral autonomy, 220, 233, 243, 254; and choice, 244
Moral equality, 21, 22, 116, 143, 144, 146; norms, 266–67
Motivation: and chronic poverty, 78–79, 83, 91, 286; and first-order discrimination, 82, 84; and members of group, 85; and racism, 90, 240, 291, 298, 300; and role models, 180; gender and, 298–99, 300
Mutual accommodation, 317, 318

Nagel, Thomas, 116, 117, 121, 123–25; on Goldman, 119–20; on Rawls, 120; and social utility as justification for affirmative action, 128–31
Natural assets/skills/talents, 27, 29, 62, 68, 69, 72, 132, 159, 234, 285, 289; and contractarian theory, 93, 284; and opportunities, 117; and egalitarian theory, 117, 120, 121, 131, 284; undeveloped due to first-order discrimination, 124, 131
Natural rights, 139; and libertarian justice, 12; and welfare-based conceptions, 12
Nepotism, 1, 161, 228
Nozick, Robert, 17, 52, 55–56, 60–64, 75, 76, 155, 224, 225–26, 229
—entitlement theory of justice, 58, 62; definition of justice, 61–62; and natural assets, 121–122; and individual autonomy, 221; and self-sufficiency, 221, 225; and welfare, 221; contractual exchange, 225. *See* Rectification, principle of

O'Connor, Sandra Day, 207, 208, 211–12, 215
O'Fallon, James M., 143

Patriotism, 242
Perelman, Chaim, 14, 147
Personnel Administrator of Massachusetts v. Feeney, 161–62
Perspective, 239–53 passim, 264, 268, 269, 277, 318; dominant, 237, 238, 240, 245, 248; of blacks, 240; of slave, 247; individual compared to collective, 251, 258; masculine, 278. *See also* Reversal test, Reversal of perspectives
Philosophical contrasted with Constitutional practice, 18–19, 135, 137–38, 140, 146, 329, 335
Plessy v. Ferguson, 143
Political equality, 143
Political philosophy, 11
Political process, 158; involvement of blacks, 205
Posner, Richard, 59
Postulate of equality, 20, 21, 26, 104, 118, 143, 145, 146, 149, 153–57 passim, 164, 219, 240, 241, 242, 284, 315; and structural grammar of equality, 20; historical perspective, 21; and distribution of scarce goods, 23, 27; and quotas, 46; and equal protection clause, 135–36, 143; and constitutional interpretation, 146; and autonomy and welfare, 220–21, 229; and identity and difference, 220; and reciprocity, 242, 243, 247, 252, 255, 275, 276; extends to individuals, 243, 298; and communicative ethics, 265, 267, 268; challenged by Gilligan's theory, 278; and innocent white male, 283
—and libertarian justice: maximizing freedom, 53; defined, 220; and refusal to outlaw first-order discrimination, 224–25, 226, 228
—and egalitarian justice, 230
Powell, Lewis F., Jr., 168–70, 175, 179–82, 184, 196, 207, 214, 215; and equal protection, 166, 180
Preferences: distinction between personal and external, 105–08, 164, 231, 233; personal, defined, 106; external, defined, 106; individual, 231, 233, 257; society's net aggregate preference, 231; and differences, 232; and necessities compared to luxuries, 232
Preferential treatment, 47, 69, 77, 90; for veterans, 3, 161; defined, 43–44; and compensatory justice, 44–45, 76, 77; and distributive justice, 45; as benefiting the best qualified of the victims, 69, 89–90, 91–92; psychological benefits of, 92, 97–98, 102, 130; and utilitarian justice, 95–96, 99, 102, 103, 108, 109, 110, 111, 112, 114, 115; in allocating government contracts, 103, 174–75, 176, 205; negative consequences of, 108–09, 122, 164; and intent of framers, 142; and antidiscrimination principle, 153; compared to school integration, 164–65; in promotions, 177, 192–97; and promotions, 192, 202; of blacks as compared to women, 198, 203–04, 327–28; for nonvictims, 210
—in hiring, 3; defined, 44; economic consequences, 96; high-medium-low-skill jobs contrasted, 110–11, 182, 295; compared to racial segregation law, 153; and role models to remedy societal discrimination, 179–80; as compared to layoffs, 181–85 passim, 326
—in education, 75, 89, 103, 142, 154, 164; university admissions, 168, 170; and Harvard plan, 169; to promote diversity, 169, 170
—in employment, 75, 89, 90, 96, 99, 102, 103, 109–15 passim, 143, 153, 164
—in layoffs, 3, 178–88; and distributive goals of affirmative action, 176; reverse seniority system, 176–78, 182–84; as compared to hiring, 181–85 passim, 326; compared to employment, 182

Preferential treatment (*continued*)
—for women, 197–204; compared to preferential treatment based on race, 198, 203–04
Priority of needs, 116, 122
Procedural justice, 14, 41, 42, 84, 88, 275, 276–77, 301
Property rights, 52–53, 55, 226–27; and welfare, 54, 56, 57, 58, 224, 228; and autonomy, 225; and perpetuation of inferior status, 227; and large corporation, 228. *See also* Locke, John
Prospect-regarding equality of opportunity, 72, 125, 127, 284, 285; defined, 25; distinguished from means-regarding equality of opportunity, 25, 73; compared to subject-regarding equality of result, 72; and job lotteries, 73; and political events, 158; and preferential treatment, 172
—for the individual, 188; and forward-looking distributive preferential layoff plans, 188; prospect-regarding inequality of opportunity, 288
Prospects of success, 125, 126, 127, 171, 185, 188, 203, 204, 288–90 passim, 298–300, 313, 316, 324, 328, 333; and equality of opportunity, 103, 159, 172; and innocent white male, 103, 175, 307–08, 325; and utilitarian justice, 103; and contractarian justice, 120; group-regarding, 124; and nonracial factors, 212, 213; and racism, 298–300; and sexism, 298–300
Public Works Employment Act of *1977*, 174
Pure utilitarianism, 95–100; and benefits of affirmative action, 95; and preferential treatment in hiring, 95, 96, 97; and zero-sum result, 96

Quotas, 42, 47, 103, 137–38, 169, 172, 173, 186, 192, 193; defined, 45–46; duration of, 45, 194, 196; flexible, 46, 194; rigid, 46, 169, 211; compared to lottery system, 126; beneficiary of quota, 174; remedial as compared to punitive, 195; impermissible in university admissions, 214

Race-conscious policies, 113, 163, 164, 165; and color-blind end, 187, 207; exclusionary, 187–88, 196, 201, 306; inclusionary, 187–88, 201, 306
Race-conscious remedies, 165, 189
Race-neutral remedies, 212, 213
Race relations: goal of, 287, 207; history in United States, 236
Racial classifications, 14, 143, 154
Racial discrimination: justifications, 104, 108; history of, 189, 190, 192, 205, 211, 237; effects of, 194, 311; compared to gender-based discrimination, 200, 203–04, 300; in housing, 205; private, 208–09, 210, 212, 228, 334; racial segregation as compared to racial integration, 241; and the role of black positions of affirmative action, 311–16 passim. *See also* Societal discrimination
Racism, 59, 87, 104, 123, 127, 129, 149, 153, 164, 174, 213, 225, 227, 228, 233, 302, 306, 307, 311, 312, 322; and libertarian property theory, 59, 226, 227; and idea that all blacks are victims, 92, 298; and motivation or self-image, 92, 240, 261, 298; use of stereotypes to perpetuate domination, 261
Rae, Douglas, 12–13, 15–19, 23–27 passim
"Radical Black Assimilationist," 321–27
"Radical Female Assimilationist," 321–27
Radical feminists, 321
Rawls, John, 28, 29, 41, 65–67, 68,

73, 139, 145, 233–35, 251. *See* Veil of ignorance
Reagan administration, and affirmative action plans, 1
Reciprocity, 244, 247; norm of, 234, 243–44, 249, 252, 268, 275
—of perspectives, 245, 246, 248, 249, 252, 253, 318, 321; limited, 253–54, 309, 310
—mere reciprocity, 247–48, 252, 255, 309; and dominant perspective, 248; compared to nonreciprocity, 253; compared to reciprocity of perspectives, 253, 256; compared to limited reciprocity of perspectives, 310. *See also* Reversal test; Justice as reversibility; Justice as reversible reciprocity
—nonreciprocity, 253; master and slave paradigm, 246–47
—and white male, 309–10; compared to mere reciprocity, 253, 256; unlimited, 253–54, 309, 311
Rectification, principle of, 61–62, 63, 75, 76
Redistribution, 40, 131, 284; and invasion of autonomy, 230
Regents of University of California v. Bakke, 1, 62, 143, 159, 166, 167–72, 174, 179, 180, 202, 207, 214, 283, 328, 330, 331, 332, 339*n.8,* 340*n.1,* 341*n.10;* purpose of admissions program, 167–68; global equality position, 168, 170, 209; marginal equality position, 168–70, 208
Rehnquist, William, 14, 141
Rescher, Nicolas, 24, 30
Retribution, as contrasted to compensation, 87
Reversal test, 70–71, 239–41, 242, 244, 245
—limited role switch, 240–41, 255; as contrasted with complete role switch, 70–71, 240–41; and dominant perspective, 240; and ego, 247
—Reversal of perspectives, 241, 242, 244, 247, 248, 256, 257, 285, 287, 315, 316, 317–21 passim, 324–26 passim; and differentiation, 241, 242, 244; compared to norm of reciprocity, 244; and concrete ego, 244; compared to hypothetical contractor, 245; compared to mere reciprocity, 248; and communicative ethics, 260, 262, 265, 268, 270, 271, 273; and layoffs, 326; and priority among conflicting claims, 327. *See also* Justice as reversibility; Justice as reversible reciprocity; Reciprocity
Reverse (benign) discrimination, 4; defined, 42–43; compared to first-order discrimination, 43; principle of, 93; rearranging inequalities, 123
Right to vote, 205, 303
Role model objective, 179–81; and compensatory justifications for affirmative action, 180, 181
Rothbard, Murray, 17
Rousseau, Jean-Jacques, 65, 66
Rule-utilitarianism: compared to act-utilitarianism, 113; defined, 113, 114; and argument against affirmative action, 113–14

San Antonio Independent School District v. Rodriguez, 162
Scalia, Antonin E., 199–200, 207, 215, 330; and comparison between racial- and gender-based job segregation, 199–200, 203; and compensation, 206, 303
Segregation, 205; "separate but equal" doctrine, 143; and legislation, 149; and goal of integration, 163; and association of inequality with inferiority, 164
—of public schools, 90, 146, 153, 160, 161, 163, 164, 165, 173, 291; and intent of framers, 141–42
"Separate but equal," 143
Separatism, 309, 320, 321
Sexism. *See* Women

Shelley v. Kraemer, 340*n.15*
Sher, George, 123
Simon, Robert, 107–08
Slavery, 62, 145, 146, 205, 232–33, 247, 302
Social contract, 65; actual contract compared to hypothetical contract, 53; classical theory, 65; and natural talents, 69; and relationship between individual contractor and corporate employer, 227
Social utility, 94, 96, 106, 114, 115, 131; maximization of, 96, 98, 100, 110, 111, 113; long-term compared to short-term, 109, 110–12, 113; universal as compared to utilities based on biases and misperceptions, 111, 112
Societal discrimination, 169, 179, 333; compared to actual, 170; compared to first-order discrimination, 203
—against blacks, 169, 170, 179, 180, 211, 237, 306; rejected by some justices as justification for affirmative action, 292
—against women, 200–201, 202, 203, 204, 237, 306; based on sex-based attitudes, 199, 200, 201, 204; use of preferential treatment to combat stereotypes, 201, 204
—and the white male from a standpoint of reciprocity, 310; as compared to the Supreme Court's view, 310
Sowell, Thomas, 311, 312–13, 314
Sphere of allocation, 301–02, 309, 314, 315
Sphere of interaction, 285, 292
State: obligations of, 60, 76, 155, 156, 157, 158, 159, 329–30; sponsored affirmative action programs, 67; as agent of allocation, 136; constitutional limitations on, 152; intervention, 293, 330
—mandated or supported discrimination, 59, 62–63, 146, 156, 164, 172, 212, 330, 334; repeal of, 164; and denial of formal equality of opportunity, 172; history of, 211
State action, 18, 148, 155, 156; and lot-regarding marginal equality, 136; requirement, 157
Stereotypes, 82, 100, 109, 114, 261, 312; victims of, 298–300; racial, based on notions of culture rather than genetics, 312
Stevens, John Paul, 186–88, 196; purely forward-looking distributive justification for affirmative action, 186–87, 201, 214, 294
Stewart, Potter, 339*n.8*, 340*n.1*
Strict scrutiny test, 151, 152, 167, 168, 179, 180, 195, 209, 286, 331; racial classifications, 154, 287; and compensation, 166, 169, 287, 292; Supreme Court standard in race-based affirmative action cases, 167, 204, 206, 210, 214, 292; requirements of test, 210–11; problems with test, 210, 214
Structural grammar of equality, 6, 12, 15, 16, 17, 19, 135
Subject of equality, 16; defined, 15
Subject-regarding equality: of opportunity, 341*n.22*
—of result, 72, 117, 124, 230, 238; compared to prospect-regarding equality of result, 72; and allocation of unequal lots of goods, 117; and the individual, 231
Subject-regarding inequality, 164
Substantive equality, 136, 219, 283, 331, 332, 335
Substantive justice, 14, 15, 41
Supreme Court: and individual as subject of equality, 21; adoption of antidiscrimination principle for analysis of equal protection claims, 136, 147, 287; adoption of standards of fit for assessment of means/end analysis, 150; and equality of opportunity, 159, 160–61, 170, 207, 332; and inconsistent opinions in affirmative action area, 159, 160, 166, 167, 168, 188; race-

based compared to gender-based classifications, 160–61; and equality of result, 162; promotion of global equality by some justices, 166, 170, 182, 209; promotion of marginal equality by some justices, 166, 169, 207–08, 310, 332; departures from equal treatment principle, 170, 208; and compensatory justifications for affirmative action, 287. *See also* Intermediate level scrutiny; Minimum rationality standard; Strict scrutiny test
Suspect classification, 161
System of allocation, 124; and equality of opportunity, 122; of education, 123; of employment, 123; meritocratic, 129, 131, 132

TenBroek, Jacobus, 21
Tests, as determinants of merit, 83, 84
Thalberg, Irving, 91–93
Thomson, Judith Jarvis, 100–102, 104
Trimble v. Gordon, 340nn.4,5

Unemployment, 174
United Jewish Organizations v. Carey, 303–04
United States v. Paradise, 192, 193–97
United Steelworkers v. Weber, 172–74

Veil of ignorance, 66–67, 234–35, 237, 240, 250, 264, 265; defined, 66, 67
—Limited (partial) veil of ignorance, 67–68, 84, 237, 255; lifting the veil, 68–69, 72; and Rawls' maximin principle, 68; defined, 236. *See also* Goldman, Alan; Hypothetical social contract; Rawls, John
Voting rights, 155, 157, 205, 303; Act of *1965*, 303

Walzer, Michael, 285
Weinrib, Ernest, 31–32, 33–34, 36
Welfare: and libertarian justice, 53, 55, 56, 57, 220, 224; social, 54, 56; state, 55, 110, 155, 220; needs, 58; benefits, 158; and contractual exchange, 225; personal (individual), 225
—Rights, 58, 228; and Supreme Court, 155. *See also* Autonomy and welfare
—and utilitarian justice: maximization of, 94, 109, 113; and race-conscious policies, 113
—and egalitarian justice, 220, 221; priority system, 116; and Nozick's entitlement theory of justice, 221
Westen, Peter, 26
White hate groups, 312
White supremacists, 312
Women:
—sexism, 87, 123, 129, 225, 227, 228, 233, 261, 298, 301, 302, 306, 307, 311, 312, 319, 322; and job discrimination, 76, 201; as insufficient to require duty to compensate, 86; and libertarian property theory, 226, 227; and use of stereotypes to perpetuate domination, 261; and self-image, 298; traditional concepts of sex roles, 298–99; every woman affected, 299; and discriminatory effect, 324
—feminine perspectives on affirmative action, 264–65, 311–21 passim; suppression of feminine voice, 277; feminine as compared to masculine perspectives, 277–79; and male domination, 314–15, 318; assimilationist ideology, 314–21 passim; traditionalist ideology, 314–21 passim; comparison between traditionalist and assimilationist, 318–21. *See also* Gender-based discrimination; Gender-blind policies; Intermediate level scrutiny; Preferential treatment
Wygant v. Jackson Board of Education, 178–89, 196, 202, 207, 331

Yick Wo v. Hopkins, 341n.11